Pro PHP MVC

Chris Pitt

Apress

Pro PHP MVC

ISBN-13 (pbk): 978-1-4302-4164-5

ISBN-13 (electronic): 978-1-4302-4165-2

President and Publisher: Paul Manning
Lead Editor: Ewan Buckingham
Technical Reviewer: Wim Mostrey
Editorial Board: Steve Anglin, Ewan Buckingham, Gary Cornell, Louise Corrigan, Morgan Ertel, Jonathan Gennick, Jonathan Hassell, Robert Hutchinson, Michelle Lowman, James Markham, Matthew Moodie, Jeff Olson, Jeffrey Pepper, Douglas Pundick, Ben Renow-Clarke, Dominic Shakeshaft, Gwenan Spearing, Matt Wade, Tom Welsh
Coordinating Editor: Katie Sullivan
Copy Editor: Vanessa Moore
Compositor: SPi Global
Indexer: SPi Global
Artist: SPi Global
Cover Designer: Anna Ishchenko

Distributed to the book trade worldwide by Springer Science+Business Media New York, 233 Spring Street, 6th Floor, New York, NY 10013. Phone 1-800-SPRINGER, fax (201) 348-4505, e-mail `orders-ny@springer-sbm.com`, or visit `www.springeronline.com`.

For information on translations, please e-mail `rights@apress.com`, or visit `www.apress.com`.

Apress and friends of ED books may be purchased in bulk for academic, corporate, or promotional use. eBook versions and licenses are also available for most titles. For more information, reference our Special Bulk Sales–eBook Licensing web page at `www.apress.com/bulk-sales`.

Any source code or other supplementary materials referenced by the author in this text is available to readers at `www.apress.com`. For detailed information about how to locate your book's source code, go to `www.apress.com/source-code`.

For my family.

—Chris Pitt

Contents at a Glance

Contents

About the Author

Christopher Pitt is an experienced developer living in Cape Town, South Africa. Having developed and maintained a plethora of high-traffic web sites in PHP, he has built up a collection of skills and tools to tackle many of the problems new PHP developers still face.

He works for a company called Knnktr, that specializes in long-term, social and mobile development; here, he spends his time shared between open source development and client-based projects.

He is a husband and a father of two; he is a Christian, and a dreamer.

About the Technical Reviewer

Wim Mostrey has more than a decade of experience building web applications in PHP. He loves enabling organizations to switch to open source software.

Acknowledgments

"Let the words of my mouth and the meditation of my heart be acceptable in your sight, O Lord, my rock and my redeemer." (Psalms 14:19, ESV)

I would like to thank my Lord for giving me the opportunity and skill with which to write this book, and letting me see it to completion.

I would like to thank my wife for countless cups of coffee, good council and lots of patience, and for her encouragement and prayer.

I would like to thank my mom and dad for their hope and love, and for their encouragement and prayer.

I would like to thank my friends and mentors, especially Grant and Wayne.

I would like to thank the team at Apress, especially Katie Sullivan; they have worked tirelessly to turn scribbles into something to be proud of.

Finally, to everyone who has helped despite my failure to mention them here, "No man is an island, entire of itself. Each is a piece of the continent, a part of the main." (John Donne, *Meditation XVII*)

Introduction

Who This Book Is For

This book is for new and old developers alike. It's designed in such a way that the basics are first explained and then advanced topics are covered. This means that more experienced developers might find certain sections (such as those explaining design patterns) to be old hat. If this is you, feel at liberty to skip ahead to the more challenging stuff.

If you are new to object-oriented programming, framework building, or PHP in general, I would recommend reading everything and taking breaks between reading to recap what you have learned by coding something.

What This Book Won't Teach You

This book won't teach you PHP. It assumes you have basic knowledge of PHP and are at least comfortable with building PHP web sites. If you are new to PHP or have never even used it, may I suggest that you take a look at *Beginning PHP 5 and MySQL* by W. Jason Gilmore (Apress, 2010) (`www.apress.com/9781893115514`), as it will give you an excellent understanding of PHP.

This book will not teach you how to be a CodeIgniter, Zend Framework, or CakePHP expert. While these frameworks are discussed and used in the course of this book, the purpose of their use is to illustrate the differences between their approaches and the approach we take when building our own framework.

Consequently, there are a variety of ways in which they could be used more efficiently or in a style recommended by their respective communities and documentation. The purpose of their use here is purely illustrative.

What This Book Will Teach You

If you are curious about learning how to better develop using object-oriented programming, or by building frameworks, or by designing clear and consistent APIs, then you will enjoy this book.

If you are curious about what goes into the making of popular MVC frameworks (such as those demonstrated in the later chapters) or why they have chosen certain paths of development, then you will enjoy this book.

If you want to become a better programmer, then it is my hope that you will find this book invaluable.

Source Code

Every line of code in this book is mirrored by the code contained within the archives (which can be downloaded from the companion site).

While great effort has been made to ensure that the code is syntactically sound (and will therefore run directly in your code editor), there might be times when dependencies are omitted to aid in shortening some of the longer code listings. When this is the case, you can be assured that the code omitted is already that which has been explained and created in previous chapters or on previous pages within the same chapter.

When in doubt, or if you are having problems executing source code, refer to the source code archives.

CHAPTER 1

Introduction to MVC

Software development is not a new idea. Ada Lovelace is said to have written the first computer program in the mid-nineteenth century for the Analytical Engine, the first mechanical computer prototyped by Charles Babbage. Much time has passed since then, and software development has grown into what is arguably one of the largest contributors to the development of our species.

Designing good software is hard. It involves taking into consideration all aspects of the application you need to build, and is complicated further by the need to be specific enough to your current requirements to get the job done, while being generic enough to address future problems. Many experienced developers have had these problems and, over time, common patterns have emerged that assist in solving them.

Christopher Alexander, a structural architect, first described patterns in such a way that they can be applied to software development. He said, "Each pattern describes a problem which occurs over and over again in our environment, and then describes the core of the solution to that problem, in such a way that you can use this solution a million times over, without ever doing it the same way twice." He might have been talking about houses or cities, but his words capture the essence of what we intend to do when considering how we can build a solid, secure, and reusable framework for web applications.

What Is MVC?

MVC (Model-View-Controller) is a software design pattern built around the interconnection of three main component types, in a programming language such as PHP, often with a strong focus on object-oriented programming (OOP) software paradigms. The three component types are loosely termed models, views, and controllers. Let's talk about them individually and then see how they fit together.

The model is where all the business logic of an application is kept. Business logic can be anything specific to how an application stores data, or uses third-party services, in order to fulfill its business requirements. If the application should access information in a database, the code to do that would be kept in the model. If it needed, for example, to fetch stock data or tweet about a new product, that code would also be kept in the model.

The view is where all of the user interface elements of our application are kept. This can include our HTML markup, CSS style sheets, and JavaScript files. Anything a user sees or interacts with can be kept in a view, and sometimes what the user sees is actually a combination of many different views in the same request.

The controller is the component that connects models and views together. Controllers isolate the business logic of a model from the user interface elements of a view, and handle how the application will respond to user interaction in the view. Controllers are the first point of entry into this trio of components, because the request is first passed to a controller, which will then instantiate the models and views required to fulfill a request to the application. See Figure 1-1.

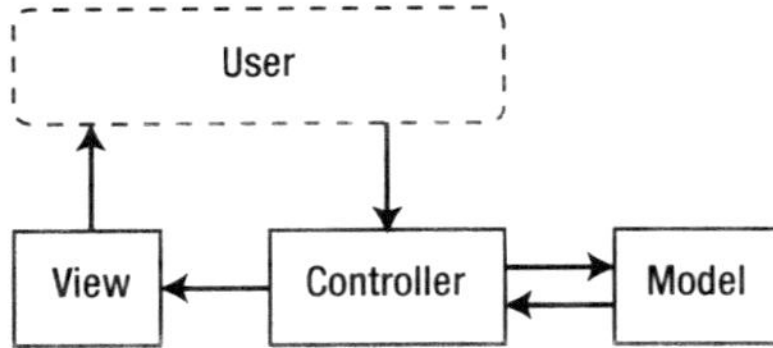

Figure 1-1. *Model-View-Controller in a nutshell*

■ **Note** Not every request to the application will require a model or a view. Which elements are loaded depends on the type of request and the resources required to fulfill it. The URL requested defines this, in a process called *routing*, which we will cover in Chapter 7. A controller could, for instance, serve only to toggle an application's state, or to return unparsed data directly from a third-party service. In such cases, there would be no need for models or views!

Let's look at an example application that illustrates the use of these classes. Social networks are usually simple to use, but can be quite complicated behind the scenes. If we were to build a simple social network, we would have to consider not only the user interface elements, but also how the user data is stored and how the user interface reacts to user input. We would need to consider the following aspects:

- Our social network is likely to maintain user data within a database. It will also need to access user photos from a third-party service, such as Flickr. The code for both these operations should be kept in models, as these operations directly relate to our business requirements.
- Our social network should be easy to use, and attractive to its users. Because we are building it for the Web, we will use standard web site technologies such as HTML for markup, externally linked CSS style sheets, and externally linked JavaScript files for behavior. All of these elements will be present in views.
- Our application's models and views must be connected together without interfering with one another. Additionally, the application needs a way to respond to user interaction in views and persist the relevant data to models. Controllers are used for this purpose.

Hopefully, this illustrates the concept in a way that makes sense. We will be looking at each part in much more detail throughout this book. The simple social network will also be used as a consistent example as we unpack the code required to make our framework work.

Benefits of MVC

There is no point explaining what MVC is without knowing why you should use it. Remember Christopher Alexander's patterns that I mentioned earlier? MVC is one of the many patterns that will be explained in this book, but to understand the usefulness of this design pattern, we must look toward the problems it helps to alleviate.

If you think of a sports team, you might realize that it is essentially a large group of players who fulfill their individual roles in order to drive the team forward. Good sports teams require the effort of each player performing their role to the best of their individual abilities to drive the team forward as a whole.

The Web is an open playing field. It allows businesses, both large and small, to compete against each other without size being a factor in the quality of work. This means many small companies with small developer pools can get the chance to build big web applications. It also means many big companies can have many people working on big web applications at the same time. In all this multitasking and/or group participation, the aspects of an application (which should be separate) often interfere with each other and require more time and effort than strictly necessary to drive forward.

There are many aspects to any complicated web application. There is design, which piques user interest in the product. There is business logic required to do practical things such as process sale items and invoice shoppers. Then there is the continual process of improving, updating, bug-fixing, and general streamlining of the application.

In any unstructured application, these areas tend to melt together in an incoherent mess. When the database needs to be changed to accommodate a new product line, or the company decides to rebrand, it doesn't only affect the code it should. More developers have to get involved to make sure that changes in one part of the application don't immediately break other parts of the application. Changes that should only affect a tiny section of code end up spilling into all sorts of strange and problematic areas.

This is the problem that MVC seeks to address. It defines strict containers for all of an application's code and features. When changes to database code are isolated in a model, views and controllers will not break. When an application's artwork changes drastically, its controller and model will be safe from breaking changes.

■ **Note** A good MVC-based application needs more than just a good MVC framework to succeed. It needs developers who are prepared to play by the rules and think carefully where they keep their code, instead of just throwing it in the codebase. We can only design the structure, just like an architect designing a beautiful house. It is up to the developers that use our framework to keep things in order.

Now that we know more about why we should be using MVC, let's look at some popular alternatives to writing our own framework.

Popular MVC Frameworks

There are many great PHP frameworks availible, but if we limit our view to just three, I think we can get a good idea of what they have in common, and what makes each special. These are not the best or the only PHP MVC frameworks, but simply a good cross-section of the different approaches to PHP MVC development.

CodeIgniter

CodeIgniter is the first and simplest of the frameworks we will be looking into. It is developed and maintained by EllisLab and can be described as an open source (though, tightly controlled) framework that forms the base for EllisLab's premium CMS (Content Management System) ExpressionEngine.

It has been around for ages, yet its ideals have changed very little in all the years since first I used it. It strives to maintain a tiny footprint, excellent developer documentation, and high code quality. It does not enjoy the same levels of popularity as some of the other frameworks we will talk about, and this is partly due to how EllisLab has managed the CodeIgniter community. They have recently begun to address this issue with new conferences and staff, and things are looking up for this framework.

It has also inspired other frameworks, giving birth to projects such as KohanaPHP.

■ **Note** You can download CodeIgniter at `http://codeigniter.com`. You can also learn more about EllisLab and ExpressionEngine at `http://ellislab.com`. Finally, you can learn more about KohanaPHP at `http://kohanaframework.org`.

Zend Framework

Zend Framework is an extensive collection of loosely coupled code libraries that can form the basis of an MVC architecture. Zend Framework takes quite a bit of effort to understand and master relative to other popular MVC frameworks. It is developed by Zend Technologies and enjoys all the benefits of a large, stable community and wide adoption.

Whereas frameworks like CodeIgniter strive to be lightweight, favoring just the essentials, Zend Framework includes libraries that help developers utilize a wide range of third-party services and APIs.

Note You can download Zend Framework at `http://framework.zend.com`. You can also learn more about Zend at `http://zend.com`.

CakePHP

CakePHP is arguably the most popular of the three frameworks. Unlike the previous two frameworks, it is not governed by any one corporate entity. It has a large community and is widely adopted.

It favors convention over configuration, which means a lot of the finer details are assumed and automated. This is apparent in every area of the framework, and you will often find yourself wondering how CakePHP is doing something you didn't ask it to do, both good and bad. This means you can develop an application quickly, but also that you might have a hard time when you need to make very specific changes.

This is even seen in the code-generation command-line tool: Bake. Within minutes, it can generate a working application, just by following command-line prompts and filling in the blanks with default parameters and behaviors.

Note You can download CakePHP at `http://cakephp.org`.

Design Patterns

We will be focusing on the MVC design pattern, and in order to achieve it, we will need to use other simpler design patterns for the libraries on which the framework is built. The design patterns we will review can often be applied to procedural development, but we will be looking at them in the context of object-oriented programming.

This means we will be dealing with classes (blueprints containing properties and performing functions), and how they interact with each other. If you are unfamiliar with some of the concepts that follow, you might want to refer to a language primer, or reference site.

Note If you would like to know more about object-oriented programming, or any of the other keywords/concepts that follow, you can read more at `http://en.wikipedia.org/wiki/Object-oriented_programming`.

Singleton

When we build OOP software, we deal with many classes. While it is ideal to design these classes in such a way that many instances can be active simultaneously, there will be times when we only practically need one instance of a class, for a specific purpose or context.

Singleton is a design pattern that ensures a class can have only one instance at a time. A traditional Singleton class maintains one instance of itself in an internal static property, and cannot be instantiated (or cloned) in the usual way that a non-Singleton class can. Singletons have a special instance accessor method, which returns the internal instance property, or creates a new instance to return and store. See Figure 1-2.

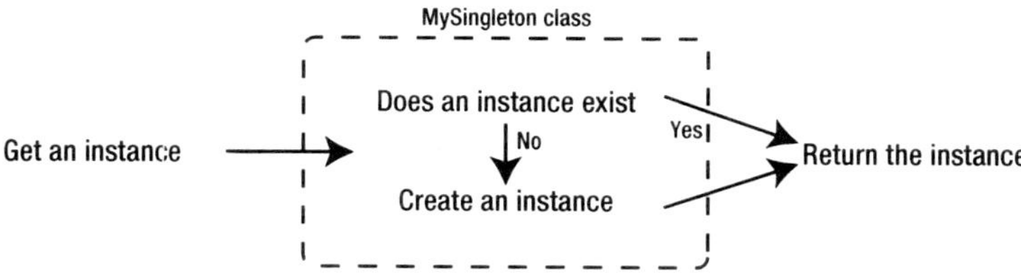

Figure 1-2. *The Singleton process*

Note You can read more about the Singleton at `http://en.wikipedia.org/wiki/Singleton_pattern`.

Registry

A Registry is a class that can store and return instances of standard classes. Think of it like a team manager that brings players off the playing field and sends new ones in as required. We use Registry classes to manage a finite amount of class instances, so that we don't need to keep on reinstantiating classes that the Registry already contains instances of.

Another way to think of a Registry class is that it helps us to treat normal classes like Singletons, without having to make those normal classes Singletons. We might find ourselves in a situation where we need two instances of a class. Perhaps we need to connect to two separate databases, but we don't want to keep on connecting to them, so we use a Registry. See Figure 1-3.

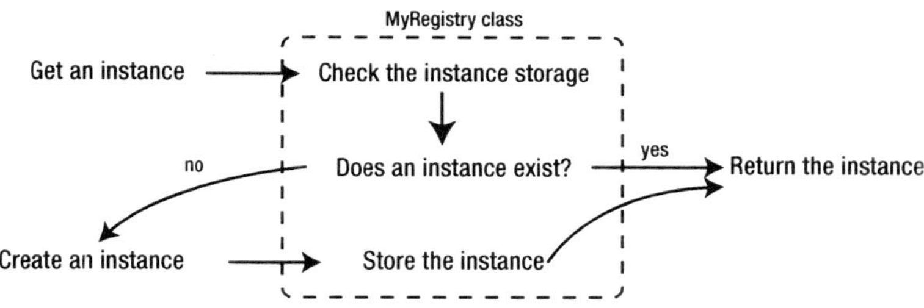

Figure 1-3. *The Registry process*

Note You can read more about the Registry pattern at `http://blog.fedecarg.com/2007/10/26/registry-pattern-or-dependency-injection-container`.

Factory

A Factory is a class that provides a singular interface for creating any number of instances, without actually needing to specify the type of class the instances should be. A Factory will choose which class to instantiate based on input or internal logic.

Factories are useful when we need to perform database work, but could be dealing with any number of different database drivers. We use a Factory class to give us the correct driver class, ensuring that all of our drivers conform to a standard interface. See Figure 1-4.

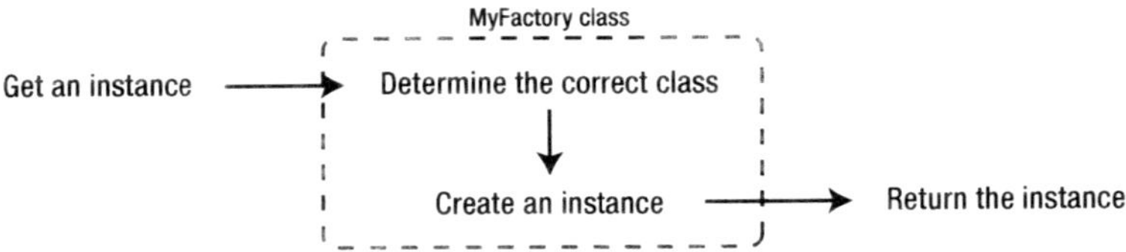

Figure 1-4. *The Factory process*

Note You can read more about the Factory pattern at `http://en.wikipedia.org/wiki/Factory_method_pattern`.

Observer

The Observer pattern describes a structure in which there are senders and receivers. When something changes in the state of a sender, it sends a message to the receivers associated with it, usually by calling one of their functions.

The most practical uses of this pattern are to implement event-based (asynchronous) software, and to facilitate loose coupling in classes only related by changes in application state. See Figure 1-5.

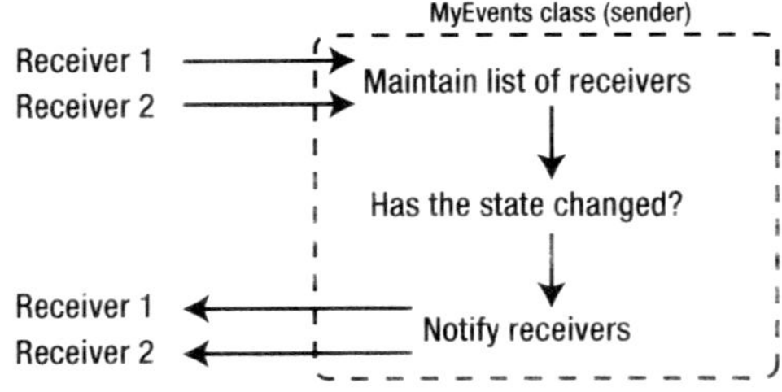

Figure 1-5. *The Observer process*

Note You can read more about the Observer pattern at `http://en.wikipedia.org/wiki/Observer_pattern`.

Creating Our Own Framework

You might be wondering why we would even need to create our own framework, when there are already so many good choices out there. The reason for this is so that we can gain an understanding of the underlying principles of MVC.

As we learn more about these principles, we will grow in our understanding of why the excellent MVC frameworks currently available do things the way they do. We are not learning how to create an application in Zend Framework, or in CakePHP. We are learning how MVC works, and by extension, how these frameworks have built upon (or deviated from) the way in which we would expect an MVC framework to be built.

Our goal isn't to add to the list of frameworks readily available for production use. Our goal is to learn how and why these frameworks do what they do, so that we can make informed decisions when it comes to selecting a framework for our next big project.

■ **Note** You are welcome to use the framework we build in a production environment, but I would caution against it unless you are prepared to invest a lot of time in the security and stability requirements of your framework, as these popular frameworks have taken years to do.

Goals

I have already mentioned our first goal, which is to learn. Above all else, our framework should teach us the core concepts that no MVC framework can do without. We will do this first by looking at some basic components, and later we will create an actual application upon these components. The important thing is that the core concepts of our framework should remain the same no matter what applications we build with it.

This will naturally inspire the second goal, which is to create a framework that is easy to configure, and makes the least assumptions possible about the applications we will build with it. This will be seen in both the application configuration later, as well as the underlying system code. We should try to only enable the configuration options where they make sense.

Our last goal is to create an abstract platform, capable enough of executing in many different environments, but focused only on those we can expect in our testing environment. To phrase it differently, I want us to allow for any color but start by painting it blue. This means we should create the infrastructure to be able to interface with many different kinds of databases, but to begin with, we will write only one database driver. It means we should create the infrastructure to be able store cache in a variety of places, but only be concerned with the first type we will deal with.

I want to get us in the mindset of dealing with the root of the problem, and all the ways in which we can solve it. I want us to learn what a true MVC framework should look like. I want us to strive for ways in which we can allow flexibility when it makes the most sense, and predictability when it makes the most sense. I want us to be concerned with all of this, while dealing with as few concrete cases as possible. When we have a good handle on everything, we can begin to branch out into multiple environments and services, but until then, we have our three goals.

CHAPTER 2

Foundation

We will begin our framework by looking at some foundational (OOP-focused) code on which the core components will be based. The first thing we will look at is how to execute code that is spread over multiple files. We will also look at what to do when we encounter errors. Finally, we will create a convenient means of sorting and retrieving class metadata.

Goals

- We need to develop a means to load classes automatically. Classes should be located based on their names, and these names should translate into a folder hierarchy.
- We need to understand and define custom `Exception` subclasses, so that we can handle the most common types of errors that could occur.
- We should also define a system of static classes that include utility methods for a number of data types.
- We should also develop a means to identify the structure (and intended use) of our framework classes that depends on the use of special code comments.

Autoloading

Because we are going to be writing a lot of code, it is safe to assume that we would want to structure the code clearly, to avoid confusion as the amount of code increases. There are a few ways in which we could do this, and one of them is keeping separate chunks of code in separate files. A problem that arises from this approach to code structure is that we will need to reference these external chunks of code from a single point of entry.

Requests to a web server tend to be routed to a single file in the server's webroot directory. For example, Apache web servers are usually configured to route default requests to `index.php`. We can keep all our framework code in this single file, or we can split it into multiple files and reference them from within `index.php`. PHP provides four basic statements for us to include external scripts within the program flow. These are shown in Listing 2-1.

Listing 2-1. The Four Basic require/include Functions

```
include("events.php");
include_once("inflection.php");
require("flash.php");
require_once("twitter.php");
```

The first statement will look for `events.php` within the PHP `include` path, and if it exists, PHP will load the file. If it cannot find the file, it will emit a warning. The second statement is the same as the first, except that it will only ever attempt to load the file `inflection.php` once. You can run the second statement as many times as you want, but the file will only be loaded the first time.

The third statement is much the same as the first, except that PHP will emit a fatal error (if uncaught it will stop execution of the script). The fourth statement is the same as the second, except that it will also emit a fatal error if the file cannot be found.

This means loading of classes is sufficient on a small scale, but it does have the following few drawbacks:

- You will always need to require/include the files that contain your scripts before you can use them. This sounds easy at first, but in a large system it is actually quite a painful process. You need to remember the path to each script and the right time to include them.
- If you opt to include all the scripts at the same time (usually at the top of each file), they will be in scope for the entire time the script is executing. They will be loaded first, before the script that requires them, and fully evaluated before anything else can happen. This is fine on a small scale, but can quickly slow your page load times.

Namespaces

One particularly useful new addition to PHP 5.3.0 is namespaces. Namespaces allow developers to sandbox their code, outside of the global namespace, to avoid class name conflicts and help organize their code better.

We will make use of namespaces in almost all of the classes we write, and they are not particularly tricky to use. Consider the example presented in Listing 2-2.

Listing 2-2. Namespaces

```
namespace Framework
{
    class Hello
    {
        public function world()
        {
            echo "Hello world!";
        }
    }
}

namespace Foo
{
    // allows us to refer to the Hello class
    // without specifying its namespace each time
    use Framework\Hello as Hello;

    class Bar
    {
        function __construct()
        {
            // here we can refer to Framework\Hello as simply Hello
            // due to the preceding "use" statement
            $hello = new Hello();
            $hello->world();
        }
    }
```

```
}
namespace
{
    $hello = new Framework\Hello();
    $hello->world(); //... prints "Hello world!"

    $foo = new Foo\Bar();
    $foo->bar(); //... prints "Hello world!"
}
```

As I mentioned before, namespaces help to remove classes from the global namespace. The namespace itself remains within the global namespace, so it must remain unique; however, it can contain any number of classes, which can reuse class names that are in the global namespace, or within other namespaces.

Note Namespaces are not a requirement of the MVC design pattern, but they certainly do help to avoid class and function name collisions. Some popular MVC frameworks (such as Symphony) already organize their classes in namespaces.

Lazy Loading

We can use the `require/include` methods to load our classes, or we can use another method PHP gives us: the `spl_autoload_register()` function. This built-in function allows us to provide our own code, to use as a means of loading a class based on the name of the class requested.

The pattern we will use to find class files will be the title-case class name with a directory separator between each word and `.php` at the end. So if we need to load the `Framework\Database\Driver\Mysql` class, we will look for the file `framework/database/driver/mysql.php` (assuming our `framework` folder is in the PHP include path). See Listing 2-3 for an example.

Listing 2-3. Using spl_autoload_register

```
function autoload($class)
{
    $paths = explode(PATH_SEPARATOR, get_include_path());

    $flags = PREG_SPLIT_NO_EMPTY | PREG_SPLIT_DELIM_CAPTURE;
    $file = strtolower(str_replace("\\", DIRECTORY_SEPARATOR, trim($class, "\\"))).".php";

    foreach ($paths as $path)
    {
        $combined = $path.DIRECTORY_SEPARATOR.$file;

        if (file_exists($combined))
        {
            include($combined);
            return;
        }
    }

    throw new Exception("{$class} not found");
}

class Autoloader
{
    public static function autoload($class)
```

```
    {
        autoload($class);
    }
}
spl_autoload_register('autoload');
spl_autoload_register(array('autoloader', 'autoload'));

// these can only be called within a class context…
// spl_autoload_register(array($this, 'autoload'));
// spl_autoload_register(__CLASS__.'::load');
```

The first call to `spl_autoload_register()` tells PHP to use the `autoload()` method to load a class file by name. The second call to `spl_autoload_register()` tells PHP to use the `Autoloader::autoload()` method to load a class file by name. The third and fourth calls to `spl_autoload_register()` tell PHP to use the `autoload()` method, belonging to the class in which these `spl_autoload_register()` calls occur, to load a class file by name.

The `autoload()` function first splits the returned string of PHP's `get_include_path()` function into separate directories. It then constructs the target file name by splitting the requested class name on the second, third, fourth, and so on, uppercase letters and joining the words together using the `PATH_SEPARATOR` constant.

If it finds the target file within any of the `$paths` directories, it will include the file and end function execution with a `return` statement. If the file is not found by the end of the loop, through `$paths`, an `Exception` will be thrown. If no exception is thrown, you can assume that a file matching the class name was found (in one of the directories in the `include` path) and was included successfully.

Note If you would like to know more about PHP namespaces, you can see the full documentation (and some examples) at `http://php.net/manual/en/language.namespaces.php`.

Exceptions

One of the ways in which PHP deals with special conditions that change the normal flow of a program (e.g., runtime errors) is to raise exceptions. Along with the built-in `Exception` class, PHP also has a mechanism of detecting that an `Exception` has occurred, and doing something useful when it does. Listing 2-4 shows an example.

Listing 2-4. Try/Catch Control Flow Statement

```
try
{
    throw new Exception();
}
catch (Exception $e)
{
    echo "An exception was raised.";
}
```

Throughout this book, we will see code that deals with a wide range of `Exception` subclasses. Most of those subclasses we will make ourselves, though they will be subclasses of those found in the SPL. You might be wondering why we would ever need to subclass `Exception` (or any of the SPL `Exception` subclasses) if we can just `try/catch Exception` to deal with errors in our framework, as shown in Listing 2-5.

Listing 2-5. Catching Multiple Exception Types

```
try
{
    throw new LogicException();
}
catch (ClassDidNotLoadException $e)
{
    // runs only if the Exception thrown
    // is of type "LogicException"
    echo "LogicException raised!";
}
catch (Exception $e)
{
    // runs only if an Exception was thrown which
    // was not caught by any previous catch blocks
    echo "Something went wrong, and we don't know what it was…";
}
```

As you can see, PHP's `try/catch` statement allows us to catch multiple types of `Exception`. This isn't really valuable to us when we can only expect one type of `Exception` to occur, but in a complicated framework of many classes and contexts, it becomes quite valuable in maintaining a stable system.

Think of a situation in which we are interacting with a database. A simple record update can fail in a number of contextually separate ways. There could be a problem connecting to the database, missing data preventing successful validation, or even a syntax error in the underlying SQL we send to the database. All of these contexts can have different `Exception` subclasses, and can be trapped in the same `try/catch` statement, with minimal effort.

One final benefit of creating many `Exception` subclasses is that we can respond to the user interface based on what `Exception` subclass is being thrown. We might want to display different views depending on whether the `Exception` thrown is caused by a problem in the database, or caused by a problem in the caching classes, and so forth.

It is important to remember that any time you see a class instance being thrown that contains the word `Exception`, it is likely an `Exception` subclass that we have created to signify a specific error. We won't always cover the code for individual `Exception` subclasses, but at least we know the reasons for creating them, and that they resemble the original `Exception` class.

Type Methods

In the remainder of this chapter, and the following chapters, we will be using many utility methods for working with the basic data types we find in PHP. To keep the code organized, we will include these utility methods as static methods on static type classes; for example, `string` methods on the `StringMethods` class (see Listing 2-6), `array` methods on the `ArrayMethods` class (see Listing 2-7), and so forth. We will be adding to these classes over time, but for now they will contain the methods given in Listings 2-6 and 2-7.

Listing 2-6. The StringMethods Class

```
namespace Framework
{
    class StringMethods
    {
        private static $_delimiter = "#";

        private function __construct()
```

```
        {
            // do nothing
        }
        private function __clone()
        {
            // do nothing
        }

        private static function _normalize($pattern)
        {
            return self::$_delimiter.trim($pattern, self::$_delimiter).self::$_delimiter;
        }

        public static function getDelimiter()
        {
            return self::$_delimiter;
        }

        public static function setDelimiter($delimiter)
        {
            self::$_delimiter = $delimiter;
        }

        public static function match($string, $pattern)
        {
            preg_match_all(self::_normalize($pattern), $string, $matches, PREG_PATTERN_ORDER);

            if (!empty($matches[1]))
            {
                return $matches[1];
            }

            if (!empty($matches[0]))
            {
                return $matches[0];
            }

            return null;
        }

        public static function split($string, $pattern, $limit = null)
        {
            $flags = PREG_SPLIT_NO_EMPTY | PREG_SPLIT_DELIM_CAPTURE;
            return preg_split(self::_normalize($pattern), $string, $limit, $flags);
        }
    }
}
```

The `$delimiter` and `_normalize()` members are all for the normalization of regular expression strings, so that the remaining methods can operate on them without first having to check or normalize them. The `match()` and `split()` methods perform similarly to the `preg_match_all()` and `preg_split()` functions, but require less formal structure to the regular expressions, and return a more predictable set of results. The `match()` method will return the first captured substring, the entire substring match, or null. The `split()` method will return the results of a call to the `preg_split()` function, after setting some flags and normalizing the regular expression.

Listing 2-7. The ArrayMethods Class

```
namespace Framework
{
    class ArrayMethods
    {
        private function __construct()
        {
            // do nothing
        }

        private function __clone()
        {
            // do nothing
        }

        public static function clean($array)
        {
            return array_filter($array, function($item) {
                return !empty($item);
            });
        }

        public static function trim($array)
        {
            return array_map(function($item) {
                return trim($item);
            }, $array);
        }
    }
}
```

The `clean()` method removes all values considered `empty()` and returns the resultant array. The `trim()` method returns an array, which contains all the items of the initial array, after they have been trimmed of all whitespace.

Note We are not trying to re-create every built-in PHP function. Whenever your code can be achieved easily using built-in functions, make very sure your reasons for creating the method are worth the confusion and repetition involved. When is a good time to reinvent the wheel? Only when you have a better wheel!

Metadata

One of our goals is sensible configuration. Another goal is building an abstract platform that can cater to many different kinds of services/implementations within the same underlying structure. Some implementations will naturally need a means of specifying configuration data. The easiest way to provide this configuration is through a configuration file parser.

We will build such a parser in the chapters to come, but how do we configure all the code leading up to the parser itself, and what about configuration details that can't sensibly be stored in a separate file? To illustrate this, let us look at the example shown in Listing 2-8.

Listing 2-8. In the Doghouse

```
class Dog
{
    public $doghouse;

    public function goSleep()
    {
        $location = $this->doghouse->location;
        $smell = $this->doghouse->smell;

        echo "The doghouse is at {$location} and smells {$smell}.";
    }
}

class Doghouse
{
    public $location;
    public $smell;
}

$doghouse = new Doghouse();
$doghouse->location = "back yard";
$doghouse->smell = "bad";

$dog = new Dog();
$dog->doghouse = $doghouse;
$dog->goSleep();
```

If the `$location` and `$smell` properties are only ever used in the same context, then our classes need none of this configuration we've been speaking about. If, on the other hand, these properties can have different meaning based on the implementation, we would need a means of defining this alternative context.

Say, for instance, we wanted to create a `Doghouse` subclass in which `$location` could be defined as the location inside the `Doghouse` in which the `Dog` sleeps; or say we wanted to define `$smell` as a percentage of scents the `Dog` can smell from inside the `Doghouse` .

In these cases, we could always add additional properties to the `Doghouse` class to provide the context for the initial properties. More often, though, developers will leave it to the next guy to figure out the context, sometimes based on the variable names or comments. On the one hand, variables should be named in such a way that their context and meaning are evident. On the other hand, this seldom happens.

There could also be times when we just want the extra flexibility, or when our framework code needs to act on this kind of data, without the added benefit of being able to understand human thinking. At such times, it would be great to have some way to allow us to describe aspects of a class, from within the class.

If you have used any programming language, you are undoubtedly familiar with the concept of comments. They are there to help developers make notes that will only be visible to other developers with access to the source code. One of the standard formats in which comments can be written is the Doc Comments format. The Doc Comments variant specific to PHP is called PHPDocs. Doc Comments look similar to normal multiline comments, but start with `/**` (as opposed to `/*`). PHP also has built-in classes that allow us to inspect these kinds of comments, which will allow us to provide the configuration metadata we are after. Consider the examples shown in Listing 2-9.

Listing 2-9. Examples of Doc Comments

```
class Controller
{
    /**
    * @readwrite
```

```
    */
    protected $_view;

    /**
    * @once
    */
    public function authenticate()
    {
        // ...authenticate the current user
    }
}
```

Perhaps we could want to enforce read-only/write-only/read-write behavior on class properties. The `$_view` property is protected, so it is not accessible outside the class, but imagine we have getters/setters for our class's protected properties. We could, in those getters/setters, read the Doc Comments of our protected properties and enforce behavior based on them.

Perhaps we could want to make sure a method is executed only once. Other methods in our class could read the Doc Comments and ensure they do not call the `authenticate()` method if it has already been called.

These are two small, but effective examples of situations that we would require metadata for, and could provide it using Doc Comments. We will need to write a class that allows us to inspect these Doc Comments, and return the relevant key/value pairs for us to use elsewhere.

Let us create this class now in Listing 2-10.

Listing 2-10. Internal Properties/Methods of Inspector Class

```
namespace Framework
{
    use Framework\ArrayMethods as ArrayMethods;
    use Framework\StringMethods as StringMethods;

    class Inspector
    {
        protected $_class;

        protected $_meta = array(
            "class" => array(),
            "properties" => array(),
            "methods" => array()
        );

        protected $_properties = array();
        protected $_methods = array();

        public function __construct($class)
        {
            $this->_class = $class;
        }

        protected function _getClassComment()
        {
            $reflection = new \ReflectionClass($this->_class);
            return $reflection->getDocComment();
        }

        protected function _getClassProperties()
        {
```

```
            $reflection = new \ReflectionClass($this->_class);
            return $reflection->getProperties();
        }

        protected function _getClassMethods()
        {
            $reflection = new \ReflectionClass($this->_class);
            return $reflection->getMethods();
        }

        protected function _getPropertyComment($property)
        {
            $reflection = new \ReflectionProperty($this->_class, $property);
            return $reflection->getDocComment();
        }

        protected function _getMethodComment($method)
        {
            $reflection = new \ReflectionMethod($this->_class, $method);
            return $reflection->getDocComment();
        }
    }
}
```

The first few methods of our Inspector class use built-in PHP reflection classes to get the string values of Doc Comments, and to get a list of the properties and methods of a class. If we only wanted the string values, we could make the _getClassComment(), _getPropertyComment(), and _getMethodComment() methods public. However, we have a much better use for these methods, as demonstrated in Listing 2-11.

Listing 2-11. Internal _parse() Method

```
namespace Framework
{
    use Framework\ArrayMethods as ArrayMethods;
    use Framework\StringMethods as StringMethods;

    class Inspector
    {
        protected function _parse($comment)
        {
            $meta = array();
            $pattern = "(@[a-zA-Z]+\s*[a-zA-Z0-9, ()_]*)";
            $matches = StringMethods::match($comment, $pattern);

            if ($matches != null)
            {
                foreach ($matches as $match)
                {
                    $parts = ArrayMethods::clean(
                       ArrayMethods::trim(
                            StringMethods::split($match, "[\s]", 2)
                        )
                    );

                    $meta[$parts[0]] = true;

                    if (sizeof($parts) > 1)
```

```
                {
                    $meta[$parts[0]] = ArrayMethods::clean(
                        ArrayMethods::trim(
                            StringMethods::split($parts[1], ",")
                        )
                    );
                }
            }
        }

        return $meta;
    }
  }
}
```

The internal _parse() method uses a fairly simple regular expression to match key/value pairs within the Doc Comment string returned by any of our _get…Meta() methods. It does this using the StringMethods::match() method. It loops through all the matches, splitting them by key/value. If it finds no value component, it sets the key to a value of true. This is useful for flag keys such as @readwrite or @once. If it finds a value component, it splits the value by, and assigns an array of value parts to the key. Finally, it returns the key/value(s) associative array. These internal methods are used by the public methods shown in Listing 2-12, which will be used to return the parsed Doc Comment string data.

Listing 2-12. Public Methods

```
namespace Framework
{
    use Framework\ArrayMethods as ArrayMethods;
    use Framework\StringMethods as StringMethods;

    class Inspector
    {
        public function getClassMeta()
        {
            if (!isset($_meta["class"]))
            {
                $comment = $this->_getClassComment();

                if (!empty($comment))
                {
                    $_meta["class"] = $this->_parse($comment);
                }
                else
                {
                    $_meta["class"] = null;
                }
            }

            return $_meta["class"];
        }

        public function getClassProperties()
        {
            if (!isset($_properties))
            {
```

```
            $properties = $this->_getClassProperties();

            foreach ($properties as $property)
            {
                $_properties[] = $property->getName();
            }
        }

        return $_properties;
    }

    public function getClassMethods()
    {
        if (!isset($_methods))
        {
            $methods = $this->_getClassMethods();

            foreach ($methods as $method)
            {
                $_methods[] = $method->getName();
            }
        }

        return $_properties;
    }

    public function getPropertyMeta($property)
    {
        if (!isset($_meta["properties"][$property]))
        {
            $comment = $this->_getPropertyComment($property);

            if (!empty($comment))
            {
                $_meta["properties"][$property] = $this->_parse($comment);
            }
            else
            {
                $_meta["properties"][$property] = null;
            }
        }

        return $_meta["properties"][$property];
    }

    public function getMethodMeta($method)
    {
        if (!isset($_meta["actions"][$method]))
        {
            $comment = $this->_getMethodComment($method);

            if (!empty($comment))
            {
                $_meta["methods"][$method] = $this->_parse($comment);
            }
            else
            {
```

```
                    $_meta["methods"][$method] = null;
                }
            }

            return $_meta["methods"][$method];
        }
    }
}
```

The public methods of our Inspector class utilize all of our internal methods to return the Doc Comment string values, parse them into associative arrays, and return usable metadata. Since classes cannot change at runtime, all of the public methods cache the results of their first execution within the internal properties. Our public methods allow us to list the methods and properties of a class. They also allow us to return the key/value metadata of the class, named methods, and named properties, without the methods or properties needing to be public. Let us take a look at what the complete class looks like in Listing 2-13.

Listing 2-13. The Inspector Class

```
namespace Framework
{
    use Framework\ArrayMethods as ArrayMethods;
    use Framework\StringMethods as StringMethods;
    class Inspector
    {
        protected $_class;

        protected $_meta = array(
            "class" => array(),
            "properties" => array(),
            "methods" => array()
        );

        protected $_properties = array();
        protected $_methods = array();

        public function __construct($class)
        {
            $this->_class = $class;
        }

        protected function _getClassComment()
        {
            $reflection = new \ReflectionClass($this->_class);
            return $reflection->getDocComment();
        }

        protected function _getClassProperties()
        {
            $reflection = new \ReflectionClass($this->_class);
            return $reflection->getProperties();
        }

        protected function _getClassMethods()
        {
            $reflection = new \ReflectionClass($this->_class);
            return $reflection->getMethods();
```

```
    }

    protected function _getPropertyComment($property)
    {
        $reflection = new \ReflectionProperty($this->_class, $property);
        return $reflection->getDocComment();
    }

    protected function _getMethodComment($method)
    {
        $reflection = new \ReflectionMethod($this->_class, $method);
        return $reflection->getDocComment();
    }

    protected function _parse($comment)
    {
        $meta = array();
        $pattern = "(@[a-zA-Z]+\s*[a-zA-Z0-9, ()_]*)";
        $matches = StringMethods::match($comment, $pattern);

        if ($matches != null)
        {
            foreach ($matches as $match)
            {
                $parts = ArrayMethods::clean(
                   ArrayMethods::trim(
                        StringMethods::split($match, "[\s]", 2)
                    )
                );

                $meta[$parts[0]] = true;

                if (sizeof($parts) > 1)
                {
                    $meta[$parts[0]] = ArrayMethods::clean(
                        ArrayMethods::trim(
                            StringMethods::split($parts[1], ",")
                        )
                    );
                }
            }
        }

        return $meta;
    }

    public function getClassMeta()
    {
        if (!isset($_meta["class"]))
        {
            $comment = $this->_getClassComment();

            if (!empty($comment))
            {
                $_meta["class"] = $this->_parse($comment);
            }
```

```
        else
        {
            $_meta["class"] = null;
        }
    }

    return $_meta["class"];
}

public function getClassProperties()
{
    if (!isset($_properties))
    {
        $properties = $this->_getClassProperties();

        foreach ($properties as $property)
        {
            $_properties[] = $property->getName();
        }
    }

    return $_properties;
}

public function getClassMethods()
{
    if (!isset($_methods))
    {
        $methods = $this->_getClassMethods();

        foreach ($methods as $method)
        {
            $_methods[] = $method->getName();
        }
    }

    return $_properties;
}

public function getPropertyMeta($property)
{
    if (!isset($_meta["properties"][$property]))
    {
        $comment = $this->_getPropertyComment($property);

        if (!empty($comment))
        {
            $_meta["properties"][$property] = $this->_parse($comment);
        }
        else
        {
            $_meta["properties"][$property] = null;
        }
    }

    return $_meta["properties"][$property];
```

```
        }

        public function getMethodMeta($method)
        {
            if (!isset($_meta["actions"][$method]))
            {
                $comment = $this->_getMethodComment($method);

                if (!empty($comment))
                {
                    $_meta["methods"][$method] = $this->_parse($comment);
                }
                else
                {
                    $_meta["methods"][$method] = null;
                }
            }

            return $_meta["methods"][$method];
        }
    }
}
```

Using the `Inspector` class, we can now determine all kinds of metadata, just by looking at the comments above each property/method! We will be using this, to great effect, in the following chapters.

■ **Note** You can read more about the PHP Reflection API at `http://php.net/manual/en/book.reflection.php`.

Questions

1. Our autoloader translates between class names and folder hierarchies. What benefit is this to us, over using the four `include`/`require` statements?
2. We set up a few static classes that contain utility methods for dealing with specific data types. Why is this preferable to us creating the same methods in the global namespace?
3. With the `Inspector` class, we can now evaluate special comment blocks for information, using code. What benefit will this be to us in later chapters?

Answers

1. Class autoloading is far better than manually including/requiring classes, especially in large systems. This is due to us no longer having to remember which dependencies to manually `include`/`require`. It's also more efficient, since nothing is loaded before it needs to be used.
2. The less we put in the global namespace, the better. The static classes are the ideal approach to handling these methods in an OOP manner.

3. We will be able to define and inspect different kinds of flags and key/value pairs. This could be for something as simple as whether the method/property should be accessible from the `Router`, or something as complex as specifying whether other methods should be called before or after the method being inspected.

Exercises

1. Try adding some code to track the amount of time it takes to load dependencies, as well as which dependencies are loaded.
2. Try creating a few classes that contain special comments (with meta properties), which can then be inspected.

CHAPTER 3

Base Class

One of the excellent things about building an MVC framework, using OOP paradigms, is the ability for us to reuse code, with minimal effort. At any time, we might be required to add core functionality to the majority of our classes, and a good OOP base will help us to do this.

Imagine we build an application with our newly built framework, and we suddenly need to add new security measures across the whole application. We could make changes to every controller, invoking a repeated function, or referencing a shared function, but the best solution would be to add the shared functionality higher up the inheritance chain.

If all our framework classes inherit from one base class, we can easily add this sort of thing by merely changing one class. This is an example of how inheritance is good for our framework. We will also be looking at other uses for it, in the chapter that follows.

Goals

- We need to use the `Inspector` class, which we created last chapter, to inspect the methods/properties of our `Base` class, and any subclasses.
- With the retrieved metadata, we need to determine whether certain properties should be treated as though they have getters/setters.

Getters and Setters

In this chapter, we are going to look at how to create a solid base class, which allows us to use the inspector code we wrote, to create getters/setters. These getters/setters will be points of public access, giving access to protected class properties. Before we begin doing this, let us take a look at some examples, as shown in Listing 3-1.

Listing 3-1. Publicly Accessible Properties

```
class Car
{
    public $color;
    public $model;
}

$car = new Car();
$car->color = "blue";
$car->model = "b-class";
```

In this example, the properties of the Car class are publicly accessible. This is how PHP 4 (and earlier versions) treated all class properties and methods. Since the release of PHP 5, PHP developers have been able to start using property/method scope—something most other OOP languages have allowed for a long time.

The main reason instance/class properties are used is to influence the execution of instance/class method logic. It follows that we may often want to prevent outside interference, or at least intercept this interference with what are commonly called getters/setters.

Consider the example given in Listing 3-2.

Listing 3-2. Variables That Should Be Private/Protected

```
class Database
{
    public $instance;
    public function __construct($host, $username, $password, $schema)
    {
        $this->instance = new MySQLi($host, $username, $password, $schema);
    }

    public function query($sql)
    {
        return $this->instance->query($sql);
    }
}

// you should specify a username, password and schema that matches your database
$database = new Database("localhost", "username", "password", "schema");

$database->instance = "cheese";

$database->query("select * from pantry");
```

In this example, our class opens a connection to a MySQL database when we create a new Database instance. Since the $instance property is public, it can be modified externally, at any time. It is not a valid database connector instance; a call to the query() method will raise an exception. In fact, we do this by setting the $instance property to "cheese", which makes the following call to the query() method raise an exception. Let us see how getters/setters might help us avoid this problem, as demonstrated in Listing 3-3.

Listing 3-3. Protecting Sensitive Variables

```
class Database
{
    protected $_instance;

    public function getInstance()
    {
        throw new Exception("Instance is protected");
    }

    public function setInstance($instance)
    {
        if ($instance instanceof MySQLi)
        {
            $this->_instance = $instance;
        }

        throw new Exception("Instance must be of type MySQLi");
    }
```

```
    public function __construct($host, $username, $password, $schema)
    {
        $this->_instance = new MySQLi($host, $username, $password, $schema);
    }

    public function query($sql)
    {
        return $this->_instance->query($sql);
    }
}
```

Our database connection instance is now protected against external interference. Our class will also give some useful information about how interaction with the `$instance` property is handled, which is helpful for other developers.

Like their names suggest, getters/setters are methods that get or set something. They are usually instance methods, and are considered best practice when allowing external access to internal variables. They commonly follow the pattern `getProperty()`/`setProperty()`, where `Property` can be any noun. Let us see what our `Car` class would look like with getters/setters, as shown in Listing 3-4.

Listing 3-4. Simple Getters/Setters

```
class Car
{
    protected $_color;
    protected $_model;

    public function getColor()
    {
        return $this->_color;
    }

    public function setColor($color)
    {
        $this->_color = $color;
        return $this;
    }

    public function getModel()
    {
        return $this->_model;
    }

    public function setModel($model)
    {
        $this->_model = $model;
        return $this;
    }
}

$car = new Car();
$car->setColor("blue");
$car->setModel("b-class");
```

There are a few important things to notice here. The first is that we actually need to create the getter/setter methods ourselves. Some other languages do this automatically, or with much less code, but there is no native getters/setters support in PHP.

Instead of using public properties, we make them protected/private. The aim is to allow access only through the getters/setters. The getColor() and getModel() methods simply return the values of those protected properties. The setColor() and setModel() methods set the values for those protected properties, and return $this. Because we return $this, we can chain calls to the setter methods.

These getters/setters are really quite simple, but there is nothing stopping us from adding additional logic to them, such as validation on the setters, or transformations to the getters.

Magic Methods

What PHP lacks, in native getter/setter support, it makes up for with magic methods. As their name suggests, magic methods perform functionality in addition to that of ordinary functions/methods. We have already seen two magic methods: __construct() and __destruct().

The magic method we will be focusing on is __call(). The __call() method is an instance method, which is invoked whenever an undefined method is called on a class instance. To put it another way, if you call a method that has not been defined, the class's __call() method will be called instead. Let us look at an example in Listing 3-5.

Listing 3-5. The __call() Method

```
class Car
{
    public function __call($name, $arguments)
    {
        echo "hello world!";
    }
}

$car = new Car();
$car->hello();
```

We do not define a hello() method on the Car class, but when we execute this code, we can see that the __call() method will be run, and will output the string "hello world!". This is because __call() is automatically invoked when an undefined method is called on an instance of Car.

We can use this to our advantage. If we expect our getters/setters to follow the format of getProperty()/setProperty(), we can create a __call() method that interprets exactly which property we seek to allow access to, and make the relevant changes/return the correct data. How would we do that, exactly? Take a look at the example shown in Listing 3-6.

Listing 3-6. Using __call() for Getters/Setters

```
class Car
{
    protected $_color;
    protected $_model;

    public function __call($name, $arguments)
    {
        $first = isset($arguments[0]) ? $arguments[0] : null;

        switch ($name)
        {
            case "getColor":
                return $this->_color;
```

```
            case "setColor":
                $this->_color = $first;
                return $this;

            case "getModel":
                return $this->_model;

            case "setModel":
                $this->_model = $first;
                return $this;
        }
    }
}

$car = new Car();
$car->setColor("blue")->setModel("b-class");
echo $car->getModel();
```

In this example, we can note a few important things. First, the `__call()` method is always provided with two properties: the `$name` of the method being called, and an array of `$arguments` given during the call to the method. If no arguments are given, this array will be empty.

We then have to account for all the accessor methods that will be called, which we do with the `switch` statement. We could use a lot of `if/else` statements, but `switch` works best for a list of preset methods. You might notice that we do not need to use `break` statements, as `return` statements will prevent further cases from being executed.

In this example, the getter/setter logic differs little from property to property. It makes sense to reuse all of the surrounding code, and simply implement the few lines of code required for handling each individual property, than it does repeating the same body of code for each property.

Adding Introspection

This approach works well for a limited number of non-public properties, but wouldn't it be cool if we could account for many non-public properties, without even needing to duplicate any code? We can achieve this by utilizing a combination of the knowledge we have gained about the `__call()` method, as well as the `Inspector` class we built previously.

Imagine we could tell our `Base` class to create these getters/setters simply by adding comments around the protected properties, as in the example given in Listing 3-7.

Listing 3-7. Creating Getters/Setters with Comments

```
class Car extends Framework\Base
{
    /**
    * @readwrite
    */

    protected $_color;
    /**
    * $write
    */
    protected $_model;
}
```

```
$car = new Car();
$car->setColor("blue")->setModel("b-class");
echo $car->getColor();
```

In order for us to achieve this sort of thing, we would need to determine the name of the property that must be read/modified, and also determine whether we are allowed to read/modify it, based on the @read/@write/ @readwrite flags in the comments. Let us begin by taking a look at what our Base class will look like, as shown in Listing 3-8.

Listing 3-8. Base __construct() Method

```
namespace Framework
{
    use Framework\Inspector as Inspector;
    use Framework\ArrayMethods as ArrayMethods;
    use Framework\StringMethods as StringMethods;
    use Framework\Core\Exception as Exception;

    class Base
    {
        private $_inspector;

        public function __construct($options = array())
        {
            $this->_inspector = new Inspector($this);

            if (is_array($options) || is_object($options))
            {
                foreach ($options as $key => $value)
                {
                    $key = ucfirst($key);
                    $method = "set{$key}";
                    $this->$method($value);
                }
            }
        }
    }
}
```

■ **Note** In the Chapter 2, I said that we would be using custom Exception subclasses. The Framework\Core\ Exception class you see in Listing 3-8 is just such a class. You can define these classes yourself, and they require nothing more than to subclass the built-in exception classes already provided by PHP. You can even leave the namespace out and use \Exception("...") in the listings that follow.

Private properties and methods cannot be shared even by subclasses, so I like to keep things protected whenever possible. In the case of the $_inspector property, we declare it private because we will only ever use it for the __call() method in our Base class and we don't want to add $_inspector to the class scope for subclasses, since every other class in our framework will inherit from it. The $_inspector property really just holds an instance of our Inspector class, which we will use to identify which properties our class should overload getters/setters for. Similarly to how we implemented getters/setters in the Car class, we will use the __call() magic method in our Base class, to handle getters/setters, as demonstrated in Listing 3-9.

Listing 3-9. The __call() Method

```
namespace Framework
{
    use Framework\Inspector as Inspector;
    use Framework\ArrayMethods as ArrayMethods;
    use Framework\StringMethods as StringMethods;
    use Framework\Core\Exception as Exception;

    class Base
    {
        public function __call($name, $arguments)
        {
            if (empty($this->_inspector))
            {
                throw new Exception("Call parent::__construct!");
            }
            $getMatches = StringMethods::match($name, "^get([a-zA-Z0-9]+)$");

            if (sizeof($getMatches) > 0)
            {
                $normalized = lcfirst($getMatches[0]);
                $property = "_{$normalized}";

                if (property_exists($this, $property))
                {
                    $meta = $this->_inspector->getPropertyMeta($property);
                    if (empty($meta["@readwrite"]) && empty($meta["@read"]))
                    {
                        throw $this->_getExceptionForWriteonly($normalized);
                    }

                    if (isset($this->$property))
                    {
                        return $this->$property;
                    }

                    return null;
                }
            }

            $setMatches = StringMethods::match($name, "^set([a-zA-Z0-9]+)$");
            if (sizeof($setMatches) > 0)
            {
                $normalized = lcfirst($setMatches[0]);
                $property = "_{$normalized}";

                if (property_exists($this, $property))
                {
                    $meta = $this->_inspector->getPropertyMeta($property);

                    if (empty($meta["@readwrite"]) && empty($meta["@write"]))
                    {
                        throw $this->_getExceptionForReadonly($normalized);
                    }

                    $this->$property = $arguments[0];
                    return $this;
```

```
                }
            }

            throw $this->_getExceptionForImplementation($name);
        }
    }
}
```

There are three basic parts to our `__call()` method: checking to see that the inspector is set, handling the `getProperty()` methods, and handling the `setProperty()` methods. Here, we begin to make a few assumptions about the general structure of the classes, which will inherit from the `Base` class.

We do not assume that the inspector property is set. This will often occur when the subclass does not currently call its parent `__construct()` method. An error description is given to this effect. We do assume that any accessor method calls that reach our `__call()` method probably refer to defined, non-public properties, belonging to the subclass. We assume they will follow the format of `setProperty()`/ `getProperty()`, so we strip out the get/set parts and append an underscore to the remaining string.

This will effectively transform calls for `setColor()`/`getColor()` to `_color`. If such a property does not exist in the subclass, we throw an exception. If the method called was a getter, we determine (via the metadata) whether reading the property is permissible. This will be the case if it has either `@read` or `@readwrite` flags. Should it be permissible to read the property, the property's value will be returned.

If the method called was a setter, we determine whether writing the property is permissible. This will be the case if it has either `@write` or `@readwrite` flags. Should it be permissible to write the property, the property's value will be set to the value of the first argument. You might be wondering what these exceptions look like, since we are only throwing the results of more methods.

If we create classes that inherit from this `Base` class, we can start to use getters/setters in a straightforward manner, simply by setting `@read`/`@write`/`@readwrite` flags within the metadata of our subclasses. Sure, there was a whole bunch of code that went into the actual `Base` class, and we need not create it if we only intend to use it once or twice.

We will, however, inherit from the `Base` class in almost every other class in our framework, so it's a good investment! Now, instead of writing our own accessor methods in each class we need them, we can inherit from the `Base` class, and have all the hard work done automatically.

Transparent Getters/Setters

At the beginning of the chapter, we contrasted the use of public properties to using getters/setters. What if we could use protected properties as if they were public and still have the added data security of using getters/ setters? Well we can, using the two magic methods shown in Listing 3-10.

Listing 3-10. The __get()/__set() Magic Methods

```
public function __get($name)
{
    $function = "get".ucfirst($name);
    return $this->$function();
}

public function __set($name, $value)
{
    $function = "set".ucfirst($name);
    return $this->$function($value);
}
```

At first glance, these methods don't really do much. The `__get()` method accepts an argument that represents the name of the property being set. In the case of `$obj->property`, the argument will be `property`. Our `__get()` method then converts this to `getProperty`, which matches the pattern we defined in the `__call()` method. What this means is that `$obj->property` will first try to set a public property with the same name, then go to `__get()`, then try to call the public method `setProperty()`, then go to `__call()`, and finally set the protected `$_property`.

The `__set()` method works similarly, except that it accepts a second argument, which defines the value to be set. It might be a little easier to see what's going on if you look at the diagram shown in Figure 3-1.

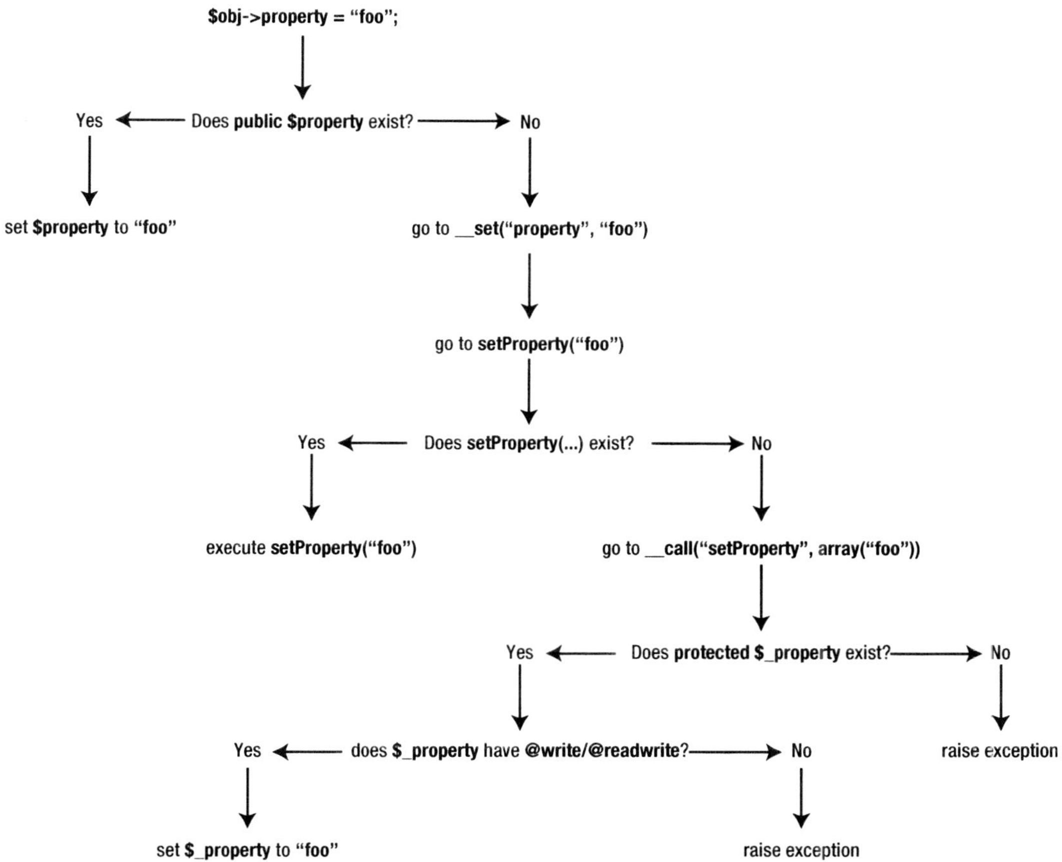

Figure 3-1. *Magic methods*

The full Base class looks like that shown in Listing 3-11.

Listing 3-11. The Base Class

```
namespace Framework
{
    use Framework\Inspector as Inspector;
    use Framework\ArrayMethods as ArrayMethods;
    use Framework\StringMethods as StringMethods;
```

```
use Framework\Core\Exception as Exception;

class Base
{
    private $_inspector;

    public function __construct($options = array())
    {
        $this->_inspector = new Inspector($this);

        if (is_array($options) || is_object($options))
        {
            foreach ($options as $key => $value)
            {
                $key = ucfirst($key);
                $method = "set{$key}";
                $this->$method($value);
            }
        }
    }

    public function __call($name, $arguments)
    {
        if (empty($this->_inspector))
        {
            throw new Exception("Call parent::__construct!");
        }

        $getMatches = StringMethods::match($name, "^get([a-zA-Z0-9]+)$");
        if (sizeof($getMatches) > 0)
        {
            $normalized = lcfirst($getMatches[0]);
            $property = "_{$normalized}";

            if (property_exists($this, $property))
            {
                $meta = $this->_inspector->getPropertyMeta($property);

                if (empty($meta["@readwrite"]) && empty($meta["@read"]))
                {
                    throw $this->_getExceptionForWriteonly($normalized);
                }

                if (isset($this->$property))
                {
                    return $this->$property;
                }

                return null;
            }
        }
        $setMatches = StringMethods::match($name, "^set([a-zA-Z0-9]+)$");
        if (sizeof($setMatches) > 0)
        {
```

```
                $normalized = lcfirst($setMatches[0]);
                $property = "_{$normalized}";

                if (property_exists($this, $property))
                {
                    $meta = $this->_inspector->getPropertyMeta($property);

                    if (empty($meta["@readwrite"]) && empty($meta["@write"]))
                    {
                        throw $this->_getExceptionForReadonly($normalized);
                    }

                    $this->$property = $arguments[0];
                    return $this;
                }
            }
            throw $this->_getExceptionForImplementation($name);
        }

        public function __get($name)
        {
            $function = "get".ucfirst($name);
            return $this->$function();
        }

        public function __set($name, $value)
        {
            $function = "set".ucfirst($name);
            return $this->$function($value);
        }

        protected function _getExceptionForReadonly($property)
        {
            return new Exception\ReadOnly("{$property} is read-only");
        }

        protected function _getExceptionForWriteonly($property)
        {
            return new Exception\WriteOnly("{$property} is write-only");
        }

        protected function _getExceptionForProperty()
        {
            return new Exception\Property("Invalid property");
        }

        protected function _getExceptionForImplementation($method)
        {
            return new Exception\Argument("{$method} method not implemented");
        }
    }
}
```

With these two magic methods in place, we can now treat protected methods as though they were public, while still using predefined (or inferred) getters/setters. Consider the example given in Listing 3-12.

Listing 3-12. Using Transparent Getters/Setters

```
class Hello extends Framework\Base
{
    /*
    * @readwrite
    */
    protected $_world;

    public function setWorld($value)
    {
        echo "your setter is being called!";
        $this->_world = $value;
    }

    public function getWorld()
    {
        echo "your getter is being called!";
        return $this->_world;
    }
}

$hello = new Hello();
$hello->world = "foo!";

echo $hello->world;
```

Amazingly, this example produces not only the expected `foo`, but also the additional strings defined in the getter/setter overrides. We don't have to define the getters/setters (as we do in this example) because our `__call()` method takes care of them. It's the best of both worlds!

Questions

1. What benefit is there to using getters and setters in our classes, when PHP doesn't even support them?
2. When we added the `Inspector` instance to the `Base` class, we stored it in a `private` variable. Why is this important?
3. We defined a few protected methods in the `Base` class, whose only purpose was to return an `Exception` subclass instance. Why could we not just deal with the `Exception` subclasses in the `__call()` method?

Answers

1. The main benefit to using getters/setters is that the protected values stored within our `Base` subclasses cannot be tampered with. Sure, `getProperty()` and `setProperty()` can be called, and will not be disallowed with the code we have defined, but what we are doing is providing a good base on which to build. Classes that should restrict access to their protected properties can do so, and the simple getters/setters will continue to work as before, with this code.

2. This `Inspector` instance will only ever be used to determine which properties should have simulated getters/setters. It could actually do more harm sitting around, accessible by subclasses, so we hide it from them by assigning it to a private property.

3. If we dealt directly with exceptions, not referencing these protected methods, then subclasses wouldn't be able to define their own exception types without overriding the `__call()` method themselves. This step is so that subclasses can easily define their own `Exception` subclasses.

Exercises

1. Our `Base` class only simulates getters and setters for properties that have the `@read/@write/@readwrite` meta flags. It doesn't provide any property validation, meaning that developers can set properties to null without any warning. Try adding another meta flag that prevents (or warns about) this.

2. Instead of defining methods that return subclass instance, try specifying the `Exception` subclasses another way. Perhaps you can use an array of strings, or a `switch` statement that will allow for the same flexibility.

CHAPTER 4

Configuration

One of our goals is to create a framework that is easy to configure, yet assumes some basic things so that it is fast to develop with and flexible to change. It follows that we would require a standard format for storing, and method for retrieving, configuration variables. There are a number of approaches to this topic, and in this chapter, we will look at two popular methods.

Goals

- We need to review different methods of configuration, and decide on the best one to use for our framework/application.
- We need to build a set of classes that we can use to parse configuration files, and provide a clear set of configuration options.

Associative Arrays

Associative arrays offer the simplest means of configuration. They are easy for any PHP developer to understand, and even simpler for our framework to parse. Listing 4-1 shows an example database settings file, and Listing 4-2 demonstrates how to parse it.

Listing 4-1. Example Associative Array Configuration File

```
$settings["database_default_provider"] = "mysql";
$settings["database_default_host"]     = "localhost";
$settings["database_default_username"] = "username";
$settings["database_default_password"] = "password";
$settings["database_default_port"]     = "3306";
$settings["database_default_schema"]   = "prophpmvc";
```

Listing 4-2. Loading Our Associative Array Configuration File

```
function parsePhp($path)
{
    $settings = array();
    include("{$path}.php");
    return $settings;
}
```

It really couldn't be simpler to parse associative arrays. All we need to do is predefine `$settings = array()`, and include the settings file. We could check whether any settings were loaded by using the `sizeof()` method on the array returned by the `parsePhp()` function, if we wanted to. The output is what you might expect, as shown in Listing 4-3.

Listing 4-3. Results of parsePhp()

```
Array
(
    [database_default_provider] => mysql
    [database_default_host] => localhost
    [database_default_username] => username
    [database_default_password] => password
    [database_default_port] => 3306
    [database_default_schema] => prophpmvc
)
```

As we can see, this method of configuration is easy to parse and change. If it sounds too good to be true, that's because it is. There are a number of reasons why we should look for another solution.

- We can only use one-dimensional configuration arrays. This is due our `parsePhp()` function needing to predefine `$settings` so that the configuration files have an array in which to store their data.
- It requires more code than is strictly necessary. All we are really interested in are the keys and values, not the PHP syntax surrounding them.

■ **Note** CakePHP and CodeIgniter use associative arrays for most of their configuration.

INI Files

The INI (**ini**tialization) file format is the standard format for configuration files in the Windows operating system. It is simple to change, and relatively simple to parse. Fortunately for us, PHP also comes with a handy `parse_ini_file()` function that will greatly simplify the creation of our settings parser. We should try to create a parser that will allow us to use dot notation for our keys/values. Listing 4-4 shows an example INI file.

Listing 4-4. Example INI Configuration File

```
database.default.type = mysql
database.default.host     = localhost
database.default.username = username
database.default.password = password
database.default.port     = 3306
database.default.schema   = prophpmvc
```

■ Note INI configuration files aren't handled in the same way as PHP files, at least not in Apache. If a user tries to access an INI file, it will probably not be modified and the user could have access to sensitive configuration settings such as username and passwords. You should always take steps to deny access to these files, and it would be best to even store them outside of a web-accessible directory.

Our configuration class will be the first factory class we create. We want to be able to extend it in the future with many different kinds of configuration possibilities, but (keeping our goals in mind) we will only be creating one driver. Let's first look at the factory class, as shown in Listing 4-5.

Listing 4-5. Configuration Factory Class

```
namespace Framework
{
    use Framework\Base as Base;
    use Framework\Configuration as Configuration;
    use Framework\Configuration\Exception as Exception;

    class Configuration extends Base
    {
        /**
        * @readwrite
        */
        protected $_type;

        /**
        * @readwrite
        */
        protected $_options;

        protected function _getExceptionForImplementation($method)
        {
            return new Exception\Implementation("{$method} method not implemented");
        }

        public function initialize()
        {
            if (!$this->type)
            {
                throw new Exception\Argument("Invalid type");
            }

            switch ($this->type)
            {
                case "ini":
                {
                    return new Configuration\Driver\Ini($this->options);
                    break;
                }
                default:
                {
                    throw new Exception\Argument("Invalid type");
                    break;
```

```
                }
            }
        }
    }
}
```

The Configuration factory class is also the first time we will use the getters/setters we created with the Base class. Both $_type and $_options can be read from and written to. If you refer back to the Base __construct() method, you will see that it takes the keys/values given in the first argument, and sets whatever protected properties it can find. If your initialization array had an options key, the protected $_options property would contain that value.

We first check to see that the $_type property value is not empty, as there is no sense trying to create a class instance if we don't know how to determine the class required. Next, we use a switch statement and the return value of $this->type, to select and instantiate the correct class type.

Because we will only support the "ini" type (for now), we throw ConfigurationExceptionArgument if the required type is not "ini". If the required type is "ini", we return a new instance, passing the instance the options supplied to the Configuration __construct() method. As you can see in Listing 4-6, the Configuration class is quite simple to use.

Listing 4-6. Creating a Configuration Object Using the Factory

```
$configuration = new Framework\Configuration(array(
    "type" => "ini"
));
$configuration = $configuration->initialize();
```

Because our factory allows many different kinds of configuration driver classes to be used, we need a way to share code across all driver classes. We achieve this by making our driver classes inherit from this base driver class, as demonstrated in Listing 4-7.

Listing 4-7. The Configuration\Driver Class

```
namespace Framework\Configuration
{
    use Framework\Base as Base;
    use Framework\Configuration\Exception as Exception;

    class Driver extends Base
    {
        protected $_parsed = array();

        public function initialize()
        {
            return $this;
        }

        protected function _getExceptionForImplementation($method)
        {
            return new Exception\Implementation("{$method} method not implemented");
        }
    }
}
```

We could get even more technical by using Interface definitions to enforce driver behavior, but we are already raising detailed implementation exceptions for calls to methods that haven't been implemented, which is enough for now. There are two basic methods for parsing our configuration files, which are demonstrated in Listings 4-8 and 4-9.

Listing 4-8. ArrayMethods::toObject() Method

```
namespace Framework
{
    class ArrayMethods
    {
        private function __construct()
        {
            // do nothing
        }

        private function __clone()
        {
            // do nothing
        }

        public static function toObject($array)
        {
            $result = new \stdClass();

            foreach ($array as $key => $value)
            {
                if (is_array($value))
                {
                    $result->{$key} = self::toObject($value);
                }
                else
                {
                    $result->{$key} = $value;
                }
            }

            return $result;
        }
    }
}
```

Listing 4-9. Configuration\Driver\Ini parse() Method

```
namespace Framework\Configuration\Driver
{
    use Framework\ArrayMethods as ArrayMethods;
    use Framework\Configuration as Configuration;
    use Framework\Configuration\Exception as Exception;

    class Ini extends Configuration\Driver
    {
        public function parse($path)
        {
            if (empty($path))
```

```
            {
                throw new Exception\Argument("\$path argument is not valid");
            }

            if (!isset($this->_parsed[$path]))
            {
                $config = array();

                ob_start();
                    include("{$path}.ini");
                    $string = ob_get_contents();
                ob_end_clean();

                $pairs = parse_ini_string($string);

                if ($pairs == false)
                {
                    throw new Exception\Syntax("Could not parse configuration file");
                }

                foreach ($pairs as $key => $value)
                {
                    $config = $this->_pair($config, $key, $value);
                }

                $this->_parsed[$path] = ArrayMethods::toObject($config);
            }

            return $this->_parsed[$path];
        }
    }
}
```

The only public method in our INI configuration parser class is a method called `parse()`. It first checks to see that the `$path` argument is not empty, throwing a `ConfigurationExceptionArgument` exception if it is. Next, it checks to see if the requested configuration file has not already been parsed, and if it has it jumps right to where it returns the configuration.

If it has not parsed the required configuration file, it uses output buffering to capture the contents of a call to `include()` the configuration file's contents. Using the `include()` method allows the configuration to be sitting anywhere relative to the paths in PHP's include path, though we will usually be loading them from a standard configuration folder.

It then parses the string contents of the configuration file using PHP's `parse_ini_string()` method, which returns an associative array of keys and values, stored in the `$pairs` variable. If nothing was returned to `$pairs`, we assume the configuration file contained invalid syntax, and raise a `ConfigurationExceptionSyntax` exception.

If it did return an associative array, we loop through the array, generating the correct hierarchy (using the `_pair()` method), finally converting the associative array to an object and caching/returning the configuration file data. You can see an example of using the `_pair()` method in Listing 4-10.

Listing 4-10. The _pair() Method

```
finamespace Framework\Configuration\Driver
{
    use Framework\ArrayMethods as ArrayMethods;
    use Framework\Configuration as Configuration;
    use Framework\Configuration\Exception as Exception;

    class Ini extends Configuration\Driver
```

```
    {
        protected function _pair($config, $key, $value)
        {
            if (strstr($key, "."))
            {
                $parts = explode(".", $key, 2);

                if (empty($config[$parts[0]]))
                {
                    $config[$parts[0]] = array();
                }
                $config[$parts[0]] = $this->_pair($config[$parts[0]], $parts[1], $value);
            }
            else
            {
                $config[$key] = $value;
            }

            return $config;
        }
    }
}
```

The `_pair()` method deconstructs the dot notation, used in the configuration file's keys, into an associative array hierarchy. If the $key variable contains a dot character (`.`), the first part will be sliced off, used to create a new array, and assigned the value of another call to `_pair()`. It's tricky at first, but works well and makes sense. Let's see what the complete driver class looks like, as shown in Listing 4-11.

Listing 4-11. The Configuration\Driver\Ini Class

```
namespace Framework\Configuration\Driver
{
    use Framework\ArrayMethods as ArrayMethods;
    use Framework\Configuration as Configuration;
    use Framework\Configuration\Exception as Exception;

    class Ini extends Configuration\Driver
    {
        protected function _pair($config, $key, $value)
        {
            if (strstr($key, "."))
            {
                $parts = explode(".", $key, 2);

                if (empty($config[$parts[0]]))
                {
                    $config[$parts[0]] = array();
                }

                $config[$parts[0]] = $this->_pair($config[$parts[0]], $parts[1], $value);
            }
            else
            {
                $config[$key] = $value;
```

```
            }
            return $config;
        }
        public function parse($path)
        {
            if (empty($path))
            {
                throw new Exception\Argument("\$path argument is not valid");
            }
            if (!isset($this->_parsed[$path]))
            {
                $config = array();
                ob_start();
                    include("{$path}.ini");
                    $string = ob_get_contents();
                ob_end_clean();
                $pairs = parse_ini_string($string);
                if ($pairs == false)
                {
                    throw new Exception\Syntax("Could not parse configuration file");
                }
                foreach ($pairs as $key => $value)
                {
                    $config = $this->_pair($config, $key, $value);
                }
                $this->_parsed[$path] = ArrayMethods::toObject($config);
            }
            return $this->_parsed[$path];
        }
    }
}
```

The configuration data looks slightly different from what we got using associative arrays, but this new format is actually much more orderly and easier to use. We don't need to keep everything in one large array. We can access the values with less code, by using object notation. The configuration files are also simpler to create and maintain, as shown in Listing 4-12.

Listing 4-12. Results of the parse() Method, with Our Previous INI Configuration File

```
stdClass Object
(
    [database] => stdClass Object
        (
            [default] => stdClass Object
                (
                    [type] => mysql
                    [host] => localhost
                    [username] => username
```

```
                [password] => password
                [port] => 3306
                [schema] => prophpmvc
            )
    )
)
```

■ **Note** Zend Framework includes a number of configuration file format parsers, but my favorite of the lot is their INI file parser.

The parser you build should reflect the needs of your framework. If associative arrays make the most sense, despite their shortcomings, then you should feel free to use them. We will make great use of the INI parsing code presented here in the remainder of this book, so if you do choose to use associative arrays (or any other kind of parser), then you need to adjust your code accordingly.

Now that we have a simple, reusable configuration system, we can begin to load all sorts of settings into our application, which will allow for a large degree of flexibility.

Questions

1. If associative arrays are easier to create and parse, why should we not use them for configuring our framework?
2. Factory classes seem to be much more work than normal classes. Why would we use them when we can just as well use normal classes for this sort of thing?

Answers

1. There might be benefits to using associative arrays for configuration, but there are also shortcomings. Associative arrays are not friendly to non-PHP programmers. They also require that the configuration file be free of syntax errors. This is not a requirement for INI configuration files.
2. The benefit of creating factory classes is that drivers can easily be added and swapped. We could add five other configuration parsers and they would all be called in much the same way as our INI configuration parser.

Exercises

1. Try creating a configuration driver to parse associative arrays. It should raise exceptions correctly, in the event that syntax errors occur.
2. Experiment with other methods of configuration. You could, for instance, try to create matching configuration drivers, further extending the framework's configuration library.

CHAPTER 5

Caching

Often, when dealing with large amounts of data, we run into performance bottlenecks. These can happen for any number of reasons, and can mostly be avoided by good *caching*. If you are wondering what I mean by *caching*, we'll look at an example in a moment.

Goals

- We should identify the need for using caching, in the first place. We will not be able to realize the full potential of caching unless we understand the problems that it solves.
- We need to learn how to access *Memcached* servers, which we will use to store cached data. This requires us writing the classes to interact with a Memcached server.

Performance Bottlenecks

Imagine a social network, where any user can have a number of friends. If a list of these friends were to be displayed on a web page, with all their relevant details, that page would have to make a database call to retrieve the friend records from the database. Now imagine that list of friends was shown on every page on the web site. Now we're talking about at least one database query for each page of the web site. Factor in thousands of users, who also have their friends lists displayed, and what you get is a lot of data.

In any application where growth or demand exceeds resources, this kind of data requirement can easily bring the application to its knees. So how could we employ caching to ease the stress on the database?

We could easily cache the list of friends, the very first time it is retrieved form the database. This means the web site will not need to make frequent, repeated requests for the same data. Instead of fetching the same data from the database every time we needed it, we could first check whether the data is stored in the cache.

Consider the configuration class we created in the Chapter 4. If we constantly need to use the configuration settings, it makes sense for us to cache them as well. The alternative is for us to load the same configuration file for every page on the web site, and for every user on the web site.

If we load the configuration data once, store it in the cache, and make subsequent requests for the configuration data from the cache, we will save much time.

Note The use of cache is not limited to storing database and configuration data. Those are simply the two examples I have used to illustrate the effectiveness of cache. Cache is useful wherever you are getting the same data repeatedly, from anything slower than the actual cache system.

The Code

If our aim is to build a framework that works fast, caching is unavoidable. We need something that stores cached data persistently, and our cache provider of choice is Memcached. It stores data in memory, in hash lookup tables so the data is quickly accessible without reading it from disk. Memcached is an open source HTTP caching system that can store huge amounts of key/value data for just such situations.

■ **Note** Memcached is not the only caching option we can use for our framework, but it is the only one you will see in this book. Consider it an exercise to create another cache driver, should you require an alternative means of caching. You can read more about Memcached at `www.memcached.org`.

Let us begin by creating our Cache factory class, as shown in Listing 5-1.

Listing 5-1. Cache Factory Class

```
namespace Framework
{
    use Framework\Base as Base;
    use Framework\Cache as Cache;
    use Framework\Cache\Exception as Exception;

    class Cache extends Base
    {
        /**
        * @readwrite
        */
        protected $_type;

        /**
        * @readwrite
        */
        protected $_options;

        protected function _getExceptionForImplementation($method)
        {
            return new Exception\Implementation("{$method} method not implemented");
        }

        public function initialize()
        {
            if (!$this->type)
            {
                throw new Exception\Argument("Invalid type");
            }
```

```
            switch ($this->type)
            {
                case "memcached":
                {
                    return new Cache\Driver\Memcached($this->options);
                    break;
                }
                default:
                {
                    throw new Exception\Argument("Invalid type");
                    break;
                }
            }
        }
    }
}
```

Our Cache factory class is very similar to our `Configuration` factory class. It accepts initialization options in exactly the same manner, and also selects the type of returned object, based on the internal `$_type` property. It raises `Cache\Exception\Argument` exceptions for invalid/unsupported types, and only supports one type of cache driver, `Cache\Driver\Memcached`. Just as we did for configuration, we will create cache driver classes, based on a standard driver class, as shown in Listing 5-2.

Listing 5-2. The Cache\Driver Class

```
namespace Framework\Cache
{
    use Framework\Base as Base;
    use Framework\Cache\Exception as Exception;

    class Driver extends Base
    {
        public function initialize()
        {
            return $this;
        }

        protected function _getExceptionForImplementation($method)
        {
            return new Exception\Implementation("{$method} method not implemented");
        }
    }
}
```

The `Cache\Driver` class is even simpler than the `Configuration\Driver` class. It only overrides Base's exception-generating methods to provide specific `Exception` subclasses for errors occurring within the `Cache\Driver` subclasses.

There are some internal properties and methods that our cache driver class will need to maintain, in order to interact successfully with a Memcached server. Take a look at these in Listing 5-3.

Listing 5-3. Cache\Driver\Memcached Internal Properties/Methods

```
namespace Framework\Cache\Driver
{
    use Framework\Cache as Cache;
    use Framework\Cache\Exception as Exception;

    class Memcached extends Cache\Driver
    {
        protected $_service;

        /**
        * @readwrite
        */
        protected $_host = "127.0.0.1";

        /**
        * @readwrite
        */
        protected $_port = "11211";

        /**
        * @readwrite
        */
        protected $_isConnected = false;

        protected function _isValidService()
        {
            $isEmpty = empty($this->_service);
            $isInstance = $this->_service instanceof \Memcache;

            if ($this->isConnected && $isInstance && !$isEmpty)
            {
                return true;
            }

            return false;
        }
    }
}
```

Unlike the `Configuration\Driver\Ini` class, the `Cache\Driver\Memcached` class actually makes use of the inherited accessor support. It defaults the `$_host` and `$_port` properties to common values, and calls the `parent::__construct($options)` method. Connections to the Memcached server are made via the `connect()` public method from within the `__construct()` method.

■ **Note** The defaults for `$_host` and `$_port` apply to the majority of installations. Yours could differ, in which case you might need to consult the documentation used to install Memcached.

The driver also has a protected `_isValidService()` method that is used ensure that the value of the `$_service` is a valid Memcached instance. Let us look at the `connect()/disconnect()` methods more closely in Listing 5-4.

Listing 5-4. Cache\Driver\Memcached connect()/disconnect() Methods

```
namespace Framework\Cache\Driver
{
    use Framework\Cache as Cache;
    use Framework\Cache\Exception as Exception;

    class Memcached extends Cache\Driver
    {
        public function connect()
        {
            try
            {
                $this->_service = new \Memcache();
                $this->_service->connect(
                    $this->host,
                    $this->port
                );
                $this->isConnected = true;
            }
            catch (\Exception $e)
            {
                throw new Exception\Service("Unable to connect to service");
            }

            return $this;
        }

        public function disconnect()
        {
            if ($this->_isValidService())
            {
                $this->_service->close();
                $this->isConnected = false;
            }

            return $this;
        }
    }
}
```

The `connect()` method attempts to connect to the Memcached server at the specified host/port. If it connects, the `$_service` property is assigned an instance of PHP's `Memcached` class, already connected to a Memcached service. If it fails to connect, a `CacheExceptionService` exception is raised.

The `disconnect()` method attempts to disconnect the `$_service` instance from the Memcached service. It will only do so if the `_isValidService()` method returns true.

Finally, we need to look at the general-purpose methods, which will be used for the majority of caching requirements. Take a look at Listing 5-5.

Listing 5-5. Cache\Driver\Memcached General-Purpose Methods

```
namespace Framework\Cache\Driver
{
    use Framework\Cache as Cache;
    use Framework\Cache\Exception as Exception;

    class Memcached extends Cache\Driver
    {
        public function get($key, $default=null)
        {
            if (!$this->_isValidService())
            {
                throw new Exception\Service("Not connected to a valid service");
            }

            $value=$this->_service->get($key, MEMCACHE_COMPRESSED);
            if ($value)
            {
                return $value;
            }
            return $default;
        }

        public function set($key, $value, $duration=120)
        {
            if (!$this->_isValidService())
            {
                throw new Exception\Service("Not connected to a valid service");
            }

            $this->_service->set($key, $value, MEMCACHE_COMPRESSED, $duration);
            return $this;
        }

        public function erase($key)
        {
            if (!$this->_isValidService())
            {
                throw new Exception\Service("Not connected to a valid service");
            }

            $this->_service->delete($key);
            return $this;
        }
    }
}
```

The `get()`, `set()`, and `erase()` methods do exactly as they say: get cached values, set values to keys, and erase values from keys, respectively. The second argument for the `get()` method allows for a default value to be supplied and returned in the event no cached value is found at the corresponding key. The second argument to the `set()` method is the duration for which the data should be cached. You can see the `Cache\Driver\Memcached` class in its entirety in Listing 5-6.

Listing 5-6. The Cache\Driver\Memcached Class

```
namespace Framework\Cache\Driver
{
    use Framework\Cache as Cache;
    use Framework\Cache\Exception as Exception;

    class Memcached extends Cache\Driver
    {
        protected $_service;

        /**
        * @readwrite
        */
        protected $_host = "127.0.0.1";

        /**
        * @readwrite
        */
        protected $_port = "11211";

        /**
        * @readwrite
        */
        protected $_isConnected = false;

        protected function _isValidService()
        {
            $isEmpty = empty($this->_service);
            $isInstance = $this->_service instanceof \Memcache;

            if ($this->isConnected && $isInstance && !$isEmpty)
            {
                return true;
            }

            return false;
        }

        public function connect()
        {
            try
            {
                $this->_service = new \Memcache();
                $this->_service->connect(
                    $this->host,
                    $this->port
                );
                $this->isConnected = true;
            }
```

```
        catch (\Exception $e)
        {
            throw new Exception\Service("Unable to connect to service");
        }
        return $this;
    }

    public function disconnect()
    {
        if ($this->_isValidService())
        {
            $this->_service->close();
            $this->isConnected = false;
        }

        return $this;
    }

    public function get($key, $default = null)
    {
        if (!$this->_isValidService())
        {
            throw new Exception\Service("Not connected to a valid service");
        }

        $value = $this->_service->get($key, MEMCACHE_COMPRESSED);

        if ($value)
        {
            return $value;
        }

        return $default;
    }

    public function set($key, $value, $duration = 120)
    {
        if (!$this->_isValidService())
        {
            throw new Exception\Service("Not connected to a valid service");
        }

        $this->_service->set($key, $value, MEMCACHE_COMPRESSED, $duration);
        return $this;
    }

    public function erase($key)
    {
        if (!$this->_isValidService())
        {
            throw new Exception\Service("Not connected to a valid service");
        }
```

```
            $this->_service->delete($key);
            return $this;
        }
    }
}
```

Using our cache classes is really quite simple. If you think back to the example we had at the beginning of the chapter, you will see how we can apply this new caching mechanism, as shown in Listing 5-7.

Listing 5-7. Using the Cache Classes

```
function getFriends()
{
    $cache = new Framework\Cache(array(
        "type" => "memcached"
    ));
    $cache->initialize();

    $friends = unserialize($cache->get("friends.{$user->id}"));
    if (empty($friends))
    {
        // get $friends from the database

        $cache->set("friends.{$user->id}", serialize($friends));
    }

    return $friends;
}
```

Caching is an important part of any large-scale application. It's also not particularly hard to create a caching solution; the hard part is using it correctly. Whenever you need to make repeated requests for data or to any third-party service, consider using caching. Whenever you need to make repeated requests to the database or file system, consider using caching. You will almost always benefit from the use of caching, provided you only cache that which would take longer to retrieve if you weren't using cache in the first place.

Questions

1. We created a cache driver that connects to a Memcached server to store, retrieve, and erase cached data. Isn't this slower than caching to files on the server?
2. Can you think of any other benefits of using Memcached over other forms of caching offered to us?

Answers

1. File I/O (storing/retrieving data from files on the server) is notoriously slow. Network requests over a fast network to an efficient server are, by comparison, much faster.
2. huge benefit of using a centralized cache server (such as Memcached) is that our application might be running over a number of load-balanced web servers. If they were to manage their own cache files, we might have a lot of work to do so that they don't needlessly re-create the cached data.

Exercises

1. Our cache driver successfully connects to and uses Memcached storage. A problem could arise where other services need to use the same Memcached storage space and could have the same key names as our cached data. Try adding a prefix to all keys stored and all keys requested.

2. Experiment with different cache mechanisms. This could mean writing new cache driver classes to have the new caching mechanisms, thereby extending our framework's caching library.

CHAPTER 6

Registry

One of the great things about object-oriented programming is the ability to reuse code by creating multiple instances of a class. When we make changes to a class, all instances will inherit those changes, so we only have to make the change once.

Goals

- We need to understand the Registry design pattern and the problems it helps us to overcome.
- We then need to build a `Registry` class to store object instances. This is an essential part of an efficient framework, so it will be our only focus in this chapter.

Singleton

There will, however, be times when we expect to only use one instance of a given class. We can achieve this in a few ways. We learned about one such way, the Singleton pattern, in Chapter 1. Let's say, for example, we had the classes shown in Listing 6-1.

Listing 6-1. Limited Instance Example

```
class Ford
{
    public $founder = "Henry Ford";
    public $headquarters = "Detroit";
    public $employees = 164000;

    public function produces($car)
    {
        return $car->producer == $this;
    }
}

class Car
{
    public $color;
    public $producer;
}
```

```
$ford = new Ford();

$car = new Car();
$car->color = "Blue";
$car->producer = $ford;

echo $ford->produces($car);
echo $ford->founder;
```

There's nothing tricky about these classes. They do serve to illustrate a point, though. Sometimes the classes we create will need only one instance at a time. Consider the Ford class. There is only one Ford company, but it will differ greatly from other car manufacturers. The logic required for the Ford class might differ much from a Toyota class. Because of this difference, and because of the uniqueness of the instance of the Ford class, we need to ensure only one instance is around at a time.

So what if we make the Ford class a Singleton, as in Listing 6-2?

Listing 6-2. Ford Singleton

```
class Ford
{
    public $founder = "Henry Ford";
    public $headquarters = "Detroit";
    public $employees = 164000;

    public function produces($car)
    {
        return $car->producer == $this;
    }

    private static $_instance;

    private function __construct()
    {
        // do nothing
    }

    private function __clone()
    {
        // do nothing
    }

    public function instance()
    {
        if (!isset(self::$_instance))
        {
            self::$_instance = new self();
        }

        return self::$_instance;
    }
}
```

To make the Ford class a Singleton, we need to do a few things. First, we need to hide both the __construct() and __clone() magic methods. The __construct() method is automatically called by PHP whenever the new keyword is used. If we make it private, any use of the new keyword will raise an exception. The __clone() method is called whenever the clone() (global) method is called, in order to duplicate a class instance. With a private __clone() method, calling clone($ford) would raise an exception.

Now that there is no external means of creating a Ford instance, we can gain access to the properties and methods of an instance only by calling the instance() method. It checks a private, static (class) property for an instance of the class. If none is set, it creates a new instance, stores it, and returns the instance. This means on first invocation, the Ford class will create and return an instance, and on every subsequent invocation, will return that instance.

Let's see how our $car instance interacts with the Ford class in Listing 6-3.

Listing 6-3. Using a Singleton

```
$ford = Ford::instance();

$car = new Car();
$car->color = "Blue";
$car->producer = $ford;

echo $ford->produces($car);
echo $ford->founder;
```

As you might have noticed, we no not create a new instance of the Ford class. We only get an instance from the instance() method. The name of the method (in this case, instance) is also not very important. You can name it getInstance() or returnTheeAnInstanceAnew(), but it needs to adhere to the same principles behind the scenes.

You might also have noticed that it's easy to make a Singleton. For the majority of limited-instance classes you create, the Singleton pattern will suffice. It does, however, have its drawbacks. For a start, there is a certain amount of code required to create a proper Singleton. In the previous examples, it amounts to 18 lines of code, but that can be squashed down to eight lines. If you are creating a lot of Singletons, even eight lines can be bothersome.

Another disadvantage to the Singleton pattern is that references to the Singleton class need to happen by name. You can no longer refer just to variables, but have to reference the class by its full name (and namespace) in order to get an instance of the class.

Registry

What if we could treat ordinary classes as limited-instance classes, without having to make them Singletons? The Registry is a Singleton, used to store instance of other "normal" classes. Another way to think of it is as a global key/instance storeroom. Instances of non-Singleton classes are given a key (identifier) and are "kept" inside the Registry's private storage. When requests are made for specific keys, the Registry checks whether there are any instances for those keys, and returns them. If no instance is found at a key, the Registry's methods will return a default value.

You might be wondering what practical use this is to our framework. There are many times when we will need to limit the amount of class instances, as they relate to shared connections to third-party services or shared resources. Consider our cache system. For most applications, one cache provider will be sufficient. You will, for instance, connect to one Memcached server. We certainly don't want to be making multiple connections to the same service when one connection will suffice.

We could build our cache system as a set of Singleton classes, or we could declare multiple instances of the Cache classes. Using Registry, we can find a neat, efficient middle ground that allows us strict control over the number of class instances, while not limiting us to single-instance use only.

Consider an application that uses a database, or one that connects to Facebook. Both of these cases would benefit from strict control and resource sharing. Registry accommodates those needs, without requiring us to write a multitude of singletons.

Let's look at some code in Listing 6-4.

Listing 6-4. The Registry Class

```
namespace Framework
{
    class Registry
    {
        private static $_instances = array();

        private function __construct()
        {
            // do nothing
        }

        private function __clone()
        {
            // do nothing
        }

        public static function get($key, $default = null)
        {
            if (isset(self::$_instances[$key]))
            {
                return self::$_instances[$key];
            }
            return $default;
        }

        public static function set($key, $instance = null)
        {
            self::$_instances[$key] = $instance;
        }

        public static function erase($key)
        {
            unset(self::$_instances[$key]);
        }
    }
}
```

I referred to the registry as a singleton, but it is actually a static class. Static classes are singletons that have no instance properties/methods or instance accessors/mutators. In fact, the only difference between a static class and our Registry is that no instance of our registry can ever be created. This is fine because we will only need our `Registry` class in a single context.

The `set()` method is used to "store" an instance with a specified key in the registry's private storage. The `get()` method searches the private storage for an instance with a matching key. If it finds an instance, it will return it, or default to the value supplied with the `$default` parameter. The `erase()` method is useful for removing an instance at a certain key.

The Registry class is easy to use with our Ford/Car classes, as demonstrated in Listing 6-5.

Listing 6-5. Using Registry

```
Framework\Registry::set("ford", new Ford());

$car = new Car();
$car->setColor("Blue")->setProducer(Framework\Registry::get("ford"));

echo Framework\Registry::get("ford")->produces($car);
echo Framework\Registry::get("ford")->founder;
```

■ **Note** Zend Framework and CakePHP both have classes dedicated to the organization of object instances—classes comparable to Registry. CodeIgniter has no such class, and depends solely on the use of the Singleton pattern.

Questions

1. The registry is an ideal place to store class instances, which helps to minimize the reinitialization of commonly used classes. Are there other uses for it?
2. Does the use of the Registry pattern preclude us from using singletons effectively in our framework?

Answers

1. Aside from storing class instances, the registry can also be used to store other data that should be globally accessible. There is nothing stopping us from storing shared data structures within the Registry.
2. The Registry pattern does not deny us the use of the singleton. It actually depends on a Singleton (or static class) to work properly. It is simply useful for managing resources, while not restricting us to the limitations of Singleton classes for everything.

Exercises

1. With our Registry class, we can set and get class instances (or any other data objects). It would be quite useful to be able to see what was already in the storage area. Try creating a method that returns a list of key/value pairs for stored objects.
2. It would be useful if there were a way that classes could know whether they have been put into (or taken out of) the registry. Try adding some logic to check whether classes could respond to these events, and which lets the class know when these events occur.

CHAPTER 7

Routing

Routing is what happens when an application determines which controllers and actions are executed based on the URL requested. Simply put, it is how the framework gets from `http://localhost/users/list.html` to the `Users` controller and the `list()` action.

Goals

- We need to understand what routes are and how they work.
- We need to build the different kinds of routes.
- We need to build the `Router` class that will manage these routes.

Defining Routes

Some routes can be inferred from the structure of the application. If the `Router` class sees that you have an `Articles` controller with a `search()` method, it can sometimes assume that the URL `http://localhost/articles/search.html` should require the execution `Articles->search()`; however, sometimes we need to define routes that aren't as easy to assume. After we've built our `Router` class, we should be able to define routes in the manner demonstrated in Listing 7-1.

Listing 7-1. Defining Routes

```
$router = new Framework\Router();
$router->addRoute(
    new Framework\Router\Route\Simple(array(
        "pattern" => ":name/profile",
        "controller" => "index",
        "action" => "home"
    ))
);

$router->url = "chris/profile";
$router->dispatch();
```

There are a few things we need for a feature-complete `Router` class. We need to manage different route objects for inferred routes. We need to be able to process any routes that don't match those we have defined, to existing controllers and actions (inferred routes) or give the appropriate error messages.

Route Classes

Route classes represent the different kinds of routes that we can define in our framework's configuration. We will cover just two kinds, but they will be able to do all that we require in our framework. Because there can be multiple types, our route classes will inherit from a base Route class, as shown in Listing 7-2.

Listing 7-2. The Router\Route Class

```
namespace Framework\Router
{
    use Framework\Base as Base;
    use Framework\Router\Exception as Exception;

    class Route extends Base
    {
        /**
        * @readwrite
        */
        protected $_pattern;

        /**
        * @readwrite
        */
        protected $_controller;

        /**
        * @readwrite
        */
        protected $_action;

        /**
        * @readwrite
        */
        protected $_parameters = array();

        public function _getExceptionForImplementation($method)
        {
            return new Exception\Implementation("{$method} method not implemented");
        }
    }
}
```

Our Router\Route class inherits from the Base class, so we can define all manner of simulated getters/setters. We also provide method overrides for our exception-generating methods. All of the protected properties relate to the variables provided when a new Router\Route (or subclass) instance are created, and contain information about the URL requested.

The Regex class extends the Router\Route class, as demonstrated in Listing 7-3.

Listing 7-3. The Router\Route\Regex Class

```
namespace Framework\Router\Route
{
    use Framework\Router as Router;

    class Regex extends Router\Route
    {
        /**
        * @readwrite
        */
        protected $_keys;

        public function matches($url)
        {
            $pattern = $this->pattern;

            // check values
            preg_match_all("#^{$pattern}$#", $url, $values);

            if (sizeof($values) && sizeof($values[0]) && sizeof($values[1]))
            {
                // values found, modify parameters and return
                $derived = array_combine($this->keys, $values[1]);
                $this->parameters = array_merge($this->parameters, $derived);

                return true;
            }

            return false;
        }
    }
}
```

The `Router\Route\Regex` class is very slim indeed. It has a `matches()` method, which the `Router` class will call on all `Router\Route` subclasses. The `matches()` method creates the correct regular expression search string and returns any matches to the provided URL.

The `ArrayMethods::flatten()` method, as demonstrated in Listing 7-4, it useful for converting a multidimensional array into a unidimensional array.

Listing 7-4. The ArrayMethods::flatten() Method

```
namespace Framework
{
    class ArrayMethods
    {
        public function flatten($array, $return = array())
        {
            foreach ($array as $key => $value)
            {
                if (is_array($value) || is_object($value))
                {
```

```
                $return = self::flatten($value, $return);
            }
            else
            {
                $return[] = $value;
            }
        }

        return $return;
    }
  }
}
```

The `Router\Route\Simple` class is slightly more detailed than the `Router\Route\Regex` class. It also has a `matches()` method that converts substrings matching the format of `:property` to regular expression wildcards. The matches properties are stored in the `$_parameters` array. The `Router\Route\Simple` class is shown in Listing 7-5.

Listing 7-5. The Router\Route\Simple Class

```
namespace Framework\Router\Route
{
    use Framework\Router as Router;
    use Framework\ArrayMethods as ArrayMethods;

    class Simple extends Router\Route
    {
        public function matches($url)
        {
            $pattern = $this->pattern;

            // get keys
            preg_match_all("#:([a-zA-Z0-9]+)#", $pattern, $keys);

            if (sizeof($keys) && sizeof($keys[0]) && sizeof($keys[1]))
            {
                $keys = $keys[1];
            }
            else
            {
                // no keys in the pattern, return a simple match
                return preg_match("#^{$pattern}$#", $url);
            }

            // normalize route pattern
            $pattern = preg_replace("#(:[a-zA-Z0-9]+)#", "([a-zA-Z0-9-_]+)", $pattern);

            // check values
            preg_match_all("#^{$pattern}$#", $url, $values);

            if (sizeof($values) && sizeof($values[0]) && sizeof($values[1]))
            {
```

```
                // unset the matched url
                unset($values[0]);

                // values found, modify parameters and return
                $derived = array_combine($keys, ArrayMethods::flatten($values));
                $this->parameters = array_merge($this->parameters, $derived);

                return true;
            }

            return false;
        }
    }
}
```

Router Class

Our Router class will use the requested URL, as well as the controller/action metadata, to determine the correct controller/action to execute. It needs to handle multiple defined routes and inferred routes if no defined routes are matched. This is demonstrated in Listing 7-6.

Listing 7-6. Route Management Methods

```
namespace Framework
{
    use Framework\Base as Base;
    use Framework\Registry as Registry;
    use Framework\Inspector as Inspector;
    use Framework\Router\Exception as Exception;

    class Router extends Base
    {
        /**
        * @readwrite
        */
        protected $_url;

        /**
        * @readwrite
        */
        protected $_extension;

        /**
        * @read
        */
        protected $_controller;

        /**
        * @read
        */
        protected $_action;
```

```
        protected $_routes = array();

        public function _getExceptionForImplementation($method)
        {
            return new Exception\Implementation("{$method} method not implemented");
        }

        public function addRoute($route)
        {
            $this->_routes[] = $route;
            return $this;
        }

        public function removeRoute($route)
        {
            foreach ($this->_routes as $i =>$stored)
            {
                if ($stored == $route)
                {
                    unset($this->_routes[$i]);
                }
            }
            return $this;
        }

        public function getRoutes()
        {
            $list = array();

            foreach ($this->_routes as $route)
            {
                $list[$route->pattern] = get_class($route);
            }

            return $list;
        }
    }
}
```

We store all the defined routes in a protected `$_routes` property, and manipulate them with the `addRoute()` and `removeRoute()` methods. The `getRoutes()` method returns a neat list of routes we have stored—their literal value as the key, and their class type as the value—which makes debugging easier.

Next, we need to work on dispatching a URL. This involves matching any defined routes, then trying to find inferred routes. See how this is accomplished in Listing 7-7.

Listing 7-7. Processing Defined Routes

```
namespace Framework
{
    use Framework\Base as Base;
    use Framework\Events as Events;
    use Framework\Registry as Registry;
    use Framework\Inspector as Inspector;
    use Framework\Router\Exception as Exception;
```

```
    class Router extends Base
    {
        public function dispatch()
        {
            $url = $this->url;
            $parameters = array();
            $controller = "index";
            $action = "index";

            foreach ($this->_routes as $route)
            {
                $matches = $route->matches($url);
                if ($matches)
                {
                    $controller = $route->controller;
                    $action = $route->action;
                    $parameters = $route->parameters;

                    $this->_pass($controller, $action, $parameters);
                    return;
                }
            }
        }
    }
}
```

This is the first part of our router's dispatch function. We start off by looping through the defined routes in the protected `$_routes` property of the `Router` class. If the route matches the URL, we get the route's controller and action (capitalizing the first letter of the controller name). Finally, we check whether the controller has the action we require and, after calculating which parameters we need to pass to the controller, execute it. This is demonstrated in Listing 7-8.

Listing 7-8. Processing Preexisting Routes

```
namespace Framework
{
    use Framework\Base as Base;
    use Framework\Events as Events;
    use Framework\Registry as Registry;
    use Framework\Inspector as Inspector;
    use Framework\Router\Exception as Exception;

    class Router extends Base
    {
        public function dispatch()
        {
            $parts = explode("/", trim($url, "/"));

            if (sizeof($parts)>0)
            {
                $controller = $parts[0];
```

```
                if (sizeof($parts) >= 2)
                {
                    $action = $parts[1];
                    $parameters = array_slice($parts, 2);
                }
            }

            $this->_pass($controller, $action, $parameters);
        }
    }
}
```

Because we only process the actual route objects in our `_pass()` method, we don't actually need to validate the route data. If none of our defined routes were matched (and function execution terminated with the `return` statement) we can assume the route can either be inferred or is invalid. Both cases will be dealt with next in Listing 7-9.

Listing 7-9. Router _pass() Method

```
namespace Framework
{
    use Framework\Base as Base;
    use Framework\Events as Events;
    use Framework\Registry as Registry;
    use Framework\Inspector as Inspector;
    use Framework\Router\Exception as Exception;

    class Router extends Base
    {
        protected function _pass($controller, $action, $parameters = array())
        {
            $name = ucfirst($controller);

            $this->_controller = $controller;
            $this->_action = $action;

            try
            {
                $instance = new $name(array(
                    "parameters" => $parameters
                ));
                Registry::set("controller", $instance);
            }
            catch (\Exception $e)
            {
                throw new Exception\Controller("Controller {$name} not found");
            }

            if (!method_exists($instance, $action))
            {
                $instance->willRenderLayoutView = false;
```

```
                $instance->willRenderActionView = false;

                throw new Exception\Action("Action {$action} not found");
            }

            $inspector = new Inspector($instance);
            $methodMeta = $inspector->getMethodMeta($action);

            if (!empty($methodMeta["@protected"]) || !empty($methodMeta["@private"]))
            {
                throw new Exception\Action("Action {$action} not found");
            }

            $hooks = function($meta, $type) use ($inspector, $instance)
            {
                if (isset($meta[$type]))
                {
                    $run = array();

                    foreach ($meta[$type] as $method)
                    {
                        $hookMeta = $inspector->getMethodMeta($method);

                        if (in_array($method, $run) && !empty($hookMeta["@once"]))
                        {
                            continue;
                        }

                        $instance->$method();
                        $run[] = $method;
                    }
                }
            };

            $hooks($methodMeta, "@before");

            call_user_func_array(array(
                $instance,
                $action
            ), is_array($parameters) ? $parameters : array());

            $hooks($methodMeta, "@after");

            // unset controller

            Registry::erase("controller");
        }
    }
}
```

Our _pass() method first modifies the requested class (passed from the _dispatch() method), so that the first letter is in uppercase. It immediately sets the protected $_controller and $_action properties to the correct values, and tries to create a new instance of the Controller class, passing in a reference to itself, and the provided $parameters array. Since our autoload() function throws an exception if the class cannot be found, we can assume that the controller was either loaded, or doesn't exist, which then raises a Router\Exception\Controller exception. Our _pass() method then checks whether the Controller class has a method that matches the $action required. If not, it will raise a Router\Exception\Action exception.

We then check whether the action is callable (checking for @protected or @private in the metadata). If either of these conditions is met, we raise a Router\Exception\Action exception. We also define an anonymous function to deal with hooks.

■ **Note** Hooks are functions that hook into a certain point within a running system, so that they can be run without changing the system itself. An example would be creating a hook function to execute before the intended action. We can change this hook function at any time without modifying the action itself.

If the action has a @before [method, [method...]] flag, our Router class will first execute that method. Likewise, if the action has an @after [method, [method...]] flag, our Router class will execute it after the action has completed.

Methods identified in @before and @after, having @once flags will be run only once, irrespective of how many times they are referenced in @before and @after. If the action has a @protected or @private flag, our Router class will throw an exception as if the action could not be found.

@before and @after are examples of how to implement hooks in our framework. The order of execution is first to execute any @before hooks, then to assign the parameters to the Controller instance and execute the controller. Finally, our _pass() method will execute any @after hooks. The full class looks like that shown in Listing 7-10.

Listing 7-10. The Router Class

```
namespace Framework
{
    use Framework\Base as Base;
    use Framework\Events as Events;
    use Framework\Registry as Registry;
    use Framework\Inspector as Inspector;
    use Framework\Router\Exception as Exception;

    class Router extends Base
    {
        /**
        * @readwrite
        */
        protected $_url;

        /**
        * @readwrite
        */
        protected $_extension;
```

```
/**
* @read
*/
protected $_controller;

/**
* @read
*/
protected $_action;

protected $_routes = array();

public function _getExceptionForImplementation($method)
{
    return new Exception\Implementation("{$method} method not implemented");
}

public function addRoute($route)
{
    $this->_routes[] = $route;
    return $this;
}

public function removeRoute($route)
{
    foreach ($this->_routes as $i => $stored)
    {
        if ($stored == $route)
        {
            unset($this->_routes[$i]);
        }
    }
    return $this;
}

public function getRoutes()
{
    $list = array();

    foreach ($this->_routes as $route)
    {
        $list[$route->pattern] = get_class($route);
    }

    return $list;
}

protected function _pass($controller, $action, $parameters = array())
{
    $name = ucfirst($controller);
```

```
$this->_controller = $controller;
$this->_action = $action;

try
{
    $instance = new $name(array(
        "parameters" => $parameters
    ));
    Registry::set("controller", $instance);
}
catch (\Exception $e)
{
    throw new Exception\Controller("Controller {$name} not found");
}

if (!method_exists($instance, $action))
{
    $instance->willRenderLayoutView = false;
    $instance->willRenderActionView = false;

    throw new Exception\Action("Action {$action} not found");
}

$inspector = new Inspector($instance);
$methodMeta = $inspector->getMethodMeta($action);

if (!empty($methodMeta["@protected"]) || !empty($methodMeta["@private"]))
{
    throw new Exception\Action("Action {$action} not found");
}

$hooks = function($meta, $type) use ($inspector, $instance)
{
    if (isset($meta[$type]))
    {
        $run = array();

        foreach ($meta[$type] as $method)
        {
            $hookMeta = $inspector->getMethodMeta($method);

            if (in_array($method, $run) && !empty($hookMeta["@once"]))
            {
                continue;
            }

            $instance->$method();
            $run[] = $method;
        }
    }
};

$hooks($methodMeta, "@before");
```

```
            call_user_func_array(array(
                $instance,
                $action
            ), is_array($parameters) ? $parameters : array());

            $hooks($methodMeta, "@after");

            // unset controller

            Registry::erase("controller");
        }

        public function dispatch()
        {
            $url = $this->url;
            $parameters = array();
            $controller = "index";
            $action = "index";

            foreach ($this->_routes as $route)
            {
                $matches = $route->matches($url);
                if ($matches)
                {
                    $controller = $route->controller;
                    $action = $route->action;
                    $parameters = $route->parameters;

                    $this->_pass($controller, $action, $parameters);
                    return;
                }
            }
            $parts = explode("/", trim($url, "/"));

            if (sizeof($parts)>0)
            {
                $controller = $parts[0];

                if (sizeof($parts)>= 2)
                {
                    $action = $parts[1];
                    $parameters = array_slice($parts, 2);
                }
            }

            $this->_pass($controller, $action, $parameters);
        }
    }
}
```

The code for the Controller class is as follows.

Listing 7-11. The Controller Class

```
namespace Framework
{
    use Framework\Base as Base;

    class Controller extends Base
    {
        /**
        * @readwrite
        */
        protected $_parameters;
    }
}
```

■ **Note** Over time, our `Controller` class will evolve to handle all sorts of things, like loading libraries and views or integrating with business logic in the model. Until then, this is all we need.

So, now that we have all the `Router\Route` code in place, let's look at how to use it, and some examples of the hooks we created. Take a look at Listing 7-12.

Listing 7-12. Example Usage of the Router Class

```
class Home extends Framework\Controller
{
    public function index()
    {
        echo "here";
    }
}

$router = new Framework\Router();
$router->addRoute(
    new Framework\Router\Route\Simple(array(
        "pattern" => ":name/profile",
        "controller" => "home",
        "action" => "index"
    ))
);

$router->url = "chris/profile";
$router->dispatch();
```

The first thing you should notice is that we will need to create instances of a `Router\Route` subclass for every route we will define. The second thing you should notice is that we refer to the `Router\Route` subclasses by their class name. We could create a `Router\Route` subclass factory, but that's a little overkill at this point, considering our applications will be constituted mostly of inferred routes.

The next example, shown in Listing 7-13, showcases the use of metadata to facilitate the use of hooks within our `Controller` subclasses. The `init()`, `authenticate()`, and `notify()` methods have `@protected` flags, so they will not be routed to, from our `Router` class. The `home()` method indicates that the methods `init()`, authenticate(), and init() (again!) should be executed before the home() method is executed. It also indicates that the notify() method should be executed after the home() method is executed. Finally, the init() method's metadata indicates that it should be run only once per URL routing. Our router accomodates all of these requirements!

Listing 7-13. Example Controller Meta Properties

```
class Index extends Framework\Controller
{
    /**
    * @once
    * @protected
    */
    public function init()
    {
        echo "init";
    }

    /**
    * @protected
    */
    public function authenticate()
    {
        echo "authenticate";
    }

    /**
    * @before init, authenticate, init
    * @after notify
    */
    public function home()
    {
        echo "hello world!";
    }

    /**
    * @protected
    */
    public function notify()
    {
        echo "notify";
    }
}

$router = new Framework\Router();
$router->addRoute(
    new Framework\Router\Route\Simple(array(
        "pattern" => ":name/profile",
        "controller" => "home",
```

```
        "action" => "index"
    ))
);

$router->url = "chris/profile";
$router->dispatch();
```

Questions

1. Why should we have both methods of defining routes if our framework could just either infer all the routes, or we could define all the required routes?
2. Are there easier ways to define `Route` instances?

Answers

3. The main reason is flexibility. There are many instances in which inferred routes are insufficient, and we do not want the hassle of defining all the simple routes ourselves.
4. We cannot use configuration files for this sort of thing, as we have not yet defined a configuration file standard that allows for the kinds of data structures we use to define routes. There are easier ways to define a large batch of routes, which you will see in Chapter 17.

Exercises

5. Routes are very application-dependent. There might be times when you need to specify different kinds of routes than those we have demonstrated in this chapter. Try creating a `Route` subclass that lets you name routes and then redirect to other named routes.
6. Defining many routes at the same time can become quite a tangled mess of code. Try simplifying the creation of ten `Router\Route\Simple` instances.

CHAPTER 8

Templates

At the heart of MVC is separation of concerns, and nowhere in our framework is that more important than between the view and the controller. Typically, when one thinks about the front end (or client side) of an application, they think of HTML, CSS, and JavaScript. Throw in server-side interaction, and an unavoidable portion of PHP enters the picture.

What's worse is we will often need to work with data, supplied to us by the controller, using PHP directly in our views. Many people have tried solving this problem with template languages (and parsers). It might not make a whole lot of sense—substituting PHP for yet another intermediary dialect—but there are advantages. Whether or not you choose to use template parsing in your framework, it remains a good exercise in the kind of analytical thinking required to build your own framework.

Goals

- We need to define a dialect on which to base our template parser. A dialect is simply another word for the grammar or commands by which a template can be defined.
- We need to formalize this dialect into a template implementation class.
- We need to build a template parser class that utilizes the template implementation class in order to convert template strings to parsed templates.

Idea

In order to build a functional template parser, we first need to define how it should work. It should accept a standardized template language, yet be flexible to change. It should be fast. It should not require a lot of learning before one can use it. Take a look at our basic template dialect in Listing 8-1.

Listing 8-1. Basic Template Dialect

```
{if $name && $address}
    name: {echo $name}
    address: {echo $address}
{/if}
{elseif $name}
    name: {echo $name}
{/elseif}
{else}
    no name or address
{/else}
```

```
{foreach $value in $stack}
    value: {echo $value}
{/foreach}
{else}
    no values in $stack
{/else}
```

Listing 8-1 demonstrates the kind of templates we are likely to need to parse in our views. We will need to jump through a few hoops before this becomes more than theoretical.

Alternatives

Creating our own template parser is merely a learning exercise. There are already so many good, free template libraries for PHP that it would make little to no sense trying to create another competing standard unless what we were creating was truly unique. If you are keen to see what's available, take a look at Smarty (`www.smarty.net`) and Twig (`http://twig.sensiolabs.org`).

Implementation

For this kind of template parser, we will need to perform three steps to get from text to template. The first is tokenizing the source template. We can achieve this in a number of ways, and it is usually done using complicated regular expressions. We will be reading the source template, piece by piece, and adding each segment to an array.

The second step our parser must take is to organize the tokenized segments into a hierarchy, so that we can put the template in terms of control structures and functions. This step looks at the contents of each segment and determines whether it is important to the template dialect, or is just another piece of data.

The last step is transforming the hierarchy into the string representation of a function, which can be converted to an actual function and called with any arbitrary data. The function is stored so that multiple data sets do not cause the template to be parsed multiple times. Since we will be working largely with strings, we need to extend our `StringMethods` class with three new methods to sanitize strings, remove duplicate characters, and determine substrings within larger strings.

Listing 8-2. Additional StringMethods Methods

```
namespace Framework
{
    class StringMethods
    {
        public static function sanitize($string, $mask)
        {
            if (is_array($mask))
            {
                $parts = $mask;
            }
            else if (is_string($mask))
            {
                $parts = str_split($mask);
            }
```

```
            else
            {
                return $string;
            }

            foreach ($parts as $part)
            {
                $normalized = self::_normalize("\\{$part}");
                $string = preg_replace(
                    "{$normalized}m",
                    "\\{$part}",
                    $string
                );
            }

            return $string;
        }

        public static function unique($string)
        {
            $unique = "";
            $parts = str_split($string);

            foreach ($parts as $part)
            {
                if (!strstr($unique, $part))
                {
                    $unique .= $part;
                }
            }

            return $unique;
        }

        public function indexOf($string, $substring, $offset = null)
        {
            $position = strpos($string, $substring, $offset);
            if (!is_int($position))
            {
                return -1;
            }
            return $position;
        }
    }
}
```

The `sanitize()` method loops through the characters of a string, replacing them with regular expression friendly character representations. The `unique()` method eliminates all duplicated characters in a string. Finally, the `indexOf()` method returns the position of a substring within a larger string, or `-1` if the substring isn't found. The reason for that last method, instead of just using PHP's native `strpos()` method, is that `strpos()` can return any number of values to represent a missing substring. Our new `indexOf()` method will always return an integer result.

■ **Note** You can read more about strpos at www.php.net/manual/en/function.strpos.php. Notice how they say [strpos] may return Boolean FALSE, but may also return a non-Boolean value, which evaluates to FALSE, such as 0 or "".

In order for our template parser to remain flexible, the structure of our template dialect needs to be in a separate class to the parser. This allows us to swap out different implementation classes for the same parser. All of our implementation classes should also inherit from a base implementation class. Let us look at that class now in Listing 8-3.

Listing 8-3. The Template\Implementation Class

```
namespace Framework\Template
{
    use Framework\Base as Base;
    use Framework\StringMethods as StringMethods;
    use Framework\Template\Exception as Exception;

    class Implementation extends Base
    {
        protected function _handler($node)
        {
            if (empty($node["delimiter"]))
            {
                return null;
            }

            if (!empty($node["tag"]))
            {
                return $this->_map[$node["delimiter"]]["tags"][$node["tag"]]["handler"];
            }

            return $this->_map[$node["delimiter"]]["handler"];
        }

        public function handle($node, $content)
        {
            try
            {
                $handler = $this->_handler($node);
                return call_user_func_array(array($this, $handler), array($node, $content));
            }
            catch (\Exception $e)
            {
                throw new Exception\Implementation();
            }
        }

        public function match($source)
        {
            $type = null;
            $delimiter = null;
```

```
            foreach ($this->_map as $_delimiter => $_type)
            {
                if (!$delimiter || StringMethods::indexOf($source, $type["opener"]) == -1)
                {
                    $delimiter = $_delimiter;
                    $type = $_type;
                }

                $indexOf = StringMethods::indexOf($source, $_type["opener"]);

                if ($indexOf > -1)
                {
                    if (StringMethods::indexOf($source, $type["opener"]) > $indexCf)
                    {
                        $delimiter = $_delimiter;
                        $type = $_type;
                    }
                }
            }

            if ($type == null)
            {
                return null;
            }

            return array(
                "type" => $type,
                "delimiter" => $delimiter
            );
        }
    }
}
```

The `_handler()` method takes a `$node` array and determines the correct handler method to execute. The `handle()` method uses the `_handler()` method to get the correct handler method, and executes it, throwing a `Template\Exception\Implementation` exception if there was a problem executing the statement's handler. The `match()` method evaluates a `$source` string to determine if it matches a tag or statement.

This class might look strange, due to the fact that we don't even know what our implementation file looks like. In fact, all three of its methods directly deal with content only found in `Template\Implementation` subclasses. Every language has rules, or grammar. We need to define that so our parser can know how to deal with the markup it needs to parse. We define that in the `Template\Implementation` subclasses. Listing 8-4 shows the grammar map for our default template parser.

Listing 8-4. The Default Template Implementation Grammar/Language Map

```
namespace Framework\Template\Implementation
{
    use Framework\Template as Template;
    use Framework\StringMethods as StringMethods;

    class Standard extends Template\Implementation
    {
        protected $_map = array(
            "echo" => array(
                "opener" => "{echo",
```

```
                "closer" => "}",
                "handler" => "_echo"
            ),
            "script" => array(
                "opener" => "{script",
                "closer" => "}",
                "handler" => "_script"
            ),
            "statement" => array(
                "opener" => "{",
                "closer" => "}",
                "tags" => array(
                    "foreach" => array(
                        "isolated" => false,
                        "arguments" => "{element} in {object}",
                        "handler" => "_each"
                    ),
                    "for" => array(
                        "isolated" => false,
                        "arguments" => "{element} in {object}",
                        "handler" => "_for"
                    ),
                    "if" => array(
                        "isolated" => false,
                        "arguments" => null,
                        "handler" => "_if"
                    ),
                    "elseif" => array(
                        "isolated" => true,
                        "arguments" => null,
                        "handler" => "_elif"
                    ),
                    "else" => array(
                        "isolated" => true,
                        "arguments" => null,
                        "handler" => "_else"
                    ),
                    "macro" => array(
                        "isolated" => false,
                        "arguments" => "{name}({args})",
                        "handler" => "_macro"
                    ),
                    "literal" => array(
                        "isolated" => false,
                        "arguments" => null,
                        "handler" => "_literal"
                    )
                )
            )
        );
    }
}
```

The code in Listing 8-4 shows what is called a grammar/language map. It is a list of language tags for our template dialect, so that the parser can know what the different types of template tags are, and how to parse them. We can see that our default template dialect only has three types of tags: `print`, `script` and `statement`.

Print tags are the most basic tags in our parser; they are simply used to add variable data to the output of the template parser. You can think of them like PHP echo statements.

Script tags are used to execute arbitrary PHP scripts. While the use of these tags is not ideal, they are there for any instances where you need to execute PHP scripts inline. You can think of them like the opening and closing `<?php ... ?>` tags.

Statement tags are used for all the control structures we want our templates to support. They include a variety of subtypes, such as `if`, `foreach`, and `else`. They also include `macro` (or function) and `literal` (cdata-esque) statement subtypes.

Each tag has an `opener` and `closer` string, which tells the parser how it should treat the beginning and end of each segment. Each tag (and subtype) has `handler` string, which tells the parser which internal function to call when it needs to evaluate the corresponding tag (or subtype).

Having defined the types of tags and statements our template parser must be able to handle, we need to implement the functions that will process the relevant tags and statements, as demonstrated in Listing 8-5.

Listing 8-5. Statement Handler Functions

```
namespace Framework\Template\Implementation
{
    use Framework\Template as Template;
    use Framework\StringMethods as StringMethods;

    class Standard extends Template\Implementation
    {
        protected function _echo($tree, $content)
        {
            $raw = $this->_script($tree, $content);
            return "\$_text[] = {$raw}";
        }

        protected function _script($tree, $content)
        {
            $raw = !empty($tree["raw"]) ? $tree["raw"] : "";
            return "{$raw};";
        }

        protected function _each($tree, $content)
        {
            $object = $tree["arguments"]["object"];
            $element = $tree["arguments"]["element"];

            return $this->_loop(
                $tree,
                "foreach ({$object} as {$element}_i => {$element}) {
                    {$content}
                }"
            );
        }
```

```
protected function _for($tree, $content)
{
    $object = $tree["arguments"]["object"];
    $element = $tree["arguments"]["element"];

    return $this->_loop(
        $tree,
        "for ({$element}_i = 0; {$element}_i < sizeof({$object}); {$element}_i++) {
            {$element} = {$object}[{$element}_i];
            {$content}
        }"
    );
}

protected function _if($tree, $content)
{
    $raw = $tree["raw"];
    return "if ({$raw}) {{$content}}";
}

protected function _elif($tree, $content)
{
    $raw = $tree["raw"];
    return "elseif ({$raw}) {{$content}}";
}

protected function _else($tree, $content)
{
    return "else {{$content}}";
}

protected function _macro($tree, $content)
{
    $arguments = $tree["arguments"];
    $name = $arguments["name"];
    $args = $arguments["args"];

    return "function {$name}({$args}) {
        \$_text = array();
        {$content}
        return implode(\$_text);
    }";
}

protected function _literal($tree, $content)
{
    $source = addslashes($tree["source"]);
    return "\$_text[] = \"{$source}\";";
}
```

```
        protected function _loop($tree, $inner)
        {
            $number = $tree["number"];
            $object = $tree["arguments"]["object"];
            $children = $tree["parent"]["children"];

            if (!empty($children[$number+1]["tag"]) && $children[$number+1]["tag"] == "else")
            {
                return "if (is_array({$object}) && sizeof({$object}) > 0) {{$inner}}";
            }
            return $inner;
        }
    }
}
```

The _echo() method converts the string "{echo $hello}" to "$_text[] = $hello", so that it is already optimized for our final evaluated function. Similarly, the _script() method converts the string "{:$foo += 1}" to "$foo += 1".

The _each() and _for() methods are also similar, but depend on the _loop() method to augment their output with checks for the contents of the arrays used by those statements, as long as an {else} tag follows them. The _each() method returns the code to perform a foreach loop through an array, while the _for() method produces the code to perform a for loop through an array.

The methods _if(), _else(), and _elif() return code to perform each of those operations within our templates. We could obviously rewrite these methods (as well as _each() and _for()) to use the alternative closing syntax (endif, endforeach, endfor, etc.), but that's really up to you.

The _macro() method creates the string representation of a function, based on the contents of a {macro...}...{/macro} tag set. It is possible, using the {macro} tag, to define functions, which we then use within our templates.

Finally, the _literal() method directly quotes any content within it. The template parser only stops directly quoting the content when it finds a {/literal} closing tag. Now that we have our template dialect implementation class (see Listing 8-6), we can begin to use it in our parser. But what does our parser look like?

Listing 8-6. The Template Class

```
namespace Framework
{
    use Framework\Base as Base;
    use Framework\ArrayMethods as ArrayMethods;
    use Framework\StringMethods as StringMethods;
    use Framework\Template\Exception as Exception;

    class Template extends Base
    {
        /**
        * @readwrite
        */
        protected $_implementation;
```

```
        /**
        * @readwrite
        */
        protected $_header = "if (is_array(\$_data) && sizeof(\$_data)) ➥
extract(\$_data); \$_text = array();";

        /**
        * @readwrite
        */
        protected $_footer = "return implode(\$_text);";

        /**
        * @read
        */
        protected $_code;

        /**
        * @read
        */
        protected $_function;

        public function _getExceptionForImplementation($method)
        {
            return new Exception\Implementation("{$method} method not implemented");
        }
    }
}
```

Our Template class begins with some adaptable properties and overrides for the exception-generation methods. We then add two utility methods to help us break down chunks of the template, separating out the tags from the text, as shown in Listing 8-7.

Listing 8-7. Tag Parsing Methods

```
namespace Framework
{
    use Framework\Base as Base;
    use Framework\ArrayMethods as ArrayMethods;
    use Framework\StringMethods as StringMethods;
    use Framework\Template\Exception as Exception;

    class Template extends Base
    {
        protected function _arguments($source, $expression)
        {
            $args = $this->_array($expression, array(
                $expression => array(
                    "opener" => "{",
                    "closer" => "}"
                )
            ));
```

```
        $tags = $args["tags"];
        $arguments = array();
        $sanitized = StringMethods::sanitize($expression, "()[],.<>*$@");

        foreach ($tags as $i => $tag)
        {
            $sanitized = str_replace($tag, "(.*)", $sanitized);
            $tags[$i] = str_replace(array("{", "}"), "", $tag);
        }

        if (preg_match("#{$sanitized}#", $source, $matches))
        {
            foreach ($tags as $i => $tag)
            {
                $arguments[$tag] = $matches[$i+1];
            }
        }

        return $arguments;
    }

    protected function _tag($source)
    {
        $tag = null;
        $arguments = array();

        $match = $this->_implementation->match($source);
        if ($match == null)
        {
            return false;
        }

        $delimiter = $match["delimiter"];
        $type = $match["type"];

        $start = strlen($type["opener"]);
        $end = strpos($source, $type["closer"]);
        $extract = substr($source, $start, $end - $start);

        if (isset($type["tags"]))
        {
            $tags = implode("|", array_keys($type["tags"]));
            $regex = "#^(/){0,1}({$tags})\s*(.*)$#";

            if (!preg_match($regex, $extract, $matches))
            {
                return false;
            }

            $tag = $matches[2];
            $extract = $matches[3];
```

```
                $closer = !!$matches[1];
            }

            if ($tag && $closer)
            {
                return array(
                    "tag" => $tag,
                    "delimiter" => $delimiter,
                    "closer" => true,
                    "source" => false,
                    "arguments" => false,
                    "isolated" => $type["tags"][$tag]["isolated"]
                );
            }

            if (isset($type["arguments"]))
            {
                $arguments = $this->_arguments($extract, $type["arguments"]);
            }
            else if ($tag && isset($type["tags"][$tag]["arguments"]))
            {
                $arguments = $this->_arguments($extract, $type["tags"][$tag]["arguments"]);
            }

            return array(
                "tag" => $tag,
                "delimiter" => $delimiter,
                "closer" => false,
                "source" => $extract,
                "arguments" => $arguments,
                "isolated" => (!empty($type["tags"]) ? $type["tags"][$tag]["isolated"]: false)
            );
        }
    }
}
```

The `_tag()` method calls the implementation's `match()` method. The `match()` method will tell our parser if the chunk of template we are parsing, is a tag or a plain string. The `match()` method will return false for a nonmatch. It then extracts all the bits between the opener and closer strings we specified in the implementation—for `{if $check}`, the `_match()` method will extract the tag (`if`), the rest of the tag data (`$check`), and whether or not it is a closing tag.

Finally, the `_tag()` method will generate a `$node` array, which contains a bit of metadata about the tag. The `_arguments()` method is used for any of the statements, if they have a specific argument format (such as `for`, `foreach`, or `macro`). It returns the bits between the `{...}` characters in a neat associative array. Now that we can tell the tags from the text, we need a method to break down the template string and pass each piece to these utility methods. Take a look at this method in Listing 8-8.

Listing 8-8. Template _array() Method

```
namespace Framework
{
    use Framework\Base as Base;
    use Framework\ArrayMethods as ArrayMethods;
```

```
use Framework\StringMethods as StringMethods;
use Framework\Template\Exception as Exception;

class Template extends Base
{
    protected function _array($source)
    {
        $parts = array();
        $tags = array();
        $all = array();

        $type = null;
        $delimiter = null;

        while ($source)
        {
            $match = $this->_implementation->match($source);

            $type = $match["type"];
            $delimiter = $match["delimiter"];

            $opener = strpos($source, $type["opener"]);
            $closer = strpos($source, $type["closer"]) + strlen($type["closer"]);

            if ($opener !== false)
            {
                $parts[] = substr($source, 0, $opener);
                $tags[] = substr($source, $opener, $closer - $opener);
                $source = substr($source, $closer);
            }
            else
            {
                $parts[] = $source;
                $source = "";
            }
        }

        foreach ($parts as $i => $part)
        {
            $all[] = $part;
            if (isset($tags[$i]))
            {
                $all[] = $tags[$i];
            }
        }
```

```
            return array(
                "text" => ArrayMethods::clean($parts),
                "tags" => ArrayMethods::clean($tags),
                "all" => ArrayMethods::clean($all)
            );
        }
    }
}
```

The _array() method essentially deconstructs a template string into arrays of tags, text, and a combination of the two. It does this with the use of the implementation's match() and ArrayMethods::clean() methods. With these arrays, we can begin to build a hierarchy of tags and text. Since our template language supports conditionals, and allows us to nest them, we need to think of our templates as tree structures, and not merely as a means for string substitution. Listing 8-9 shows our method for building this hierarchy of tags and text.

Listing 8-9. Template _tree() Method

```
namespace Framework
{
    use Framework\Base as Base;
    use Framework\ArrayMethods as ArrayMethods;
    use Framework\StringMethods as StringMethods;
    use Framework\Template\Exception as Exception;

    class Template extends Base
    {
        protected function _tree($array)
        {
            $root = array(
                "children" => array()
            );
            $current =& $root;

            foreach ($array as $i => $node)
            {
                $result = $this->_tag($node);

                if ($result)
                {
                    $tag = isset($result["tag"]) ? $result["tag"] : "";
                    $arguments = isset($result["arguments"]) ? $result["arguments"] : "";

                    if ($tag)
                    {
                        if (!$result["closer"])
                        {
                            $last = ArrayMethods::last($current["children"]);

                            if ($result["isolated"] && is_string($last))
                            {
                                array_pop($current["children"]);
                            }
```

```
                        $current["children"][]=array(
                            "index" => $i,
                            "parent" => &$current,
                            "children" => array(),
                            "raw" => $result["source"],
                            "tag" => $tag,
                            "arguments" => $arguments,
                            "delimiter" => $result["delimiter"],
                            "number" => sizeof($current["children"])
                        );
                        $current=& $current["children"][sizeof($current["children"])  - 1];
                    }
                    else if (isset($current["tag"]) && $result["tag"] == $current["tag"])
                    {
                        $start=$current["index"]+1;
                        $length=$i - $start;
                        $current["source"]=implode(array_slice($array, $start,$length));
                        $current=& $current["parent"];
                    }
                }
                else
                {
                    $current["children"][]=array(
                        "index" => $i,
                        "parent" => &$current,
                        "children" => array(),
                        "raw" => $result["source"],
                        "tag" => $tag,
                        "arguments" => $arguments,
                        "delimiter" => $result["delimiter"],
                        "number" => sizeof($current["children"])
                    );
                }
            }
            else
            {
                $current["children"][]=$node;
            }
        }

        return $root;
    }
  }
}
```

The _tree() method loops through the array of template segments, generated by the _array() method, and organizes them into a hierarchical structure. Plain text nodes are simply assigned as-is to the tree, while additional metadata is generated and assigned with the tags. One important thing to note is that certain statements have an isolated property. This specifies whether text is allowed before the statement. When the loop gets to an isolated tag, it removes the preceding segment (as long as it is a plain text segment), so that the resultant function code is syntactically correct. The last bit of template processing we need to do is convert the template tree into a PHP function. This will allow us to reuse the template without having to recompile it. Take a look at Listing 8-10 to see how we accomplish this.

Listing 8-10. The _script() Method

```
namespace Framework
{
    use Framework\Base as Base;
    use Framework\ArrayMethods as ArrayMethods;
    use Framework\StringMethods as StringMethods;
    use Framework\Template\Exception as Exception;

    class Template extends Base
    {
        protected function _script($tree)
        {
            $content = array();

            if (is_string($tree))
            {
                $tree = addslashes($tree);
                return "\$_text[] = \"{$tree}\";";
            }

            if (sizeof($tree["children"]) > 0)
            {
                foreach ($tree["children"] as $child)
                {
                    $content[] = $this->_script($child);
                }
            }

            if (isset($tree["parent"]))
            {
                return $this->_implementation->handle($tree, implode($content));
            }

            return implode($content);
        }
    }
}
```

The final protected parser method is the `_script()` method. It walks the hierarchy (generated by the `_tree()` method), parses plain text nodes, and indirectly invokes the handler for each valid tag. The `_script()` method should generate a syntactically correct function body.

Our parser is technically complete. If these protected methods were public, we could string a bunch of statements together for a variety of purposes: to convert our template to an array, to convert that array to a tree, and to convert that tree with a script. We want something easier though. We need to bear in mind that our templates are precompiled, in the sense that we need to compile them to functions before we can use them. We can, therefore, simplify our template parsing by have two public methods: one to turn the template into a function, and one to process the template in terms of an array of input data. Let's look at these two methods in Listing 8-11.

Listing 8-11. Main Public Parser Methods

```
namespace Framework
{
    use Framework\Base as Base;
    use Framework\ArrayMethods as ArrayMethods;
    use Framework\StringMethods as StringMethods;
    use Framework\Template\Exception as Exception;

    class Template extends Base
    {
        public function parse($template)
        {
            if (!is_a($this->_implementation, "Framework\Template\Implementation"))
            {
                throw new Exception\Implementation();
            }

            $array = $this->_array($template);
            $tree = $this->_tree($array["all"]);

            $this->_code = $this->header.$this->_script($tree).$this->footer;
            $this->_function = create_function("\$_data", $this->code);

            return $this;
        }

        public function process($data = array())
        {
            if ($this->_function == null)
            {
                throw new Exception\Parser();
            }

            try
            {
                $function = $this->_function;
                return $function($data);
            }
            catch (\Exception $e)
            {
                throw new Exception\Parser($e);
            }
        }
    }
}
```

Aside from assigning a template implementation to the template parser, the only public methods you will use when evaluating and populating a template will be the `parse()` and `process()` methods. The `parse()` method utilizes all of the code we have written so far (for our template parser) to create a working function. It wraps the processed template within the `$_header` and `$_footer` variables we saw earlier. This is then evaluated with a call to PHP's `create_function` method and assigned to the protected `$_function` property.

The process() method check for the existence of the protected $_function property and throws a Template\Exception\Parser exception if it is not present. It then tries to execute the generated function with the $data passed to it. If the function errors, another Template\Exception\Parser exception is thrown. Let's take a look at what our parser does, behind the scenes, with the template shown in Listing 8-12.

Listing 8-12. Example Template

```
{if $name && $address}
    name: {echo $name}<br />
    address: {echo $address}<br />
{/if}
{elseif $name}
    name: {echo $name}<br />
{/elseif}

{foreach $value in $stack}
    {foreach $item in $value}
        item ({echo $item_i}): {echo $item}<br />
    {/foreach}
{/foreach}

{foreach $value in $empty}
    <!--never printed-->
{/foreach}
{else}
    nothing in that stack!<br />
{/else}

{macro test($args)}
    this item's value is: {echo $args}<br />
{/macro}

{foreach $value in $stack["one"]}
    {echo test($value)}
{/foreach}

{if true}
    in first<br />
    {if true}
        in second<br />
        {if true}
            in third<br />
        {/if}
    {/if}
{/if}

{literal}
    {echo "hello world"}
{/literal}
```

Template parsing is only relevant in the context of data being applied to it. For our example, we will use the data array given in Listing 8-13.

Listing 8-13. Example Template Data

```
array(
    "name" => "Chris",
    "address" => "Planet Earth!",
    "stack" => array(
        "one" => array(1, 2, 3),
        "two" => array(4, 5, 6)
    ),
    "empty" =>array()
)
```

■ **Note** The function code generated by our template parser is messy. The following code might look strange, but it is simply the result of the string substitution the parser performs.

If we look at the example template, we can probably imagine the sort of heirarchy being built behind the scenes. The function our `_script()` method compiles is somewhat messy, but interesting still. Take a look at this generated function in Listing 8-14.

Listing 8-14. Generated Function

```
extract($_data); $_text=array();$_text[]="        ";if ($name && $address) {$_text[]="
    name: ";$_text[]=$name;$_text[]="<br />
    address: ";$_text[]=$address;$_text[]="<br />
";}elseif ($name) {$_text[]="
    name: ";$_text[]=$name;$_text[]="<br />
";}$_text[]="

";foreach ($stack as $value_i =>$value) {
        $_text[]="
    ";foreach ($value as $item_i =>$item) {
        $_text[]="
        item (";$_text[]=$item_i;$_text[]="): ";$_text[]=$item;$_text[]="<br />
    ";
    }$_text[]="
";
    }$_text[]="

";

// full listing shortened
```

What a mess! The biggest reason for this is that the parser accounts for the whitespace (and newlines in particular) that our original example template contains. Most of the clutter you see is that whitespace. The processed template (a parsed template with applied data) is quite neat, as you can see in Listing 8-15.

Listing 8-15. Results

```
name: Chris
address: Planet Earth!
item (0): 1
item (1): 2
item (2): 3
item (0): 4
item (1): 5
item (2): 6
nothing in that stack!
this item's value is: 1
this item's value is: 2
this item's value is: 3
in first
in second
in third
{="hello world"}
```

Benefits

You might be asking yourself what the benefits are to swapping out one template language for another. PHP is, after all, only a template language. We haven't even removed all of the PHP artifacts—the need for $ symbols and a strict syntax—so what have we really gained?

At the end of the day, we could have spent a lot more time on a simple template dialect. We could even have made our templates look and feel like regular HTML. What we have ended up with is something that is much simpler to understand and learn than regular PHP.

You want to be able to hand your code over to the average front-end tech/designer and have them immediately be able to see and understand what is going on, without a lot of experience in PHP. Our template dialect/parser helps us achieve that goal.

There are many template dialects/parsers already out there. We will likely get to use more than the simple one we have crafted here, but it is helpful to understand a bit about what goes into creating one, so we can appreciate the work others have done, and be able to customize it to the needs of our clients or project managers.

We will take one last look at the complete `Template\Implementation\Standard` and `Template` classes in Listings 8-16 and 8-17.

Listing 8-16. Template\Implementation\Standard Class

```
namespace Framework\Template\Implementation
{
    use Framework\Template as Template;
    use Framework\StringMethods as StringMethods;

    class Standard extends Template\Implementation
    {
        protected $_map = array(
            "echo" => array(
                "opener" => "{echo",
                "closer" => "}",
                "handler" => "_echo"
            ),
```

```
    "script" => array(
        "opener" => "{script",
        "closer" => "}",
        "handler" => "_script"
    ),
    "statement" => array(
        "opener" => "{",
        "closer" => "}",
        "tags" => array(
            "foreach" => array(
                "isolated" => false,
                "arguments" => "{element} in {object}",
                "handler" => "_each"
            ),
            "for" => array(
                "isolated" => false,
                "arguments" => "{element} in {object}",
                "handler" => "_for"
            ),
            "if" => array(
                "isolated" => false,
                "arguments" => null,
                "handler" => "_if"
            ),
            "elseif" => array(
                "isolated" => true,
                "arguments" => null,
                "handler" => "_elif"
            ),
            "else" => array(
                "isolated" => true,
                "arguments" => null,
                "handler" => "_else"
            ),
            "macro" => array(
                "isolated" => false,
                "arguments" => "{name}({args})",
                "handler" => "_macro"
            ),
            "literal" => array(
                "isolated" => false,
                "arguments" => null,
                "handler" => "_literal"
            )
        )
    )
);
```

```
protected function _echo($tree, $content)
{
    $raw = $this->_script($tree, $content);
    return "\$_text[] = {$raw}";
}

protected function _script($tree, $content)
{
    $raw = !empty($tree["raw"]) ? $tree["raw"] : "";
    return "{$raw};";
}

protected function _each($tree, $content)
{
    $object = $tree["arguments"]["object"];
    $element = $tree["arguments"]["element"];

    return $this->_loop(
        $tree,
        "foreach ({$object} as {$element}_i => {$element}) {
            {$content}
        }"
    );
}

protected function _for($tree, $content)
{
    $object = $tree["arguments"]["object"];
    $element = $tree["arguments"]["element"];

    return $this->_loop(
        $tree,
        "for ({$element}_i = 0; {$element}_i < sizeof({$object}); {$element}_i++) {
            {$element} = {$object}[{$element}_i];
            {$content}
        }"
    );
}

protected function _if($tree, $content)
{
    $raw = $tree["raw"];
    return "if ({$raw}) {{$content}}";
}

protected function _elif($tree, $content)
{
    $raw = $tree["raw"];
    return "elseif ({$raw}) {{$content}}";
}
```

```
        protected function _else($tree, $content)
        {
            return "else {{$content}}";
        }

        protected function _macro($tree, $content)
        {
            $arguments = $tree["arguments"];
            $name = $arguments["name"];
            $args = $arguments["args"];

            return "function {$name}({$args}) {
                \$_text = array();
                {$content}
                return implode(\$_text);
            }";
        }

        protected function _literal($tree, $content)
        {
            $source = addslashes($tree["source"]);
            return "\$_text[] = \"{$source}\";";
        }

        protected function _loop($tree, $inner)
        {
            $number = $tree["number"];
            $object = $tree["arguments"]["object"];
            $children = $tree["parent"]["children"];

            if (!empty($children[$number + 1]["tag"]) && $children[$number + 1]["tag"]== "else")
            {
                return "if (is_array({$object}) && sizeof({$object}) > 0) {{$inner}}";
            }
            return $inner;
        }
    }
}
```

Listing 8-17. Template Class

```
namespace Framework
{
    use Framework\Base as Base;
    use Framework\ArrayMethods as ArrayMethods;
    use Framework\StringMethods as StringMethods;
    use Framework\Template\Exception as Exception;
```

```
    class Template extends Base
    {
        /**
        * @readwrite
        */
        protected $_implementation;

        /**
        * @readwrite
        */
        protected $_header = "if (is_array(\$_data) && sizeof(\$_data)) ➥
extract(\$_data); \$_text = array();";

        /**
        * @readwrite
        */
        protected $_footer = "return implode(\$_text);";

        /**
        * @read
        */
        protected $_code;

        /**
        * @read
        */
        protected $_function;

        public function _getExceptionForImplementation($method)
        {
            return new Exception\Implementation("{$method} method not implemented");
        }

        protected function _arguments($source, $expression)
        {
            $args = $this->_array($expression, array(
                $expression => array(
                    "opener" => "{",
                    "closer" => "}"
                )
            ));

            $tags = $args["tags"];
            $arguments = array();
            $sanitized = StringMethods::sanitize($expression, "()[],.<>*$@");

            foreach ($tags as $i => $tag)
            {
                $sanitized = str_replace($tag, "(.*)", $sanitized);
                $tags[$i] = str_replace(array("{", "}"), "", $tag);
            }
```

```
    if (preg_match("#{$sanitized}#", $source, $matches))
    {
        foreach ($tags as $i => $tag)
        {
            $arguments[$tag] = $matches[$i + 1];
        }
    }

    return $arguments;
}

protected function _tag($source)
{
    $tag = null;
    $arguments = array();

    $match = $this->_implementation->match($source);
    if ($match == null)
    {
        return false;
    }

    $delimiter = $match["delimiter"];
    $type = $match["type"];

    $start = strlen($type["opener"]);
    $end = strpos($source, $type["closer"]);
    $extract = substr($source, $start, $end - $start);

    if (isset($type["tags"]))
    {
        $tags = implode("|", array_keys($type["tags"]));
        $regex = "#^(/){0,1}({$tags})\s*(.*)$#";

        if (!preg_match($regex, $extract, $matches))
        {
            return false;
        }

        $tag = $matches[2];
        $extract = $matches[3];
        $closer = !!$matches[1];
    }

    if ($tag && $closer)
    {
        return array(
            "tag" => $tag,
            "delimiter" => $delimiter,
            "closer" => true,
            "source" => false,
```

```
                "arguments" => false,
                "isolated" => $type["tags"][$tag]["isolated"]
            );
        }

        if (isset($type["arguments"]))
        {
            $arguments = $this->_arguments($extract, $type["arguments"]);
        }
        else if ($tag && isset($type["tags"][$tag]["arguments"]))
        {
            $arguments = $this->_arguments($extract, $type["tags"][$tag]["arguments"]);
        }

        return array(
            "tag" => $tag,
            "delimiter" => $delimiter,
            "closer" => false,
            "source" => $extract,
            "arguments" => $arguments,
            "isolated" => (!empty($type["tags"]) ? $type["tags"][$tag]["isolated"]: false)
        );
    }

    protected function _array($source)
    {
        $parts = array();
        $tags = array();
        $all = array();

        $type = null;
        $delimiter = null;

        while ($source)
        {
            $match = $this->_implementation->match($source);

            $type = $match["type"];
            $delimiter = $match["delimiter"];

            $opener = strpos($source, $type["opener"]);
            $closer = strpos($source, $type["closer"]) + strlen($type["closer"]);

            if ($opener !== false)
            {
                $parts[] = substr($source, 0, $opener);
                $tags[] = substr($source, $opener, $closer - $opener);
                $source = substr($source, $closer);
            }
```

```
        else
        {
            $parts[] = $source;
            $source = "";
        }
    }

    foreach ($parts as $i => $part)
    {
        $all[] = $part;
        if (isset($tags[$i]))
        {
            $all[] = $tags[$i];
        }
    }

    return array(
        "text" => ArrayMethods::clean($parts),
        "tags" => ArrayMethods::clean($tags),
        "all" => ArrayMethods::clean($all)
    );
}

protected function _tree($array)
{
    $root = array(
        "children" => array()
    );
    $current =& $root;

    foreach ($array as $i => $node)
    {
        $result = $this->_tag($node);

        if ($result)
        {
            $tag = isset($result["tag"]) ? $result["tag"] : "";
            $arguments = isset($result["arguments"]) ? $result["arguments"] : "";

            if ($tag)
            {
                if (!$result["closer"])
                {
                    $last = ArrayMethods::last($current["children"]);

                    if ($result["isolated"] && is_string($last))
                    {
                        array_pop($current["children"]);
                    }

                    $current["children"][] = array(
                        "index" => $i,
```

```
                                "parent" =>&$current,
                                "children" =>array(),
                                "raw" =>$result["source"],
                                "tag" =>$tag,
                                "arguments" =>$arguments,
                                "delimiter" =>$result["delimiter"],
                                "number" =>sizeof($current["children"])
                            );
                            $current=& $current["children"][sizeof($current["children"]) - 1];
                        }
                        else if (isset($current["tag"]) && $result["tag"] == $current["tag"])
                        {
                            $start=$current["index"]+1;
                            $length=$i - $start;
                            $current["source"]=implode(array_slice($array,$start, $length));
                            $current=& $current["parent"];
                        }
                    }
                    else
                    {
                        $current["children"][]=array(
                            "index" =>$i,
                            "parent" =>&$current,
                            "children" =>array(),
                            "raw" =>$result["source"],
                            "tag" =>$tag,
                            "arguments" =>$arguments,
                            "delimiter" =>$result["delimiter"],
                            "number" =>sizeof($current["children"])
                        );
                    }
                }
                else
                {
                    $current["children"][]=$node;
                }
            }

            return $root;
        }

        protected function _script($tree)
        {
            $content=array();

            if (is_string($tree))
            {
                $tree=addslashes($tree);
                return "\$_text[]=\"{$tree}\";";
            }
```

```
        if (sizeof($tree["children"])>0)
        {
            foreach ($tree["children"] as $child)
            {
                $content[]=$this->_script($child);
            }
        }

        if (isset($tree["parent"]))
        {
            return $this->_implementation->handle($tree, implode($content));
        }

        return implode($content);
    }

    public function parse($template)
    {
        if (!is_a($this->_implementation, "Framework\Template\Implementation"))
        {
            throw new Exception\Implementation();
        }

        $array=$this->_array($template);
        $tree=$this->_tree($array["all"]);

        $this->_code=$this->header.$this->_script($tree).$this->footer;
        $this->_function=create_function("\$_data", $this->code);

        return $this;
    }

    public function process($data=array())
    {
        if ($this->_function == null)
        {
            throw new Exception\Parser();
        }

        try
        {
            $function=$this->_function;
            return $function($data);
        }
        catch (\Exception $e)
        {
            throw new Exception\Parser($e);
        }
    }
  }
}
```

■ **Note** There are many ways to implement a template parser, and we have chosen one that translates well into our application requirements. We could write books on just this subject alone, so it is important to see that our approach is the most feature-rich that we can do within the constraints.

Questions

1. In this chapter, we created separate classes for implementation and parser. Why is this preferable to a single class?
2. Is there a way in which we could modify the template parser to work with variables not preceded by the PHP $ prefix?
3. Is it possible to implement other control flow structures in our template dialect, such as switch statements?

Answers

1. This is a good path to take, as it lends the template dialect and parser open to future extension. We could easily drop in a different dialect class and the parser would continue to function unaffected. We actually extend the dialect in a future chapter, so this works out nicely!
2. All the template parser is doing behind the scenes is string replacement. We could, theoretically, remove these PHP relics, but it would require intelligent parsing of the arguments provided to the control structures. We could no longer just drop these argument lists into the parsed template as we are currently doing.
3. It is possible. When adding new control flow structures to this template dialect and parser, you just need to think about how the template tags translate into executable PHP. That's what the current tags are doing.

Exercises

1. The template dialect includes a rich set of tags to control the flow of execution in templates. Try extending it with a switch tag.
2. With the classes we created in this chapter, it is now possible to parse string templates with variable data. Try this out!

CHAPTER 9

Databases

Most large applications have one thing in common: they are built to work with a database. All the calculation in the world means nothing without data to perform it on. Think of the rules of any sport. The rules are there to make sure decorum is upheld, and to determine who the winner is. Rules mean very little without the teams who make the score.

Similarly, business processes and calculations mean very little unless they involve real-world data. But in order to get at that data, or to store it, or to change it, we need code to connect to a database and perform the various functions required. That is the code we seek to create now.

Goals

- We need to build a set of classes that allow us to work with a database.
- These classes should allow us to chain method calls for expressive query generation.

Implementation

The database engine we will be focusing our efforts on, in the interest of time, is MySQL. MySQL is a relational SQL database engine. If you are not familiar with SQL, now might be a good time to brush up. Consider the example shown in Listing 9-1.

Listing 9-1. Working with PHP/MySQL

```
/*
 *    Assuming the following database tables:
 *
 *    CREATE TABLE 'users' (
 *        'id' int(11) NOT NULL AUTO_INCREMENT,
 *        'first_name' varchar(32) DEFAULT NULL,
 *        'last_name' varchar(32) DEFAULT NULL,
 *        'modified' datetime DEFAULT NULL,
 *        PRIMARY KEY ('id')
 *    ) ENGINE=InnoDB DEFAULT CHARSET=utf8 AUTO_INCREMENT=1 ;
 *
 *    CREATE TABLE 'points' (
 *        'id' int(11) DEFAULT NULL,
```

```
 *        'points' int(11) DEFAULT NULL
 *     ) ENGINE=InnoDB DEFAULT CHARSET=utf8;
 */

$database=new MySQLi(
    "localhost",
    "prophpmvc",
    "prophpmvc",
    "prophpmvc",
    3306
);

$rows=array();
$result=$database->query("SELECT first_name, last_name AS surname, points AS ➥
 discount FROM users JOIN points ON users.id=points.id WHERE first_name='chris'➥
 ORDER BY last_name DESC LIMIT 100");

for ($i=0; $i<$result->num_rows; $i++)
{
    $rows[]=(object) $result->fetch_array(MYSQLI_ASSOC);
}
```

There are two parts to this example. The first is the PHP statements used to execute the SQL statement, and the second is the statement itself. This is a very basic example of PHP and MySQL working together, but we can go a step further, as you can see in Listing 9-2.

Listing 9-2. Expressive SQL Generation

```
$all=$database->query()
   ->from("users", array(
       "name",
       "surname" =>"last_name"
   ))
   ->join("points", "points.user_id=users.id", array(
       "points" =>"rewards"
   ))
   ->where("name=?", "chris")
   ->order("last_name", "desc")
   ->limit(100)
   ->all();
```

This code demonstrates the kind of fluid query creation we are after. By the time we are done with this chapter, the second example should do exactly the same as the first, but it is much simpler to read and understand. If we build the required code well enough, we should also be able to swap to a different database engine without having to rewrite a single query!

The platform on which we build our database code needs to be robust—it will handle a lot of data. It needs to be easy to use for the majority of cases, and it needs to be secure. As with configuration and caching, we will create a database factory class, which loads a database driver. The database drivers are a little different from configuration and caching in as much as they are split into two parts: connectors and queries. Before we get too far into connectors and queries, let's take a look at the database factory shown in Listing 9-3.

Listing 9-3. The Database Factory Class

```
namespace Framework
{
    use Framework\Base as Base;
    use Framework\Database as Database;
    use Framework\Database\Exception as Exception;

    class Database extends Base
    {
        /**
        * @readwrite
        */
        protected $_type;

        /**
        * @readwrite
        */
        protected $_options;

        protected function _getExceptionForImplementation($method)
        {
            return new Exception\Implementation("{$method} method not implemented");
        }

        public function initialize()
        {
            if (!$this->type)
            {
                throw new Exception\Argument("Invalid type");
            }

            switch ($this->type)
            {
                case "mysql":
                {
                    return new Database\Connector\Mysql($this->options);
                    break;
                }
                default:
                {
                    throw new Exception\Argument("Invalid type");
                    break;
                }
            }
        }
    }
}
```

We begin our database work with the `Database` factory class. It returns a `Database\Connector` subclass (in this case `Database\Connector\Mysql`). Connectors are the classes that do the actual interfacing with the specific database engine. They execute queries and return metadata (such as last inserted ID and affected rows).

Queries are responsible for generating the actual instructions to the database engine, such as SQL queries for INSERT, UPDATE, and DELETE.

Connectors

Our database connectors are not limited to relational database engines, but since we have limited space to cover this section, we will only build MySQL connector/query classes. I leave the creating of other connectors/queries as an exercise to the reader.

■ **Note** We are not limited to working with MySQL database engine, but we will only be creating the connector/query classes that apply to MySQL database servers. Alternatively, you could use SQL Server (www.microsoft.com/sqlserver/en/us/default.aspx) or PostgreSQL (www.postgresql.org), but I have chosen to use MySQL because it is free, easy to install, and is the most popular of the three.

Similar to how our configuration and caching drivers extended a base driver class, our connector classes will inherit from the base connector class shown in Listing 9-4.

Listing 9-4. The Database\Connector Class

```
namespace Framework\Database
{
    use Framework\Base as Base;
    use Framework\Database\Exception as Exception;

    class Connector extends Base
    {
        public function initialize()
        {
            return $this;
        }

        protected function _getExceptionForImplementation($method)
        {
            return new Exception\Implementation("{$method} method not implemented");
        }
    }
}
```

The Database\Connector class is quite simple. It only overrides the exception-generation methods with database-specific variants. It is up to each vendor-specific connector class to do the actual work of connecting to the database engine and/or returning the relevant query class instances. Our MySQL connector class does quite a bit more, as you can see in Listing 9-5.

Listing 9-5. The Database\Connector\Mysql Class

```
namespace Framework\Database\Connector
{
    use Framework\Database as Database;
```

```
use Framework\Database\Exception as Exception;

class Mysql extends Database\Connector
{
    protected $_service;

    /**
    * @readwrite
    */
    protected $_host;

    /**
    * @readwrite
    */
    protected $_username;

    /**
    * @readwrite
    */
    protected $_password;

    /**
    * @readwrite
    */
    protected $_schema;

    /**
    * @readwrite
    */
    protected $_port = "3306";

    /**
    * @readwrite
    */
    protected $_charset = "utf8";

    /**
    * @readwrite
    */
    protected $_engine = "InnoDB";

    /**
    * @readwrite
    */
    protected $_isConnected = false;

    // checks if connected to the database
    protected function _isValidService()
    {
        $isEmpty = empty($this->_service);
        $isInstance = $this->_service instanceof \MySQLi;
```

```
        if ($this->isConnected && $isInstance && !$isEmpty)
        {
            return true;
        }

        return false;
    }

    // connects to the database
    public function connect()
    {
        if (!$this->_isValidService())
        {
            $this->_service=new \MySQLi(
                $this->_host,
                $this->_username,
                $this->_password,
                $this->_schema,
                $this->_port
            );

            if ($this->_service->connect_error)
            {
                throw new Exception\Service("Unable to connect to service");
            }

            $this->isConnected = true;
        }

        return $this;
    }

    // disconnects from the database
    public function disconnect()
    {
        if ($this->_isValidService())
        {
            $this->isConnected=false;
            $this->_service->close();
        }

        return $this;
    }

    // returns a corresponding query instance
    public function query()
    {
        return new Database\Query\Mysql(array(
            "connector" =>$this
        ));
    }
```

```
// executes the provided SQL statement
public function execute($sql)
{
    if (!$this->_isValidService())
    {
        throw new Exception\Service("Not connected to a valid service");
    }

    return $this->_service->query($sql);
}

// escapes the provided value to make it safe for queries
public function escape($value)
{
    if (!$this->_isValidService())
    {
        throw new Exception\Service("Not connected to a valid service");
    }

    return $this->_service->real_escape_string($value);
}

// returns the ID of the last row
// to be inserted
public function getLastInsertId()
{
    if (!$this->_isValidService())
    {
        throw new Exception\Service("Not connected to a valid service");
    }

    return $this->_service->insert_id;
}

// returns the number of rows affected
// by the last SQL query executed
public function getAffectedRows()
{
    if (!$this->_isValidService())
    {
        throw new Exception\Service("Not connected to a valid service");
    }

    return $this->_service->affected_rows;
}

// returns the last error of occur
public function getLastError()
{
    if (!$this->_isValidService())
    {
```

```
                throw new Exception\Service("Not connected to a valid service");
            }

            return $this->_service->error;
        }
    }
}
```

The Database\Connector\Mysql class is much more intense. It defines a handful of adaptable properties and methods used to perform MySQLi class-specific functions, and return MySQLi class-specific properties. We want to isolate these from the outside so that our system is essentially plug-and-play. If connectors are built for other database engines, and they implement the functions we see here, our system won't be able to tell the difference. That is what we are going for.

■ **Note** The default database engine is set to InnoDB, instead of MyISAM. There are a few differences between these two database storage engines, which you need to consider when planning your application. You can learn more about the differences between InnoDB and MyISAM here: http://en.wikipedia.org/wiki/Comparison_of_MySQL_database_engines. I find that InnoDB is usually the one I want to go with, which is why it makes a sane default value.

You will notice, therefore, that our MySQL connector class, while allowing us to execute SQL strings, and giving us various bits of useful information about recently executed SQL queries, does not actually write any SQL! That is the job of the Query class, which we will discuss next.

Queries

One more important thing to notice, in the previous listing, is that the query() method returns an instance of the Database\Query\Mysql class. It is in this class that most of our database code will go. The Query class is what writes the vendor-specific database code. In MySQL's case: UPDATE, DELETE, and SELECT queries. It begins with the code shown in Listing 9-6, which should look familiar.

Listing 9-6. The Database\Query Class

```
namespace Framework\Database
{
    use Framework\Base as Base;
    use Framework\ArrayMethods as ArrayMethods;
    use Framework\Database\Exception as Exception;

    class Query extends Base
    {
        /**
        * @readwrite
        */
        protected $_connector;

        /**
        * @read
        */
        protected $_from;
```

```
        /**
        * @read
        */
        protected $_fields;

        /**
        * @read
        */
        protected $_limit;

        /**
        * @read
        */
        protected $_offset;

        /**
        * @read
        */
        protected $_order;

        /**
        * @read
        */
        protected $_direction;

        /**
        * @read
        */
        protected $_join=array();

        /**
        * @read
        */
        protected $_where=array();

        protected function _getExceptionForImplementation($method)
        {
            return new Exception\Implementation("{$method} method not implemented");
        }
    }
}
```

Here, we can see a handful of adaptable properties and exception-generation method overrides. These properties hold the query parameters before the actual queries are generated. The methods that generate the database queries use data within these properties, which is why they are protected, and mostly read-only. We can't have developers fiddling with their content in the middle of the generation process. As in the second example we saw, we should be able to substitute the ? character with any type of data, so we also need a method to correctly quote the input data according to how MySQL will expect it. Take a look at Listing 9-7.

Listing 9-7. The _quote() Method

```
namespace Framework\Database
{
    use Framework\Base as Base;
    use Framework\ArrayMethods as ArrayMethods;
    use Framework\Database\Exception as Exception;

    class Query extends Base
    {
        protected function _quote($value)
        {
            if (is_string($value))
            {
                $escaped = $this->connector->escape($value);
                return "'{$escaped}'";
            }

            if (is_array($value))
            {
                $buffer = array();

                foreach ($value as $i)
                {
                    array_push($buffer, $this->_quote($i));
                }

                $buffer = join(", ", $buffer);
                return "({$buffer})";
            }

            if (is_null($value))
            {
                return "NULL";
            }

            if (is_bool($value))
            {
                return (int) $value;
            }

            return $this->connector->escape($value);
        }
    }
}
```

The protected `_quote()` method is used to wrap the `$value` passed to it in the applicable quotation marks, so that it can be added to the applicable query in a syntactically correct form. It has logic to deal with different value types, such as strings, arrays, and boolean values. We also need to build the convenience methods for altering queries, namely things like `from()`, `limit()`, and `join()`, as shown in Listing 9-8.

Listing 9-8. The Query Sugar Methods

```
namespace Framework\Database
{
    use Framework\Base as Base;
    use Framework\ArrayMethods as ArrayMethods;
    use Framework\Database\Exception as Exception;

    class Query extends Base
    {
        public function from($from, $fields = array("*"))
        {
            if (empty($from))
            {
                throw new Exception\Argument("Invalid argument");
            }

            $this->_from = $from;

            if ($fields)
            {
                $this->_fields[$from] = $fields;
            }

            return $this;
        }

        public function join($join, $on, $fields = array())
        {
            if (empty($join))
            {
                throw new Exception\Argument("Invalid argument");
            }

            if (empty($on))
            {
                throw new Exception\Argument("Invalid argument");
            }

            $this->_fields += array($join => $fields);
            $this->_join[] = "JOIN {$join} ON {$on}";

            return $this;
        }

        public function limit($limit, $page = 1)
        {
            if (empty($limit))
            {
                throw new Exception\Argument("Invalid argument");
            }
```

```
            $this->_limit = $limit;
            $this->_offset = $limit * ($page - 1);

            return $this;
        }

        public function order($order, $direction = "asc")
        {
            if (empty($order))
            {
                throw new Exception\Argument("Invalid argument");
            }

            $this->_order = $order;
            $this->_direction = $direction;

            return $this;
        }

        public function where()
        {
            $arguments = func_get_args();

            if (sizeof($arguments) < 1)
            {
                throw new Exception\Argument("Invalid argument");
            }

            $arguments[0] = preg_replace("#\?#", "%s", $arguments[0]);

            foreach (array_slice($arguments, 1, null, true) as $i =>$parameter)
            {
                $arguments[$i] = $this->_quote($arguments[$i]);
            }

            $this->_where[] = call_user_func_array("sprintf", $arguments);

            return $this;
        }
    }
}
```

All these methods return a reference to the class instance, so that they can be chained. The `from()` method is used to specify the table from which data should be read from, or written to (in the case of `INSERT`, `UPDATE`, and `DELETE`). It also accepts a second argument for the fields you wish to query. While these can be specified, even if you wish to perform a data modification query, they will be ignored when they do not apply to the requested query.

The `join()` method is used to specify joins across tables. It only allows a natural `JOIN`, as this should do for most cases. Once again, we are only interested in succinct code that does what we want it to most of the time. In the event that we need a complicated query, we are far likely to be better off writing one out in plain SQL or even creating a stored procedure/view to do it for us.

The second argument for the `join()` method is the fields on which the join is dependent. The last (optional) argument is similar to the `from()` method's second argument, in that it allows you to specify fields to return from the joined table. The _buildSelect() method we will see in a bit allows the $fields arguments to be simple field names, or field names with aliases. The methods are smart enough to guess the difference between $fields = array('field1') and $fields = array('field1' => 'alias1').

The where() method is the most tricky of these methods, in that it allows for variable-length arguments. It will take a string in the format of 'foo = ? and bar = ? and baz = ?' and accept a further three arguments to replace those ? characters. What it is actually doing is running PHP's sprintf, so we don't need to handle any tokenizing; but it is also quoting the values passed in the second, third, fourth (etc.) positions with that _quote() method we saw earlier, so that our database data is secure from injection attacks.

The order() method is useful for specifying which field to order the query by, and in which direction. It only handles ordering by one field, another instance of accommodating the majority of cases, and defaults the direction to asc if the second (optional) $direction parameter is not specified.

The limit() method is useful for specifying how many rows to return at once, and on which page to begin the results. This is slightly more convenient than having to provide an offset directly, as you don't have to think in terms of individual rows, but rather pages of rows (which is the typical use of the SQL LIMIT statement). The page parameter is optional.

All of these methods accept some kind of input that will later be used in the construction of a SQL query. They have minimal input validation and can probably do with proper exception messages, but we won't worry about that right now. The purpose of their names is to allow for fluid query creation (for most of the cases we are likely to encounter). It is a lot easier working out a query when you can read it in plain language.

The majority of relational SQL queries are INSERT, UPDATE, DELETE, or SELECT queries. We will create methods to handle each of these types of queries, beginning with select queries, as shown in Listing 9-9.

Listing 9-9. The _buildSelect() Method

```
namespace Framework\Database
{
    use Framework\Base as Base;
    use Framework\ArrayMethods as ArrayMethods;
    use Framework\Database\Exception as Exception;

    class Query extends Base
    {
        protected function _buildSelect()
        {
            $fields = array();
            $where = $order = $limit = $join = "";
            $template = "SELECT %s FROM %s %s %s %s %s";

            foreach ($this->fields as $table => $_fields)
            {
                foreach ($_fields as $field => $alias)
                {
                    if (is_string($field))
                    {
                        $fields[] = "{$field} AS {$alias}";
                    }
                    else
                    {
                        $fields[] = $alias;
                    }
                }
            }
```

```
            $fields = join(", ", $fields);

            $_join = $this->join;
            if (!empty($_join))
            {
                $join = join(" ", $_join);
            }

            $_where = $this->where;
            if (!empty($_where))
            {
                $joined = join(" AND ", $_where);
                $where = "WHERE {$joined}";
            }

            $_order = $this->order;
            if (!empty($_order))
            {
                $_direction = $this->direction;
                $order = "ORDER BY {$_order} {$_direction}";
            }

            $_limit = $this->limit;
            if (!empty($_limit))
            {
                $_offset = $this->offset;
                if ($_offset)
                {
                    $limit = "LIMIT {$_limit}, {$_offset}";
                }
                else
                {
                    $limit = "LIMIT {$_limit}";
                }
            }

            return sprintf($template, $fields, $this->from, $join, $where, $order, $limit);
        }
    }
}
```

This method is the heart of our query class—specifically the `all()`, `first()`, and `count()` methods. It takes into account all the data stored in those protected properties we saw earlier, and builds a MySQL compatible SQL query, from the ground up. It declares the template for our `SELECT` statement. It then loops through all the stored fields (from the `from()` and `join()` methods) and determines whether to alias them. It neatens them up by joining them into a comma-delimited string. Similarly, it joins the `$_join`, `$_where` properties. It continues by creating the correctly formatted `ORDER BY` and `LIMIT` clauses and finally running everything through `sprintf`, generating a valid SQL query.

The methods that build `INSERT`, `UPDATE`, and `DELETE` queries are a bit simpler than the `_buildSelect()` method. Take a look at Listing 9-10.

Listing 9-10. The buildInsert(), _buildUpdate(), and _buildDelete() Methods

```
namespace Framework\Database
{
    use Framework\Base as Base;
    use Framework\ArrayMethods as ArrayMethods;
    use Framework\Database\Exception as Exception;

    class Query extends Base
    {
        protected function _buildInsert($data)
        {
            $fields = array();
            $values = array();
            $template = "INSERT INTO '%s' ('%s') VALUES (%s)";

            foreach ($data as $field => $value)
            {
                $fields[] = $field;
                $values[] = $this->_quote($value);
            }

            $fields = join("', '", $fields);
            $values = join(", ", $values);

            return sprintf($template, $this->from, $fields, $values);
        }

        protected function _buildUpdate($data)
        {
            $parts = array();
            $where = $limit = "";
            $template = "UPDATE %s SET %s %s %s";

            foreach ($data as $field => $value)
            {
                $parts[] = "{$field} = ".$this->_quote($value);
            }

            $parts = join(", ", $parts);

            $_where = $this->where;
            if (!empty($_where))
            {
                $joined = join(", ", $_where);
                $where = "WHERE {$joined}";
            }

            $_limit = $this->limit;
            if (!empty($_limit))
```

```
            {
                $_offset = $this->offset;
                $limit = "LIMIT {$_limit} {$_offset}";
            }

            return sprintf($template, $this->from, $parts, $where, $limit);
        }

        protected function _buildDelete()
        {
            $where = $limit = "";
            $template = "DELETE FROM %s %s %s";

            $_where = $this->where;
            if (!empty($_where))
            {
                $joined = join(", ", $_where);
                $where = "WHERE {$joined}";
            }

            $_limit = $this->limit;
            if (!empty($_limit))
            {
                $_offset = $this->offset;
                $limit = "LIMIT {$_limit} {$_offset}";
            }

            return sprintf($template, $this->from, $where, $limit);
        }
    }
}
```

The `_buildInsert()`, `_buildUpdate()`, and `_buildDelete()` methods are relatively simple in comparison. They too construct a SQL query, but for different purposes, and utilizing different data.

The `_buildInsert()` method defines the template for a valid `INSERT` query, and then goes about splitting the passed `$data` into two arrays: for `$fields` and `$values`. It joins those arrays, and finally runs the results through `sprintf`.

The `_buildUpdate()` does pretty much the same, except it combines both the fields and values into a single array (as is consistent with MySQL `UPDATE` queries). It also has the added task of dealing with `WHERE` clauses, since most updates are done on specific sets of database rows. Failure to specify a valid `WHERE` clause, on an `UPDATE` query, will lead to all rows in the table being updated with the same data.

It also takes into account the `LIMIT` clause, so that updates can be limited to a finite amount of records that match the `WHERE` clause. It is always good to set a limit of table updates, in case your `WHERE` clause is missing, or targets more than the amount of rows you were intending for it to target.

The `_buildDelete()` method does everything the `_buildUpdate()` method does, and nothing that the `_buildInsert()` method does. This is because there is no row data to take into account except for whatever the `WHERE` clauses target. It is also recommended that you always use the `LIMIT` clause on row deletions, as you might be deleting more rows than you intend to target.

These four methods perform the bulk of the required work, but we can simplify their use with the methods shown in Listing 9-11.

Listing 9-11. Convenience Methods

```
namespace Framework\Database
{
    use Framework\Base as Base;
    use Framework\ArrayMethods as ArrayMethods;
    use Framework\Database\Exception as Exception;

    class Query extends Base
    {
        public function save($data)
        {
            $isInsert = sizeof($this->_where) == 0;

            if ($isInsert)
            {
                $sql = $this->_buildInsert($data);
            }
            else
            {
                $sql = $this->_buildUpdate($data);
            }

            $result = $this->_connector->execute($sql);

            if ($result === false)
            {
                throw new Exception\Sql();
            }

            if ($isInsert)
            {
                return $this->_connector->lastInsertId;
            }
            return 0;
        }

        public function delete()
        {
            $sql = $this->_buildDelete();
            $result = $this->_connector->execute($sql);

            if ($result === false)
            {
                throw new Exception\Sql();
            }

            return $this->_connector->affectedRows;
        }
    }
}
```

The save() method determines what kind of query you need by looking at whether you have called the where() method on this query object. If you have, it assumes it is to specify a row ID (or other row-specific criteria), and calls the _buildUpdate() method accordingly. If the INSERT/UPDATE query fails to execute, a Database\Exception\Sql exception is thrown. If they do execute correctly, and an INSERT query was performed, the last inserted ID will be returned. If an UPDATE query was performed, 0 is returned (as a means of specifying that the operation was successful).

■ **Note** We don't return affected rows or Boolean values with the save() method—those would make this function's results ambiguous. You can find the affected rows of an UPDATE query, by calling the getAffectedRows() method on the database connector.

The delete() method simply calls the _buildDelete() method and executes its result. If the query could not execute, a Database\Exception\Sql exception is thrown; otherwise, the number of affected rows are returned. The last three public methods we need return all rows matching a query, the first row matching a query, and a count of all rows to be returned by a query. You can see how this is demonstrated in Listings 9-12 and 9-13.

Listing 9-12. Database\Driver Data Access Methods

```
namespace Framework\Database
{
    use Framework\Base as Base;
    use Framework\ArrayMethods as ArrayMethods;
    use Framework\Database\Exception as Exception;

    class Query extends Base
    {
        public function first()
        {
            $limit = $this->_limit;
            $offset = $this->_offset;

            $this->limit(1);

            $all = $this->all();
            $first = ArrayMethods::first($all);

            if ($limit)
            {
                $this->_limit = $limit;
            }
            if ($offset)
            {
                $this->_offset = $offset;
            }

            return $first;
        }
```

```
        public function count()
        {
            $limit = $this->limit;
            $offset = $this->offset;
            $fields = $this->fields;

            $this->_fields = array($this->from => array("COUNT(1)" => "rows"));

            $this->limit(1);
            $row = $this->first();

            $this->_fields = $fields;

            if ($fields)
            {
                $this->_fields = $fields;
            }
            if ($limit)
            {
                $this->_limit = $limit;
            }
            if ($offset)
            {
                $this->_offset = $offset;
            }

            return $row["rows"];
        }
    }
}
```

Listing 9-13. Database\Driver\Mysql Data Access Method

```
namespace Framework\Database\Query
{
    use Framework\Database as Database;
    use Framework\Database\Exception as Exception;
    class Mysql extends Database\Query
    {
        public function all()
        {
            $sql = $this->_buildSelect();
            $result = $this->connector->execute($sql);

            if ($result === false)
            {
                $error = $this->connector->lastError;
                throw new Exception\Sql("There was an error with your SQL query: {$error}");
            }

            $rows = array();
```

```
            for ($i=0; $i<$result->num_rows; $i++)
            {
                $rows[]=$result->fetch_array(MYSQLI_ASSOC);
            }

            return $rows;
        }
    }
}
```

The all() method is responsible for returning a variable number of rows, based on the SELECT query performed. It calls the _buildSelect() method and attempts to execute it. If it fails, a Database\Exception\Sql exception is thrown. If it gets valid results, it will loop through them and assign the object representation of the returned associative arrays to the $rows array.

The first() and count() methods are both based on the all() method. The first() method alters the $_limit and $_offset properties so that only one row is returned. Those properties are then reset to their original values, and then that single row is returned.

The count() method also alters the $_limit and $_offset properties, and also the $_fields property. It adds the field count(1) (the most efficient way to return the number of rows in a single query on a table). It calls all(), gets the first row, gets the count value and then resets the $_limit, $_offset, and $_fields properties to their original values.

With all of this database code in place, we can now perform many different kinds of queries using our stable, polymorphic database library. The code in Listing 9-14 gives a good all-around example of that.

Listing 9-14. Example Database Usage

```
$database=new Database(array(
    "type" =>"mysql",
    "options" =>array(
        "host" =>"localhost",
        "username" =>"prophpmvc",
        "password" =>"prophpmvc",
        "schema" =>"prophpmvc",
        "port" =>"3306"
    )
));
$database=$database->initialize();

$all=$database->query()
    ->from("users", array(
        "first_name",
        "last_name" =>"surname"
    ))
    ->join("points", "points.id=users.id", array(
        "points" =>"rewards"
    ))
    ->where("first_name=?", "chris")
    ->order("last_name", "desc")
    ->limit(100)
    ->all();
```

```
$print=print_r($all, true);
echo "all =>{$print}";

$id=$database->query()
    ->from("users")
    ->save(array(
        "first_name" =>"Liz",
        "last_name" =>"Pitt"
    ));

echo "id =>{$id}\n";

$affected=$database->query()
    ->from("users")
    ->where("first_name=?", "Liz")
    ->delete();

echo "affected =>{$affected}\n";

$id=$database->query()
    ->from("users")
    ->where("first_name=?", "Chris")
    ->save(array(
        "modified" =>date("Y-m-d H:i:s")
    ));

echo "id =>{$id}\n";

$count=$database->query()
    ->from("users")
    ->count();

echo "count =>{$count}\n";
```

Depending on the kinds of database engines you are likely to support, you may choose to keep minimal code within the base Query class, and have each Query subclass implement similar logic for the engine in question.

■ **Note** The collation you choose to apply to your database tables will determine whether your SQL queries will be case sensitive, in terms of the comparison between string values and table column data. This can be overridden on a per-query basis, but this sort of advanced SQL falls outside the scope of this book.

As I am familiar with more relational SQL database engines than not, I have opted to keep all the reusable SQL creation code in the base Query class, and only need one method in the actual MySQL Query subclass. Let's take a look at the complete Query class in Listing 9-15.

Listing 9-15. The Database\Query Class

```
namespace Framework\Database
{
    use Framework\Base as Base;
    use Framework\ArrayMethods as ArrayMethods;
    use Framework\Database\Exception as Exception;

    class Query extends Base
    {
        /**
        * @readwrite
        */
        protected $_connector;

        /**
        * @read
        */
        protected $_from;

        /**
        * @read
        */
        protected $_fields;

        /**
        * @read
        */
        protected $_limit;

        /**
        * @read
        */
        protected $_offset;

        /**
        * @read
        */
        protected $_order;

        /**
        * @read
        */
        protected $_direction;

        /**
        * @read
        */
        protected $_join = array();
```

```
/**
* @read
*/
protected $_where = array();

protected function _getExceptionForImplementation($method)
{
    return new Exception\Implementation("{$method} method not implemented");
}

protected function _quote($value)
{
    if (is_string($value))
    {
        $escaped = $this->connector->escape($value);
        return "'{$escaped}'";
    }

    if (is_array($value))
    {
        $buffer = array();

        foreach ($value as $i)
        {
            array_push($buffer, $this->_quote($i));
        }

        $buffer = join(", ", $buffer);
        return "({$buffer})";
    }

    if (is_null($value))
    {
        return "NULL";
    }

    if (is_bool($value))
    {
        return (int) $value;
    }

    return $this->connector->escape($value);
}

protected function _buildSelect()
{
    $fields = array();
    $where = $order = $limit = $join = "";
    $template = "SELECT %s FROM %s %s %s %s %s";
```

```
foreach ($this->fields as $table =>$_fields)
{
    foreach ($_fields as $field =>$alias)
    {
        if (is_string($field))
        {
            $fields[]="{$field} AS {$alias}";
        }
        else
        {
            $fields[]=$alias;
        }
    }
}

$fields=join(", ", $fields);

$_join=$this->join;
if (!empty($_join))
{
    $join=join(" ", $_join);
}

$_where=$this->where;
if (!empty($_where))
{
    $joined=join(" AND ", $_where);
    $where="WHERE {$joined}";
}

$_order=$this->order;
if (!empty($_order))
{
    $_direction=$this->direction;
    $order="ORDER BY {$_order} {$_direction}";
}

$_limit=$this->limit;
if (!empty($_limit))
{
    $_offset=$this->offset;

    if ($_offset)
    {
        $limit="LIMIT {$_limit}, {$_offset}";
    }
    else
    {
        $limit="LIMIT {$_limit}";
    }
}
```

```
    return sprintf($template, $fields, $this->from, $join, $where, $order, $limit);
}

protected function _buildInsert($data)
{
    $fields = array();
    $values = array();
    $template = "INSERT INTO '%s' ('%s') VALUES (%s)";

    foreach ($data as $field => $value)
    {
        $fields[] = $field;
        $values[] = $this->_quote($value);
    }

    $fields = join("', '", $fields);
    $values = join(", ", $values);

    return sprintf($template, $this->from, $fields, $values);
}

protected function _buildUpdate($data)
{
    $parts = array();
    $where = $limit = "";
    $template = "UPDATE %s SET %s %s %s";

    foreach ($data as $field => $value)
    {
        $parts[] = "{$field} = ".$this->_quote($value);
    }

    $parts = join(", ", $parts);

    $_where = $this->where;
    if (!empty($_where))
    {
        $joined = join(", ", $_where);
        $where = "WHERE {$joined}";
    }

    $_limit = $this->limit;
    if (!empty($_limit))
    {
        $_offset = $this->offset;
        $limit = "LIMIT {$_limit} {$_offset}";
    }

    return sprintf($template, $this->from, $parts, $where, $limit);
}
```

```
        protected function _buildDelete()
        {
            $where = $limit = "";
            $template = "DELETE FROM %s %s %s";

            $_where = $this->where;
            if (!empty($_where))
            {
                $joined = join(", ", $_where);
                $where = "WHERE {$joined}";
            }

            $_limit = $this->limit;
            if (!empty($_limit))
            {
                $_offset = $this->offset;
                $limit = "LIMIT {$_limit} {$_offset}";
            }

            return sprintf($template, $this->from, $where, $limit);
        }

        public function save($data)
        {
            $isInsert = sizeof($this->_where) == 0;

            if ($isInsert)
            {
                $sql = $this->_buildInsert($data);
            }
            else
            {
                $sql = $this->_buildUpdate($data);
            }
            $result = $this->_connector->execute($sql);

            if ($result === false)
            {
                throw new Exception\Sql();
            }

            if ($isInsert)
            {
                return $this->_connector->lastInsertId;
            }
            return 0;
        }

        public function delete()
        {
            $sql = $this->_buildDelete();
            $result = $this->_connector->execute($sql);
```

```
    if ($result === false)
    {
        throw new Exception\Sql();
    }

    return $this->_connector->affectedRows;
}

public function from($from, $fields=array("*"))
{
    if (empty($from))
    {
        throw new Exception\Argument("Invalid argument");
    }

    $this->_from=$from;

    if ($fields)
    {
        $this->_fields[$from]=$fields;
    }

    return $this;
}

public function join($join, $on, $fields=array())
{
    if (empty($join))
    {
        throw new Exception\Argument("Invalid argument");
    }

    if (empty($on))
    {
        throw new Exception\Argument("Invalid argument");
    }

    $this->_fields += array($join =>$fields);
    $this->_join[]="JOIN {$join} ON {$on}";
    return $this;
}

public function limit($limit, $page=1)
{
    if (empty($limit))
    {
        throw new Exception\Argument("Invalid argument");
    }
```

```
        $this->_limit = $limit;
        $this->_offset = $limit * ($page - 1);

        return $this;
    }

    public function order($order, $direction = "asc")
    {
        if (empty($order))
        {
            throw new Exception\Argument("Invalid argument");
        }

        $this->_order = $order;
        $this->_direction = $direction;

        return $this;
    }

    public function where()
    {
        $arguments = func_get_args();

        if (sizeof($arguments) < 1)
        {
            throw new Exception\Argument("Invalid argument");
        }

        $arguments[0] = preg_replace("#\?#", "%s", $arguments[0]);

        foreach (array_slice($arguments, 1, null, true) as $i => $parameter)
        {
            $arguments[$i] = $this->_quote($arguments[$i]);
        }

        $this->_where[] = call_user_func_array("sprintf", $arguments);

        return $this;
    }

    public function first()
    {
        $limit = $this->_limit;
        $offset = $this->_offset;

        $this->limit(1);

        $all = $this->all();
        $first = ArrayMethods::first($all);
```

```
            if ($limit)
            {
                $this->_limit = $limit;
            }
            if ($offset)
            {
                $this->_offset = $offset;
            }

            return $first;
        }

        public function count()
        {
            $limit = $this->limit;
            $offset = $this->offset;
            $fields = $this->fields;

            $this->_fields = array($this->from => array("COUNT(1)" => "rows"));

            $this->limit(1);
            $row = $this->first();

            $this->_fields = $fields;

            if ($fields)
            {
                $this->_fields = $fields;
            }
            if ($limit)
            {
                $this->_limit = $limit;
            }
            if ($offset)
            {
                $this->_offset = $offset;
            }

            return $row["rows"];
        }
    }
}
```

If you are planning to use nonrelational, or non-SQL database engines, feel free to have a relatively empty Query class, and a full Query subclass.

■ **Note** The process of escaping query values is quite important. It prevents SQL injection attacks by ensuring that special query characters are securely escaped to their literal string representations. SQL injection attacks are a fairly common security problem, which you can read more about at `http://en.wikipedia.org/wiki/SQL_injection`.

Questions

1. In this chapter, we built a database engine in three parts: factory, connector, and driver. Why is this preferable to a single class or just a factory-driver combination?
2. The `Connector` class is much simpler than the `Connector\Mysql` class, yet the `Query\Mysql` class is much simpler than the `Query` class. Why is this?
3. Why does the `Query` class need to substitute query values for the ? character?

Answers

1. The factory is a good idea if we plan on having multiple connector or query classes. The connector-query combination is a good idea because they deal with different things. The `Connector` class is an intermediary between PHP and a MySQL server. The `Query` class builds SQL queries. Combining them into a single class would limit the library significantly.
2. Every database engine you access through PHP will require unique method and class names. This means that very little can be abstracted to apply to all database engines. Relational SQL, on the other hand, is not unique to a specific database engine, so it can be abstracted for use in multiple relational SQL database engines.
3. This is a security measure we put in place to validate the query parameters that we provide to MySQL. We could use basic string substitution, but that would be less secure.

Exercises

1. This chapter is all about MySQL. The structure we built can be used for other relational SQL database engines, so try creating another connector-driver combination for another relational SQL database engine.
2. The `WHERE` clauses generated with the `Driver\Mysql` class does not handle `OR`, `WHERE`, or `LIKE` clauses. Try creating methods for these.

CHAPTER 10

Models

Up until now, we have created classes and libraries that form the foundation of our framework, but that aren't particularly concerned with how applications will use them. All that is about to change.

As I mentioned before, calculation is nothing without data to calculate on. Most projects you will work on have one thing in common: they need to store, manipulate, and return and display data. You can achieve this with the use of a database.

In Chapter 9, we learned how to create an extensible database library, and wrote a MySQL connector/query class pair. Talking directly to the database is one way to get the job done, but it is hardly ideal to do so directly in our controller. This is just one of the reasons for using models.

Goals

- We need to understand what models are.
- We need to build the model class to handle general, repeated tasks easily.

Idea

Models allow us to isolate all the direct database communication, and most communication with third-party web services. The models we build, in this chapter, will present a simple interface for performing changes to our database.

Note The way in which we define our models in this chapter, is sometimes referred to as Object-Relational Mapping (ORM). An ORM library creates an opaque communication layer between two data-related systems. You can read more about ORM at `http://en.wikipedia.org/wiki/Object-relational_mapping`.

It is important to understand that models are not limited to database work. Models can connect to any number of third-party data services, and provide a simple interface for use in our controllers. We just happen to be focusing our models into the ORM paradigm.

We could just as easily need to build a model that connects to Flickr to download photos, or a model that allows us to upload/download files from a cloud computing network like Amazon S3. Models are meant to contain any and every resource not presented directly in a view, or used by a controller to connect views and models together.

Implementation

Database engines can store many different types of data. We are only going to need the following few for our models.

- **Autonumber**
  Autonumber fields generate an automatically incremented numeric value, and are most often used for identity fields.
- **Text**
  Text fields relate to either the varchar or text data types, depending on the required field length.
- **Integer**
  The default field length of our integer type is 11.
- **Decimal**
  Decimal fields contain float values.
- **Boolean**
  Boolean fields are actually tinyint fields. When assigning true/false to them, the Boolean value will be cast to an integer value.
- **Datetime**

The reason we have chosen such a small subset of data types to support in our ORM is because it keeps things simple. We can also be confident that the vast majority of database engines support these data types. How do we use these data types in our models? The example shown in Listing 10-1 illustrates a way for us to define the different data types our model needs.

Listing 10-1. The User Model

```
class User extends Framework\Model
{
    /**
    * @column
    * @readwrite
    * @primary
    * @type autonumber
    */
    protected $_id;

    /**
    * @column
    * @readwrite
    * @type text
    * @length 100
    */
    protected $_first;

    /**
    * @column
    * @readwrite
    * @type text
    * @length 100
    */
    protected $_last;
```

```
    /**
    * @column
    * @readwrite
    * @type text
    * @length 100
    * @index
    */
    protected $_email;

    /**
    * @column
    * @readwrite
    * @type text
    * @length 100
    * @index
    */
    protected $_password;

    /**
    * @column
    * @readwrite
    * @type text
    */
    protected $_notes;

    /**
    * @column
    * @readwrite
    * @type boolean
    * @index
    */
    protected $_live;

    /**
    * @column
    * @readwrite
    * @type boolean
    * @index
    */
    protected $_deleted;

    /**
    * @column
    * @readwrite
    * @type datetime
    */
    protected $_created;

    /**
    * @column
    * @readwrite
    * @type datetime
    */
    protected $_modified;
}
```

The first thing we notice about this example model is that it contains only a handful of properties, and is really easy to understand. Each of these protected properties includes the @readwrite flag, which we have seen before. This means we will be able to call getter/setter methods like setFirst() and getCreated() without having to define them in our Model class.

The new properties are what we are really interested in. Every class property, which translates into a column in the database, is identified with an @column flag. Our model initialization code will ignore all class properties that do not have this flag. The $_id class property has an @primary flag which identifies it as the primary key column. The $_email, $_password, $_live, and $_deleted properties all have an @index flag to show that they should be indexed in the database table.

The remaining flags are @type and @length. These show what data type the class property should be, and the field length (which we will only use in the case of text fields, to decide whether they should be varchar or text).

This structure needs to translate into an actual database table, if it is to be of any use to us. Our database/model layer needs to turn the columns we created into the underlying SQL in order for it to be committed to the database. When we are done, it should resemble the SQL shown in Listing 10-2.

Listing 10-2. The MySQL Table Representation of the User Model

```
CREATE TABLE 'user' (
'id' int(11) NOT NULL AUTO_INCREMENT,
'first' varchar(100) DEFAULT NULL,
'last' varchar(100) DEFAULT NULL,
'email' varchar(100) DEFAULT NULL,
'password' varchar(100) DEFAULT NULL,
'notes' text,
'live' tinyint(4) DEFAULT NULL,
'deleted' tinyint(4) DEFAULT NULL,
'created' datetime DEFAULT NULL,
'modified' datetime DEFAULT NULL,
PRIMARY KEY ('id'),
KEY 'email' ('email'),
KEY 'password' ('password'),
KEY 'live' ('live'),
KEY 'deleted' ('deleted')
) ENGINE=InnoDB DEFAULT CHARSET=utf8;
```

Note Passwords should never be stored in plain text. We forgo this best practice in order to keep things simple and focused. You should take the time to learn how to encrypt or hash passwords to make sure they cannot be stolen and used for nefarious purposes.

Building the SQL

The SQL in Listing 10-2 is what we expect our model to look like in the database. It illustrates the data type conversion our Model class makes between the simple types we outlined (text, integer, Boolean, etc.), and the actual field types in the database. So let us begin our Model class, as demonstrated in Listing 10-3.

Listing 10-3. The Model class

```
namespace Framework
{
    use Framework\Base as Base;
```

```
    use Framework\Registry as Registry;
    use Framework\Inspector as Inspector;
    use Framework\StringMethods as StringMethods;
    use Framework\Model\Exception as Exception;

    class Model extends Base
    {
        /**
        * @readwrite
        */
        protected $_table;

        /**
        * @readwrite
        */
        protected $_connector;

        /**
        * @read
        */
        protected $_types = array(
            "autonumber",
            "text",
            "integer",
            "decimal",
            "boolean",
            "datetime"
        );

        protected $_columns;
        protected $_primary;

        public function _getExceptionForImplementation($method)
        {
            return new Exception\Implementation("{$method} method not implemented");
        }
    }
}
```

Our Model class begins simply enough, with the properties we want getters/setters for, and the exception-generation override methods. The $_types property holds the simple data types our models understand, and is used both internally and externally, for validation. Before we can create the SQL for our model/database table, we need to create some utility methods, in the StringMethods class, as shown in Listing 10-4.

Listing 10-4. StringMethods Inflection Methods

```
namespace Framework
{
    class StringMethods
    {
        private static $_singular = array(
            "(matr)ices$" => "\\1ix",
            "(vert|ind)ices$" => "\\1ex",
            "^(ox)en" => "\\1",
            "(alias)es$" => "\\1",
```

```
        "([octop|vir])i$" => "\\1us",
        "(cris|ax|test)es$" => "\\1is",
        "(shoe)s$" => "\\1",
        "(o)es$" => "\\1",
        "(bus|campus)es$" => "\\1",
        "([m|l])ice$" => "\\1ouse",
        "(x|ch|ss|sh)es$" => "\\1",
        "(m)ovies$" => "\\1\\2ovie",
        "(s)eries$" => "\\1\\2eries",
        "([^aeiouy]|qu)ies$" => "\\1y",
        "([lr])ves$" => "\\1f",
        "(tive)s$" => "\\1",
        "(hive)s$" => "\\1",
        "([^f])ves$" => "\\1fe",
        "(^analy)ses$" => "\\1sis",
        "((a)naly|(b)a|(d)iagno|(p)arenthe|(p)rogno|(s)ynop|(t)he)ses$" => "\\1\\2sis",
        "([ti])a$" => "\\1um",
        "(p)eople$" => "\\1\\2erson",
        "(m)en$" => "\\1an",
        "(s)tatuses$" => "\\1\\2tatus",
        "(c)hildren$" => "\\1\\2hild",
        "(n)ews$" => "\\1\\2ews",
        "([^u])s$" => "\\1"
    );

    private static $_plural = array(
        "^(ox)$" => "\\1\\2en",
        "([m|l])ouse$" => "\\1ice",
        "(matr|vert|ind)ix|ex$" => "\\1ices",
        "(x|ch|ss|sh)$" => "\\1es",
        "([^aeiouy]|qu)y$" => "\\1ies",
        "(hive)$" => "\\1s",
        "(?:([^f])fe|([lr])f)$" => "\\1\\2ves",
        "sis$" => "ses",
        "([ti])um$" => "\\1a",
        "(p)erson$" => "\\1eople",
        "(m)an$" => "\\1en",
        "(c)hild$" => "\\1hildren",
        "(buffal|tomat)o$" => "\\1\\2oes",
        "(bu|campu)s$" => "\\1\\2ses",
        "(alias|status|virus)" => "\\1es",
        "(octop)us$" => "\\1i",
        "(ax|cris|test)is$" => "\\1es",
        "s$" => "s",
        "$" => "s"
    );

    public static function singular($string)
    {
        $result = $string;

        foreach (self::$_singular as $rule => $replacement)
        {
            $rule = self::_normalize($rule);
```

```
                if (preg_match($rule, $string))
                {
                    $result = preg_replace($rule, $replacement, $string);
                    break;
                }
            }

            return $result;
        }

        function plural($string)
        {
            $result = $string;

            foreach (self::$_plural as $rule => $replacement)
            {
                $rule = self::_normalize($rule);

                if (preg_match($rule, $string))
                {
                    $result = preg_replace($rule, $replacement, $string);
                    break;
                }
            }
            return $result;
        }
    }
}
```

We also need to add some methods to the `Model` class we created previously, as demonstrated in Listing 10-5.

Listing 10-5. Getter Overrides

```
namespace Framework
{
  use Framework\Base as Base;
  use Framework\Registry as Registry;
  use Framework\Inspector as Inspector;
  use Framework\StringMethods as StringMethods;
  use Framework\Model\Exception as Exception;

  class Model extends Base
  {
    public function getTable()
    {
        if (empty($this->_table))
        {
            $this->_table = strtolower(StringMethods::singular(get_class($this)));
        }

        return $this->_table;
      }

      public function getConnector()
      {
          if (empty($this->_connector))
```

```
            {
                $database = Registry::get("database");

                if (!$database)
                {
                    throw new Exception\Connector("No connector availible");
                }

                $this->_connector = $database->initialize();
            }

            return $this->_connector;
        }
    }
}
```

We add two new methods (called *inflection* methods) to the StringMethods class. These methods convert a string to either its singular or plural form, using a bunch of regular expressions. Next, we override the getters for both the $_table and $_connector properties in the Model class. In the case of the getTable() method, we want to return a user-defined table name or else default to the singular form of the current Model's class name (using PHP's get_class() method, and one of the new inflection methods we added to the StringMethods class).

We override the getConnector() method so that we can return the contents of the $_connector property, a connector instance stored in the Registry class, or raise a Model\Exception\Connector. This is the first time we are retrieving anything from the Registry class, and we do it here because it is very possible that a database connection would already have been initialized, at this point.

We also need to create a method that returns the columns, as defined with all their metadata, in an orderly array, so we can construct the SQL. Take a look at Listing 10-6 to see how we accomplish this.

Listing 10-6. The getColumns() Method

```
namespace Framework
{
    use Framework\Base as Base;
    use Framework\Registry as Registry;
    use Framework\Inspector as Inspector;
    use Framework\StringMethods as StringMethods;
    use Framework\Model\Exception as Exception;

    class Model extends Base
    {
        public function getColumns()
        {
            if (empty($_columns))
            {
                $primaries = 0;
                $columns = array();
                $class = get_class($this);
                $types = $this->types;

                $inspector = new Inspector($this);
                $properties = $inspector->getClassProperties();

                $first = function($array, $key)
                {
                    if (!empty($array[$key]) && sizeof($array[$key]) == 1)
                    {
```

```
                return $array[$key][0];
            }
            return null;
        };

        foreach ($properties as $property)
        {
            $propertyMeta = $inspector->getPropertyMeta($property);

            if (!empty($propertyMeta["@column"]))
            {
                $name = preg_replace("#^_#", "", $property);
                $primary = !empty($propertyMeta["@primary"]);
                $type = $first($propertyMeta, "@type");
                $length = $first($propertyMeta, "@length");
                $index = !empty($propertyMeta["@index"]);
                $readwrite = !empty($propertyMeta["@readwrite"]);
                $read = !empty($propertyMeta["@read"]) || $readwrite;
                $write = !empty($propertyMeta["@write"]) || $readwrite;

                $validate = !empty($propertyMeta["@validate"]) ➥
? $propertyMeta["@validate"] : false;
                $label = $first($propertyMeta, "@label");

                if (!in_array($type, $types))
                {
                    throw new Exception\Type("{$type} is not a valid type");
                }

                if ($primary)
                {
                    $primaries++;
                }

                $columns[$name] = array(
                    "raw" => $property,
                    "name" => $name,
                    "primary" => $primary,
                    "type" => $type,
                    "length" => $length,
                    "index" => $index,
                    "read" => $read,
                    "write" => $write,

                    "validate" => $validate,
                    "label" => $label
                );
            }
        }

        if ($primaries !== 1)
        {
            throw new Exception\Primary("{$class} must have exactly one ➥
@primary column");
        }
```

```
                $this->_columns = $columns;
            }

            return $this->_columns;
        }
    }
}
```

The getColumns() method might look like something out of the Template library we built in a previous chapter, but it is actually quite simple. It creates an Inspector instance and a utility function ($first) to return the first item in a metadata array. Next, it loops through all the properties in the model, and sifts out all that have an @column flag. Any other properties are ignored at this point.

The column's @type flag is checked to make sure it is valid, raising a Model\Exception\Type in the event that it is not. If the column's type is valid, it is added to the $_columns property. Every valid $primary column leads to the incrementing of the $primaries variable, which is checked at the end of the method to make sure that exactly one primary column has been defined. In essence, this method takes the User model definition and returns an associative array of column data. We can also create two convenience methods to return individual columns from this associative array, as shown in Listing 10-7.

Listing 10-7. Column Getters

```
namespace Framework
{
    use Framework\Base as Base;
    use Framework\Registry as Registry;
    use Framework\Inspector as Inspector;
    use Framework\StringMethods as StringMethods;
    use Framework\Model\Exception as Exception;

    class Model extends Base
    {
        public function getColumn($name)
        {
            if (!empty($this->_columns[$name]))
            {
                return $this->_columns[$name];
            }
            return null;
        }

        public function getPrimaryColumn()
        {
            if (!isset($this->_primary))
            {
                $primary;

                foreach ($this->columns as $column)
                {
                    if ($column["primary"])
                    {
                        $primary = $column;
                        break;
                    }
                }
```

```
                $this->_primary = $primary;
            }

            return $this->_primary;
        }
    }
}
```

The getColumn() method returns a column by name. One thing you might have noticed is that column class properties are assumed to begin with an underscore (_) character. This assumption is continued by the getColumn() method, which checks for a column without the _ character. When declared as a column property, columns will look like _firstName, but referenced by any public getters/setters/methods, they will look like setFirstName/firstName. The getPrimaryColumn() method loops through the columns, returning the one marked as primary.

Now that we have the means to describe and iterate over our model properties (and, therefore, our database table), we can begin to construct the SQL that will eventually lead to a physical table. As the table is created using SQL syntax, and since that syntax is usually database specific, we will create a method on our connector classes that we can use to sync the structure to the database. This method will convert the array of columns into the SQL we require, as shown in Listing 10-8.

Listing 10-8. Database\Connector\Mysql sync() Method

```
namespace Framework\Database\Connector
{
    use Framework\Database as Database;
    use Framework\Database\Exception as Exception;

    class Mysql extends Database\Connector
    {
        public function sync($model)
        {
            $lines = array();
            $indices = array();
            $columns = $model->columns;
            $template = "CREATE TABLE '%s' (\n%s,\n%s\n) ENGINE=%s DEFAULT CHARSET=%s;";
            foreach ($columns as $column)
            {
                $raw = $column["raw"];
                $name = $column["name"];
                $type = $column["type"];
                $length = $column["length"];

                if ($column["primary"])
                {
                    $indices[] = "PRIMARY KEY ('{$name}')";
                }
                if ($column["index"])
                {
                    $indices[] = "KEY '{$name}' ('{$name}')";
                }

                switch ($type)
                {
                    case "autonumber":
                    {
```

```
                    $lines[] = "'{$name}' int(11) NOT NULL AUTO_INCREMENT";
                    break;
                }
                case "text":
                {
                    if ($length !== null && $length <= 255)
                    {
                        $lines[] = "'{$name}' varchar({$length}) DEFAULT NULL";
                    }
                    else
                    {
                        $lines[] = "'{$name}' text";
                    }
                    break;
                }
                case "integer":
                {
                    $lines[] = "'{$name}' int(11) DEFAULT NULL";
                    break;
                }
                case "decimal":
                {
                    $lines[] = "'{$name}' float DEFAULT NULL";
                    break;
                }
                case "boolean":
                {
                    $lines[] = "'{$name}' tinyint(4) DEFAULT NULL";
                    break;
                }
                case "datetime":
                {
                    $lines[] = "'{$name}' datetime DEFAULT NULL";
                    break;
                }
            }
        }

        $table = $model->table;
        $sql = sprintf(
            $template,
            $table,
            join(",\n", $lines),
            join(",\n", $indices),
            $this->_engine,
            $this->_charset
        );

        $result = $this->execute("DROP TABLE IF EXISTS {$table};");
        if ($result === false)
        {
            $error = $this->lastError;
```

```
                throw new Exception\Sql("There was an error in the query: {$error}");
            }

            $result = $this->execute($sql);
            if ($result === false)
            {
                $error = $this->lastError;
                throw new Exception\Sql("There was an error in the query: {$error}");
            }

            return $this;
        }
    }
}
```

The sync() method we have created converts the class/properties into a valid SQL query, and ultimately into a physical database table. It does this by first getting a list of the columns, by calling the model's getColumns() method. Looping over the columns, it creates arrays of indices and field strings.

■ **Note** This CREATE TABLE SQL is made with MySQL in mind, and can be found in the Database\Connector class. If the database engine you are working with is having trouble executing the final SQL query, you might need to override the sync() method in your Database\Connector subclass, providing the correct SQL query syntax for the database engine you are working with.

After all the field strings have been created, they are joined (along with the indices), and applied to the CREATE TABLE $template string. A DROP TABLE statement is created and executed, to clear the way for the new table, and then the final SQL query (to create the table) is executed. Any SQL errors will lead to raised Database\Exception\Sql exceptions. We can see an example of the sync method in Listing 10-9.

Listing 10-9. Example Usage of the sync() Method

```
$database = new Database(array(
    "type" => "mysql",
    "options" => array(
        "host" => "localhost",
        "username" => "prophpmvc",
        "password" => "prophpmvc",
        "schema" => "prophpmvc"
    )
));
$database = $database->initialize()->connect();

$user = new User(array(
    "connector" => $database
));
$database->sync($user);
```

In Listing 10-9, we see how we first create an active database connection, and assign it (as the connector) to the new User model instance. Finally, we call the sync() method on the User model instance, and the database table is created. Since we checked for the existence of the database key in the Registry class, we can also achieve the same results with the code shown in Listing 10-10.

Listing 10-10. Alternative Connector Usage

```
$database = new Database(array(
    "type" => "mysql",
    "options" => array(
        "host" => "localhost",
        "username" => "prophpmvc",
        "password" => "prophpmvc",
        "schema" => "prophpmvc"
    )
));

Registry::set("database", $database->initialize()->connect());
$database->sync(new User());
```

Modifying Records

Now that we have a viable database table, we need to extend our model to deal directly with the database, and provide us with a simple interface. The first thing we want to enable is for our model to load a record if the primary column's value has been provided. We do this by modifying the constructor and adding a `load()` method, as demonstrated in Listing 10-11.

Listing 10-11. Model __construct() and load() Methods

```
namespace Framework
{
    use Framework\Base as Base;
    use Framework\Registry as Registry;
    use Framework\Inspector as Inspector;
    use Framework\StringMethods as StringMethods;
    use Framework\Model\Exception as Exception;

    class Model extends Base
    {
        public function __construct($options = array())
        {
            parent::__construct($options);
            $this->load();
        }

        public function load()
        {
            $primary = $this->primaryColumn;

            $raw = $primary["raw"];
            $name = $primary["name"];

            if (!empty($this->$raw))
            {
                $previous = $this->connector
                    ->query()
                    ->from($this->table)
                    ->where("{$name} = ?", $this->$raw)
                    ->first();
```

```
                if ($previous == null)
                {
                    throw new Exception\Primary("Primary key value invalid");
                }
                foreach ($previous as $key => $value)
                {
                    $prop = "_{$key}";
                    if (!empty($previous->$key) && !isset($this->$prop))
                    {
                        $this->$key = $previous->$key;
                    }
                }
            }
        }
    }
}
```

If we look back at the Base class, we will remind ourselves that the associative array we pass to the constructor is applied to the getters/setters present. This means we could load an existing record by providing the correct key/value pair, which matches the primary column name as well as a value corresponding with an existing record, to the constructor function.

The `load()` method greatly simplifies record retrieval for us. It determines the model's primary column and checks to see whether it is not empty. This tells us whether the primary key has been provided, which gives us a viable means of finding the intended record. If the primary key class property is empty, we assume this model instance is intended for the creation of a new record, and do nothing further.

To load the database record, we get the current model's connector, which halts execution if none is found. We create a database query for the record, based on the primary key column property's value. If no record is found, the `Model\Exception\Primary` exception is raised. This happens when a primary key column value is provided, but does not represent a valid identifier for a record in the database table.

Finally, we loop over the loaded record's data and only set property values that were not set in the `__construct()` method. This ensures no data is lost, after the model was initialized. Another useful method for our model to have is one that allows for records to be created or updated, as shown in Listing 10-12.

Listing 10-12. The save() Method

```
namespace Framework
{
    use Framework\Base as Base;
    use Framework\Registry as Registry;
    use Framework\Inspector as Inspector;
    use Framework\StringMethods as StringMethods;
    use Framework\Model\Exception as Exception;

    class Model extends Base
    {
        public function save()
        {
            $primary = $this->primaryColumn;

            $raw = $primary["raw"];
            $name = $primary["name"];

            $query = $this->connector
```

```
                ->query()
                ->from($this->table);

            if (!empty($this->$raw))
            {
                $query->where("{$name} = ?", $this->$raw);
            }

            $data = array();
            foreach ($this->columns as $key => $column)
            {
                if (!$column["read"])
                {
                    $prop = $column["raw"];
                    $data[$key] = $this->$prop;
                    continue;
                }

                if ($column != $this->primaryColumn && $column)
                {
                    $method = "get".ucfirst($key);
                    $data[$key] = $this->$method();
                    continue;
                }
            }

            $result = $query->save($data);
            if ($result > 0)
            {
                $this->$raw = $result;
            }
            return $result;
        }
    }
}
```

The save() method creates a query instance, and targets the table related to the Model class. It applies a WHERE clause if the primary key property value is not empty, and builds a data array based on columns returned by the getColumns() method. Finally, it calls the query instance's save()method to commit the data to the database. Since the Database\Connector class executes either an INSERT or UPDATE statement, based on the WHERE clause criteria, this method will either insert a new record, or update an existing record, depending on whether the primary key property has a value or not. The last modifier methods we need are the delete() and deleteAll() methods, which remove records from the database. You can see these methods in Listing 10-13.

Listing 10-13. The delete() and deleteAll() Methods

```
namespace Framework
{
    use Framework\Base as Base;
    use Framework\Registry as Registry;
    use Framework\Inspector as Inspector;
    use Framework\StringMethods as StringMethods;
    use Framework\Model\Exception as Exception;

    class Model extends Base
```

```
    {
        public function delete()
        {
            $primary = $this->primaryColumn;

            $raw = $primary["raw"];
            $name = $primary["name"];

            if (!empty($this->$raw))
            {
                return $this->connector
                    ->query()
                    ->from($this->table)
                    ->where("{$name} = ?", $this->$raw)
                    ->delete();
            }
        }

        public static function deleteAll($where = array())
        {
            $instance = new static();

            $query = $instance->connector
                ->query()
                ->from($instance->table);

            foreach ($where as $clause => $value)
            {
                $query->where($clause, $value);
            }

            return $query->delete();
        }
    }
}
```

The delete() method is the simplest of our model's modifier methods. It creates a query object, only if the primary key property value is not empty, and executes the query's delete() method. The deleteAll() method does pretty much the same thing, except it is called statically. So far, we have looked at single-record interactions, but we would do well to allow for multiple-record operations, similar to our database's all(), first(), and count() methods. The first one we will create is the all() method, as shown in Listing 10-14.

Listing 10-14. The all() Method all() method

```
namespace Framework
{
    use Framework\Base as Base;
    use Framework\Registry as Registry;
    use Framework\Inspector as Inspector;
    use Framework\StringMethods as StringMethods;
    use Framework\Model\Exception as Exception;

    class Model extends Base
    {
        public static function all($where = array(), $fields = array("*"),➥
$order = null, $direction = null, $limit = null, $page = null)
```

```
        {
            $model = new static();
            return $model->_all($where, $fields, $order, $direction, $limit, $page);
        }

        protected function _all($where = array(), $fields = array("*"),➥
$order = null, $direction = null, $limit = null, $page = null)
        {
            $query = $this
                ->connector
                ->query()
                ->from($this->table, $fields);

            foreach ($where as $clause => $value)
            {
                $query->where($clause, $value);
            }

            if ($order != null)
            {
                $query->order($order, $direction);
            }

            if ($limit != null)
            {
                $query->limit($limit, $page);
            }

            $rows = array();
            $class = get_class($this);

            foreach ($query->all() as $row)
            {
                $rows[] = new $class(
                    $row
                );
            }

            return $rows;
        }
    }
}
```

The `all()` method is a simple, static wrapper method for the protected `_all()` method. The `_all()` method creates a query, taking into account the various filters and flags, to return all matching records.

The reason we go to the trouble of wrapping an instance method within a static method is because we have created a context wherein a model instance is equal to a database record. Multirecord operations make more sense as class methods, in this context.

The `first()` method is similar to the `all()` method in that it is a simple, static wrapper method to a protected instance method. The `_first()` method simply returns the first matched record, as demonstrated in Listing 10-15.

Listing 10-15. The first() Method

```
namespace Framework
{
    use Framework\Base as Base;
    use Framework\Registry as Registry;
    use Framework\Inspector as Inspector;
    use Framework\StringMethods as StringMethods;
    use Framework\Model\Exception as Exception;

    class Model extends Base
    {
        public static function first($where = array(), $fields = array("*"),↩
$order = null, $direction = null)
        {
            $model = new static();
            return $model->_first($where, $fields, $order, $direction);
        }

        protected function _first($where = array(), $fields = array("*"),↩
$order = null, $direction = null)
        {
            $query = $this
                ->connector
                ->query()
                ->from($this->table, $fields);

            foreach ($where as $clause => $value)
            {
                $query->where($clause, $value);
            }

            if ($order != null)
            {
                $query->order($order, $direction);
            }

            $first = $query->first();
            $class = get_class($this);

            if ($first)
            {
                return new $class(
                    $query->first()
                );
            }

            return null;
        }
    }
}
```

The `count()` method is similar to the previous two static methods. The `_count()` method returns a count of the matched records. Listing 10-16 shows the `count()` method.

Listing 10-16. The count() Method

```
namespace Framework
{
    use Framework\Base as Base;
    use Framework\Registry as Registry;
    use Framework\Inspector as Inspector;
    use Framework\StringMethods as StringMethods;
    use Framework\Model\Exception as Exception;

    class Model extends Base
    {
        public static function count($where = array())
        {
            $model = new static();
            return $model->_count($where);
        }

        protected function _count($where = array())
        {
            $query = $this
                ->connector
                ->query()
                ->from($this->table);

            foreach ($where as $clause => $value)
            {
                $query->where($clause, $value);
            }

            return $query->count();
        }
    }
}
```

With all this code in place, let's take a look at how we can use our model, as demonstrated in Listing 10-17.

Listing 10-17. Example Model Usage

```
$database = new Database(array(
    "type" => "mysql",
    "options" => array(
        "host" => "localhost",
        "username" => "prophpmvc",
        "password" => "prophpmvc",
        "schema" => "prophpmvc"
    )
));
$database = $database->initialize();

$user = new User(array(
    "connector" => $database
));
$database->sync($user);

$elijah = new User(array(
```

```
    "connector" => $database,
    "first" => "Chris",
    "last" => "Pitt",
    "email" => "chris@example.com",
    "password" => "password",
    "live" => true,
    "deleted" => false,
    "created" => date("Y-m-d H:i:s"),
    "modified" => date("Y-m-d H:i:s")
));

$elijah->save();

$all = User::all(array(
    "last = ?" => "Pitt"
));

$elijah->delete();
```

This is certainly a lot easier than using a `Database\Connector` or `Database\Query` directly. It provides a way to keep our database tables in check with our ORM code. We can query or modify database records with simple, OOP code. Listing 10-18 shows the complete `Model` class.

Listing 10-18. The Model Class

```
namespace Framework
{
    use Framework\Base as Base;
    use Framework\Registry as Registry;
    use Framework\Inspector as Inspector;
    use Framework\StringMethods as StringMethods;
    use Framework\Model\Exception as Exception;

    class Model extends Base
    {
        /**
        * @readwrite
        */
        protected $_table;

        /**
        * @readwrite
        */
        protected $_connector;

        /**
        * @read
        */
        protected $_types = array(
            "autonumber",
            "text",
            "integer",
            "decimal",
            "boolean",
            "datetime"
```

```
);

protected $_columns;
protected $_primary;

public function _getExceptionForImplementation($method)
{
    return new Exception\Implementation("{$method} method not implemented");
}

public function __construct($options = array())
{
    parent::__construct($options);
    $this->load();
}

public function load()
{
    $primary = $this->primaryColumn;

    $raw = $primary["raw"];
    $name = $primary["name"];

    if (!empty($this->$raw))
    {
        $previous = $this->connector
            ->query()
            ->from($this->table)
            ->where("{$name} = ?", $this->$raw)
            ->first();

        if ($previous == null)
        {
            throw new Exception\Primary("Primary key value invalid");
        }

        foreach ($previous as $key => $value)
        {
            $prop = "_{$key}";
            if (!empty($previous->$key) && !isset($this->$prop))
            {
                $this->$key = $previous->$key;
            }
        }
    }
}

public function delete()
{
    $primary = $this->primaryColumn;

    $raw = $primary["raw"];
    $name = $primary["name"];

    if (!empty($this->$raw))
    {
        return $this->connector
```

```
                ->query()
                ->from($this->table)
                ->where("{$name} = ?", $this->$raw)
                ->delete();
        }
    }

    public static function deleteAll($where = array())
    {
        $instance = new static();

        $query = $instance->connector
            ->query()
            ->from($instance->table);

        foreach ($where as $clause => $value)
        {
            $query->where($clause, $value);
        }

        return $query->delete();
    }

    public function save()
    {
        $primary = $this->primaryColumn;

        $raw = $primary["raw"];
        $name = $primary["name"];

        $query = $this->connector
            ->query()
            ->from($this->table);

        if (!empty($this->$raw))
        {
            $query->where("{$name} = ?", $this->$raw);
        }

        $data = array();
        foreach ($this->columns as $key => $column)
        {
            if (!$column["read"])
            {
                $prop = $column["raw"];
                $data[$key] = $this->$prop;
                continue;
            }

            if ($column != $this->primaryColumn && $column)
            {
                $method = "get".ucfirst($key);
                $data[$key] = $this->$method();
                continue;
            }
        }
```

```
        $result = $query->save($data);

        if ($result > 0)
        {
            $this->$raw = $result;
        }

        return $result;
    }

    public function getTable()
    {
        if (empty($this->_table))
        {
            $this->_table = strtolower(StringMethods::singular(get_class($this)));
        }
        return $this->_table;
    }

    public function getConnector()
    {
        if (empty($this->_connector))
        {
            $database = Registry::get("database");

            if (!$database)
            {
                throw new Exception\Connector("No connector availible");
            }

            $this->_connector = $database->initialize();
        }

        return $this->_connector;
    }

    public function getColumns()
    {
        if (empty($_columns))
        {
            $primaries = 0;
            $columns = array();
            $class = get_class($this);
            $types = $this->types;

            $inspector = new Inspector($this);
            $properties = $inspector->getClassProperties();
            $first = function($array, $key)
            {
                if (!empty($array[$key]) && sizeof($array[$key]) == 1)
                {
                    return $array[$key][0];
                }
                return null;
            };
```

```
                foreach ($properties as $property)
                {
                    $propertyMeta = $inspector->getPropertyMeta($property);

                    if (!empty($propertyMeta["@column"]))
                    {
                        $name = preg_replace("#^_#", "", $property);
                        $primary = !empty($propertyMeta["@primary"]);
                        $type = $first($propertyMeta, "@type");
                        $length = $first($propertyMeta, "@length");
                        $index = !empty($propertyMeta["@index"]);
                        $readwrite = !empty($propertyMeta["@readwrite"]);
                        $read = !empty($propertyMeta["@read"]) || $readwrite;
                        $write = !empty($propertyMeta["@write"]) || $readwrite;

                        $validate = !empty($propertyMeta["@validate"]) ➥
? $propertyMeta["@validate"] : false;
                        $label = $first($propertyMeta, "@label");

                        if (!in_array($type, $types))
                        {
                            throw new Exception\Type("{$type} is not a valid type");
                        }

                        if ($primary)
                        {
                            $primaries++;
                        }

                        $columns[$name] = array(
                            "raw" => $property,
                            "name" => $name,
                            "primary" => $primary,
                            "type" => $type,
                            "length" => $length,
                            "index" => $index,
                            "read" => $read,
                            "write" => $write,

                            "validate" => $validate,
                            "label" => $label
                        );
                    }
                }

                if ($primaries !== 1)
                {
                    throw new Exception\Primary("{$class} must have exactly one ➥
@primary column");
                }

                $this->_columns = $columns;
            }
            return $this->_columns;
        }
```

```
        public function getColumn($name)
        {
            if (!empty($this->_columns[$name]))
            {
                return $this->_columns[$name];
            }
            return null;
        }

        public function getPrimaryColumn()
        {
            if (!isset($this->_primary))
            {
                $primary;

                foreach ($this->columns as $column)
                {
                    if ($column["primary"])
                    {
                        $primary = $column;
                        break;
                    }
                }

                $this->_primary = $primary;
            }

            return $this->_primary;
        }

        public static function first($where = array(), $fields = array("*"),➥
$order = null, $direction = null)
        {
            $model = new static();
            return $model->_first($where, $fields, $order, $direction);
        }

        protected function _first($where = array(), $fields = array("*"),➥
$order = null, $direction = null)
        {
            $query = $this
                ->connector
                ->query()
                ->from($this->table, $fields);

            foreach ($where as $clause => $value)
            {
                $query->where($clause, $value);
            }

            if ($order != null)
            {
                $query->order($order, $direction);
            }
```

```
            $first = $query->first();
            $class = get_class($this);

            if ($first)
            {
                return new $class(
                    $query->first()
                );
            }

            return null;
        }

        public static function all($where = array(), $fields = array("*"),➥
$order = null, $direction = null, $limit = null, $page = null)
        {
            $model = new static();
            return $model->_all($where, $fields, $order, $direction, $limit, $page);
        }

        protected function _all($where = array(), $fields = array("*"),➥
$order = null, $direction = null, $limit = null, $page = null)
        {
            $query = $this
                ->connector
                ->query()
                ->from($this->table, $fields);

            foreach ($where as $clause => $value)
            {
                $query->where($clause, $value);
            }

            if ($order != null)
            {
                $query->order($order, $direction);
            }

            if ($limit != null)
            {
                $query->limit($limit, $page);
            }

            $rows = array();
            $class = get_class($this);

            foreach ($query->all() as $row)
            {
                $rows[] = new $class(
                    $row
                );
            }

            return $rows;
        }

        public static function count($where = array())
```

```
        {
            $model = new static();
            return $model->_count($where);
        }

        protected function _count($where = array())
        {
            $query = $this
                ->connector
                ->query()
                ->from($this->table);

            foreach ($where as $clause => $value)
            {
                $query->where($clause, $value);
            }

            return $query->count();
        }
    }
}
```

No Relation of Mine!

This is the point at which we could start to get really bogged down in details. It would be really neat if our models could identify linked tables and join types, querying not only for single records, but all the related records in other tables. We could certainly create all that code, but it isn't essential to understanding the concept of ORM, or how it fits into our framework.

Indeed, many ORM libraries implement just such code, allowing immense control over related database data. We could decide to extend our model library in the future, or even to use a larger, more feature-complete ORM library, but what we have now does everything we want and there is no need to get bogged down in details just yet.

Questions

1. Are models only for working with databases?
2. The `Model` class we created has a mix of instance and class methods for working with database rows. Why do we not pick either instance or class methods with which to do all row manipulation?

Answers

1. No! Models can handle all sorts of things, such as connecting to a third-party API or modifying file system information. Models are not the same thing as ORM.
2. There are times when it is syntactically attractive to work with multiple rows at the same time, such as when fetching multiple rows from the database or deleting multiple rows. Other actions involve individual rows, such as with `INSERT` or `UPDATE` queries.

Exercises

1. The `Model` class gives us a few good methods that make database development easier. There are more convenience methods that can be added, such as a method which returns the amount of pages for a given limit and `WHERE` clause. Try adding this method.

2. While we can use `Model` subclasses to easily insert or update database rows, there is no way for us to validate that data. Try adding a few methods that could be used to check for valid data before an `INSERT` or `UPDATE` query is created.

CHAPTER 11

Testing

We have written an enormous amount of code, so far. That's an achievement, but it can quickly turn into a burden if our code needs to be changed. For anything as complex as a complete MVC framework, you can expect a lot of interconnected code. The more connected the code is, even with the separation that MVC affords our framework, the more likely that changes to code can break other code.

Imagine we wanted to add a few ORM methods to our `Model` class. They could require changes to methods we already created, and may subtly change the functionality already established. Usually, this will lead to unexpected breaks in our application.

Or imagine we needed to add additional configuration or caching drivers. It would be ideal to have a consistent way of comparing the functionality of existing drivers to new ones, in such a way that the comparisons could be repeated with the addition of further drivers, in the future.

The solution is to provide a set of reusable tests that can be periodically run to ensure that our classes continue to function in a predictable manner.

Goals

- We need to build a simple testing class.
- We need to set up tests that cover the classes we have already created.

Unit Testing

Unit testing is the process of breaking down a big system into small parts that can be tested in isolation from the rest of the system. It's tough testing a full user-driven web application, but testing a single command to the database, or evaluating a single template tag is easy.

Unit tests are, by definition, an endless task. The more code you write, the more unit tests you should be writing. When you find a situation in which functionality isn't already covered by a test, you should create that test case so that it will be covered.

Test Class

Before we start writing tests for our code-base, we need to create a simple class that will help to organize the tests and evaluate the results. Listing 11-1 shows this `Test` class.

Listing 11-1. The Test Class

```
namespace Framework
{
    class Test
    {
        private static $_tests = array();

        public static function add($callback, $title = "Unnamed Test", $set = "General")
        {
          self::$_tests[] = array(
            "set" => $set,
            "title" => $title,
            "callback" => $callback
          );
        }

        public static function run($before = null, $after = null)
        {
          if ($before)
          {
              $before($this->_tests);
          }

          $passed = array();
          $failed = array();
          $exceptions = array();

          foreach (self::$_tests as $test)
          {
            try
            {
               $result = call_user_func($test["callback"]);

               if ($result)
               {
                   $passed[] = array(
                     "set" => $test["set"],
                     "title" => $test["title"]
                   );
               }
               else
               {
                 $failed[] = array(
                   "set" => $test["set"],
                   "title" => $test["title"]
                 );
               }
            }
            catch (\Exception $e)
            {
              $exceptions[] = array(
                "set" => $test["set"],
                "title" => $test["title"],
                "type" => get_class($e)
```

```
                );
            }
        }
        if ($after)
        {
            $after($this->_tests);
        }
        return array(
          "passed" => $passed,
          "failed" => $failed,
          "exceptions" => $exceptions
        );
    }
  }
}
```

This class is all that we need to write unit tests. The add() method accepts a $callback, a $title (which describes the test), and a $set (which describes which group of tests the test belongs to). The tests are stored in an internal $_tests array.

The run() method loops through the tests and executes them. If the test passes, it is added to an array of passed tests. If it fails, it is added to an array of failed tests. If, during any test, an exception occurs, the test title/set/exception type will be added to an array of exceptions. These three arrays are returned when the run() method ends. The $before and $after parameters refer to callbacks that can optionally be provided, which will be run before and after the tests.

Cache

We will test the Cache classes first. We need to test the factory functionality, to ensure that a valid instance of the Memcached cache driver is returned. We need to test whether the driver can connect and disconnect to the Memcached server.

If it can, we will check whether the driver can successfully send data to the server, and then read it back. We also need to test whether the data expires after a certain amount of time, and finally, if the driver can erase previously stored data from the Memcached server.

Coverage

We should create tests that cover the following requirements:

- The Cache factory class can be created.
- The Cache\Driver\Memcached class can initialize.
- The Cache\Driver\Memcached class can connect and return itself.
- The Cache\Driver\Memcached class can disconnect and return itself.
- The Cache\Driver\Memcached class can set values and return itself.
- The Cache\Driver\Memcached class can retrieve values.
- The Cache\Driver\Memcached class can return default values.
- The Cache\Driver\Memcached class will adhere to the expiry time on values.
- The Cache\Driver\Memcached class can erase values and return itself.

Tests

The initial cache tests, shown in Listing 11-2, test the factory class, and the initialization method.

Listing 11-2. Initial Cache Tests

```
Framework\Test::add(
  function()
  {
    $cache = new Framework\Cache();
    return ($cache instanceof Framework\Cache);
  },
  "Cache instantiates in uninitialized state",
  "Cache"
);

Framework\Test::add(
  function()
  {
    $cache = new Framework\Cache(array(
      "type" => "memcached"
    ));

    $cache = $cache->initialize();
    return ($cache instanceof Framework\Cache\Driver\Memcached);
  },
  "Cache\Driver\Memcached initializes",
  "Cache\Driver\Memcached"
);
```

While we only deal with the Cache class name in our application, what it is doing is returning the driver when we call `initialize()`. We now need to check whether the driver can connect to/disconnect from a running Memcached server. Listing 11-3 shows we accomplish this. You should already have Memcached running locally, as well as the details to connect to a running server.

Listing 11-3. Connect/Disconnect from Memcached Server

```
Framework\Test::add(
  function()
  {
    $cache = new Framework\Cache(array(
      "type" => "memcached"
    ));

    $cache = $cache->initialize();
    return ($cache->connect() instanceof Framework\Cache\Driver\Memcached);
  },
  "Cache\Driver\Memcached connects and returns self",
  "Cache\Driver\Memcached"
);

Framework\Test::add(
  function()
  {
    $cache = new Framework\Cache(array(
      "type" => "memcached"
```

```
    ));

    $cache = $cache->initialize();
    $cache = $cache->connect();
    $cache = $cache->disconnect();

    try
    {
      $cache->get("anything");
    }
    catch (Framework\Cache\Exception\Service $e)
    {
      return ($cache instanceof Framework\Cache\Driver\Memcached);
    }

    return false;
  },
  "Cache\Driver\Memcached disconnects and returns self",
  "Cache\Driver\Memcached"
);
```

If these tests pass, we can test the remaining Memcached class functionality, as demonstrated in Listing 11-4.

Listing 11-4. Reading/Writing to a Memcached Server

```
Framework\Test::add(
  function()
  {
    $cache = new Framework\Cache(array(
        "type" => "memcached"
    ));

    $cache = $cache->initialize();
    $cache = $cache->connect();

    return ($cache->set("foo", "bar", 1) instanceof ➥
Framework\Cache\Driver\Memcached);
  },
  "Cache\Driver\Memcached sets values and returns self",
  "Cache\Driver\Memcached"
);

Framework\Test::add(
  function()
  {
    $cache = new Framework\Cache(array(
      "type" => "memcached"
    ));

    $cache = $cache->initialize();
    $cache = $cache->connect();

    return ($cache->get("foo") == "bar");
  },
  "Cache\Driver\Memcached retrieves values",
  "Cache\Driver\Memcached"
```

```
);
Framework\Test::add(
  function()
  {
    $cache = new Framework\Cache(array(
      "type" => "memcached"
    ));

    $cache = $cache->initialize();
    $cache = $cache->connect();

    return ($cache->get("404", "baz") == "baz");
  },
  "Cache\Driver\Memcached returns default values",
  "Cache\Driver\Memcached"
);

Framework\Test::add(
  function()
  {
    $cache = new Framework\Cache(array(
      "type" => "memcached"
    ));

    $cache = $cache->initialize();
    $cache = $cache->connect();

    // we sleep to void the 1 second cache key/value above
    sleep(1);

    return ($cache->get("foo") == null);
  },
  "Cache\Driver\Memcached expires values",
  "Cache\Driver\Memcached"
);

Framework\Test::add(
  function()
  {
    $cache = new Framework\Cache(array(
      "type" => "memcached"
    ));

    $cache = $cache->initialize();
    $cache = $cache->connect();

    $cache = $cache->set("hello", "world");
    $cache = $cache->erase("hello");

    return ($cache->get("hello") == null && ➥
$cache instanceof Framework\Cache\Driver\Memcached);
  },
  "Cache\Driver\Memcached erases values and returns self",
  "Cache\Driver\Memcached"
);
```

Configuration

Next, we will test our Configuration classes. We will again test the factory functionality, to ensure that a valid instance of the Ini cache driver is returned. We will also check whether it can parse a configuration file. The final (parsed) data should correlate with our configuration file's hierarchy.

Coverage

We should create tests that cover the following requirements:

- The Configuration factory class can be created.
- The Configuration\Driver\Ini class can initialize.
- The Configuration\Driver\Ini class can parse() a configuration file.

Tests

The initial configuration tests, shown in Listing 11-5, test the factory class and the initialization method.

Listing 11-5. Initial Configuration Testing

```
Framework\Test::add(
  function()
  {
    $configuration = new Framework\Configuration();
    return ($configuration instanceof Framework\Configuration);
  },
  "Configuration instantiates in uninitialized state",
  "Configuration"
);

Framework\Test::add(
  function()
  {
    $configuration = new Framework\Configuration(array(
      "type" => "ini"
    ));

    $configuration = $configuration->initialize();
    return ($configuration instanceof ➥
Framework\Configuration\Driver\Ini);
  },
  "Configuration\Driver\Ini initializes",
  "Configuration\Driver\Ini"
);
```

We now need to check whether the driver can parse an INI configuration file, and that the final data conforms to the correct hierarchical structure, as demonstrated in Listing 11-6.

Listing 11-6. Parsing Configuration Files

```
Framework\Test::add(
  function()
```

```
  {
    $configuration = new Framework\Configuration(array(
      "type" => "ini"
    ));

    $configuration = $configuration->initialize();
    $parsed = $configuration->parse("_configuration");

    return ($parsed->config->first == "hello" && ➥
$parsed->config->second->second == "bar");
  },
  "Configuration\Driver\Ini parses configuration files",
  "Configuration\Driver\Ini"
);
```

Database

The database tests are quite a bit more complicated. We do the usual factory class test. We also need to account for the connector/query concept we explored in the Chapter 9. The query class also includes many methods that need to be tested.

Coverage

We should create tests that cover the following requirements:

- The `Database` factory class can be created.
- The `Database\Connector\Mysql` class can initialize.
- The `Database\Connector\Mysql` class can connect and return itself.
- The `Database\Connector\Mysql` class can disconnect and return itself.
- The `Database\Connector\Mysql` class can escape values.
- The `Database\Connector\Mysql` class can execute SQL queries.
- The `Database\Connector\Mysql` class can return the last inserted ID.
- The `Database\Connector\Mysql` class can return the number of affected rows.
- The `Database\Connector\Mysql` class can return the last SQL error.
- The `Database\Connector\Mysql` class can return a `Database\Connector\Mysql` instance.
- The `Database\Query\Mysql` class references a connector.
- The `Database\Query\Mysql` class can fetch the first row in a table.
- The `Database\Query\Mysql` class can fetch multiple rows in a table.
- The `Database\Query\Mysql` class can use limit, offset, order, and direction.
- The `Database\Query\Mysql` class can get the number of rows in a table.
- The `Database\Query\Mysql` class can use multiple `WHERE` clauses.
- The `Database\Query\Mysql` class can specify and alias fields.
- The `Database\Query\Mysql` class can join tables and alias joined fields.

- The Database\Query\Mysql class can insert rows.
- The Database\Query\Mysql class can update rows.
- The Database\Query\Mysql class can delete rows.

Tests

The initial database tests, shown in Listing 11-7, also test the factory class and the initialization method.

Listing 11-7. Initial Database Tests

```
$options = array(
  "type" => "mysql",
  "options" => array(
     "host" => "localhost",
     "username" => "prophpmvc",
     "password" => "prophpmvc",
     "schema" => "prophpmvc"
  )
);

Framework\Test::add(
  function()
  {
    $database = new Framework\Database();
    return ($database instanceof Framework\Database);
  },
  "Database instantiates in uninitialized state",
  "Database"
);

Framework\Test::add(
  function() use ($options)
  {
    $database = new Framework\Database($options);
    $database = $database->initialize();

    return ($database instanceof ➥
Framework\Database\Connector\Mysql);
  },
  "Database\Connector\Mysql initializes",
  "Database\Connector\Mysql"
);
```

We now need to check whether the driver can connect to/disconnect from a running MySQL server. Listing 11-8 shows how we accomplish this. You should already have MySQL running locally, or have the details to connect to a running server.

Listing 11-8. Connecting, Disconnecting, and Sanitizing Data

```
Framework\Test::add(
  function() use ($options)
  {
```

```
    $database = new Framework\Database($options);
    $database = $database->initialize();
    $database = $database->connect();

    return ($database instanceof ➥
Framework\Database\Connector\Mysql);
  },
  "Database\Connector\Mysql connects and returns self",
  "Database\Connector\Mysql"
);

Framework\Test::add(
  function() use ($options)
  {
    $database = new Framework\Database($options);
    $database = $database->initialize();
    $database = $database->connect();
    $database = $database->disconnect();

    try
    {
       $database->execute("SELECT 1");
    }
    catch (Framework\Database\Exception\Service $e)
    {
      return ($database instanceof ➥
Framework\Database\Connector\Mysql);
    }

  return false;
  },
  "Database\Connector\Mysql disconnects and returns self",
  "Database\Connector\Mysql"
);

Framework\Test::add(
  function() use ($options)
  {
    $database = new Framework\Database($options);
    $database = $database->initialize();
    $database = $database->connect();

    return ($database->escape("foo'".'bar"') == "foo\\'bar\\"");
  },
  "Database\Connector\Mysql escapes values",
  "Database\Connector\Mysql"
);
```

These tests resemble those we created for the cache driver, but they are targeted at an instance of the MySQL driver. The `connect()`/`disconnect()` methods are simple, and we have seen their like before. The `escape()` method, however, is new. When dealing with databases, we need to protect the information they hold, from SQL injection attacks. SQL injection (and often just bad data) is the number-one cause of application instability and security breaches.

These problems occur, most often, when data does not conform to the correct data type, or attempts to perform a database query from within the body of another. We can avoid this by escaping the parameters we pass the database, within queries. That is the purpose of the escape() method.

Next, we need to test whether the driver (connector) is capable of executing SQL queries, and whether if can return the correct metadata after executing those queries. Listing 11-9 shows how we do this.

Listing 11-9. Executing SQL and Returning Metadata

```
Framework\Test::add(
  function() use ($options)
  {
    $database = new Framework\Database($options);
    $database = $database->initialize();
    $database = $database->connect();

    $database->execute("
      SOME INVALID SQL
    ");

    return (bool) $database->lastError;
  },
  "Database\Connector\Mysql returns last error",
  "Database\Connector\Mysql"
);

Framework\Test::add(
  function() use ($options)
  {
    $database = new Framework\Database($options);
    $database = $database->initialize();
    $database = $database->connect();

    $database->execute("
      DROP TABLE IF EXISTS 'tests';
    ");
    $database->execute("
      CREATE TABLE 'tests' (
        'id' int(11) NOT NULL AUTO_INCREMENT,
        'number' int(11) NOT NULL,
        'text' varchar(255) NOT NULL,
        'boolean' tinyint(4) NOT NULL,
        PRIMARY KEY ('id')
      ) ENGINE=InnoDB DEFAULT CHARSET=utf8;
    ");

    return !$database->lastError;
  },
  "Database\Connector\Mysql executes queries",
  "Database\Connector\Mysql"
);

Framework\Test::add(
  function() use ($options)
  {
```

```
    $database = new Framework\Database($options);
    $database = $database->initialize();
    $database = $database->connect();

    for ($i = 0; $i < 4; $i++)
    {
    $database->execute("
        INSERT INTO 'tests' ('number', 'text', 'boolean') VALUES ➥
('1337', 'text', '0');
        ");
    }

    return $database->lastInsertId;
  },
  "Database\Connector\Mysql returns last inserted ID",
  "Database\Connector\Mysql"
);

Framework\Test::add(
  function() use ($options)
  {
    $database = new Framework\Database($options);
    $database = $database->initialize();
    $database = $database->connect();

    $database->execute("
        UPDATE 'tests' SET 'number' = 1338;
    ");

    return $database->affectedRows;
  },
  "Database\Connector\Mysql returns affected rows",
  "Database\Connector\Mysql"
);
```

The first two tests drop and create a testing table, and then insert some rows. These are basic SQL commands, and the tests are comparably simple. The third test checks whether the last inserted ID is returned, and the fourth checks whether the last error message is returned.

Because we are working with both connectors and queries, we need to check the associations between the two, as shown in Listing 11-10.

Listing 11-10. Returning a Query with the Correct References

```
Framework\Test::add(
  function() use ($options)
  {
    $database = new Framework\Database($options);
    $database = $database->initialize();
    $database = $database->connect();
    $query = $database->query();

    return ($query instanceof Framework\Database\Query\Mysql);
    },
    "Database\Connector\Mysql returns instance of Database\Query\Mysql",
    "Database\Query\Mysql"
);
```

```
Framework\Test::add(
  function() use ($options)
  {
    $database = new Framework\Database($options);
    $database = $database->initialize();
    $database = $database->connect();
    $query = $database->query();

    return ($query->connector instanceof ➥
Framework\Database\Connector\Mysql);
  },
  "Database\Query\Mysql references connector",
  "Database\Query\Mysql"
);
```

Next, we need to test whether the query class can return the rows we just inserted, and whether it can return the correct row count. Listing 11-11 demonstrates how we accomplish this.

Listing 11-11. Fetching Rows/Counts

```
Framework\Test::add(
  function() use ($options)
  {
    $database = new Framework\Database($options);
    $database = $database->initialize();
    $database = $database->connect();

    $row = $database->query()
        ->from("tests")
        ->first();

    return ($row["id"] == 1);
  },
  "Database\Query\Mysql fetches first row",
  "Database\Query\Mysql"
);

Framework\Test::add(
  function() use ($options)
  {
    $database = new Framework\Database($options);
    $database = $database->initialize();
    $database = $database->connect();

    $rows = $database->query()
        ->from("tests")
        ->all();

    return (sizeof($rows) == 4);
  },
  "Database\Query\Mysql fetches multiple rows",
  "Database\Query\Mysql"
);

Framework\Test::add(
  function() use ($options)
```

```
  {
    $database = new Framework\Database($options);
    $database = $database->initialize();
    $database = $database->connect();

    $count = $database
      ->query()
      ->from("tests")
      ->count();

    return ($count == 4);
  },
  "Database\Query\Mysql fetches number of rows",
  "Database\Query\Mysql"
);
```

We also need to test the convenience methods we added to the Query class, as shown in Listing 11-12.

Listing 11-12. Query Convenience Methods

```
Framework\Test::add(
  function() use ($options)
  {
    $database = new Framework\Database($options);
    $database = $database->initialize();
    $database = $database->connect();

    $rows = $database->query()
      ->from("tests")
      ->limit(1, 2)
      ->order("id", "desc")
      ->all();

    return (sizeof($rows) == 1 && $rows[0]["id"] == 3);
  },
  "Database\Query\Mysql accepts LIMIT, OFFSET, ➥
ORDER and DIRECTION clauses",
  "Database\Query\Mysql"
);

Framework\Test::add(
  function() use ($options)
  {
    $database = new Framework\Database($options);
    $database = $database->initialize();
    $database = $database->connect();

    $rows = $database->query()
        ->from("tests")
        ->where("id != ?", 1)
        ->where("id != ?", 3)
        ->where("id != ?", 4)
        ->all();

    return (sizeof($rows) == 1 && $rows[0]["id"] == 2);
  },
```

```
  "Database\Query\Mysql accepts WHERE clauses",
  "Database\Query\Mysql"
);

Framework\Test::add(
  function() use ($options)
  {
    $database = new Framework\Database($options);
    $database = $database->initialize();
    $database = $database->connect();

    $rows = $database->query()
      ->from("tests", array(
        "id" => "foo"
      ))
      ->all();

    return (sizeof($rows) && isset($rows[0]["foo"]) && ➥
$rows[0]["foo"] == 1);
  },
  "Database\Query\Mysql can alias fields",
  "Database\Query\Mysql"
);

Framework\Test::add(
  function() use ($options)
  {
    $database = new Framework\Database($options);
    $database = $database->initialize();
    $database = $database->connect();

    $rows = $database->query()
      ->from("tests", array(
        "tests.id" => "foo"
      ))
      ->join("tests AS baz", "tests.id = baz.id", array(
        "baz.id" => "bar"
      ))
       ->all();

    return (sizeof($rows) && $rows[0]->foo == $rows[0]->bar);
  },
  "Database\Query\Mysql can join tables and alias joined fields",
  "Database\Query\Mysql"
);
```

Finally, we need to test the methods responsible for modifying rows. Rows are typically inserted, updated, and deleted from database tables, and we have methods for all three actions, as you can see in Listing 11-13.

Listing 11-13. Modifying Rows

```
Framework\Test::add(
  function() use ($options)
  {
```

```
    $database = new Framework\Database($options);
    $database = $database->initialize();
    $database = $database->connect();

    $result = $database->query()
      ->from("tests")
      ->save(array(
        "number" => 3,
        "text" => "foo",
        "boolean" => true
      ));

    return ($result == 5);
  },
  "Database\Query\Mysql can insert rows",
  "Database\Query\Mysql"
);

Framework\Test::add(
  function() use ($options)
  {
    $database = new Framework\Database($options);
    $database = $database->initialize();
    $database = $database->connect();

    $result = $database->query()
        ->from("tests")
        ->where("id = ?", 5)
        ->save(array(
          "number" => 3,
          "text" => "foo",
          "boolean" => false
        ));

    return ($result == 0);
  },
  "Database\Query\Mysql can update rows",
  "Database\Query\Mysql"
);

Framework\Test::add(
  function() use ($options)
  {
    $database = new Framework\Database($options);
    $database = $database->initialize();
    $database = $database->connect();

    $database->query()
     ->from("tests")
     ->delete();

    return ($database->query()->from("tests")->count() == 0);
  },
  "Database\Query\Mysql can delete rows",
  "Database\Query\Mysql"
);
```

Consider, again, the database methods we created for inserting/updating rows. If a WHERE clause is provided, the database will attempt to update a row. If no WHERE conditions are present, a row will be inserted. A call to the delete() method will remove rows matching the WHERE conditions, or all rows if there are no conditions.

Model

Because we have chosen to create an ORM, and to store it within the Model class, most of the model tests involve the ORM methods. The Model class is not a factory, so we don't need those tests, leaving a simple set of model tests to create.

We need to test that the model structure syncs correctly to the database. We need to test whether rows can be inserted, updated, and deleted from the database. We also test whether rows can be returned form the database, matching WHERE conditions.

Coverage

We should create tests that cover the following requirements:

- The Model class syncs with the database.
- The Model class can insert rows.
- The Model class can fetch the number of rows.
- The Model class can save a row multiple times.
- The Model class can update rows.
- The Model class can delete rows.

Tests

First, we need to define a model to sync to the database, as shown in Listing 11-14. It follows the same format we learned in the Chapter 10.

Listing 11-14. Syncing the Model to the Database

```
$database = new Framework\Database(array(
  "type" => "mysql",
  "options" => array(
    "host" => "localhost",
    "username" => "prophpmvc",
    "password" => "prophpmvc",
    "schema" => "prophpmvc"
  )
));
$database = $database->initialize();
$database = $database->connect();

Framework\Registry::set("database", $database);

class Example extends Framework\Model
{
  /**
  * @readwrite
```

```
 * @column
 * @type autonumber
 * @primary
 */
 protected $_id;

 /**
 * @readwrite
 * @column
 * @type text
 * @length 32
 */
 protected $_name;

 /**
 * @readwrite
 * @column
 * @type datetime
 */
 protected $_created;
}

Framework\Test::add(
  function() use ($database)
  {
    $example = new Example();
    return ($database->sync($example) instanceof ➥
Framework\Database\Connector\Mysql);
  },
  "Model syncs",
  "Model"
);
```

The first test syncs this model to the database. With the correct table structure, we can then begin to insert rows, as demonstrated in Listing 11-15.

Listing 11-15. Inserting and Returning Rowsfrom the Database

```
Framework\Test::add(
  function() use ($database)
  {
    $example = new Example(array(
        "name" => "foo",
        "created" => date("Y-m-d H:i:s")
    ));

    return ($example->save() > 0);
  },
  "Model inserts rows",
  "Model"
);

Framework\Test::add(
  function() use ($database)
```

```
  {
    return (Example::count() == 1);
  },
  "Model fetches number of rows",
  "Model"
);
```

Inserting rows to in the database is a simple check, and we also test the `count()` method as a kind of double-check for the inserting behavior. The last few tests we need check the updating/deleting behavior, as shown in Listing 11-16.

Listing 11-16. Updating/Deleting Rows

```
Framework\Test::add(
  function() use ($database)
  {
    $example = new Example(array(
      "name" => "foo",
      "created" => date("Y-m-d H:i:s")
    ));

    $example->save();
    $example->save();
    $example->save();

    return (Example::count() == 2);
  },
  "Model saves single row multiple times",
  "Model"
);

Framework\Test::add(
  function() use ($database)
  {
    $example = new Example(array(
     "id" => 1,
     "name" => "hello",
     "created" => date("Y-m-d H:i:s")
    ));
    $example->save();

    return (Example::first()->name == "hello");
  },
  "Model updates rows",
  "Model"
);

Framework\Test::add(
  function() use ($database)
  {
    $example = new Example(array(
      "id" => 2
    ));
    $example->delete();

    return (Example::count() == 1);
```

```
  },
  "Model deletes rows",
  "Model"
);
```

Template

Testing the template parser we create is really a case of testing the individual template tags. This is due to the template parser being a complicated bit of code that performs a relatively simple task.

We need to test each of the common template tags, to ensure they all return the correct output when provided with data.

Coverage

We should create tests that cover the following requirements:

- The `Template` class can be created.
- The `Template` class can parse `echo` tags.
- The `Template` class can parse `script` tags.
- The `Template` class can parse `foreach` tags.
- The `Template` class can parse `for` tags.
- The `Template` class can parse `if`, `else`, and `elseif` tags.
- The `Template` class can parse `macro` tags.
- The `Template` class can parse `literal` tags.

Tests

There is nothing particularly tricky about these template parser tests, which you can see in Listing 11-17. They all address a specific template tag, and ensure the output conforms to what can be expected from the tag's use.

Listing 11-17. Testing Template Tags

```
$template = new Framework\Template(array(
  "implementation" => new Framework\Template\Implementation\Standard()
));

Framework\Test::add(
  function() use ($template)
  {
    return ($template instanceof Framework\Template);
  },
  "Template instantiates",
  "Template"
);

Framework\Test::add(
  function() use ($template)
  {
```

```
        $template->parse("{echo 'hello world'}");
        $processed = $template->process();

        return ($processed == "hello world");
    },
    "Template parses echo tag",
    "Template"
);

Framework\Test::add(
    function() use ($template)
    {
        $template->parse("{script \$_text[] = 'foo bar' }");
        $processed = $template->process();

        return ($processed == "foo bar");
    },
    "Template parses script tag",
    "Template"
);

Framework\Test::add(
    function() use ($template)
    {
        $template->parse("
            {foreach \$number in \$numbers}{echo \$number_i},{echo \$number},{/foreach}"
        );
        $processed = $template->process(array(
            "numbers" => array(1, 2, 3)
        ));

        return (trim($processed) == "0,1,1,2,2,3,");
    },
    "Template parses foreach tag",
    "Template"
);

Framework\Test::add(
    function() use ($template)
    {
        $template->parse("
            {for \$number in \$numbers}{echo \$number_i},{echo \$number},{/for}
        ");
        $processed = $template->process(array(
            "numbers" => array(1, 2, 3)
        ));

        return (trim($processed) == "0,1,1,2,2,3,");
    },
    "Template parses for tag",
    "Template"
);

Framework\Test::add(
    function() use ($template)
    {
        $template->parse("
```

```
        {if \$check == \"yes\"}yes{/if}
        {elseif \$check == \"maybe\"}yes{/elseif}
        {else}yes{/else}
      ");

      $yes = $template->process(array(
        "check" => "yes"
      ));

      $maybe = $template->process(array(
        "check" => "maybe"
      ));

      $no = $template->process(array(
        "check" => null
      ));

      return ($yes == $maybe && $maybe == $no);
  },
  "Template parses if, else and elseif tags",
  "Template"
);

Framework\Test::add(
  function() use ($template)
  {
    $template->parse("
       {macro foo(\$number)}
           {echo \$number + 2}
       {/macro}

       {echo foo(2)}
    ");
    $processed = $template->process();

    return ($processed == 4);
  },
  "Template parses macro tag",
  "Template"
);

Framework\Test::add(
  function() use ($template)
  {
    $template->parse("
      {literal}
          {echo \"hello world\"}
      {/literal}
    ");
    $processed = $template->process();

    return (trim($processed) == "{echo \"hello world\"}");
  },
  "Template parses literal tag",
  "Template"
);
```

Holy Code, Batman!

One of the excellent things about about tests, apart from the fact that they provide a reliable means of ensuring our code continues working, is that they also help us identify shortfalls in our code, and how best to use the bits we are testing.

I spent hours writing these tests, not because they are by any means complicated, but because it pointed out many bugs I could fix and improvements I could make to the code in the previous chapters.

Questions

1. The unit tests we created seem to repeat a lot of code. This is especially true of the unit tests of the `Database` and `Model` classes. Why is this necessary?
2. Should these kinds of tests be written in parallel or after the classes they test have been written?

Answers

1. The reason our testing occurs outside of the MVC structure our framework facilitates is the same reason we repeat code within the individual unit tests. The less our tests depend on external variables, the more accurate they will be at pointing out breaking changes to the classes we cover in the unit tests.
2. The decision of when to write these tests isn't nearly as important as having them in the first place. Forgetting or neglecting to unit test code is an easy trap to fall into. Writing tests in parallel, or after the classes they are meant to test, makes little difference.

Exercises

1. We created tests for the biggest class libraries in our framework. Now try covering some smaller ones, like the `Registry`, `StringMethods`, or `ArrayMethods` classes.
2. The `Test` class we created is a nice tool for running unit tests, but does not handle any output formatting. Try putting together a presentable overview of passed tests as well as tests that failed or raised exceptions.

CHAPTER 12

Structure

We now get to step out of the realm of theory, and into a practical application. We used the concept of a social network in some of the examples so far, and now we will build one.

To better plan our application, we need to look at some of the things common to most social networks. First and foremost is the concept of user profiles. User profiles contain some information about the users they belong to, such as their hobbies or country of origin. Depending on the focus of the network, this information can be anything ranging from employment history and credentials, to previous vacation destinations and favorite bands.

Social networks also serve as a platform for sharing—links to photos, music tracks, and videos are easily shared . If you have something to show off, or want to know what your friends are looking at, social networks are the place to be.

The last area in which these networks can vary is how well they moderate their users and the information that is shared. Very exclusive social networks may moderate the kinds of things their users share, while others allow users to share (and see) anything!

Goals

- We need to build the pages/actions for users to register, log in, update their settings, and view their profiles.
- Users should be able to view the profiles of others, and befriend them.
- Users should be able to share status messages and photos, upload their own photos, and search for users through a number of different fields.
- There should be an administration interface through which system administrators can review and/or modify information stored in the database.

Our application will need to store a fair amount of user-related data, and it is ideal for testing our database/ORM code. It will also require quite a few views, which will allow us to test (and extend) our template parser. The photo-sharing functionality allows us to tie into third-party image editing libraries, while the link-sharing and friends functionalities allow us to connect to third-party web services.

Database

We can represent the database for our social network as depicted in Figure 12-1.

Users can have multiple friends, which are essentially other users. They can own multiple photos, which can then be shared with their friends. Links and status messages can also be shared with their friends. Friends can be added/removed following user interaction, and users can also report photos, shared links, and other users as inappropriate.

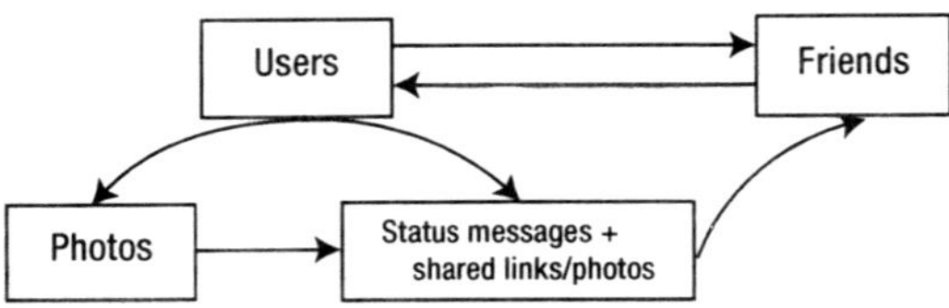

Figure 12-1. *Data structure*

All users and content can be managed via an administration interface, which will require authentication of a valid administrative user account. We will create the individual model structures, as they are needed.

Folders

We need to establish the folder structure for our application, so that files are stored in predictable locations. We have already arranged our framework within a folder of that same name, but the rest of our application should follow the neat organizational pattern shown in Figure 12-2.

Figure 12-2. *Folder structure*

The application folder is where we will keep everything that crosses the line, from framework code to application code. The HTML views we create will be kept in the `views` folder, while any third-party libraries will be kept in the `libraries` folder.

The `configuration` folder will hold the configuration files for our application's classes, while the model and controller files will be kept in their respective folders.

The `public` folder will hold all the publicly accessible files, which are not directly loading in the course of the application's execution. This includes images, JavaScript files, and cascading style sheets.

One interesting thing to notice is that our application `tests` are kept in the `public` folder. We do this to keep our tests completely separate from both our framework and application code bases. Our tests will ultimately use framework code and test both framework/application code, but it is important to try and keep all these aspects (tests, framework, and application) separate.

Questions

1. We have defined a rough structure for the database tables/data objects in our social network. What is the significance in planning data structures before we begin coding?
2. The folder structure we use depends largely on the kind of application we're building. Why do we need to decide this when it is likely to change, in varying degrees, for each application we begin to develop?

Answers

1. The more time spent planning any application, the smoother the development will progress. This is even more apparent in an MVC application. When our application uses a database, we're not merely using PHP to query the database; we're building models and interacting with the database as if it were any other class. We need to know, beforehand, what those classes should look like.
2. The folder structure is important in two areas. The first is that it keeps everything neat and tidy. The second is that we can know where to find things quickly. Whether we are looking for a model, a controller, or even a third-party library, we can find it quickly by understanding the folder structure.

CHAPTER 13

Bootstrapping

Bootstrapping is a metaphor for self-sustaining processes that proceed without external help. In terms of our framework, bootstrapping is a collective term for the processes our framework will perform in order to get from a web address to a specific set of controllers, models, and views.

These processes are required by virtue of the fact that our framework is heavily focused on OOP practices, in which we attempt to isolate as much functionality as we can within individual classes. If we were to attempt a functional approach to MVC framework construction, it would imply that our code is executed in a top-down fashion, and requires no initial code to stitch the individual classes together in a meaningful application.

So far, we have built many individual classes, which are foundational to a solid framework. The moment we start to build applications on top of our framework, we need to start thinking of how each part interacts with all the others it needs to. This begins with bootstrapping.

Goals

- We need to intercept requests to our application (with `.htaccess`) and reroute these to the bootstrap file.
- The bootstrap file needs to instantiate the classes required to get the application running. These include configuration, cache, and router, to name a few.
- The router will then decide which controller and action to load. The controller will first allow the action to execute and then render the action's view (if a matching view is found).

When a File Is Not a File...

Developers venturing into the realms of framework development might be surprised to find that unique web addresses do not necessarily point to unique files on a web server. It is commonplace for multiple domain names to point to the same web site. Likewise, it is commonplace for addresses with varying querystring parameters to point to the same file. The kind of address-to-file relationship I am talking about is the ability of a web server to redirect addresses (of any kind) to any files they choose, based on pattern matching. This is a process known as *URL rewriting.*

URL rewriting is something the server can do, if sufficient instructions are given to it, telling it what addresses to match, and where to send the corresponding requests to. Requests can be rerouted to files/scripts within the local file system, or even remote files and/or addresses. These instructions are usually given within the configuration files of the specific web server.

Some web servers, such as Apache2, allow these configuration files to be loaded at the same time as the server is started. These servers may also allow configuration files to be stored within each directory, as is the case with Apache2.

URL Rewriting

The reason URL rewriting is important to us is that we will be using it to funnel all requests into a single index.php file. This is because we want to handle all requests through the same bootstrapping code (contained in this index.php file), so that we can select the best response with no repeated code.

I mentioned the directory-based configuration files we could use to initialize the URL rewriting, and we will be creating one now. This should be in the public directory, and your web server's root directory should point to within the public directory. This will ensure that our application code can read all the framework files, while only the files contained within the public directory will be publicly accessible to the outside world. Let's see what that file looks like in Listing 13-1.

Listing 13-1. URL Rewriting in Apache2

```
RewriteEngine On
RewriteCond %{REQUEST_FILENAME} !-d
RewriteCond %{REQUEST_FILENAME} !-f
RewriteCond %{REQUEST_URI} !=/favicon.ico
RewriteRule ^([a-zA-Z0-9\/\-_]+)\.?([a-zA-Z]+)?$ index.php?url=$1&extension=$2 [QSA,L]
```

These five lines might look complicated, but their meaning is simple. The first instructs Apache2 to enable URL rewriting for this directory. It assumes that the module is installed and enabled at the time the server starts.

The second instruction tells Apache2 to ignore all requests made to actual directories within this directory. For example, if there is a scripts directory within the public directory, and a request is made to http://localhost/scripts, Apache2 will ignore the rewriting and let the request execute as normal. The third instruction is similar, but refers to files. If a request is made to http://localhost/scripts/shared.js, the request will be executed as normal.

The fourth instruction tells Apache2 to ignore all requests to http://localhost/favicon.ico. Browsers frequently request standard files such as this, and we don't want this additional traffic triggering 404 error pages because our framework doesn't cater to the address.

The last instruction is the most important. It tells Apache2 to match all addresses that contain the characters a-zA-Z0-9/-_ (all alphanumeric characters in both upper- and lowercase), and relay them to the index.php file, as a querystring parameter. It also tells Apache2 to send whatever file extension was mentioned as a querystring parameter to the index.php file.

For example, a request to http://localhost/users/add.html will pass through this .htaccess file, and Apache2 will send the request (with querystring parameters and form data) to the address http://localhost/index.php?url=users/add&extension=html.

You might be wondering why we would want to isolate all requests to the public directory, and not simply have the index.php file in the same directory as our application/framework directories. The reason is that our .htaccess can't tell the difference between files that can legitimately be accessed from outside (scripts, style sheets, and images), and those that should be secure. We don't want people tampering with our framework and application code.

We should remove any possibility for our web server to return sensitive PHP code, and this is a step in the right direction!

■ **Note** If you are having trouble getting the web server to use the public directory as its root directory, you can also try creating a secondary .htaccess file to redirect all requests to the public directory, but Apache needs mod_rewrite enabled in order for you to use URL rewriting.

Index.php

We now need to create a script that will send rerouted requests to a controller/action. That file is, as you can guess, index.php. This is a simple task, and forms the bulk of the bootstrapping code we will need to create in this chapter.

You might see bootstrapping code as an extension of the framework code we already created, but it is really the first application-specific code we will create. You see, the framework is largely complete, at this stage. It has the means of routing requests to controllers and loading models. It can persist those model structures (ORM data objects) to the database. We have created code to parse templates, code to manage cache and configuration files, even code to handle sessions and inspect class structures and store class instances. However, in order for our application to utilize these framework classes, it must first load them into memory and string them together. This is at the heart of the bootstrapping code we are about to create.

There are a few framework classes that we can expect to use throughout our framework. The first step toward getting out application off the ground is to instantiate these classes and store them in the registry. We do this after establishing an application directory (so that our class loader knows where to start looking for the framework classes), and promptly dispatch the request thereafter. In terms of code, our index.php should look like that shown in Listing 13-2.

Listing 13-2. Bootstrapping

```
// 1. define the default path for includes
define("APP_PATH", dirname(dirname(__FILE__)));

// 2. load the Core class that includes an autoloader
require("../framework/core.php");
Framework\Core::initialize();

// 3. load and initialize the Configuration class
$configuration = new Framework\Configuration(array(
    "type" => "ini"
));
Framework\Registry::set("configuration", $configuration->initialize());

// 4. load and initialize the Database class - does not connect
$database = new Framework\Database();
Framework\Registry::set("database", $database->initialize());

// 5. load and initialize the Cache class - does not connect
$cache = new Framework\Cache();
Framework\Registry::set("cache", $cache->initialize());

// 6. load and initialize the Session class
$session = new Framework\Session();
Framework\Registry::set("session", $session->initialize());

// 7. load the Router class and provide the url+extension
$router = new Framework\Router(array(
    "url" => isset($_GET["url"]) ? $_GET["url"] : "index/index",
    "extension" => isset($_GET["url"]) ? $_GET["url"] : "html"
));
Framework\Registry::set("router", $router);

// 8. dispatch the current request
$router->dispatch();
```

```
// 9. unset global variables
unset($configuration);
unset($database);
unset($cache);
unset($session);
unset($router);
```

As I mentioned earlier, the first step is to define the application's base file path. This is so that our class autoloader, `Core::autoload()`, can know where to start looking for the framework files. I have marked this statement as (1), and will refer to similar markings in further explanation of this listing.

The next things we do (2) are to include the Core class file and call the `Core::initialize()` method. This will set up the include paths for class autoloading and register the `Core::autoload()` method as a class autoloader for our framework classes.

Following this, we instantiate four of our framework classes (3, 4, 5, 6), beginning with `Configuration` and ending with `Session`. We only provide construction options for the `Configuration` instance—a curious fact that we will explore in a bit.

Next, we instantiate the `Router` class (7), and pass the `url/extension` parameters (with defaults) as construction options. If you refer back to Chapter 7 in which we create the `Router` class, you will remember that these options are used to determine the applicable controller/action that should be invoked.

We also need to call the `Router->dispatch()` method (8) to tell the `Router` that we want it to go about getting the right controller/action. It is the essential indication that we are handing over control to the `Router`.

The remaining statements (9) are simply to remove global references to the class instances we created in this script. Because these instances are already referenced in the `Registry`, we no longer need them hanging around in their global form.

In summary, our `index.php` file set the application file path, initialized Core (the autoloader), defined some instances (which we will use later), and handed the request over to the `Router`.

■ **Note** If you have been following, and wish to see what the bootstrapping returns to your browser, you are in for a bit of a surprise. The `index.php` file does everything we need it to, but the address `http://localhost` will return an error. Look, again, at the `Router` code (7). We provide the `url` querystring parameters as the only clue as to which controller/action to load. We also provide it with a default (`index/index`) in the event that no `url` querystring parameter is found. This means our `Router` instance will attempt to load the `Index` controller and the `index` action, or `Index->index()`. Unless that controller and action have already been created, the `Router` will throw either a `Router/Exception/Controller` or a `Router/Exception/Action` exception.

Configuration

Half of the four classes we just used were provided no configuration when we instantiate them. To recap, they were `Database`, `Cache`, and `Session`. We have not yet covered the `Session` class, but it is sufficient to understand that it is quite similar to the Cache classes we created in Chapter 5. When we begin creating the user accounts, we will learn how it differs.

What is safe to assume is that instances of `Database` and `Cache` (and even `Session`) require configuration parameters that we have not provided. They are required for our framework classes to have even the faintest idea of what services to connect to, and what credentials to connect with. Those details need to be provided, but we do not see them mentioned here. This is due to a bit of code we are about to add to each of the big class factories.

Database

We can begin with the Database factory class. At a minimum, the factory needs to know what type of database driver it is to create. We can achieve that with a modification to the Database::initialize() method, as demonstrated in Listing 13-3.

Listing 13-3. Automatic Database Configuration

```
public function initialize()
{
    $type = $this->getType();
    if (empty($type))
    {
        $configuration = Registry::get("configuration");

        if ($configuration)
        {
            $configuration = $configuration->initialize();
            $parsed = $configuration->parse("configuration/database");

            if (!empty($parsed->database->default) && ➥
!empty($parsed->database->default->type))
            {
                $type = $parsed->database->default->type;
                unset($parsed->database->default->type);

                $this->__construct(array(
                    "type" => $type,
                    "options" => (array) $parsed->database->default
                ));
            }
        }
    }

    if (empty($type))
    {
        throw new Exception\Argument("Invalid type");
    }

    switch ($type)
    {
        case "mysql":
        {
            return new Database\Connector\Mysql($this->getOptions());
            break;
        }
        default:
        {
            throw new Exception\Argument("Invalid type");
            break;
        }
    }
}
```

Where previously we simply rejected any requests for class instances (via the Database::initialize() method), we now first check to see whether it has been provided. If it is not found within the construction options, we attempt to load the database configuration file application/configuration/database.ini. If the parsed configuration data defines a default database type, that type is used in the initialization of the database connector class.

This modified method ensures that, should there be a database configuration file, and should it contain a default array that defines a default database connector type, a connector instance of that type will be returned. This will only occur if type is not found within the construction options.

■ **Note** When it comes to the Database factory, it is important to remember that initialization is not the same as connecting to the database. It is perfectly reasonable that the factory can return a valid connector instance, which then fails to connect to the database with the credentials provided.

Cache

Automatic configuration of the Cache class factory is much the same as that of the Database class factory. It involves a similar change to the Cache::initialize() method, which you can see in Listing 13-4.

Listing 13-4. Automatic Cache Configuration

```
public function initialize()
{
    $type = $this->getType();

    if (empty($type))
    {
        $configuration = Registry::get("configuration");

        if ($configuration)
        {
            $configuration = $configuration->initialize();
            $parsed = $configuration->parse("configuration/cache");

            if (!empty($parsed->cache->default) && !empty($parsed->cache->default->type))
            {
                $type = $parsed->cache->default->type;
                unset($parsed->cache->default->type);

                $this->__construct(array(
                    "type" => $type,
                    "options" => (array) $parsed->cache->default
                ));
            }
        }
    }

    if (empty($type))
    {
        throw new Exception\Argument("Invalid type");
    }

    switch ($type)
    {
```

```
            case "memcached":
            {
                return new Cache\Driver\Memcached($this->getOptions());
                break;
            }
            default:
            {
                throw new Exception\Argument("Invalid type");
                break;
            }
        }
    }
```

The default type of cache driver is defined within the application/configuration/cache.ini file, and will obviously be a list of cache driver classes, instead of database connector classes. Other than that, the automatic configuration follows the same pattern as that of the Database class factory.

Note Depending on the Cache driver, the same distinction could exist between Cache::initialize() and Cache->connect(). In the case of Memcached, there are no user credentials, but there are addresses and ports involved, so it is possible to have a valid cache instance that then fails to connect to a valid server Always refer to the type of exception generated when a factory class fails to preform—they are likely to be of a type similar to Database/Exception/Service or Cache/Exception/Service, which would indicate a valid instance that cannot connect to the required server/service.

Controller

The final piece of the bootstrapping puzzle is not strictly about bootstrapping or our framework. It is actually about how each controller will render views. Let me demystify this topic by saying that this code belongs equally within the realms of application and framework code.

If we refer back to the three goals of our framework, we will remember that the second is to create a framework that is easy to use, and makes few assumptions about the applications we will use it to create. There are, however, times when these two statements counter each other. A very practical example is that of view rendering.

We can assume that all of our application's actions will elicit a response. Moreover, this response should be in a form that conveys itself to the application's users. This can take the form of HTML, or JavaScript (JSON), or XML, and so on. The point is that all (or near as makes no difference) of our actions will require output, which is likely to occur in the form of views.

For this reason, the MVC paradigm is an excellent choice for a framework. We are expecting many controllers/actions and each will require a significant level of view rendering. We have good separation here, but we also have a lot of repeated behavior. If each action should output to a view, we either need to render a view within the body of each action (method), or we need to hook it into a common point in the framework's execution so that it becomes standard behavior.

At this point, we could choose to create an application-specific Controller subclass, from which all of our application's controllers will inherit the view-rendering behavior, or we can make the decision to incorporate this commonplace behavior in the default Controller class. I think, at this stage, it would be best simply to modify the Controller class.

■ **Note** We will learn how to extend framework classes in later chapters, but for now you should simply extend the default `Controller` class along with me.

Views

Before we can begin to modify the `Controller` class, we must first create a class for handling (and rendering) views. In order to keep this class simple, we will assume that it deals with classes that resemble that of the template parser we have already built; namely, a class that has `parse()` and `process()` methods, and looks like that shown in Listing 13-5.

Listing 13-5. The View Class

```
namespace Framework
{
    use Framework\Base as Base;
    use Framework\Template as Template;
    use Framework\View\Exception as Exception;

    class View extends Base
    {
        /**
        * @readwrite
        */
        protected $_file;

        /**
        * @read
        */
        protected $_template;

        protected $_data = array();

        public function _getExceptionForImplementation($method)
        {
            return new Exception\Implementation("{$method} method not implemented");
        }

        public function _getExceptionForArgument()
        {
            return new Exception\Argument("Invalid argument");
        }

        public function __construct($options = array())
        {
            parent::__construct($options);
            $this->_template = new Template(array(
                "implementation" => new Template\Implementation\Standard()
            ));
        }

        public function render()
        {
```

```
            if (!file_exists($this->getFile()))
            {
                return "";
            }

            $content = file_get_contents($this->getFile());

            $this->_template->parse($content);
            return $this->_template->process($this->_data);
        }

        public function get($key, $default = "")
        {
            if (isset($this->_data[$key]))
            {
                return $this->_data[$key];
            }
            return $default;
        }

        protected function _set($key, $value)
        {
            if (!is_string($key) && !is_numeric($key))
            {
                throw new Exception\Data("Key must be a string or a number");
            }

            $this->_data[$key] = $value;
        }

        public function set($key, $value = null)
        {
            if (is_array($key))
            {
                foreach ($key as $_key => $value)
                {
                    $this->_set($_key, $value);
                }
                return $this;
            }

            $this->_set($key, $value);
            return $this;
        }

        public function erase($key)
        {
            unset($this->_data[$key]);
            return $this;
        }
    }
}
```

There are a few important things to note about the View class. First, its constructor method will create a Template instance, which it will later use to parse the view templates. Second, it has methods for storing, retrieving, and erasing key/value pairs of template data, which it provides to the template parser. You can think of the View class as a combination of something resembling a cache driver, and the template parser usage examples we saw previously.

We are making the assumption that our views will be sent through the template parser we created. If we wanted something different to happen, we could easily subclass this View class, overriding the __construct() and render() methods with our alternative logic. This class does, however, provide a convenient façade for our template parsing.

Note The façade design pattern we used previously can be described as having one class that provides a simple interface to a more complicated set of functionality. You can read more about the façade pattern at http://en.wikipedia.org/wiki/Facade_pattern.

Rendering

The View class is only half the work required for automatically rendering the correct view. We now need to use it within a modified Controller class, in order for each action to render its own view. The changes needed to the Controller are fairly extensive, so we will review each section. We begin with a few embellishments on the previous Controller skeleton, as shown in Listing 13-6.

Listing 13-6. Fleshing Out the Controller

```
namespace Framework
{
    use Framework\Base as Base;
    use Framework\View as View;
    use Framework\Registry as Registry;
    use Framework\Template as Template;
    use Framework\Controller\Exception as Exception;

    class Controller extends Base
    {
        /**
        * @readwrite
        */
        protected $_parameters;

        /**
        * @readwrite
        */
        protected $_layoutView;

        /**
        * @readwrite
        */
        protected $_actionView;

        /**
        * @readwrite
        */
        protected $_willRenderLayoutView=true;
```

```
        /**
        * @readwrite
        */
        protected $_willRenderActionView = true;

        /**
        * @readwrite
        */
        protected $_defaultPath = "application/views";

        /**
        * @readwrite
        */
        protected $_defaultLayout = "layouts/standard";

        /**
        * @readwrite
        */
        protected $_defaultExtension = "html";

        /**
        * @readwrite
        */
        protected $_defaultContentType = "text/html";

        protected function _getExceptionForImplementation($method)
        {
            return new Exception\Implementation("{$method} method not implemented");
        }

        protected function _getExceptionForArgument()
        {
            return new Exception\Argument("Invalid argument");
        }
    }
}
```

We add three additional getter/setter properties: `layoutView`, `actionView`, and `willRenderLayoutView/willRenderActionView`. The `layoutView` property is a placeholder for a layout's view, the `actionView` property is a placeholder for the action's view, and the `willRenderLayoutView/willRenderActionView` properties are flags that will be used to disable automatic view rendering.

Layouts address a problem you might not even have known existed. In terms of interface design, a consistent layout is essential for a good user experience. I did say that we would ignore (most) interface design, but this is a functional requirement of any good application, so we are adding it now.

Layouts are essentially views that are shared. They are frames within which the views of individual actions are rendered, and serve to reduce repeated HTML across the application's view files. You can understand them better by the process in which they are used.

The controller, should it be required to attempt automatic view rendering, will first render the current action's view, and then the layout's view. The action's view and the layout's view are both `View` instances, but the action's view markup is placed smack-dab in the middle of the layout view's markup. We will now look at the methods responsible for rendering the views in Listing 13-7.

Listing 13-7. Render Methods

```
public function render()
{
```

```
    $defaultContentType = $this->getDefaultContentType();
    $results = null;

    $doAction = $this->getWillRenderActionView() && $this->getActionView();
    $doLayout = $this->getWillRenderLayoutView() && $this->getLayoutView();

    try
    {
        if ($doAction)
        {
            $view = $this->getActionView();
            $results = $view->render();
        }

        if ($doLayout)
        {
            $view = $this->getLayoutView();
            $view->set("template", $results);
            $results = $view->render();

            header("Content-type: {$defaultContentType}");
            echo $results;
        }
        else if ($doAction)
        {
            header("Content-type: {$defaultContentType}");
            echo $results;

            $this->setWillRenderLayoutView(false);
            $this->setWillRenderActionView(false);
        }
    }
    catch (\Exception $e)
    {
        throw new View\Exception\Renderer("Invalid layout/template syntax");
    }
}

public function __destruct()
{
    $this->render();
}
```

The `__destruct()` method is responsible for calling the `render()` method. This means the `render()` method will be called at the end of each action's execution. If `willRenderLayoutView` and `layoutView` are true, then the layout will be rendered. The same can be said of the action's view if `willRenderActionView` and `actionView` are true. If both the layout and action views are rendered, then the action view's content is assigned to the layout's template, else the action view's content is returned to the browser. As a precaution against multiple `render()` calls, `willRenderLayoutView`/`willRenderActionView` are set to false to prevent rerendering the layout/action views.

The last `Controller` method we need to modify is the `__construct()` method, as shown in Listing 13-8.

Listing 13-8. __construct() Method

```
public function __construct($options = array())
{
```

```
    parent::__construct($options);

    if ($this->getWillRenderLayoutView())
    {
        $defaultPath = $this->getDefaultPath();
        $defaultLayout = $this->getDefaultLayout();
        $defaultExtension = $this->getDefaultExtension();

        $view = new View(array(
            "file" => APP_PATH."/{$defaultPath}/{$defaultLayout}.{$defaultExtension}"
        ));

        $this->setLayoutView($view);
    }

    if ($this->getWillRenderLayoutView())
    {
        $router = Registry::get("router");
        $controller = $router->getController();
        $action = $router->getAction();

        $view = new View(array(
            "file" => APP_PATH."/{$defaultPath}/{$controller}/{$action}.{$defaultExtension}"
        ));

        $this->setActionView($view);
    }
}
```

This new `__construct()` method does two important things. First, it defines the location of the layout template, which is passed to the new `View` instance, which is then passed into the `setLayoutView()` setter method.

Second, it gets the controller/action names from the router. It gets the router instance from the registry, and uses getters for the names. It then builds a path from the controller/action names, to a template it can render. For example, if the user requests the URL `http://localhost/users/add.html`, the new `__construct()` method will define the location as `APP_PATH/application/views/users/add.html`. The correlation between the two is merely coincidental to our naming and organizational structures.

To gain an understanding of the full structure of the new `Controller` class, I have included the full code in Listing 13-9.

Listing 13-9. The Modified Controller Class

```
namespace Framework
{
    use Framework\Base as Base;
    use Framework\View as View;
    use Framework\Event as Event;
    use Framework\Registry as Registry;
    use Framework\Template as Template;
    use Framework\Controller\Exception as Exception;

    class Controller extends Base
    {
        /**
        * @readwrite
        */
```

```
protected $_parameters;

/**
* @readwrite
*/
protected $_layoutView;

/**
* @readwrite
*/
protected $_actionView;

/**
* @readwrite
*/
protected $_willRenderLayoutView = true;

/**
* @readwrite
*/
protected $_willRenderActionView = true;

/**
* @readwrite
*/
protected $_defaultPath = "application/views";

/**
* @readwrite
*/
protected $_defaultLayout = "layouts/standard";

/**
* @readwrite
*/
protected $_defaultExtension = "html";

/**
* @readwrite
*/
protected $_defaultContentType = "text/html";

protected function _getExceptionForImplementation($method)
{
    return new Exception\Implementation("{$method} method not implemented");
}

protected function _getExceptionForArgument()
{
    return new Exception\Argument("Invalid argument");
}

public function __construct($options = array())
{
    parent::__construct($options);
```

```
        if ($this->getWillRenderLayoutView())
        {
            $defaultPath = $this->getDefaultPath();
            $defaultLayout = $this->getDefaultLayout();
            $defaultExtension = $this->getDefaultExtension();

            $view = new View(array(
                "file" => APP_PATH."/{$defaultPath}/{$defaultLayout}.{$defaultExtension}"
            ));

            $this->setLayoutView($view);
        }

        if ($this->getWillRenderLayoutView())
        {
            $router = Registry::get("router");
            $controller = $router->getController();
            $action = $router->getAction();

            $view = new View(array(
                "file" => APP_PATH. ➥
"/{$defaultPath}/{$controller}/{$action}.{$defaultExtension}"
            ));

            $this->setActionView($view);
        }
    }

    public function render()
    {
        $defaultContentType = $this->getDefaultContentType();
        $results = null;

        $doAction = $this->getWillRenderActionView() && $this->getActionView();
        $doLayout = $this->getWillRenderLayoutView() && $this->getLayoutView();

        try
        {
            if ($doAction)
            {
                $view = $this->getActionView();
                $results = $view->render();
            }

            if ($doLayout)
            {
                $view = $this->getLayoutView();
                $view->set("template", $results);
                $results = $view->render();

                header("Content-type: {$defaultContentType}");
                echo $results;
            }
            else if ($doAction)
            {
```

```
                    header("Content-type: {$defaultContentType}");
                    echo $results;
                }

                $this->setWillRenderLayoutView(false);
                $this->setWillRenderActionView(false);
            }
            catch (\Exception $e)
            {
                throw new View\Exception\Renderer("Invalid layout/template syntax");
            }
        }

        public function __destruct()
        {
            $this->render();
        }
    }
}
```

Questions

1. We used URL rewriting to reroute application requests to a single `index.php` file. Why was this required?
2. Our bootstrap file references many classes by their full namespace (e.g., `Framework\Configuration`) instead of utilizing use statements. It also unsets the variables we define. Why are these steps necessary?
3. We added automatic configuration of the `Database` and `Cache` classes. This is useful for configuring these classes exclusively with configuration files. What are the benefits of this approach to configuration?
4. Our `Controller` class has been modified to attempt automatic rendering, should a matching view be found. It will also try to wrap the results in a layout file. Can you think of a practical use for this behavior?

Answers

1. URL rewriting is not strictly required. All application requests are handled through the same file, but there is nothing stopping you from addressing the `index.php` file directly. The difference is apparent in the URLs `http://localhost/users/view.html` and `http://localhost/index.php?url=users/view&extension=html`. The benefit of using URL rewriting is that the URLs will be simpler and neater.
2. One of the benefits of namespaces is that our framework classes are no longer in the global namespace. Instead of 20+ classes (`Database`, `Cache`, `Configuration`, etc.) we only have to add one to the global `Framework` namespace. This avoids the many pitfalls of namespace collision.

   When we begin using use statements, we negate this benefit, adding more things to the global namespace. This is not a problem if it is done within a namespace block (e.g., `namespace ACME\TNT { use ACME\Glue as Glue; }`), but less so if the use statements are in the global namespace. We unset the variables because we don't want them polluting the global namespace either.

3. Adding automatic configuration to classes within our framework allows other developers to customize the behavior of those classes without changing their code.

4. Layouts offer us a way to give our views a consistent framework, without repeating any markup. A good example is using layouts for navigation.

Exercises

1. We used automatic configuration to initialize some of our framework classes. Now try configuring the `View` class to allow for different view-rendering engines.

2. Our bootstrapping file will attempt to execute the most applicable controller/action, but it has no way of channeling raised exceptions so that applicable error pages can be shown. Now attempt handling exceptions so that custom error pages can be used.

CHAPTER 14

Registration and Login

A social network is built around the concept of users with profiles. Profiles are a place for users to share with other users, and in order for users to have profiles they need to have user accounts. In this chapter, we will be creating the pages and classes required for users to be able to create accounts, and log in to those accounts.

Goals

- Users need to be able to register new accounts. This will involve a form that they need to complete. After they have completed it, a new database row will be created with the information, and they should be able to log in.
- Naturally, this means users need to be able to log in to their accounts. This will require another form, which secures their profile, allowing access through the verification of valid user credentials. For the sake of simplicity, we will require users to provide their e-mail address and password in order to log in.

Shared Libraries

Depending on the kind of application we want to build, the need may exist to share controller and model logic across multiple controllers and models. I am not talking about what we have already added to the `Controller` class for view rendering. What I am referring to here are actions such as connecting to a database or sharing common model fields.

These examples are exactly the kinds of details we need to achieve in this chapter, so we will begin by adding them! The first class we would like to share common functionality with is the `Controller` class. If the needs of the shared code were application-agnostic, we might consider adding them as an extension of the `Controller` class. This is the approach we chose for the view rendering, assuming that the majority of actions would render in the same way.

Unfortunately, it would seem that opening a persistent connection to the database is not the kind of decision we can make for all applications using our framework. Some applications might not want the constant connection, and some applications might not even need a database in order to fulfill their ORM/model requirements.

For this reason, we will subclass the `Controller` class, to add the database functionality we require. This sounds trickier than it really is. Consider the code shown in Listing 14-1.

Listing 14-1. application/libraries/shared/controller.php

```
namespace Shared
{
    class Controller extends \Framework\Controller
    {
        public function __construct($options = array())
        {
            parent::__construct($options);

            $database = \Framework\Registry::get("database");
            $database->connect();
        }
    }
}
```

As Listing 14-1 demonstrates, it is fairly easy to subclass the `Controller` class within our application. The `libraries` directory was added as a possible `include` directory (in the `Core::initialize()` method), so it will be loaded easily enough, and we can even keep the shared `Controller` subclass namespaced.

We override the `__construct()` method (making sure to call the appropriate parent method), retrieving the database instance from the registry, and then connecting to the database server with it. At first glance, it might appear that we are mixing concerns by talking to the database from within a generic, shared `Controller` subclass. It does, however, make sense to do so. After all, both this shared `Controller` subclass and the (bootstrap) `index.php` file are part of the same application codebase. They are concerned with the application, and sharing this database connection code is far preferable to adding it in each database-aware action.

■ **Note** If our application controllers are to utilize this shared `Controller` subclass, they should extend it. Be sure to change the `Controller` reference (in each application controller) from `Framework\Controller` to `Shared\Controller`.

After creating this subclass, we can comfortably assume that the registry's `Database` instance is connected by the time we need to do any database work within our actions.

User Model

Because we are going to be working with user accounts (database rows), now would be a good time to define what fields constitute a valid user account. I suggest we use the structure shown in Listing 14-2 for our `User` model.

Listing 14-2. application/models/user.php

```
class User extends Framework\Model
{
    /**
    * @column
    * @readwrite
    * @primary
    * @type autonumber
    */
    protected $_id;
```

```
/**
* @column
* @readwrite
* @type text
* @length 100
*/
protected $_first;

/**
* @column
* @readwrite
* @type text
* @length 100
*/
protected $_last;

/**
* @column
* @readwrite
* @type text
* @length 100
* @index
*/
protected $_email;

/**
* @column
* @readwrite
* @type text
* @length 100
* @index
*/
protected $_password;

/**
* @column
* @readwrite
* @type boolean
* @index
*/
protected $_live;

/**
* @column
* @readwrite
* @type boolean
* @index
*/
protected $_deleted;
```

```
    /**
    * @column
    * @readwrite
    * @type datetime
    */
    protected $_created;

    /**
    * @column
    * @readwrite
    * @type datetime
    */
    protected $_modified;
}
```

The first few fields (from `first` to `password`) are fairly straightforward text fields. The fields that follow these are a convention I like to follow. They contain a small amount of metadata about the rows in my database tables (e.g., when they were created and changed, whether they should be displayed in a public listing, etc.)

The `User` model expects that the `user` database table will have the structure shown in Listing 14-3.

Listing 14-3. Table Structure for user Table

```
CREATE TABLE `user` (
  `first` varchar(100) DEFAULT NULL,
  `last` varchar(100) DEFAULT NULL,
  `email` varchar(100) DEFAULT NULL,
  `password` varchar(100) DEFAULT NULL,
  `id` int(11) NOT NULL AUTO_INCREMENT,
  `live` tinyint(4) DEFAULT NULL,
  `deleted` tinyint(4) DEFAULT NULL,
  `created` datetime DEFAULT NULL,
  `modified` datetime DEFAULT NULL,
  PRIMARY KEY (`id`),
  KEY `email` (`email`),
  KEY `password` (`password`),
  KEY `live` (`live`),
  KEY `deleted` (`deleted`)
) ENGINE=InnoDB  DEFAULT CHARSET=utf8;
```

These fields are not a requirement of our framework in general, or social networks specifically. They are just a bunch of fields I like to add. That being said, I tend to add them to every database table (and in this case, every model). It would be a shame if we need to repeat these fields for every model, though. Fear not, as we can create a shared model, as demonstrated in Listing 14-4.

Listing 14-4. application/libraries/shared/model.php

```
namespace Shared
{
    class Model extends \Framework\Model
    {
        /**
        * @column
```

```
        * @readwrite
        * @primary
        * @type autonumber
        */
        protected $_id;

        /**
        * @column
        * @readwrite
        * @type boolean
        * @index
        */
        protected $_live;

        /**
        * @column
        * @readwrite
        * @type boolean
        * @index
        */
        protected $_deleted;

        /**
        * @column
        * @readwrite
        * @type datetime
        */
        protected $_created;

        /**
        * @column
        * @readwrite
        * @type datetime
        */
        protected $_modified;
    }
}
```

As you can tell, these fields have been placed in a shared Model subclass. This subclass acts in much the same way as the shared Controller subclass we created, in that our models extend the shared Model class, and in which the shared Model class extends the framework Model class. Shared classes allow us to hook in extra functionality without needless repetition in every controller and/or model.

■ **Note** Remember to also update your models to reference Shared\Model instead of Framework\Model.

Registration

Another step we need to take before user accounts can be created, is to create the form that new users will use to register. Listing 14-5 shows how we do this by creating a template file, which is mostly just ordinary HTML.

Listing 14-5. application/views/users/register.html

```
<h1>Register</h1>
{if isset($success)}
    Your account has been created!
{/if}
{else}
    <form method="post">
        <ol>
            <li>
                <label>
                    First name:
                    <input type="text" name="first" />
                    {if isset($first_error)}
                        {echo $first_error}
                    {/if}
                </label>
            </li>
            <li>
                <label>
                    Last name:
                    <input type="text" name="last" />
                    {if isset($last_error)}
                        {echo $last_error}
                    {/if}
                </label>
            </li>
            <li>
                <label>
                    Email:
                    <input type="text" name="email" />
                    {if isset($email_error)}
                        {echo $email_error}
                    {/if}
                </label>
            </li>
            <li>
                <label>
                    Password:
                    <input type="password" name="password" />
                    {if isset($password_error)}
                        {echo $password_error}
                    {/if}
                </label>
            </li>
            <li>
                <input type="submit" name="register" value="register" />
            </li>
        </ol>
    </form>
{/else}
```

This template is a simple form, with four fields and a button. If the success property is set (on the view) the success message will be displayed, otherwise the registration form will be displayed. Each field is composed of a label, an input, and an error message. We will set these error messages within the controller, but we want them to render in the view, in case there are any errors to display. You might notice that we are using some of the template tags our template parser supports.

Now that we have an HTML form for capturing the user's account data, we need an action to process this data. The perfect place for this is the `Users` controller, and the `register()` action. Before we can access the posted form data, we need to create a utility class that has the methods we will use. Listing 14-6 demonstrates how we accomplish this.

Listing 14-6. The RequestMethods Class

```
namespace Framework
{
    class RequestMethods
    {
        private function __construct()
        {
            // do nothing
        }

        private function __clone()
        {
            // do nothing
        }

        public static function get($key, $default = "")
        {
            if (!empty($_GET[$key]))
            {
                return $_GET[$key];
            }
            return $default;
        }

        public static function post($key, $default = "")
        {
            if (!empty($_POST[$key]))
            {
                return $_POST[$key];
            }
            return $default;
        }
```

```
        public static function server($key, $default = "")
        {
            if (!empty($_SERVER[$key]))
            {
                return $_SERVER[$key];
            }
            return $default;
        }
    }
}
```

This RequestMethods class is quite simple. It has methods for returning get/post/server variables, based on a key. If that key is not present, the default value will be returned. We use these methods to return our posted form data to the controller. Let's look at the Users->register() method, as shown in Listing 14-7.

Listing 14-7. The Users->register() Method

```
use Shared\Controller as Controller;
use Framework\Registry as Registry;
use Framework\RequestMethods as RequestMethods;

class Users extends Controller
{
    public function register()
    {
        if (RequestMethods::post("register"))
        {
            $first = RequestMethods::post("first");
            $last = RequestMethods::post("last");
            $email = RequestMethods::post("email");
            $password = RequestMethods::post("password");

            $view = $this->getActionView();
            $error = false;

            if (empty($first))
            {
                $view->set("first_error", "First name not provided");
                $error = true;
            }

            if (empty($last))
            {
                $view->set("last_error", "Last name not provided");
                $error = true;
            }

            if (empty($email))
            {
                $view->set("email_error", "Email not provided");
                $error = true;
            }
```

```
            if (empty($password))
            {
                $view->set("password_error", "Password not provided");
                $error = true;
            }

            if (!$error)
            {
                $user = new User(array(
                    "first" => $first,
                    "last" => $last,
                    "email" => $email,
                    "password" => $password
                ));

                $user->save();
                $view->set("success", true);
            }
        }
    }
}
```

The register() method does three important things. The first is retrieving the posted form data, for which it uses the RequestMethods::post() method. The second is checking each form field's value and creating error messages for missing values. The third thing it does is to create a new user row in the database, as long as no errors were found in the form data.

■ **Note** This is the most basic kind of validation. All we are doing is making sure the user has entered some value for each of the fields. Later, we will see how to extend our ORM to allow for more accurate data validation.

Now, completing the form and clicking the register button should insert a row into the user database table. If you see this row, give yourself a pat on the back. What you might also notice if that four of the fields have null values.

This may be permissible in terms of the database structure, but what we really want is for these values to be populated when the row is created, and then optionally updated from that point on. To achieve this automatic data population, we need to override the Shared\Model->save() method, as shown in Listing 14-8.

Listing 14-8. Overriding the save() Method for Default Population

```
public function save()
{
    $primary = $this->getPrimaryColumn();
    $raw = $primary["raw"];

    if (empty($this->$raw))
    {
        $this->setCreated(date("Y-m-d H:i:s"));
        $this->setDeleted(false);
```

```
        $this->setLive(true);
    }
    $this->setModified(date("Y-m-d H:i:s"));

    parent::save();
}
```

With this new method, every time a row is created these fields should be populated with default values. The next user account you register should now have these values in the row, even though we didn't explicitly set them within the controller.

Sessions

Sessions are temporary storage areas, which are linked to a web browser. The data stored in a session persists across different pages (on the same web site), and can be engineered to even survive browser restarts. For this reason, sessions are the perfect way to keep track of whether a user is logged in, or not.

The `Session` class, which we will now create, is very similar to the `Cache` class we created in Chapter 5. It is even possible to combine the two, but that's not something we are going to distract ourselves with. The `Session` class follows the factory patten we have seen in `Cache`, `Configuration`, and `Database`. Because you should already be familiar with the concepts involved, I will cover it only briefly. We begin with the `Session` factory class, as shown in Listing 14-9.

Listing 14-9. The Session Class

```
namespace Framework
{
    use Framework\Base as Base;
    use Framework\Registry as Registry;
    use Framework\Session as Session;
    use Framework\Session\Exception as Exception;

    class Session extends Base
    {
        /**
        * @readwrite
        */
        protected $_type;

        /**
        * @readwrite
        */
        protected $_options;

        protected function _getExceptionForImplementation($method)
        {
            return new Exception\Implementation("{$method} method not implemented");
        }

        protected function _getExceptionForArgument()
        {
            return new Exception\Argument("Invalid argument");
        }
```

```
        public function initialize()
        {
            $type = $this->getType();

            if (empty($type))
            {
                $configuration = Registry::get("configuration");

                if ($configuration)
                {
                    $configuration = $configuration->initialize();
                    $parsed = $configuration->parse("configuration/session");

                    if (!empty($parsed->session->default) && ➥
!empty($parsed->session->default->type))
                    {
                        $type = $parsed->session->default->type;
                        unset($parsed->session->default->type);

                        $this->__construct(array(
                            "type" => $type,
                            "options" => (array) $parsed->session->default
                        ));
                    }
                }
            }

            if (empty($type))
            {
                throw new Exception\Argument("Invalid type");
            }

            switch ($type)
            {
                case "server":
                {
                    return new Session\Driver\Server($this->getOptions());
                    break;
                }
                default:
                {
                    throw new Exception\Argument("Invalid type");
                    break;
                }
            }
        }
    }
}
```

The factory class begins with the automatic configuration we recently added to Cache and Configuration. The "server" driver is the only one we will create and it will be returned as an instance of Session\Driver\

Server. The Session\Driver class is virtually identical to the Cache\Driver and Configuration\Driver classes. The server driver, shown in Listing 14-10, is also fairly simple.

Listing 14-10. The Session\Driver\Server Class

```
namespace Framework\Session\Driver
{
    use Framework\Session as Session;

    class Server extends Session\Driver
    {
        /**
        * @readwrite
        */
        protected $_prefix = "app_";

        public function __construct($options = array())
        {
            parent::__construct($options);
            session_start();
        }

        public function get($key, $default = null)
        {
            $prefix = $this->getPrefix();

            if (isset($_SESSION[$prefix.$key]))
            {
                return $_SESSION[$prefix.$key];
            }

            return $default;
        }

        public function set($key, $value)
        {
            $prefix = $this->getPrefix();
            $_SESSION[$prefix.$key] = $value;
            return $this;
        }

        public function erase($key)
        {
            $prefix = $this->getPrefix();
            unset($_SESSION[$prefix.$key]);
            return $this;
        }

        public function __destruct()
        {
            session_commit();
        }
    }
}
```

The driver class uses PHP's built-in $_SESSION array, which contains key/value pairs of session data. Session values can be stored with the set() method. They can be retreived with the get() method, and removed with the erase() method. As social networks are all about user accounts, and are therefore deeply connected with user sessions, it makes sense that we added it to the bootstrap index.php.

Login

Login works similarly to how registration works, in as much as there is an HTML form and a special action to handle the creation of a session. The first step is to create the login template, as shown in Listing 14-11.

Listing 14-11. application/views/users/login.html

```
<h1>Login</h1>
<form method="post">
    <ol>
        <li>
            <label>
                Email:
                <input type="text" name="email" />
                {if isset($email_error)}
                    {echo $email_error}
                {/if}
            </label>
        </li>
        <li>
            <label>
                Password:
                <input type="password" name="password" />
                {if isset($password_error)}
                    {echo $password_error}
                {/if}
            </label>
        </li>
        <li>
            <input type="submit" name="login" value="login" />
        </li>
    </ol>
</form>
```

The login form is quite straightforward. It has just two fields, for e-mail address and password, which we will use in the Users->login() action, as demonstrated in Listing 14-12.

Listing 14-12. The Users->login() Action

```
public function login()
{
    if (RequestMethods::post("login"))
    {
        $email=RequestMethods::post("email");
        $password=RequestMethods::post("password");
```

```
        $view = $this->getActionView();
        $error = false;

        if (empty($email))
        {
            $view->set("email_error", "Email not provided");
            $error = true;
        }

        if (empty($password))
        {
           $view->set("password_error", "Password not provided");
           $error = true;
        }

        if (!$error)
        {
            $user = User::first(array(
                "email = ?" => $email,
                "password = ?" => $password,
                "live = ?" => true,
                "deleted = ?" => false
            ));

            if (!empty($user))
            {
                echo "success!";
            }
            else
            {
                echo "error!";
            }

            exit();
        }
    }
}
```

The `login()` action begins by retreiving the posted form values, and making sure they were provided. This happens in the same was as it did for the `register()` action. If the fields were provided, we use the `User::first()` model method to return the first matching database row. If a row is found, with the provided e-mail and password fields, we echo "`success!`", otherwise we echo "`error!`".

You might have noticed that our example is missing two very important things: the user's session must still be created, and we need this action to do something based on whether the user logged in successfully or not.

Let's first concentrate on what the `login()` action should do when the user successfully logs in. One option would be to present a message to the user, in the template, telling them they successfully logged in. It's not very user-friendly, though. It doesn't encourage them to go anywhere else, or do anything else. What would be better is if we redirected them to their profile page. For this to work, we need to create a basic profile page for them, as shown in Listing 14-13.

Listing 14-13. application/views/users/profile.html

```
<h1>{echo $user->first} {echo $user->last}</h1>
This is a profile page!
```

This is the most basic form of the profile page. It presents the user's first and last names, as well as a short description of what it is. If you are following me so far, you might be curious as to why the first and last names are not shown (in the h1 tag). The reason is that we are not yet creating or assigning the user session to the template. Let us do that by adding the `Users->profile()` action, which you can see in Listing 14-14.

Listing 14-14. The Users->profile() Action

```
public function profile()
{
    $session = Registry::get("session");
    $user = unserialize($session->get("user", null));

    if (empty($user))
    {
        $user = new StdClass();
        $user->first = "Mr.";
        $user->last = "Smith";
    }

    $this->getActionView()->set("user", $user);
}
```

The profile method gets the `Session` instance from the registry (the use statement allows me to use an alias of `Framework\Registry`). From out of the session, it gets the value for the `"user"` key, and unserializes it. If there is no `$user`, a default `$user` object is created, and finally the `$user` object is assigned to the template. Because we have not yet assigned the user row to the session, you should see Mr. Smith (in the h1 tag).

Let's assign the user row to the session, and complete this section. We modify the `login()` action to resemble that shown in Listing 14-15.

Listing 14-15. Extract of the Modified login() Action

```
if (!$error)
{
    $user = User::first(array(
        "email = ?" => $email,
        "password = ?" => $password,
        "live = ?" => true,
        "deleted = ?" => false
    ));

    if (!empty($user))
    {
        $session = Registry::get("session");
        $session->set("user", serialize($user));

        header("Location: /users/profile.html");
        exit();
    }
```

```
    else
    {
        $view->set("password_error", "Email address and/or password are incorrect");
    }
}
```

If the user row is found, the row object is serialized into a string representation of the original object. It is then stored in the session, and the user is redirected to the `/users/profile.html` controller/action. After the user gets to their destination, it will be possible for the `profile()` action to retreive the user object, and present the correct information on the profile page.

This completes the requirements set forth by our goals for this chapter. By now, you should have a fully functional registration and login system, which creates database records and saves to a session. It could do with a lot of polish (which we will be adding later on), but is, nonetheless, a fair achievement!

Note The PHP serialize/unserialize methods are useful for turning many kinds of PHP data types into their string representations. This is most useful for taking objects (in memory) and turning them into a format that is easy to store. We save the string representation of the user object to the session, as it is much easier to imagine saving such data to any kind of session provider. It's not strictly needed with server sessions, but the more portable we make the session management, the easier it will be to develop (and utilize) other session drivers. Think ahead!

I have included the following listings, for the sake of completeness. They outline the full structure of the `Users` controller (Listing 14-16), the `User` model (Listing 14-17), and the `Shared\Model` subclass (Listing 14-18).

Listing 14-16. The Users Controller

```
use Shared\Controller as Controller;
use Framework\Registry as Registry;
use Framework\RequestMethods as RequestMethods;

class Users extends Controller
{
    public function register()
    {
        if (RequestMethods::post("register"))
        {
            $first = RequestMethods::post("first");
            $last = RequestMethods::post("last");
            $email = RequestMethods::post("email");
            $password = RequestMethods::post("password");

            $view = $this->getActionView();
            $error = false;

            if (empty($first))
            {
                $view->set("first_error", "First name not provided");
                $error = true;
            }
```

```
        if (empty($last))
        {
            $view->set("last_error", "Last name not provided");
            $error=true;
        }

        if (empty($email))
        {
            $view->set("email_error", "Email not provided");
            $error=true;
        }

        if (empty($password))
        {
           $view->set("password_error", "Password not provided");
           $error=true;
        }

        if (!$error)
        {
            $user=new User(array(
                "first" =>$first,
                "last" =>$last,
                "email" =>$email,
                "password" =>$password
            ));

            $user->save();
            $view->set("success", true);
        }
    }
}

public function login()
{
    if (RequestMethods::post("login"))
    {
        $email=RequestMethods::post("email");
        $password=RequestMethods::post("password");

        $view=$this->getActionView();
        $error=false;

        if (empty($email))
        {
            $view->set("email_error", "Email not provided");
            $error=true;
        }
```

```
            if (empty($password))
            {
                $view->set("password_error", "Password not provided");
                $error = true;
            }

            if (!$error)
            {
                $user = User::first(array(
                    "email = ?" => $email,
                    "password = ?" => $password,
                    "live = ?" => true,
                    "deleted = ?" => false
                ));

                if (!empty($user))
                {
                    $session = Registry::get("session");
                    $session->set("user", serialize($user));

                    header("Location: /users/profile.html");
                    exit();
                }
                else
                {
                    $view->set("password_error", "Email address and/or password are incorrect");
                }
            }
        }
    }

    public function profile()
    {
        $session = Registry::get("session");
        $user = unserialize($session->get("user", null));

        if (empty($user))
        {
            $user = new StdClass();
            $user->first = "Mr.";
            $user->last = "Smith";
        }

        $this->getActionView()->set("user", $user);
    }
}
```

Listing 14-17. The User Model

```
class User extends Shared\Model
{
    /**
    * @column
    * @readwrite
    * @primary
    * @type autonumber
    */
    protected $_id;

    /**
    * @column
    * @readwrite
    * @type text
    * @length 100
    */
    protected $_first;

    /**
    * @column
    * @readwrite
    * @type text
    * @length 100
    */
    protected $_last;

    /**
    * @column
    * @readwrite
    * @type text
    * @length 100
    * @index
    */
    protected $_email;

    /**
    * @column
    * @readwrite
    * @type text
    * @length 100
    * @index
    */
    protected $_password;
}
```

Listing 14-18. The Shared\Model Class

```
namespace Shared
{
    class Model extends \Framework\Model
    {
        /**
        * @column
        * @readwrite
        * @type boolean
        * @index
        */
        protected $_live;

        /**
        * @column
        * @readwrite
        * @type boolean
        * @index
        */
        protected $_deleted;

        /**
        * @column
        * @readwrite
        * @type datetime
        */
        protected $_created;

        /**
        * @column
        * @readwrite
        * @type datetime
        */
        protected $_modified;

        public function save()
        {
            $primary = $this->getPrimaryColumn();
            $raw = $primary["raw"];

            if (empty($this->$raw))
            {
                $this->setCreated(date("Y-m-d H:i:s"));
                $this->setDeleted(false);
                $this->setLive(true);
            }
            $this->setModified(date("Y-m-d H:i:s"));

            parent::save();
        }
    }
}
```

Questions

1. Why did we subclass the `Controller` class to add database functionality?
2. PHP has built-in session management functions, some of which are even used in the `Session` classes we created. Why do we even need to create these `Session` classes?
3. What is the purpose of the `$_prefix` property of the `Session` driver class?

Answers

1. First, we chose the `Controller` class as the ideal place for the database code due to the fact that all of our application controllers will need access to the database. Second, the reason we subclass `Controller`, instead of modifying the original, is because this is clearly in the territory of application requirements. Not all applications will require a database connection; therefore, it should be decided per application.
2. We do, in fact, use some of PHP's built-in session management code, but there are two reasons why it is still a good idea to create these classes. The first is that working with sessions (in PHP) requires opening the session before, and closing the session after, any changes to the session data. We no longer have to repeat that code every time we work with the session. The second reason is that we are free to create any number of session drivers, which might not use the default session management code.
3. We prefix all session keys for the same reason that all our framework code is organized in namespaces. Namely, we don't know what other server code will be running alongside our framework. Likewise, we do not know what other systems will be using the same session space. The best thing for us to do is avoid collisions by prefixing all session keys.

Exercises

1. Our `Controller` subclass opens a connection to the database, but does not close it. This isn't usually a problem (for systems with many resources to throw around), but it would be ideal for the connection to be closed when no longer in use. Now add the additional code to close the connection to the database. Be careful not to close the connection too early.
2. Our `Session` classes only use the native PHP sessions. Now add another driver that uses some other form of storage to manage sessions. You can use files or cache, or anything you like. Just be sure to keep each user's session data private!

CHAPTER 15

Search

In the last chapter, we took our first look at how to use basic views, and perform basic validation. In this chapter, we will look at a few ways to extend our views, as well as building a user search page.

Goals

- We need to improve our template renderer to be able to include subtemplates, load third-party HTML, and store and retrieve data.
- We need to create the necessary action and view to facilitate user searching.

In order for us to understand the new template language constructs we will be adding to the template implementation, we need to look at the examples shown in Listing 15-1.

Listing 15-1. Additional Template Grammar

```
{include tracking.html}

{partial messages/feed.html}

{set scripts}
    <script src="/scripts/shared.js"></script>
{/set}

{prepend meta.title}
    Social Network
{/prepend}

{append styles}
    <link rel="stylesheet" type="text/css" href="/styles/widget.css" />
{/append}

{yield meta.title}
{yield scripts}
{yield styles}
```

The `include` construct should instruct the template parser to fetch the contents of the `tracking.html` file (within the default application view folder) and place its contents directly into the template (to be processed with the main template).

Similarly, the partial construct should instruct the template parser to make a GET request to the provided URL, and place the results into the main template. While the include construct will return executable (subtemplate) code to the main template, the partial construct should return only the string results of a GET request to the main template.

The set construct should instruct the template parser to take the data, contained within the opening/closing tags, and store it. This storage should be shared between all parsed templates, and any template should be able to retrieve the data stored. The append/prepend constructs are similar to the set construct, but they will not replace the data stored in a key. The prepend construct will insert the provided data before anything already stored in the same key, while the append construct will place the provided data after anything already stored in the same key.

Finally, the yield construct will return any data stored, for that key, in the shared storage area.

Extended Implementation

We begin our extended template implementation by adding a few new protected properties to our implementation subclass. We also need to adjust the language map, which defines that grammar of our template language. Take a look at Listing 15-2 to see how we accomplish this.

Listing 15-2. The Template\Implementation\Extended Class

```
namespace Framework\Template\Implementation
{
    use Framework\Request as Request;
    use Framework\Registry as Registry;
    use Framework\Template as Template;
    use Framework\StringMethods as StringMethods;
    use Framework\RequestMethods as RequestMethods;

    class Extended extends Standard
    {
        /**
        * @readwrite
        */
        protected $_defaultPath = "application/views";

        /**
        * @readwrite
        */
        protected $_defaultKey = "_data";

        /**
        * @readwrite
        */
        protected $_index = 0;

        public function __construct($options = array())
        {
            parent::__construct($options);

            $this->_map = array(
                "partial" =>array(
                    "opener" => "{partial",
```

```
                "closer" => "}",
                "handler" => "_partial"
            ),
            "include" => array(
                "opener" => "{include",
                "closer" => "}",
                "handler" => "_include"
            ),
            "yield" => array(
                "opener" => "{yield",
                "closer" => "}",
                "handler" => "yield"
            )
        ) + $this->_map;

        $this->_map["statement"]["tags"] = array(
            "set" => array(
                "isolated" => false,
                "arguments" => "{key}",
                "handler" => "set"
            ),
            "append" => array(
                "isolated" => false,
                "arguments" => "{key}",
                "handler" => "append"
            ),
            "prepend" => array(
                "isolated" => false,
                "arguments" => "{key}",
                "handler" => "prepend"
            )
        ) + $this->_map["statement"]["tags"];
    }
  }
}
```

The first three template constructs we want to add are single-tag constructs, so we add them to the main `$_map` array. This means our template parser won't go looking for closing tags, or creating hierarchies from the child data.

The last three template constructs, on the other hand, are statements (with opening/closing tags and child data). These we add to the statements subarray, where they will be parsed in the same way as the `if/else` loop constructs are parsed.

Next, we need to create the handlers for each of these new constructs. The first one we will tackle is the `_include()` handler, shown in Listing 15-3.

Listing 15-3. The _include() Handler

```
protected function _include($tree, $content)
{
    $template = new Template(array(
        "implementation" => new self()
    ));
```

```
    $file = trim($tree["raw"]);
    $path = $this->getDefaultPath();
    $content = file_get_contents(APP_PATH."/{$path}/{$file}");

    $template->parse($content);
    $index = $this->_index++;

    return "function anon_{$index}(\$_data){
        ".$template->getCode()."
    };\$_text[] = anon_{$index}(\$_data);";
}
```

The goal of this construct is to fetch a subtemplate and place it within the main template. The subtemplate should be processed at the same time as the main template, so that any logic can happen at the same time. This is one way that the templates can communicate with each other to share data.

We begin by creating a new `Template` instance, using this implementation. That means the subtemplates can have subtemplates of their own, and also have access to the other new template constructs.

We fetch the contents of the file (the name of which is provided in the `include` tag). We then parse the template instance, providing the template file contents. The trick is to create a new method for each included template, so that the processing can all happen at the same time. The functions generated by each `Template` instance return a string, so all we need to do is wrap this functionality within a new function and call it immediately (adding its return value to the `$_text` array). This means the main template will call the results of the subtemplate, when the main template is processed. This is perhaps the trickiest of all the new template constructs we are adding.

URL Requests

The next construct requires a new set of classes that will allow us to make HTTP requests to remote URLs. You can see the first of these `Request` classes in Listing 15-4.

Listing 15-4. The Request Class

```
namespace Framework
{
    use Framework\Base as Base;
    use Framework\StringMethods as StringMethods;
    use Framework\RequestMethods as RequestMethods;
    use Framework\Request\Exception as Exception;

    class Request extends Base
    {
        protected $_request;

        /**
        * @readwrite
        */
        public $_willFollow = true;

        /**
        * @readwrite
        */
        protected $_headers = array();
```

```
        /**
        * @readwrite
        */
        protected $_options = array();

        /**
        * @readwrite
        */
        protected $_referer;

        /**
        * @readwrite
        */
        protected $_agent;

        protected function _getExceptionForImplementation($method)
        {
            return new Exception\Implementation("{$method} not implemented");
        }

        protected function _getExceptionForArgument()
        {
            return new Exception\Argument("Invalid argument");
        }

        public function __construct($options = array())
        {
            parent::__construct($options);
            $this->setAgent(RequestMethods::server("HTTP_USER_AGENT", ➥
"Curl/PHP ".PHP_VERSION));
        }

        public function delete($url, $parameters = array())
        {
            return $this->request("DELETE", $url, $parameters);
        }

        function get($url, $parameters = array())
        {
            if (!empty($parameters))
            {
                $url .= StringMethods::indexOf($url, "?") ? "&" : "?";
                $url .= is_string($parameters) ? $parameters : ➥
http_build_query($parameters, "", "&");
            }
            return $this->request("GET", $url);
        }

        function head($url, $parameters = array())
        {
            return $this->request("HEAD", $url, $parameters);
        }
```

```
        function post($url, $parameters = array())
        {
            return $this->request("POST", $url, $parameters);
        }

        function put($url, $parameters = array())
        {
            return $this->request("PUT", $url, $parameters);
        }
    }
}
```

The Request class has all of the usual Base subclass goodies, as well as some request methods (get, post, put, delete, and head). These represent the different types of request methods, but ultimately they all call the same request() method. Other things to note are that the constructor sets the user agent, and the get method turns a provided parameter array into a valid querystring.

The request() method, shown in Listing 15-5, is responsible for doing (or delegating) the real work.

Listing 15-5. The request() Method

```
function request($method, $url, $parameters = array())
{
    $request = $this->_request = curl_init();

    if (is_array($parameters))
    {
        $parameters = http_build_query($parameters, "", "&");
    }

    $this
        ->_setRequestMethod($method)
        ->_setRequestOptions($url, $parameters)
        ->_setRequestHeaders();

    $response = curl_exec($request);

    if ($response)
    {
        $response = new Request\Response(array(
            "response" => $response
        ));
    }
    else
    {
        throw new Exception\Response(curl_errno($request).' - '.curl_error($request));
    }

    curl_close($request);
    return $response;
}
```

The `request()` method (and the `Request` classes in general) use *Curl* to make the HTTP requests. The method begins by creating a new `curl` resource instance and continues by setting some parameters of the instance. It then makes the request, and if the request is successful, it will be returned in the form of a `Request\Response` class instance. If the request fails, an exception will be raised.

Finally, the `curl` resource is destroyed and the response is returned. Before we dive into the `Request\Response` class, we need to look at those setter methods shown in Listing 15-6.

Listing 15-6. Request Setter Methods

```
protected function _setOption($key, $value)
{
    curl_setopt($this->_request, $key, $value);
    return $this;
}

protected function _normalize($key)
{
    return "CURLOPT_".str_replace("CURLOPT_", "", strtoupper($key));
}

protected function _setRequestMethod($method)
{
    switch (strtoupper($method))
    {
        case "HEAD":
            $this->_setOption(CURLOPT_NOBODY, true);
            break;
        case "GET":
            $this->_setOption(CURLOPT_HTTPGET, true);
            break;
        case "POST":
            $this->_setOption(CURLOPT_POST, true);
            break;
        default:
            $this->_setOption(CURLOPT_CUSTOMREQUEST, $method);
            break;
    }

    return $this;
}

protected function _setRequestOptions($url, $parameters)
{
    $this
        ->_setOption(CURLOPT_URL, $url)
        ->_setOption(CURLOPT_HEADER, true)
        ->_setOption(CURLOPT_RETURNTRANSFER, true)
        ->_setOption(CURLOPT_USERAGENT, $this->getAgent());

    if (!empty($parameters))
```

```
    {
        $this->_setOption(CURLOPT_POSTFIELDS, $parameters);
    }

    if ($this->getWillFollow())
    {
        $this->_setOption(CURLOPT_FOLLOWLOCATION, true);
    }

    if ($this->getReferer())
    {
        $this->_setOption(CURLOPT_REFERER, $this->getReferer());
    }

    foreach ($this->_options as $key => $value)
    {
        $this->_setOption(constant($this->_normalize($key)), $value);
    }

    return $this;
}

protected function _setRequestHeaders()
{
    $headers = array();

    foreach ($this->getHeaders() as $key =>$value)
    {
        $headers[] = $key.': '.$value;
    }

    $this->_setOption(CURLOPT_HTTPHEADER, $headers);
    return $this;
}
```

The `_setOption()` and `_normalize()` methods are convenience methods for tasks that we will perform within the three important `Request` setter methods. If you are familiar with the PHP Curl class, they will be old hat to you.

■ **Note** You can read more about the PHP Curl class at `http://www.php.net/manual/en/book.curl.php`.

The `_setRequestMethod()` method sets Curl parameters relating to each of the different request methods. Some request methods need additional parameters set (such as `GET` and `POST`), while others need things excluded from the response (such as `HEAD`).

The `_setRequestOptions()` method iterates through all the request-specific parameters that need to be set. This includes the URL, the user agent, whether the request should follow redirects, and so on. It even adds any options specified by the use of the `setOptions()` setter method (or construction option).

Finally, the `_setRequestHeaders()` method iterates through the headers specified by the `setHeaders()` setter method (or construction options) to add any custom headers to the request.

The Request\Response class is responsible for processing the results of the HTTP request, as shown in Listing 15-7.

Listing 15-7. The Request\Response Class

```
namespace Framework\Request
{
    use Framework\Base as Base;
    use Framework\Request\Exception as Exception;

    class Response extends Base
    {
        protected $_response;

        /**
        * @read
        */
        protected $_body = null;

        /**
        * @read
        */
        protected $_headers = array();

        protected function _getExceptionForImplementation($method)
        {
            return new Exception\Implementation("{$method} not implemented");
        }

        protected function _getExceptionForArgument()
        {
            return new Exception\Argument("Invalid argument");
        }

        function __construct($options = array())
        {
            if (!empty($options["response"]))
            {
                $response = $this->_response = $options["response"];
                unset($options["response"]);
            }

            parent::__construct($options);

            $pattern = '#HTTP/\d\.\d.*?$.*?\r\n\r\n#ims';
            preg_match_all($pattern, $response, $matches);

            $headers = array_pop($matches[0]);
            $headers = explode("\r\n", str_replace("\r\n\r\n", "", $headers));

            $this->_body = str_replace($headers, "", $response);
```

```
            $version = array_shift($headers);
            preg_match('#HTTP/(\d\.\d)\s(\d\d\d)\s(.*)#', $version, $matches);

            $this->_headers["Http-Version"] = $matches[1];
            $this->_headers["Status-Code"] = $matches[2];
            $this->_headers["Status"] = $matches[2]." ".$matches[3];

            foreach ($headers as $header)
            {
                preg_match('#(.*?)\:\s(.*)#', $header, $matches);
                $this->_headers[$matches[1]] = $matches[2];
            }
        }

        function __toString()
        {
            return $this->getBody();
        }
    }
}
```

The Request\Response class is relatively simple. It accepts a response constructor option, which is the result of an HTTP request. It splits this response string into headers and a body, which are available through getter methods.

Listing 15-8 shows how these classes are used in the creation of our second template construct: the partial construct.

Listing 15-8. The _partial() Handler

```
protected function _partial($tree, $content)
{
    $address = trim($tree["raw"], " /");
    if (StringMethods::indexOf($address, "http") != 0)
    {
        $host = RequestMethods::server("HTTP_HOST");
        $address = "http://{$host}/{$address}";
    }

    $request = new Request();
    $response = addslashes(trim($request->get($address)));
    return "\$_text[] = \"{$response}\";";
}
```

The `_partial()` handler accepts a URL (`$address`) that can either be absolute (e.g., `http://www.google.com`) or relative to the same application (e.g., `http://localhost/messages/feed.html`). If the URL does not start with http then we will treat it as a relative URL and adjust it accordingly. We make a `GET` request to the URL and return the results to the template's `$_text` array, where it will be rendered to the final template output.

Next, we need to add the three utility methods shown in Listing 15-9, which we will then use in the remaining template constructs.

Listing 15-9. Extended Implementation Utility Methods

```
protected function _getKey($tree)
{
    if (empty($tree["arguments"]["key"]))
    {

        return null;
    }

    return trim($tree["arguments"]["key"]);
}

protected function _setValue($key, $value)
{
    if (!empty($key))
    {
        $default = $this->getDefaultKey();

        $data = Registry::get($default, array());
        $data[$key] = $value;

        Registry::set($default, $data);
    }
}

protected function _getValue($key)
{
    $data = Registry::get($this->getDefaultKey());

    if (isset($data[$key]))
    {
        return $data[$key];
    }

    return "";
}
```

The `_getKey()` method simply extracts the provided storage key from the language constructs. The `_setValue()` method offers the solution to storage that can be accessed from everywhere. In the past, we have used the `Registry` class to store class instances, but the beauty of this is that we can also store plain objects and arrays. This method retrieves the data array (or defaults with a blank array) and sets the `$key`/`$value` provided. It then stores the data array back in the registry. Finally, the `_getValue()` method queries the stored data array for the value matching the provided `$key`.

With these methods created, we can look at the final template constructs, beginning with the `set` construct shown in Listing 15-10.

Listing 15-10. The set() Handler

```
public function set($key, $value)
{
    if (StringMethods::indexOf($value, "\$_text") > -1)
```

```
    {
        $first = StringMethods::indexOf($value, "\"");
        $last = StringMethods::lastIndexOf($value, "\"");
        $value = stripslashes(substr($value, $first+1, ($last - $first) - 1));
    }

    if (is_array($key))
    {
        $key = $this->_getKey($key);
    }

    $this->_setValue($key, $value);
}
```

The `set()` handler is curious for two reasons. The first is that it is the first public construct handler we have used in any of our template implementations. This is because we want to allow for the shared storage to be accessed not only within our template files, but also from within our application's controllers and actions.

The second reason the `set()` method is interesting is that it modifies the value string from something resembling `$_text = "foo";` to something resembling `foo`. This is because of how our `Template` class parses text nodes within our template files. If you refer back to the `Template->_script()` method, you will see one of the first things we do is convert plain text nodes to code that adds them directly to the `$_text` array. This is desired behavior, which we need to revert in this fringe case.

We do this by removing everything up to the first " character and everything after the last " character. This gives us the raw data, which is what we want to store.

Next, we tackle the `prepend()` and `append()` handlers, shown in Listing 15-11.

Listing 15-11. The prepend() and append() Handlers

```
public function append($key, $value)
{
    if (is_array($key))
    {
        $key = $this->_getKey($key);
    }

    $previous = $this->_getValue($key);
    $this->set($key, $previous.$value);
}

public function prepend($key, $value)
{
    if (is_array($key))
    {
        $key = $this->_getKey($key);
    }

    $previous = $this->_getValue($key);
    $this->set($key, $value.$previous);
}
```

Like the `set()` handler, these handler methods are also public. They too allow either a string or node tree to be supplied as the `$key`. If a node tree is provided, the `_getKey()` method will be used to extract the storage key needed.

The final, new template construct is the yield construct, shown in Listing 15-12.

Listing 15-12. The yield() Handler

```
public function yield($tree, $content)
{
    $key = trim($tree["raw"]);
    $value = addslashes($this->_getValue($key));
    return "\$_text[] = \"{$value}\";";
}
```

The yield() handler is the simplest of all the new constructs, and does pretty much the same thing as the standard implementation's _literal() handler method.

■ **Note** Remember to adjust the View class to utilize this new Template\Implementation\Extended class or you will not be able to use the new constructs.

Search

Adding the search page is going to be quite a bit easier after the work we have just done. We already have a login page, and we can now use the partial template rendering we just added to the extended template implementation.

The goal is simple: we should add consistent navigation to the application, which will allow logged in users to get to logout/settings/profile, and logged out users to get to login/register/search. We start by generating the navigation links in a new view file, as shown in Listing 15-13.

Listing 15-13. application/views/nagivation.html

```
<a href="/">home</a>
{if (isset($user))}
    <a href = "/users/profile.html">profile</a>
    <a href = "/users/settings.html">settings</a>
    <a href = "/users/logout.html">logout</a>
{/if}
{else}
    <a href = "/users/register.html">register</a>
    <a href = "/users/login.html">login</a>
{/else}
```

The logic is simple: if the template has a $user variable, then the user is logged in and we should present alternate links. You might be wondering where this variable is set, so let's recap how the login system works.

A user enters their e-mail address and password. These fields are then submitted to the login() action, which requests a user row from the database. If a row is returned, the row will be serialized and stored in the session.

It might seem strange to depend on the presence of a variable, within a file that will be included in almost every page of our application. Doesn't that mean we will constantly have to draw the serialized user row from the session and assign it to the view? In a manner of speaking, that is exactly what we need to do. The way we will achieve this is to add the logic for the retrieval and deserialization to the shared Controller subclass, by altering the __construct() method, as shown in Listing 15-14.

Listing 15-14. Modified __construct() Method

```
/**
* @readwrite
*/
protected $_user;

public function __construct($options = array())
{
    parent::__construct($options);

    $database = \Framework\Registry::get("database");
    $database->connect();

    $session = \Framework\Registry::get("session");
    $user = unserialize($session->get("user", null));
    $this->setUser($user);
}
```

We add a new property to the `Shared\Controller` class. In the `__construct()` method, after setting up the database, we draw the user row from the session and deserialize it. After this, we set the controller's `$_user` property, so it will effectively be available to every application controller.

How then do we assign it to the view? Our original framework `Controller` class has a render method, which is responsible for issuing the render commands on the layout and action views. We can override this method, and add our user logic to it, as demonstrated in Listing 15-15.

Listing 15-15. Modified render() Method

```
public function render()
{
    if ($this->getUser())
    {
        if ($this->getActionView())
        {
            $this->getActionView()
                ->set("user", $this->getUser());
        }

        if ($this->getLayoutView())
        {
            $this->getLayoutView()
                ->set("user", $this->getUser());
        }
    }

    parent::render();
}
```

After checking whether the user is set, we assign it to both the layout and action views. This is so that it can be used in both. We could store it in the shared storage, but we would be limited to yielding the whole object. Doing it this way lets us access the properties of the session user object.

Note Other than determining which links to show in our navigation, we don't really make heavy use of the user session in this chapter. It will come in handy in the next chapter when we create the user settings page.

We can now build the action and view for searching, as shown in Listing 15-16.

Listing 15-16. The search() Action

```
public function search()
{
    $view = $this->getActionView();

    $query = RequestMethods::post("query");
    $order = RequestMethods::post("order", "modified");
    $direction = RequestMethods::post("direction", "desc");
    $page = RequestMethods::post("page", 1);
    $limit = RequestMethods::post("limit", 10);

    $count = 0;
    $users = false;

    if (RequestMethods::post("search"))
    {
        $where = array(
            "SOUNDEX(first) = SOUNDEX(?)" => $query,
            "live = ?" => true,
            "deleted = ?" => false
        );

        $fields = array(
            "id", "first", "last"
        );

        $count = User::count($where);
        $users = User::all($where, $fields, $order, $direction, $limit, $page);
    }

    $view
        ->set("query", $query)
        ->set("order", $order)
        ->set("direction", $direction)
        ->set("page", $page)
        ->set("limit", $limit)
        ->set("count", $count)
        ->set("users", $users);
}
```

The `search()` action does a few important things. It begins by setting some defaults that will be overridden by posted form field data. It is good to remember that our search form will have fields by default, and then populate these fields with whatever form data was previously submitted. The defaults need to be sensible, and will be used for the first (and subsequent) queries.

If there is posted form data available, it then attempts to draw database user rows, based on a query. We are actually performing two queries: first getting a count of rows matching the conditions, and then returning a limited set (or page) of user rows.

The reason we need to get a count of all the matching rows is so that we can render accurate page counts, so users can navigate beyond the first page of rows. The `search()` action ends by assigning all of the variables we worked with, to the view.

Next, we need to create a fairly large view, in two main parts. We begin with the form fields that will be used to search for user rows, as shown in Listing 15-17.

Listing 15-17. application/views/users/search.html (Extract)

```
<h1>Search</h1>
<form method="post">
    <ol>
        <li>
            <label>
                Query:
                <input type="text" name="query" value="{echo $query}" />
            </label>
        </li>
        <li>
            <label>
                Order:
                <select name="order">
                    <option {if $order == "created"}selected="selected"{/if} ➥
value="created">Created</option>
                    <option {if $order == "modified"}selected="selected"{/if} ➥
value="modified">Modified</option>
                    <option {if $order == "first"}selected="selected"{/if} ➥
 value="first">First name</option>
                    <option {if $order == "last"}selected="selected"{/if} ➥
 value="last">Last name</option>
                 </select>
             </label>
         </li>
         <li>
             <label>
                 Direction:
                 <select name="direction">
                     <option {if $direction == "asc"}selected="selected"{/if} ➥
value="asc">Ascending</option>
                    <option {if $direction == "desc"}selected="selected"{/if} ➥
value="desc">Descending</option>
                 </select>
             </label>
         </li>
         <li>
             <label>
                 Page:
                 <select name = "page">
                     {if $count == 0}
                         <option value = "1">1</option>
```

```
                {/if}
                {else}
                    {foreach $_page in range(1, ceil($count / $limit))}
                        <option {if $page == $_page}selected = "selected"{/if} ➥
value= "{echo $_page}">{echo $_page}</option>
                    {/foreach}
                {/else}
            </select>
        </label>
    </li>
    <li>
        <label>
            Limit:
            <select name= "limit">
                <option {if $limit == "10"}selected= "selected"{/if} value= "10" >10</option>
                <option {if $limit == "20"}selected= "selected"{/if} value= "20" >20</option>
                <option {if $limit == "30"}selected= "selected"{/if} value= "30" >30</option>
            </select>
        </label>
    </li>
    <li>
        <input type= "submit" name= "search" value= "search" />
    </li>
</ol>
</form>
```

The first thing you should notice is that we do not wrap the form in any conditionals. It should always be visible (and prepopulated with previously posted data, where available). We can populate the fields with the variables we assigned, even if the form has not been posted, since we chose sensible default values.

The order and direction fields are relatively straightforward to understand—they are simply static fields. If any of the options match their respective post fields, they are selected by default. This helps to indicate to users which options were previously selected.

The page field is a little tricky. If there are no user rows in the `$users` variable, then this field applies only to the following query, in which case it only makes sense to go to page 1. If, on the other hand, there are user rows, this needs to take into account how many total matching rows there are, and render a list of possible page numbers. This is done by generating a range of page numbers between 1 and the total rows divided by the page size. We round this number up to account for a partial set of rows, at the end of the list. The limit field is a simple, static list of page sizes. All of these fields feed back into the query of user rows.

We also need to create a list of found user rows, as shown in Listing 15-18.

Listing 15-18. application/views/users/search.html (Extract)

```
{if $users != false}
    <table>
        <tr>
            <th>Name</th>
        </tr>
        {foreach $row in $users}
            <tr>
                <td>{echo $row->first} {echo $row->last}</td>
            </tr>
```

```
        {/foreach}
    </table>
{/if}
```

This code generates a simple table, containing the first/last names of the found users. In the next chapter, we will look at how to visit the users' profile pages, and add them as friends, so this serves as a good basis for that code.

Let us take one final look at the complete search template, as shown in Listing 15-19.

Listing 15-19. application/views/users/search.html (Complete)

```
<h1>Search</h1>
<form method = "post">
    <ol>
        <li>
            <label>
                Query:
                <input type="text" name="query" value="{echo $query}" />
            </label>
        </li>
        <li>
            <label>
                Order:
                <select name="order">
                    <option {if $order == "created"}selected="selected"{/if} ➥
 value="created">Created</option>
                    <option {if $order == "modified"}selected="selected"{/if} ➥
 value="modified">Modified</option>
                    <option {if $order == "first"}selected="selected"{/if} ➥
 value="first">First name</option>
                    <option {if $order == "last"}selected="selected"{/if} ➥
 value="last">Last name</option>
                </select>
            </label>
        </li>
        <li>
            <label>
                Direction:
                <select name = "direction">
                    <option {if $direction == "asc"}selected = "selected"{/if} ➥
 value="asc">Ascending</option>
                    <option {if $direction == "desc"}selected = "selected"{/if} ➥
 value="desc">Descending</option>
                </select>
            </label>
        </li>
        <li>
            <label>
                Page:
                <select name = "page">
                    {if $count == 0}
                        <option value = "1">1</option>
```

```
                {/if}
                {else}
                    {foreach $_page in range(1, ceil($count / $limit))}
                        <option {if $page == $_page}selected = "selected"{/if} ➥
value = "{echo $_page}">{echo $_page}</option>
                    {/foreach}
                {/else}
            </select>
        </label>
    </li>
    <li>
        <label>
            Limit:
            <select name="limit">
                <option {if $limit == "10"}selected="selected"{/if} value="10">10</option>
                <option {if $limit == "20"}selected="selected"{/if} value="20">20</option>
                <option {if $limit == "30"}selected="selected"{/if} value="30">30</option>
            </select>
        </label>
    </li>
    <li>
        <input type="submit" name="search" value="search" />
    </li>
  </ol>
</form>
{if $users != false}
    <table>
        <tr>
            <th>Name</th>
        </tr>
        {foreach $row in $users}
            <tr>
                <td>{echo $row->first} {echo $row->last}</td>
            </tr>
        {/foreach}
    </table>
{/if}
```

Questions

1. Why do we create a new template implementation for the new template tags we used in this chapter?
2. What is the difference between the partial/include template tags?
3. What is the difference between shared storage (prepend, set, append, yield) and template data values?

Answers

1. Our previous template implementation was actually sufficient for basic template rendering. It might not have been built with layouts or partial views in mind, but it is still a valid implementation. The extra tags take template rendering a step further, so it is better to have a good distinction between the standard template tags and the enhanced (extended) template tags.

2. The `include` tag makes an HTTP request to a URL, and injects the resulting text/html into the current template. The `partial` tag fetches the contents of another template and places it within the current template, so that both templates will be evaluated when the main template is rendered.

3. Assigning data to the shared storage (`prepend`, `set`, `append`, `yield`) allows the data to be accessed from any template scope, be it within the layout, action, or partials. It is best used for single-dimensional data, like strings or integers, since our tags do not allow the retrieval of subitems within a stored object. Template data values are assigned to an individual template, and are not accessible outside of that template's scope.

Exercises

1. We have discussed the difference between shared data storage (`prepend`, `set`, `append`, `yield`) and template data values. Now try creating additional (extended) template tags that allow for subitem access (e.g., `{yield scripts.shared}`) to objects in the shared storage.

2. Our `search()` action only searches by first names that sound the same (using `SOUNDEX`). Now add the last name field to the query.

3. Our `Request` class does not manage cookies. Try adding support for them now!

CHAPTER 16

Settings

In this chapter, we will be looking at how to better validate posted form data, by extending the Model class. This allows us to delegate a task typically involved with the data of our application to the model where data (or business logic) should dwell.

Goals

- We need to extend our Model class to include methods of posted form data validation, and to apply this validation before allowing rows to be added, updated, or deleted.
- We need to create the action and view for the settings page.

Validation

Getting validation right can be a tricky thing, particularly when the aim of MVC is to allow for good separation of concerns. Validation is connected to a number of unrelated components, mainly data types and views. The basic function of validation is to secure user input, but that has to come from somewhere (such as views/form data). That data has to relate to predefined data structures (such as database table fields), and validation needs to facilitate feedback to the user in such a way that they know what was wrong with the data they submitted.

Because we already have a fairly extensive ORM library, which we have contained in our model layer, we will be adding validation logic to the model layer. What we want to do is be able to define not only our database fields (at a model level), but also the validation through which their data must pass. Consider the example model shown in Listing 16-1.

Listing 16-1. Validating the Model

```
class User extends Shared\Model
{
    /**
    * @column
    * @readwrite
    * @primary
    * @type autonumber
    */
    protected $_id;
```

```
    /**
    * @column
    * @readwrite
    * @type text
    * @length 100
    *
    * @validate required, alpha, min(3), max(32)
    * @label first name
    */
    protected $_first;

    /**
    * @column
    * @readwrite
    * @type text
    * @length 100
    *
    * @validate required, alpha, min(3), max(32)
    * @label last name
    */
    protected $_last;

    /**
    * @column
    * @readwrite
    * @type text
    * @length 100
    * @index
    *
    * @validate required, max(100)
    * @label email address
    */
    protected $_email;

    /**
    * @column
    * @readwrite
    * @type text
    * @length 100
    * @index
    *
    * @validate required, min(8), max(32)
    * @label password
    */
    protected $_password;
}
```

We added two new metadata fields: `@validate` and `@label`. It would be ideal if these fields could be used to (1) define the validation that should be performed on the contained data, and (2) customize the validation error message that could be presented to the user. In order for us to achieve these two requirements, we need to modify the `Model` class.

■ **Note** Validation is a common requirement of web applications, so we can safely add it to the framework codebase. If the requirements were application-specific, we would consider creating a shared application library.

The first change we need to make to the Model class is to add a map of validation methods and messages, as shown in Listing 16-2.

Listing 16-2. Validation Map

```
/**
* @read
*/
protected $_validators = array(
    "required" =>array(
        "handler" => "_validateRequired",
        "message" => "The {0} field is required"
    ),
    "alpha" =>array(
        "handler" => "_validateAlpha",
        "message" => "The {0} field can only contain letters"
    ),
    "numeric" =>array(
        "handler" => "_validateNumeric",
        "message" => "The {0} field can only contain numbers"
    ),
    "alphanumeric" => array(
        "handler" => "_validateAlphaNumeric",
        "message" => "The {0} field can only contain letters and numbers"
    ),
    "max" =>array(
        "handler" => "_validateMax",
        "message" => "The {0} field must contain less than {2} characters"
    ),
    "min" =>array(
        "handler" => "_validateMin",
        "message" => "The {0} field must contain more than {2} characters"
    )
);

/**
* @read
*/
protected $_errors = array();
```

The $_validators array will be used by the Model class to determine the appropriate validation methods to perform (based on metadata). To illustrate this, a metadata flag resembling @validate required would lead to the execution of the _validateRequired() method (on the Model class), and present the error The {0} field is required. We will be substituting {0} with a proper value in a bit.

Next, we need to create the validation methods defined in the $_validators array, as demonstrated in Listing 16-3.

Listing 16-3. Validation Methods

```
protected function _validateRequired($value)
{
    return !empty($value);
}

protected function _validateAlpha($value)
{
    return StringMethods::match($value, "#^([a-zA-Z]+)$#");
}

protected function _validateNumeric($value)
{
    return StringMethods::match($value, "#^([0-9]+)$#");
}

protected function _validateAlphaNumeric($value)
{
    return StringMethods::match($value, "#^([a-zA-Z0-9]+)$#");
}

protected function _validateMax($value, $number)
{
    return strlen($value) <= (int) $number;
}

protected function _validateMin($value, $number)
{
    return strlen($value) >= (int) $number;
}
```

These validation methods are all reasonably simple, each performing the required validation and returning true for success or false for failure. We will want to remember this important behavior when we add custom field validation, in later chapters.

The basic functionality of the `validate()` method can be understood with the pseudocode shown in Listing 16-4.

Listing 16-4. How the validate() Method Functions

```
function validate
{
    set error flag to false

    for each column
    {
        if column must validate
        {
            for each condition
            {
                run condition validate method
```

```
                if validation failed
                {
                    make error message and save to array

                    set error flag to true
                }
            }
        }
    }

    return error flag
}
```

The actual validate() method, shown in Listing 16-5, is essentially the same, but with a few more details.

Listing 16-5. The validate() Method

```
public function validate()
{
    $this->_errors = array();
    $columns = $this->getColumns();

    foreach ($columns as $column)
    {
        if ($column["validate"])
        {
            $error = false;
            $pattern = "#[a-z]+\(([a-zA-Z0-9, ]+)\)#";

            $raw = $column["raw"];
            $name = $column["name"];
            $validators = $column["validate"];
            $label = $column["label"];

            $defined = $this->getValidators();

            foreach ($validators as $validator)
            {
                $function = $validator;
                $arguments = array(
                    $this->$raw
                );

                $match = StringMethods::match($validator, $pattern);

                if (count($match)>0)
                {
                    $matches = StringMethods::split($match[0], ",\s*");
                    $arguments = array_merge($arguments, $matches);
                    $offset = StringMethods::indexOf($validator, "(");
                    $function = substr($validator, 0, $offset);
                }
```

```
                if (!isset($defined[$function]))
                {
                    throw new Exception\Validation("The {$function} validator is not defined");
                }

                $template = $defined[$function];

                if (!call_user_func_array(array($this, $template["handler"]), $arguments))
                {
                    $replacements = array_merge(array(
                        $label ? $label : $raw
                    ), $arguments);

                    $message = $template["message"];
                    foreach ($replacements as $i => $replacement)
                    {
                        $message = str_replace("{{$i}}", $replacement, $message);
                    }

                    if (!isset($this->_errors[$name]))
                    {
                        $this->_errors[$name] = array();
                    }
                    $this->_errors[$name][] = $message;
                    $error = true;
                }
            }
        }
    }

    return !$error;
}
```

The `validate()` method begins by getting a list of columns and iterating over that list. For each column, we determine whether validation should occur. We then split the `@validate` metadata into a list of validation conditions. If a condition has arguments (e.g., `max(100)`), we extract the arguments.

We then run each validation method on the column data and generate error messages for those validation conditions that failed. We return a final `true/false` to indicate whether the complete validation passed or failed.

This changes a few things in our controllers. First, we no longer need to create separate validation logic in each action. The validation logic is defined in our models and applies any time we call the `validate()` method. Let us see how to modify the `register()` action, in our `Users` controller, as demonstrated in Listing 16-6.

Listing 16-6. The register() Action

```
public function register()
{
    $view = $this->getActionView();

    if (RequestMethods::post("register"))
    {
        $user = new User(array(
            "first" =>RequestMethods::post("first"),
```

```
            "last" =>RequestMethods::post("last"),
            "email" =>RequestMethods::post("email"),
            "password" =>RequestMethods::post("password")
        ));

        if ($user->validate())
        {
            $user->save();
            $view->set("success", true);
        }

        $view->set("errors", $user->getErrors());
    }
}
```

There are two main differences in this new `register()` action. The first is that we have removed the validation code from each of the form fields. This is now handled by the new `Model` validation logic. Furthermore, we can do all sorts of validation, instead of the simple (required) validation conditions we had before.

The second big change is that we first check the results of the `validate()` method before we save the `$user` row. Where before, we only created the new `User` instance after all our data was correct, we now do it before checking the data. As long as we don't save incorrect data, this difference doesn't matter much.

Our `register()` action is significantly shorter than the previous iteration. Future actions (which concern saving data to a database) should also be significantly shorter with this new validation code.

Validate As Required

You might be wondering why we didn't change our `login()` action. The `login()` action actually remains completely unmodified for two reasons:

- It gives more information than the user needs at login. They don't need to know what constitutes good first/last name data, or how many characters a password should be; they just need to know if their credentials allowed them to log in (or not).
- The new validation requires us to create a `User` instance before validating. This is the opposite of how the login should work. We want to return a user row if the credentials were valid, not the other way around.

It is important that we use this new validation at the right time. Adding it to the `login()` action is not ideal (for these reasons), and working around them will only further complicate our `login()` action.

Settings

In the previous chapter, we refactored the controller to automatically load the user session, and modified the navigation by adding a link to the settings page we were expecting to create. Now, we need to create a view for the settings page. It will resemble the registration page, since we want to be able to edit all of those fields. Take a look at Listing 16-7 to see how we accomplish this.

Listing 16-7. application/views/users/settings.html

```
<h1>Settings</h1>
{if isset($success)}
    Your account has been updated!
{/if}
```

```
{else}
    <form method="post">
        <ol>
            <li>
                <label>
                    First name:
                    <input type="text" name="first" value="{echo $user->first}" />
                </label>
            </li>
            <li>
                <label>
                    Last name:
                    <input type="text" name="last" value="{echo $user->last}" />
                </label>
            </li>
            <li>
                <label>
                    Email:
                    <input type="text" name="email" value="{echo $user->email}" />
                </label>
            </li>
            <li>
                <label>
                    Password:
                    <input type="password" name="password" value="{echo $user->password}" />
                </label>
            </li>
            <li>
                <input type="submit" name="update" value="update" />
            </li>
        </ol>
    </form>
{/else}
```

The only important deviation here is that we are populating all of the fields with their respective data, stored in the session user object.

■ **Note** It is better not to show the password in a production application, but it is done here for demonstration purposes. Passwords shouldn't even be saved in the user session, but it's not critical in our example application.

The `settings()` action also looks similar to the `register()` action, and is shown in Listing 16-8.

Listing 16-8. The settings() Method

```
public function settings()
{
    $view = $this->getActionView();
    $user = $this->getUser();
```

```
    if (RequestMethods::post("update"))
    {
        $user = new User(array(
            "first" => RequestMethods::post("first", $user->first),
            "last" => RequestMethods::post("last", $user->last),
            "email" => RequestMethods::post("email", $user->email),
            "password" => RequestMethods::post("password", $user->password)
        ));

        if ($user->validate())
        {
            $user->save();
            $view->set("success", true);
        }

        $view->set("errors", $user->getErrors());
    }
}
```

The `settings()` action is essentially identical to the `register()` action. If we look back to the registration view, we will remember that we had pretty simple error reporting (in the view). This is because we only had a single error message for each field, due to the simple validation.

If we had to incorporate the new validation mechanics, our registration page would look even more bloated, as demonstrated in Listing 16-9.

Listing 16-9. Bloated Registration View

```
<h1>Register</h1>
{if isset($success)}
    Your account has been created!
{/if}
{else}
    <form method="post">
        <ol>
            <li>
                <label>
                    First name:
                    <input type="text" name="first" />
                    {if (isset($errors["first"]))}
                        <br />{echo join("<br />", $errors["first"])}
                    {/if}
                </label>
            </li>
            <li>
                <label>
                    Last name:
                    <input type="text" name="last" />
                    {if (isset($errors["last"]))}
                        <br />{echo join("<br />", $errors["last"])}
                    {/if}
                </label>
```

```
            </li>
            <li>
                <label>
                    Email:
                    <input type="text" name="email" />
                    {if (isset($errors["email"]))}
                        <br />{echo join("<br />", $errors["email"])}
                    {/if}
                </label>
            </li>
            <li>
                <label>
                    Password:
                    <input type="password" name="password" />
                    {if (isset($errors["password"]))}
                        <br />{echo join("<br />", $errors["password"])}
                    {/if}
                </label>
            </li>
            <li>
                <input type="submit" name="register" value="register" />
            </li>
        </ol>
    </form>
{/else}
```

You might notice the repeated logic for iterating over the error messages. This can be separated out into a shared library, as shown in Listing 16-10.

Listing 16-10. application/libraries/shared/markup.php

```
namespace Shared
{
    class Markup
    {
        public function __construct()
        {
            // do nothing
        }

        public function __clone()
        {
            // do nothing
        }

        public static function errors($array, $key, $separator = "<br />", $before = ➥
"<br />", $after = "")
        {
            if (isset($array[$key]))
            {
                return $before.join($separator, $array[$key]).$after;
            }
```

```
            return "";
        }
    }
}
```

With this shared code available to all our views, we no longer have to deal with all the bloat. Both the settings/registration views are now a lot cleaner, as shown in Listing 16-11.

Listing 16-11. application/views/users/register.html (Extract)

```
<li>
    <label>
        First name:
        <input type="text" name ="first" />
        {echo Shared\Markup::errors($errors, "first")}
    </label>
</li>
<li>
    <label>
        Last name:
        <input type="text" name="last" />
        {echo Shared\Markup::errors($errors, "last")}
    </label>
</li>
<li>
    <label>
        Email:
        <input type="text" name="email" />
        {echo Shared\Markup::errors($errors, "email")}
    </label>
</li>
<li>
    <label>
        Password:
        <input type="password" name="password" />
        {echo Shared\Markup::errors($errors, "password")}
    </label>
</li>
```

■ **Note** Remember to update your settings view as well!

Before we tackle search, we need to take a look at our navigation links again. There is a link for logout, but we don't actually have that action yet. It's quite simple, as shown in Listing 16-12.

Listing 16-12. The logout() Action

```
public function logout()
{
    $this->setUser(false);
```

```
    $session = Registry::get("session");
    $session->erase("user");

    header("Location: /users/login.html");
    exit();
}
```

All this action does is set the controller's `$_user` property to false. It erases the user session object and redirects back to the login page. In other words, the user session will no longer exist after this action is called, which is exactly what we want!

Questions

1. In the previous chapters, all the form validation was done in the controller layer. Why did we move the form validation from the controller layer to the model layer?
2. Why should we bother with complicated password hashing when our database is protected by shell passwords and MySQL passwords?

Answers

1. Validation straddles the fine line between views/controllers and models. It concerns form data, so that makes it a good fit for the controller. The form data does, however, directly relate to the model structure, so it fits equally with the model code. Either is fine, but there is already a solid model/ORM structure defined, which is why I have chosen to package the code within the `Model` class.
2. Passwords should never be saved in plain-text format. All secure applications perform a nonreversible hash conversion of the password. This prevents them from knowing what the password is, but allows them to repeat the process in order to check whether a submitted password matches a password stored in the database.

Exercises

1. We added some basic validation types, but there are many more we could add. Try adding validation methods for e-mail addresses and date formats.
2. Try modifying the `login()`, `register()`, and `settings()` actions to perform this one-way conversion, while still allowing the user to log in successfully.

CHAPTER 17

Sharing

Relationships are at the heart of any social network. In the Chapter 16, we had a brief look at how to search for other social network users, and in this chapter we will make a way to befriend them! We will also explore the topic of status/link sharing, and integrate it all into an activity feed.

Goals

- We will create user-friendly error pages that present exception stack traces when the application is in debugging mode.
- We will create the models, actions, and views necessary to support adding/removing friends from our account.
- We will create the models, actions, and views necessary to be able to share messages, and read messages our friends have shared.

Error Pages

Error pages are an unavoidable part of any large application. We deal with them when programming, usually in the form of exceptions. We have already seen (and created) a number of `Exception` subclasses, but they aren't really useful to us unless we have a nice way to present the exception data (in the case of debugging) or a user-friendly error page, in the case of a public-facing application.

The difference between these two representations of errors is quite important. If you are intending on building a secure application, one of the first things you should do is disable error reporting. You don't want users seeing why your application is failing. This is not to say that users shouldn't be given advice on how to better use the system, as in the case of validation errors, but the average user should not be made aware that your application failed to connect to a database, or that a crucial class could not be loaded.

We will solve this problem by creating (and loading) special pages to inform the user that something has gone wrong. We will achieve this by first modifying the `public/index.php` bootstrap file, as shown in Listing 17-1.

Listing 17-1. public/index.php (Modified)

```
// constants

define("DEBUG", TRUE);
define("APP_PATH", dirname(dirname(__FILE__)));
```

```
try
{
    // core

    require("../framework/core.php");
    Framework\Core::initialize();

    // configuration

    $configuration = new Framework\Configuration(array(
        "type" => "ini"
    ));
    Framework\Registry::set("configuration", $configuration->initialize());

    // database

    $database = new Framework\Database();
    Framework\Registry::set("database", $database->initialize());

    // cache

    $cache = new Framework\Cache();
    Framework\Registry::set("cache", $cache->initialize());

    // session

    $session = new Framework\Session();
    Framework\Registry::set("session", $session->initialize());

    // router

    $router = new Framework\Router(array(
        "url" => isset($_GET["url"]) ? $_GET["url"] : "home/index",
        "extension" => isset($_GET["url"]) ? $_GET["url"] : "html"
    ));
    Framework\Registry::set("router", $router);

    $router->dispatch();

    // unset globals

    unset($configuration);
    unset($database);
    unset($cache);
    unset($session);
    unset($router);
}
catch (Exception $e)
{
    // list exceptions
```

```
$exceptions = array(
    "500" => array(
        "Framework\Cache\Exception",
        "Framework\Cache\Exception\Argument",
        "Framework\Cache\Exception\Implementation",
        "Framework\Cache\Exception\Service",

        "Framework\Configuration\Exception",
        "Framework\Configuration\Exception\Argument",
        "Framework\Configuration\Exception\Implementation",
        "Framework\Configuration\Exception\Syntax",

        "Framework\Controller\Exception",
        "Framework\Controller\Exception\Argument",
        "Framework\Controller\Exception\Implementation",

        "Framework\Core\Exception",
        "Framework\Core\Exception\Argument",
        "Framework\Core\Exception\Implementation",
        "Framework\Core\Exception\Property",
        "Framework\Core\Exception\ReadOnly",
        "Framework\Core\Exception\WriteOnly",

        "Framework\Database\Exception",
        "Framework\Database\Exception\Argument",
        "Framework\Database\Exception\Implementation",
        "Framework\Database\Exception\Service",
        "Framework\Database\Exception\Sql",

        "Framework\Model\Exception",
        "Framework\Model\Exception\Argument",
        "Framework\Model\Exception\Connector",
        "Framework\Model\Exception\Implementation",
        "Framework\Model\Exception\Primary",
        "Framework\Model\Exception\Type",
        "Framework\Model\Exception\Validation",

        "Framework\Request\Exception",
        "Framework\Request\Exception\Argument",
        "Framework\Request\Exception\Implementation",
        "Framework\Request\Exception\Response",

        "Framework\Router\Exception",
        "Framework\Router\Exception\Argument",
        "Framework\Router\Exception\Implementation",

        "Framework\Session\Exception",
        "Framework\Session\Exception\Argument",
        "Framework\Session\Exception\Implementation",

        "Framework\Template\Exception",
        "Framework\Template\Exception\Argument",
```

```
            "Framework\Template\Exception\Implementation",
            "Framework\Template\Exception\Parser",

            "Framework\View\Exception",
            "Framework\View\Exception\Argument",
            "Framework\View\Exception\Data",
            "Framework\View\Exception\Implementation",
            "Framework\View\Exception\Renderer",
            "Framework\View\Exception\Syntax"
        ),
        "404" => array(
            "Framework\Router\Exception\Action",
            "Framework\Router\Exception\Controller"
        )
    );

    $exception = get_class($e);

    // attempt to find the approapriate template, and render

    foreach ($exceptions as $template => $classes)
    {
        foreach ($classes as $class)
        {
            if ($class == $exception)
            {
                header("Content-type: text/html");
                include(APP_PATH."/application/views/errors/{$template}.php");
                exit;
            }
        }
    }

    // render fallback template

    header("Content-type: text/html");
    echo "An error occurred.";
    exit;
}
```

Our original `index.php` file has basically been wrapped in a giant `try/catch` control statement. This is so that we can intercept every exception the framework could raise, and display the appropriate error page. For this reason, we will ignore all of the old code, and focus on the error page presentation.

We begin by defining a full list of templates that correlate to the exceptions that should invoke them. This simple list defines two error page templates, but you are welcome to define as many as you see fit. After determining the class name of the exception, we iterate through this list of templates/exceptions in an attempt to find the appropriate template to display. If the class name of the raised exception matches one on the list, the corresponding template is rendered. Failing this, a fallback template is rendered.

■ **Note** If we need to perform additional logic, such as e-mailing an error report to an administrator, this will be the place to do so, and the added flexibility of exception types will only help the process! We may restrict this e-mail functionality if the type of exception is not important enough to warrant it.

There are two important points yet to note about this added code. The first is that we render the error page templates using an `include` statement. You might be wondering why we do that, if we have gone through the effort of creating an awesome view/template system. The reason is that the exceptions should be raised in the `View/Template` classes. It is hardly ideal that the exceptions we are trying to address could be caused by the code used to address them. For this reason, we need to use as little as possible of our framework code in order to render the error pages.

This brings us to the second important point, which is that the error page templates are PHP files. Using PHP files, we can use the error pages to present the PHP exception data, and act on the DEBUG constant we created. We can see this in action, by looking at the general layout of an error page, as demonstrated in Listing 17-2.

Listing 17-2. application/views/errors/404.php

```
<!DOCTYPE html>
<html>
    <head>
        <title>Social Network</title>
    </head>
    <body>
        error 404
        <?php if (DEBUG): ?>
            <pre><?php print_r($e); ?></pre>
        <?php endif; ?>
    </body>
</html>
```

The reality is that changes to the layouts will not affect these error documents. The result is that we will have some repeated view markup. On the other hand, we will have a secure application, which helps us debug the application, and presents user-friendly error pages.

■ **Note** Remember to set DEBUG to `false` when your code is in a production environment. You don't want the average Joe knowing the details of your code malfunctions.

Friends

Social networks are made of friends. Sometimes they are called *connections* or *followers*, but they are usually the same thing: other users. We have already built most of the details required to register and log into the application, but now we need to add the ability to connect with other users.

The first step is to create a `Friend` model, as shown in Listing 17-3.

Listing 17-3. The Friend Model

```
class Friend extends Shared\Model
{
    /**
    * @column
    * @readwrite
    * @type integer
    */
    protected $_user;

    /**
    * @column
    * @readwrite
    * @type integer
    */
    protected $_friend;
}
```

This Friend model expects the database table shown in Listing 17-4.

Listing 17-4. The friend table

```
CREATE TABLE `friend` (
  `user` int(11) DEFAULT NULL,
  `friend` int(11) DEFAULT NULL,
  `id` int(11) NOT NULL AUTO_INCREMENT,
  `live` tinyint(4) DEFAULT NULL,
  `deleted` tinyint(4) DEFAULT NULL,
  `created` datetime DEFAULT NULL,
  `modified` datetime DEFAULT NULL,
  PRIMARY KEY (`id`),
  KEY `live` (`live`),
  KEY `deleted` (`deleted`)
) ENGINE=InnoDB  DEFAULT CHARSET=utf8
```

Aside from this simple model, we need to create the actions to handle friending and unfriending. We add these to the `Users` controller, as demonstrated in Listing 17-5.

Listing 17-5. The friend()/unfriend() Actions

```
public function friend($id)
{
    $user = $this->getUser();

    $friend = new Friend(array(
        "user" => $user->id,
        "friend" => $id
    ));

    $friend->save();
```

```
    header("Location: /search.html");
    exit();
}

public function unfriend($id)
{
    $user = $this->getUser();

    $friend = Friend::first(array(
        "user" => $user->id,
        "friend" => $id
    ));

    if ($friend)
    {
        $friend = new Friend(array(
            "id" => $friend->id
        ));
        $friend->delete();
    }

    header("Location: /search.html");
    exit();
}
```

Using the `Friend` model that we just created, the actions for friending/unfriending are quite simple. In both, we retrieve the user session, so that we can get the ID of the logged in user. Combining this with the passed `$id` parameter, we either create a new friend row, or delete an existing friend row.

You might be curious as to why we redirect to `/search.html` instead of `/users/search.html`. Well, the simple answer is that we need to create custom routes to handle the friend/unfriend actions, so we will use this opportunity to shorten many of the URLs we have already seen, as shown in Listing 17-6.

Listing 17-6. public/routes.php

```
// define routes

$routes = array(
    array(
        "pattern" => "register",
        "controller" => "users",
        "action" => "register"
    ),
    array(
        "pattern" => "login",
        "controller" => "users",
        "action" => "login"
    ),
    array(
        "pattern" => "logout",
        "controller" => "users",
        "action" => "logout"
    ),
```

```
    array(
        "pattern" => "search",
        "controller" => "users",
        "action" => "search"
    ),
    array(
        "pattern" => "profile",
        "controller" => "users",
        "action" => "profile"
    ),
    array(
        "pattern" => "settings",
        "controller" => "users",
        "action" => "settings"
    ),
    array(
        "pattern" => "unfriend/?",
        "controller" => "users",
        "action" => "friend",
        "parameters" => array("id")
    ),
    array(
        "pattern" => "friend/?",
        "controller" => "users",
        "action" => "friend",
        "parameters" => array("id")
    )
);

// add defined routes

foreach ($routes as $route)
{
    $router->addRoute(new Framework\Router\Route\Simple($route));
}

// unset globals

unset($routes);
```

We begin creating our custom routes by defining an array of custom route initialization arrays. Right at the bottom you can see where we define the routes for the `friend()`/`unfriend()` actions. We simply iterate over this list of custom routes, creating and assigning instances of `Router\Route\Simple` to our router. Finally, we unset the array we define, so that the global namespace stays clean.

Before we move on, we need to plug this custom routes file into the bootstrap file, as demonstrated in Listing 17-7.

Listing 17-7. public/index.php (Extract)

```
// router

$router = new Framework\Router(array(
    "url" => isset($_GET["url"]) ? $_GET["url"] : "home/index",
    "extension" => isset($_GET["url"]) ? $_GET["url"] : "html"
```

```
));
Framework\Registry::set("router", $router);

// include custom routes

include("routes.php");

// dispatch request

$router->dispatch();
```

With these custom routes, we can now shorten the navigation links we created in Chapter 16, as shown in Listing 17-8.

Listing 17-8. application/views/navigation.html

```
<a href="/">home</a>
<a href="/search.html">search</a>
{if (isset($user))}
    <a href="/profile.html">profile</a>
    <a href="/settings.html">settings</a>
    <a href="/logout.html">logout</a>
{/if}
{else}
    <a href="/register.html">register</a>
    <a href="/login.html">login</a>
{/else}
```

The most logical place for users to friend/unfriend other users is on the search page. Remember that we created a list of users returned in the search results. We can modify this page by adding new links, as shown in Listing 17-9.

Listing 17-9. application/views/users/search.html (Extract)

```
<table>
    <tr>
        <th>Name</th>
        <th> </th>
    </tr>
    {foreach $row in $users}
        <tr>
            <td>{echo $row->first} {echo $row->last}</td>
            <td>
                <a href="/friend/{echo $row->id}.html">friend</a>
                <a href="/unfriend/{echo $row->id}.html">unfriend</a>
            </td>
        </tr>
    {/foreach}
</table>
```

At this point, if you are not logged in, you should see an error. This is because we are not yet securing actions by checking whether a valid user session exists. If you are wondering how we can easily do this, you should check back to when we created the `Inspector` class (in Chapter 3) and how we instantiated controllers (in Chapter 7). Let's look at the code required to secure our actions, as shown in Listing 17-10.

Listing 17-10. application/controllers/users.php (Extract)

```
/**
* @before _secure
*/
public function friend($id)
{
    // friend code
}

/**
* @before _secure
*/
public function unfriend($id)
{
    // unfriend code
}

/**
* @protected
*/
public function _secure()
{
    $user = $this->getUser();
    if (!$user)
    {
        header("Location: /login.html");
        exit();
    }
}
```

Adding the `@before` meta flag will tell the `Router` class that we want this method run before these actions. The `_secure()` has an `@protected` flag that will allow the `Inspector` class to discover it, while disallowing access through the router. This means that `_secure()`, while not accessible from a routing point of view, will be run before both the `friend()` and `unfriend()` actions. If the user session is not present, the user will be redirected to the login page.

■ **Note** It only makes sense to redirect to `/login.html` if your application is in the webroot. If it is within another folder, then a destination such as `/site/login.html` makes more sense. Be sure to secure the settings and profile actions, as these should also require a valid user session.

Being able to make friends isn't nearly as important as knowing who your friends are! At this point, we can use the friend/unfriend methods to modify database rows, but we also need to be able to tell whether another user is a friend of the current user. What we need to add, to the `User` model, is a method that will tell us this. Take a look at Listing 17-11 to see how we accomplish this.

Listing 17-11. The isFriend()/hasFriend() Methods

```
public function isFriend($id)
{
    $friend = Friend::first(array(
        "user" => $this->getId(),
        "friend" => $id
    ));

    if ($friend)
    {
        return true;
    }
    return false;
}

public static function hasFriend($id, $friend)
{
    $user = new self(array(
        "id" => $id
    ));
    return $user->isFriend($friend);
}
```

The `isFriend()` method does a simple database lookup to see where a linking record exists between the two users. The `hasFriend()` method is a convenient, static representation of the same method. If we plug this into our search page, it should look something like that shown in Listing 17-12.

Listing 17-12. application/views/users/search.html (Extract)

```
<table>
    <tr>
        <th>Name</th>
        <th> </th>
    </tr>
    {foreach $row in $users}
        <tr>
            <td>{echo $row->first} {echo $row->last}</td>
            <td>
                {if User::hasFriend($user->id, $row->id)}
                    <a href="/unfriend/{echo $row->id}.html">unfriend</a>
                {/if}
                {else}
                    <a href="/friend/{echo $row->id}.html">friend</a>
                {/else}
            </td>
        </tr>
    {/foreach}
</table>
```

With these new methods, displaying the correct link is an easy task. They also complete this section, as we can now easily search for and add new friends.

■ **Note** It would be a good idea to first check for preexisting links between users, before adding new ones.

Sharing

Sharing is a pretty huge deal. It is arguably the number-one reason people even use social networks in the first place. We are going to be creating a means for users to share status messages. We'll even allow them to comment on shared messages, and present all relevant messages in an activity feed for each user.

In order to store the message information, we need to create another model, as shown in Listing 17-13.

Listing 17-13. The Message Model

```
class Message extends Shared\Model
{
    /**
    * @column
    * @readwrite
    * @type text
    * @length 256
    *
    * @validate required
    * @label body
    */
    protected $_body;

    /**
    * @column
    * @readwrite
    * @type integer
    */
    protected $_message;

    /**
    * @column
    * @readwrite
    * @type integer
    */
    protected $_user;
}
```

This message model expects the database table shown in Listing 17-14.

Listing 17-14. The message table

```
CREATE TABLE `message` (
  `user` int(11) DEFAULT NULL,
  `message` int(11) DEFAULT NULL,
  `body` text DEFAULT NULL,
  `id` int(11) NOT NULL AUTO_INCREMENT,
  `live` tinyint(4) DEFAULT NULL,
  `deleted` tinyint(4) DEFAULT NULL,
```

```
  `created` datetime DEFAULT NULL,
  `modified` datetime DEFAULT NULL,
  PRIMARY KEY (`id`),
  KEY `live` (`live`),
  KEY `deleted` (`deleted`)
) ENGINE=InnoDB  DEFAULT CHARSET=utf8
```

Each message has a body, belongs to a user, and can be related to another message (which was shared earlier). Creating the actual messages is pretty easy: we first need to modify the home page to present all relevant, shared messages to the current user.

Let's see how to customize the Home controller to display a stream of messages from friends, as shown in Listing 17-15.

Listing 17-15. Message stream

```
public function index()
{
    $user = $this->getUser();
    $view = $this->getActionView();

    if ($user)
    {
        $friends = Friend::all(array(
            "user = ?" => $user->id,
            "live = ?" => true,
            "deleted = ?" => false
        ), array("friend"));

        $ids = array();
        foreach($friends as $friend)
        {
            $ids[] = $friend->friend;
        }

        $messages = Message::all(array(
            "user in ?" => $ids,
            "live = ?" => true,
            "deleted = ?" => false
        ), array(
            "*",
            "(SELECT CONCAT(first, \" \", last) FROM user WHERE user.id = message.user)" ➥
 => "user_name"
        ), "created", "asc");

        $view->set("messages", $messages);
    }
}
```

In order to get relevant messages, our modified index() action first needs to get all the linking rows. We then fetch all the messages linked to those users, after flattening the friend rows into a single-dimensional array of friend IDs. Finally, we assign the messages to the action view. The view markup is also quite simple, as you can see in Listing 17-16.

Listing 17-16. application/views/home/index.html

```
<h1>Home</h1>
{if isset($messages)}
    {foreach $message in $messages}
        {echo $message->body}<br />
    {/foreach}
{/if}
```

It's good that we have a way for users to see their friends' messages, but we also need to allow them to share their own messages. The first step is a new action on the `Messages` controller, as shown in Listing 17-17.

Listing 17-17. application/controllers/messages.php

```
use Shared\Controller as Controller;
use Framework\RequestMethods as RequestMethods;

class Messages extends Controller
{
    public function add()
    {
        $user = $this->getUser();

        if (RequestMethods::post("share"))
        {
            $message = new Message(array(
                "body" => RequestMethods::post("body"),
                "message" => RequestMethods::post("message"),
                "user" => $user->id
            ));

            if ($message->validate())
            {
                $message->save();
                header("Location: /");
                exit();
            }
        }
    }
}
```

The `Messages::add()` action is responsible for collecting posted form data into a new message database row. It performs the required validation, and if everything looks good will save the record and redirect back to the home page. Now we need to add a form to the home page, which users can use to post new messages. Take a look at Listing 17-18 to see how we do this.

Listing 17-18. application/views/home/index.html (Extract)

```
{if (isset($user))}
    <form method="post" action="/messages/add.html">
        <textarea name="body"></textarea>
        <input type="submit" name="share" value="share" />
    </form>
{/if}
```

This is one of the few forms we will create that posts to a different action. Because the `Messages::add()` action redirects back to this page, the journey won't be apparent to users. We don't specify a message field here, as any messages added through this form are not in reply to another message.

We do want to be able to reply to earlier messages, though. We also want to display replies, at the same time. Before we modify the home page further, we need to add some methods to the `Message` model, as demonstrated in Listing 17-19.

Listing 17-19. Message Model Methods

```
public function getReplies()
{
    return self::all(array(
        "message = ?" => $this->getId(),
        "live = ?" => true,
        "deleted = ?" => false
    ), array("*"), "created", "desc");
}
public static function fetchReplies($id)
{
    $message = new Message(array(
        "id" => $id
    ));
    return $message->getReplies();
}
```

The first method fetches a list of replies to a message. It also returns the `user_name` of the user who replied, and sorts the replies by their creation date, so that newer messages are displayed first. With these two methods, let's see how the home page changes, as shown in Listing 17-20.

Listing 17-20. application/views/home/index.html (Extract)

```
{if isset($messages)}
    {foreach $message in $messages}
        {echo $message->body}<br />
        {foreach $reply in Message::fetchReplies($message->id)}
                 {echo $reply->body}<br />
        {/foreach}
        <form method="post" action="/messages/add.html">
            <textarea name="body"></textarea>
            <input type="hidden" value="{echo $message->id}" name="message" />
            <input type="submit" name="share" value="share" />
        </form>
    {/foreach}
{/if}
```

The first thing to note is that nested messages/replies are rendered (using the methods we just created). The second thing to note is that we have a form for each main message. This is because each form needs a different message field to convey the message to which a user may be replying. The `Messages::add()` action handles both top-level messages, as well as replies.

Questions

1. Error pages are a common feature of most applications. Why do we add the logic to display them in the application bootstrap file?
2. Why is it important not to use a `Template` or `View` instance to render the error pages?
3. We created a large array of exception classes in the bootstrap file. Wouldn't this be better in a configuration file?
4. When we wanted to get replies, or check whether another user was our friend, we did so via model methods. Why not just check that sort of thing in the view or the controller?

Answers

1. Yes, error pages are a common feature of most of today's applications. However, the means for handling errors are not. We have chosen to raise exceptions in almost every instance where errors prevent the normal functioning of the application. For this reason, and in order to present the correct error pages, we inspect the type of exception that has been raised. How other applications handle their errors might differ. For this reason, the code is no longer application-agnostic, and the bootstrap becomes the most reasonable place for this logic.
2. We use an `include` statement to avoid any possible errors with using a `Template` or `View` instance. This is similar to how our testing code resides in the public folder. The more framework code required for handling error pages, the less we can afford for errors to occur within that code. The simplest solution is, therefore, to use as little framework code to test for/report on framework errors.
3. If an exception occurs in the configuration classes, and the error pages require those classes, the error pages won't be displayed.
4. The main goal of MVC is the separation of concerns. Fetching friends/replies are the concern of the model, and the corresponding code should be contained in the applicable models.

Exercises

1. The list of exception classes is quite specific, and quite lengthy. Now try specifying which error page must be displayed (within the exception class) and modifying the bootstrap file accordingly.
2. We created the `isFriend()`/`hasFriend()` methods to be able to tell which actions to present the user, but when we wanted to fetch a user's friends, we did so in the controller. Now see if you can create methods to fetch the friends straight from the `User` model.
3. To be able to reply to earlier messages, we had to create individual forms for each top-level message shared. The problem is that these forms are always visible, leading to an ugly page. Now try employing some PHP/JavaScript to show/hide different reply forms, by allowing the user to click a "reply" link.

CHAPTER 18

Photos

User profiles and status messages are only parts of the puzzle of social networks. As a developer, you cannot go far without encountering file uploads, and they form a large portion of many types of enterprise applications, social networks included.

However, file uploads are a strange beast. The logic required to achieve them varies greatly from platform to platform. Some platforms, such as ColdFusion, handle file uploads almost implicitly. Other platforms, like ASP classic, are nightmarish when it comes to this area of development.

PHP, on the other hand, requires a bit of work, but after you have the hang of it, file uploads are a breeze. We will begin this chapter with a brief introduction to the logic required for file uploads, and then progress to adding file-upload capabilities to our application.

Goals

- We will review the processes required to facilitate file uploads.
- We will then add upload functionality to the registration and settings pages (for profile photos).
- Finally, we will display these photos on the profile and the user search pages.

How to Upload Files

The basic idea is that files need to get from the users to the server. This happens in a few steps, and while the order is important, there is plenty of room for adding extras, like validation for the following:

- The user posts a form, containing a file input with a selected file.
- The server checks for a posted form, then checks for a posted file.
- If a file was posted, the server checks whether it can move the file from temporary storage to a permanent location.
- If the file was moved, the server performs any postprocessing on the file, such as returning the dimensions, modifying any relevant database rows, and so forth.

These four simple steps can be represented with the code shown in Listing 18-1.

Listing 18-1. Uploading a File

```
if (isset($_FILES["photo_field"]))
{
    $file = $_FILES["photo_field"];
    $newFile = "path/to/permanent/file";
    $uploaded = move_uploaded_file($file["tmp_name"], $newFile);

    if ($uploaded)
    {
        $meta = getimagesize($newFile);
        // do something with the new file/metadata
    }
}
```

This code appears pretty simple, but how does it fit into our application? Let's move along to find out.

User Photos

For a start, we will have many users, who are all allowed to upload their own photos. This means we can expect many file uploads. It also means that we could probably benefit from storing a reference to each upload within a database table.

Let's begin integrating the photo-upload functionality into our application, by creating a new model that will serve as a means to storing uploaded file references in the database. Take a look at Listing 18-2 to see this new File model.

Listing 18-2. The File Model

```
class File extends Shared\Model
{
    /**
    * @column
    * @readwrite
    * @type text
    * @length 255
    */
    protected $_name;

    /**
    * @column
    * @readwrite
    * @type text
    * @length 32
    */
    protected $_mime;

    /**
    * @column
    * @readwrite
    * @type integer
    */
    protected $_size;
```

```
    /**
    * @column
    * @readwrite
    * @type integer
    */
    protected $_width;

    /**
    * @column
    * @readwrite
    * @type integer
    */
    protected $_height;

    /**
    * @column
    * @readwrite
    * @type integer
    */
    protected $_user;
}
```

This model is similar to the Friend model we created in Chapter 17, in that it has no validation. That is not because validation is unimportant to us, but simply because it could complicate things at this stage. The File model has fields for file name, mime type, file size, width, height, and user. With the exception of the user field, all the fields relate to specific uploads, and we will populate them after a file has successfully been uploaded.

If this model is persisted to the database (using the Connector->sync() method), it should produce a table like that shown in Listing 18-3.

Listing 18-3. The file Table

```
CREATE TABLE `file` (
  `name` varchar(255) DEFAULT NULL,
  `mime` varchar(32) DEFAULT NULL,
  `size` int(11) DEFAULT NULL,
  `width` int(11) DEFAULT NULL,
  `height` int(11) DEFAULT NULL,
  `user` int(11) DEFAULT NULL,
  `id` int(11) NOT NULL AUTO_INCREMENT,
  `live` tinyint(4) DEFAULT NULL,
  `deleted` tinyint(4) DEFAULT NULL,
  `created` datetime DEFAULT NULL,
  `modified` datetime DEFAULT NULL,
  PRIMARY KEY (`id`),
  KEY `live` (`live`),
  KEY `deleted` (`deleted`)
) ENGINE = InnoDB DEFAULT CHARSET = utf8 ;
```

Because we want to add the upload functionality to the places where users register and update their settings, we should add a central function to perform the upload. We will add this function to the Users model, as shown in Listing 18-4.

Listing 18-4. The _upload() Method

```
use Shared\Controller as Controller;

class Users extends Controller
{
    protected function _upload($name, $user)
    {
        if (isset($_FILES[$name]))
        {
            $file = $_FILES[$name];
            $path = APP_PATH."/public/uploads/";

            $time = time();
            $extension = pathinfo($file["name"], PATHINFO_EXTENSION);
            $filename = "{$user}-{$time}.{$extension}";

            if (move_uploaded_file($file["tmp_name"], $path.$filename))
            {
                $meta = getimagesize($path.$filename);

                if ($meta)
                {
                    $width = $meta[0];
                    $height = $meta[1];

                    $file = new File(array(
                        "name" => $filename,
                        "mime" => $file["type"],
                        "size" => $file["size"],
                        "width" => $width,
                        "height" => $height,
                        "user" => $user
                    ));
                    $file->save();
                }
            }
        }
    }
}
```

There are a few important things to note about this method. The first thing is that file uploads may only differ in two areas, specifically the name of the form input and the ID of the user who is uploading files. The second thing to note is the method defines a path for the new file within the `public/uploads` folder. This will allow the files to be directly accessible via URL.

As with our example code, the method checks whether a file has been uploaded. If it has, the method attempts to move the file to a permanent location.

■ **Note** When a file cannot be moved to permanent storage, it might be a sign that the upload is insecure and/or invalid. This would be a good time to raise an exception, making the developer aware that something has gone wrong.

After the file is moved to the permanent storage, a new `File` instance is created and a row is saved to the database. We also determine the width/height of the uploaded file. Now that we have a reusable method for uploading, it is a good time to integrate it into the register() and settings() actions of our Users controller. The methods should resemble those shown in Listings 18-5 and 18-6.

Listing 18-5. The register() Action

```
use Framework\RequestMethods as RequestMethods;
use Shared\Controller as Controller;

class Users extends Controller
{
    public function register()
    {
        if (RequestMethods::post("save"))
        {
            $user = new User(array(
                "first" => RequestMethods::post("first"),
                "last" => RequestMethods::post("last"),
                "email" => RequestMethods::post("email"),
                "password" => RequestMethods::post("password")
            ));

            if ($user->validate())
            {
                $user->save();
                $this->_upload("photo", $user->id);
                $this->actionView->set("success", true);
            }

            $this->actionView->set("errors", $user->errors);
        }
    }
}
```

Listing 18-6. The settings() Action

```
use Framework\RequestMethods as RequestMethods;
use Shared\Controller as Controller;

class Users extends Controller
{
    /**
    * @before _secure
    */
    public function settings()
    {
        $errors = array();

        if (RequestMethods::post("save"))
        {
            $this->user->first = RequestMethods::post("first");
            $this->user->last = RequestMethods::post("last");
            $this->user->email = RequestMethods::post("email");
```

```
            if (RequestMethods::post("password"))
            {
                $this->user->password = RequestMethods::post("password");
            }

            if ($this->user->validate())
            {
                $this->user->save();
                $this->_upload("photo", $this->user->id);
                $this->actionView->set("success", true);
            }

            $errors = $this->user->errors;
        }
        $this->actionView->set("errors", $errors);
    }
}
```

The integration of our reusable `_upload()` method is rather simple. In each case, we simply need to supply the correct form input name and user ID in order for the file upload to take place. We also need to add the form input to our `register.html` and `settings.html` views, as shown in Listing 18-7.

Listing 18-7. The File Input

```
<li>
    <label>
        Photo:
        <input type = "file" name = "photo" />
    </label>
</li>
```

If you have completed these steps, created an `uploads` folder (with the correct file permissions required for upload), and submitted either the register or settings forms, you should now see files being created in that folder. You also need to add the enctype = `"multipart/form-data"` attribute to your `settings.html` and `register.html` forms.

■ **Note** If you were adding validation to the file-upload mechanism, you would need to add some `echo` logic (below the file input) to display any validation errors.

Showing Off, a Little

Now that we have working file uploads, we should add these files to the profile and search pages. The first thing we need to do is create a new method, on the `User` model, to return the latest `File` row. Take a look at Listing 18-8 to see how we do this.

Listing 18-8. The getFile() Method

```
use Shared\Model as Model;

class User extends Model
{
    public function getFile()
```

```
    {
        return File::first(array(
            "user = ?" =>$this->id,
            "live = ?" =>true,
            "deleted = ?" =>false
        ), array("*"), "id", "DESC");
    }
}
```

This method simply returns the latest file from the database, which is linked to the current user row. The next thing we should do is update the `search.html` template to include photos, as demonstrated in Listing 18-9.

Listing 18-9. The search.html Template (Extract)

```
{foreach $_user in $users}
    {script $file = $_user->file}
    <tr>
        <td>{if $file}<img src = "/uploads/{echo $file->name}" />{/if}</td>
        <td>{echo $_user->first} {echo $_user->last}</td>
        <td>
            {if $_user->isFriend($user->id)}
                <a href = "/unfriend/{echo $_user->id}.html">unfriend</a>
            {/if}
            {else}
                <a href = "/friend/{echo $_user->id}.html">friend</a>
            {/else}
        </td>
    </tr>
{/foreach}
```

Because the `getFile()` method matches the pattern specified in the `__get()` method of the `Base` class, we can simply reference it by `$_user->file`. If a file is found, we echo the file name into the `src` of an image element, rendering the image in the search results list. The final task is to modify the `profile.html` view, as demonstrated in Listing 18-10.

Listing 18-10. The profile.html Template (Extract)

```
{script $file = $user->file}
{if $file}<img src = "/uploads/{echo $file->name}" />{/if}
<h1>{echo $user->first} {echo $user->last}</h1>
This is a profile page!
```

This completes the steps required to allow users to upload their own files, and to see these files reflected on the search and profile pages.

Questions

1. Why was it necessary to save a reference to the uploaded files in the database?
2. We uploaded files to the `public/uploads` folder, and didn't check whether they were valid images. What prevents users from uploading malicious files to the server?
3. What was the purpose of determining and storing the file width and height?

4. How would we modify this functionality to allow for uploads to cloud services like Amazon CloudFront or Rackspace Cloud Files?

Answers

1. It is not strictly necessary, but rather recommended. One of the biggest bottlenecks in any PHP application is reading from and writing to files. If we didn't save these file references in the database, we would have to iterate through all the files in the `uploads` folder, matching those that had the user's ID in the file name. This is way too intensive to be practical. With the database rows, we can simply query for all rows linked to the user and return the corresponding files by reference.
2. We do not validate and, therefore, cannot prevent this sort of thing from happening. There are a number of steps you should take when securing your application—from denying execution of any files within the `uploads` directory, to validating the mime type, size, and file name of the files you let users upload. These processes should take place before the file is moved to permanent storage, and will not prevent any of the other steps from taking place.
3. We spoke much about files, but what we really meant was photos. The idea is that users can upload multiple photos, and that these are referenced in the database. Width and height are useful photo characteristics for determining how the photo should be rendered and/or modified. We didn't use them here, but they can be used in a number of practical ways, such as for creating thumbnails or rendering in a slideshow.
4. We would begin by checking whether a file has been uploaded. After performing any required file validation, we would then post the file to the cloud server, instead of moving it to permanent storage (on our own server). The steps of determining metadata and saving references to the database would still apply, but might be subtly different in terms of how they get the information.

Exercises

1. Our code is quite minimal, in terms of file validation. Try adding some checks for things such as file size, mime type, and file name, to ensure that the files being uploaded are indeed valid images.
2. Using the stored width and height properties, try creating thumbnails for the uploaded photos, so that the search and profile pages don't break when large photos are uploaded. One PHP function that might help you is `imagecopyresized()`.
3. We spoke a little about using cloud-based storage servers. If you are feeling particularly adventurous, try connecting to, and utilizing one of these services to store the uploaded files.

■ **Note** You can read more about the `imagecopyresized()` method at `www.php.net/manual/en/function.imagecopyresized.php`.

CHAPTER 19

Extending

One of the biggest differentiators of popular frameworks is how easily they can be extended with third-party libraries. Up until now, all the classes we have developed have belonged either to the framework or to the application.

Goals

- We need to understand how we can create our own libraries.
- We need to understand how we can use libraries from other developers.
- We need to understand what the Observer design pattern is and why it's relevant to our application.
- We need to build a means of listening for and emitting events within our applications.

Foxy

The first kind of library we will look at is the kind we create ourselves. While these libraries are not strictly third party, the potential exists for us to reuse them in many projects. They aren't "application" enough that we would want to bundle them with the rest of the application code, but they aren't "framework" enough that we would want to add them to the framework code either.

A few years ago, I created a library for the express purpose of determining a user's browser, and serving a targeted style sheet that would allow for custom fonts to be used in CSS. This is similar to Google's Web Fonts (`www.google.com/webfonts`); in fact, I think that's what inspired me to write the library in the first place.

I decided to call this library Foxy (a portmanteau of the words *font* and *proxy*). This library will inspire our own font proxy library, which will be slightly simpler, but essentially the same.

Custom CSS Fonts

CSS, while not the focus of this book, is an inescapable part of the modern web. If you are unfamiliar, think of it as the dress code for elements in an HTML page. Style declarations (which are instructions for the appearance of certain aspects of an element) are targeted to specific elements, by way of CSS selectors. CSS selectors are string representations of structured element markup.

Modern browsers have fairly good support for custom fonts, and the concept is by no means new. There are also some good alternatives to this library, which are very good at what they do. We're not building this library because we think we can do better, but rather to gain a basic understanding of how we can extend our framework.

With all of that in mind, take a look at the CSS required to utilize these custom fonts, as shown in Listing 19-1.

Listing 19-1. CSS Custom Font Declarations

```
@font-face
{
    font-family: "LuxiSans";
    src: url("/fonts/LuxiSans.eot");
    src: url("/fonts/LuxiSans.eot?#iefix") format("embedded-opentype"),
         url("/fonts/LuxiSans.woff") format("woff"),
         url("/fonts/LuxiSans.ttf") format("truetype"),
         url("/fonts/LuxiSans.svg#LuxiSans") format("svg");
    font-style: normal;
}
```

While this is easy enough hard-code, for a handful of fonts, it is not very extensible. For a start, each font would require an additional 10 lines of CSS, not to mention each font variant (bold, oblique/italic, etc.). This is further complicated by the fact that certain browsers (such as Internet Explorer) have a hard time dealing with multiple `src` values, leaving this approach a little unstable.

What we really want is for the application to detect which browser we are using, and return CSS only for the relevant file type. For this to happen, we need to a) be able to register multiple font types/variants, b) detect the browser type, and c) serve only the applicable font formats.

Building the Proxy

We begin by adding a fonts directory, containing two PHP class files, to the `application/libraries` directory. The first, `application/libraries/fonts/types.php` contains some constants, which represent different format types. You can see this file in Listing 19-2.

Listing 19-2. application/libraries/fonts/types.php

```
namespace Fonts
{
    class Types
    {
        const OTF = "opentype";
        const TTF = "truetype";
        const EOT = "eot";
    }
}
```

The second class is a little trickier. It begins with the code shown in Listing 19-3, which is used for adding font formats/variants to the proxy.

Listing 19-3. application/libraries/fonts/proxy.php (Extract)

```
namespace Fonts
{
    use Fonts\Types as Types;

    class Proxy
    {
        protected $_fonts = array();
```

```
        public function addFont($key, $type, $file)
        {
            if (!isset($this->_fonts[$type]))
            {
                $this->_fonts[$type] = array();
            }

            $this->_fonts[$type][$key] = $file;
            return $this;
        }

        public function addFontTypes($key, $types)
        {
            foreach ($types as $type => $file)
            {
                $this->addFont($key, $type, $file);
            }
            return $this;
        }

        public function removeFont($key, $type)
        {
            if (isset($this->_fonts[$type][$key]))
            {
                unset($this->_fonts[$type][$key]);
            }

            return $this;
        }

        public function getFont($key, $type)
        {
            if (isset($this->_fonts[$type][$key]))
            {
                return $this->_fonts[$type][$key];
            }
            return null;
        }
    }
}
```

The `addFont()` method adds a single font to the protected `$_fonts` array. Similarly, the `addFontTypes()` method adds an array of font types for each font face. The `getFont()` method returns a named font from the `$_fonts` array, and the `deleteFont()` method removes a named font from the `$_fonts` array.

These methods don't really do anything useful. For us to know which fonts to serve, we need to know which browser is trying to load them. That's where the next method fits in, as demonstrated in Listing 19-4.

Listing 19-4. application/libraries/fonts/proxy.php (Extract)

```
namespace Fonts
{
    use Fonts\Types as Types;
```

```
    class Proxy
    {
        public function sniff($agent)
        {
            $browser = "#(opera|ie|firefox|chrome|version)[\s\/:]([\w\d\.]+)?.*?➥
(safari|version[\s\/:]([\w\d\.]+)|$)#i";
            $platform = "#(ipod|iphone|ipad|webos|android|win|mac|linux)#i";

            if (preg_match($browser, $agent, $browsers))
            {
                if (preg_match($platform, $agent, $platforms))
                {
                    $platform = $platforms[1];
                }
                else
                {
                    $platform = "other";
                }

                return array(
                    "browser" => (strtolower($browsers[1]) == "version") ? ➥
strtolower($browsers[3]) : strtolower($browsers[1]),
                    "version" => (float) (strtolower($browsers[1]) == "opera") ? ➥
strtolower($browsers[4]) : strtolower($browsers[2]),
                    "platform" => strtolower($platform)
                );
            }

            return false;
        }
    }
}
```

The `sniff()` method does just that: it sniffs the browser's user agent string in an attempt to identify the characteristics (type, version, and platform) of the browser.

■ **Note** Browser identification by user agent detection is not bulletproof. Browsers can change their own user agents, and new browsers (with new user agent strings) are constantly being released. At best, this method will need to be updated regularly. At worst, it could provide false negatives for browsers that actually do support some of the available formats. Use at your own peril!

So, we have a way to add font formats and a means of identifying which browser is looking for the custom fonts. We tie these two aspects together with the method shown in Listing 19-5.

Listing 19-5. application/libraries/fonts/proxy.php (Extract)

```
namespace Fonts
{
    use Fonts\Types as Types;
```

```
    class Proxy
    {
        public function detectSupport($agent)
        {
            $sniff=$this->sniff($agent);

            if ($sniff)
            {
                switch ($sniff["platform"])
                {
                    case "win":
                    case "mac":
                    case "linux":
                    {
                        switch ($sniff["browser"])
                        {
                            case "opera":
                            {
                                return ($sniff["version"]>10) ? array(Types::TTF, ➥
Types::OTF, Types::SVG) : false;
                            }
                            case "safari":
                            {
                                return ($sniff["version"]>3.1) ? array(Types::TTF, ➥
Types::OTF) : false;
                            }
                            case "chrome":
                            {
                                return ($sniff["version"]>4) ? array(Types::TTF, ➥
Types::OTF) : false;
                            }
                            case "firefox":
                            {
                                return ($sniff["version"]>3.5) ? array(Types::TTF, ➥
Types::OTF) : false;
                            }
                            case "ie":
                            {
                                return ($sniff["version"]>4) ? array(Types::EOT) : false;
                            }
                        }
                    }
                }
            }

            return false;
        }
    }
}
```

The detectSupport() method begins with a call to the sniff() method. Then, it jumps straight into some nested switch statements, which return either an array of known supported formats, or false. This will provide the best guess for what fonts are supported for the browser.

With these methods, we are just about ready to start serving our custom fonts, but there is one convenience method I think we should add. Take a look at Listing 19-6 to see this method.

Listing 19-6. application/libraries/fonts/proxy.php (Extract)

```
namespace Fonts
{
    use Fonts\Types as Types;

    class Proxy
    {
        public function serve($key, $agent)
        {
            $support = $this->detectSupport($agent);

            if ($support)
            {
                $fonts = array();

                foreach ($support as $type)
                {
                    $font = $this->getFont($key, $type);

                    if ($font)
                    {
                        $fonts[$type] = $this->getFont($key, $type);
                    }
                }

                return $fonts;
            }

            return array();
        }
    }
}
```

The serve() method accepts a $key (referring to a font face, stored in the $_fonts array) and an $agent (referring to the user agent), so that it can detect support and return an array of supported fonts.

Using the Proxy

Now we need to use the font proxy we've just built. To do this, we are going to create a new Files controller, with a fonts() action. In order to get to this action, we will add a custom route to the routes.php file we created in Chapter 17 (in public/routes.php). The custom route has the configuration parameters shown in Listing 19-7.

Listing 19-7. Custom Fonts Route

```
array(
    "pattern" => "fonts/:id",
    "controller" => "files",
    "action" => "fonts"
)
```

The idea is that we add an external style sheet (which points to this route). The `fonts()` action then generates this style sheet that is then passed back to the browser. Let's see what the `fonts()` action looks like, as shown in Listing 19-8.

Listing 19-8. The Files Controller

```
use Shared\Controller as Controller;
use Fonts\Proxy as Proxy;
use Fonts\Types as Types;

class Files extends Controller
{
    public function fonts($name)
    {
        $path = "/fonts";

        if (!file_exists("{$path}/{$name}"))
        {
            $proxy = new Proxy();

            $proxy->addFontTypes("{$name}", array(
                Types::OTF => "{$path}/{$name}.otf",
                Types::EOT => "{$path}/{$name}.eot",
                Types::TTF => "{$path}/{$name}.ttf"
            ));

            $weight = "";
            $style = "";
            $font = explode("-", $name);

            if (sizeof($font) > 1)
            {
                switch (strtolower($font[1]))
                {
                    case "Bold":
                        $weight = "bold";
                        break;
                    case "Oblique":
                        $style = "oblique";
                        break;
                    case "BoldOblique":
                        $weight = "bold";
                        $style = "oblique";
                        break;
                }
            }
```

```
        $declarations = "";
        $font = join("-", $font);
        $sniff = $proxy->sniff($_SERVER["HTTP_USER_AGENT"]);
        $served = $proxy->serve($font, $_SERVER["HTTP_USER_AGENT"]);

        if (sizeof($served) > 0)
        {
            $keys = array_keys($served);
            $declarations .= "@font-face {";
            $declarations .= "font-family: \"{$font}\";";

            if ($weight)
            {
                $declarations .= "font-weight: {$weight};";
            }
            if ($style)
            {
                $declarations .= "font-style: {$style};";
            }

            $type = $keys[0];
            $url = $served[$type];

            if ($sniff && strtolower($sniff["browser"]) == "ie")
            {
                $declarations .= "src: url(\"{$url}\");";
            }
            else
            {
                $declarations .= "src: url(\"{$url}\") format(\"{$type}\");";
            }

            $declarations .= "}";
        }

        header("Content-type: text/css");

        if ($declarations)
        {
            echo $declarations;
        }
        else
        {
            echo "/* no fonts to show */";
        }

        $this->willRenderLayoutView = false;
        $this->willRenderActionView = false;
    }
```

```
        else
        {
            header("Location: {$path}/{$name}");
        }
    }
}
```

The `fonts()` action is quite long, so we will break it up into the following five main parts:

1. We begin by checking whether the requested file actually exists. If it does, we redirect to it. We do not actually create the file if it does not exist (as the style sheet must be recreated every time it is requested by a new browser), but this is in case the font files are in a directory called `fonts` within the `public` directory.
2. If the requested font has a trailing variant indicator (`-Oblique`, `-Bold` or `-BoldOblique`), we adjust weight and style properties accordingly.
3. After we know which fonts must be served (thanks to a call to the `server()` proxy method), we compile the CSS style declaration.
4. Finally, we set the correct `Content-type` and return the style declaration to the browser.

Assuming you have a `fonts` directory (within your `public` directory) and it is populated with font variants of a matching naming scheme, a request to `http://localhost/fonts/fontname.css` should return browser-specific custom font CSS declarations.

Imagine

The second kind of library we will look at integrating into our framework is a third-party library called Imagine. Imagine is an image-editing library (based on the façade design pattern), which strives to provide a consistent interface for working with the various image libraries available to PHP.

One of the benefits of using Imagine is that it is already namespaced, which fits well with our framework's design philosophy. We will be using Imagine to perform changes to the uploaded photos, creating thumbnails in particular. To begin using Imagine, we need to download the source (`https://github.com/avalanche123/Imagine`), extract the contents, and copy the contents of the extracted `lib` directory to the `application/libraries/imagine` directory. The files are arranged rather neatly within the new `imagine` directory, but the class names differ slightly from our naming conventions. For this reason, our class autoloader (`Core::_autoload()`) will not work for them. In order to get the Imagine classes to load, we will need to add another autoload function to the `spl_autoload_register`, as demonstrated in Listing 19-9.

Listing 19-9. Autoloading Imagine Classes

```
spl_autoload_register(function($class)
{
    $path = lcfirst(str_replace("\\", DIRECTORY_SEPARATOR, $class));
    $file = APP_PATH."/application/libraries/{$path}.php";

    if (file_exists($file))
    {
        require_once $file;
        return true;
    }
});
```

This new autoloader function is not particularly tricky, but it does need to be placed above the call to `Core::initialize()`. The reason for this is that we have told `Core::_autoload()` to raise an exception when it can't find a class file. If `Core::_autoload()` is run before this new autoloader method, an exception will be raised.

At this point, we can start using the Imagine classes (as demonstrated in their documentation). Because we already have a `Files` controller, we will add a new `thumbnails()` action to it, and make it navigable by adding the custom route shown in Listing 19-10.

Listing 19-10. Custom Thumbnails Route

```
array(
    "pattern" => "thumbnails/:id",
    "controller" => "files",
    "action" => "thumbnails"
)
```

With this route in place, we can now create (and use) the `thumbnails()` action, as demonstrated in Listing 19-11.

Listing 19-11. The thumbnails() Action

```
use Shared\Controller as Controller;
use Fonts\Proxy as Proxy;
use Fonts\Types as Types;

class Files extends Controller
{
    public function thumbnails($id)
    {
        $path = APP_PATH."/public/uploads";

        $file = File::first(array(
            "id = ?" => $id
        ));

        if ($file)
        {
            $width = 64;
            $height = 64;

            $name = $file->name;
            $filename = pathinfo($name, PATHINFO_FILENAME);
            $extension = pathinfo($name, PATHINFO_EXTENSION);

            if ($filename && $extension)
            {
                $thumbnail = "{$filename}-{$width}x{$height}.{$extension}";

                if (!file_exists("{$path}/{$thumbnail}"))
                {
                    $imagine = new Imagine\Gd\Imagine();

                    $size = new Imagine\Image\Box($width, $height);
                    $mode = Imagine\Image\ImageInterface::THUMBNAIL_OUTBOUND;
```

```
                $imagine
                    ->open("{$path}/{$name}")
                    ->thumbnail($size, $mode)
                    ->save("{$path}/{$thumbnail}");
            }

            header("Location: /uploads/{$thumbnail}");
            exit();
        }

        header("Location: /uploads/{$name}");
        exit();
    }
  }
}
```

The thumbnails() action begins with an attempt to find the File database row matching the provided $id. If no row is found, no thumbnail is returned. It then proceeds to split the $file->name into $filename and $extension. This is so that a thumbnail file name can be constructed.

If the thumbnail already exists, the browser is simply redirected to it, avoiding any further execution of code. If it does not exist, we create a new Imagine\Gd\Imagine instance and use it to a) open the uploaded photo, b) resize the photo into a thumbnail of $width and $height, and c) save the thumbnail file.

■ **Note** You can get more details about how to use these methods/properties at http://imagine.readthedocs.org/en/latest/index.html.

The only thing left to do is modify the search.html and profile.html templates to use the new thumbnail files. Listing 19-12 shows how we accomplish this.

Listing 19-12. application/views/users/profile.html (Extract)

```
{script $file=$user->file}
{if $file}<img src="/thumbnails/{echo $file->id}" />{/if}
```

We now know how to build our own reusable application libraries, as well as how to integrate third-party libraries into our applications.

Observer

In Chapter 1, we learned about some of the design patterns we are using in our framework. In this chapter we will see another of those in action, specifically the Observer pattern. A brief summary of the Observer pattern is that receivers wait for the state of something to change (an event), and senders notify receivers (emit an event) of changes in state.

Synchronicity

There are many things that separate modern programming languages (and platforms). One difference that has recently picked up a lot of attention is the distinction modern platforms make between synchronous (sometimes threaded) and asynchronous (sometimes multithreaded or nonthreaded) execution of code.

Synchronous languages/platforms are those in which code is executed in a linear manner, each statement concluding before execution of the next statement can begin. Consider the example shown in Listing 19-13.

Listing 19-13. Synchronous Apache/PHP Execution

```
echo "opening file...";
$contents=file_get_contents("/path/to/some/file.txt");
echo "got contents: " . $contents;
```

The first statement will be executed almost immediately. The implications are clear and simple: output the contents of a string. The second statement, on the other hand, is a little trickier. It requires that the server open a file and assign the contents of the file to a variable. In programming terms, this is referred to as a *bottleneck*. The server must halt execution while it locates the file. It must open the file and read the contents before execution can resume.

This has two implications:

- The second echo statement does not execute until the second is complete.
- All code execution, in PHP/Apache, will behave similarly.

Now, let's consider asynchronous languages/platforms such as JavaScript/Node.JS. Asynchronous languages/platforms are those in which code is also executed in a linear manner, but where execution can be suspended (to be continued at a later time, after a state change). In other words, the server will continue execution until a point at which it reaches a potential bottleneck. It will move on to other processing until it needs to return to the current "request." Consider the example shown in Listing 19-14.

Listing 19-14. Asynchronous Node.JS/JavaScript Execution

```
var fs=require("fs");

console.log("opening file...");

fs.readFile("/path/to/some/file.txt", function(error, data)
{
    if (!error)
    {
        console.log("got contents: "+data);
    }
});
```

This example does basically the same thing as the previous one, but with one major difference. We begin by outputting the contents of a string, and even request that the server read the contents of a file. We also provide a function (or callback) that the server should execute after it resumes. The second output statement (`console.log`) still waits for the file to be read, but execution is not halted while the server fetches the file. This means the server can continue to process other requests until this one can resume (after the file is read).

■ **Note** I am very careful to specify not only the language but also the "server" on which these languages run. This is because other "servers" exist that can blur the line between synchronous/asynchronous. There is Nginx (for PHP) and it is even possible to create JavaScript (at least on the client side) that blocks/halts execution. The important thing is to understand the difference.

How does this understanding help us? For a start, it will help to explain why things freeze while PHP is executing blocking code. Blocking code can be anything as simple as a loop or anything as complicated as connecting to a TCP server. While it is possible to simulate asynchronous execution of PHP code, it will always be synchronous, no matter how swiftly executed or how many requests are served in parallel.

In languages like JavaScript, this is overcome by passing functions (or callbacks) that will be executed when the intensive operations are completed. PHP 5.3 also supports callbacks, but they aren't nearly as useful, considering the language itself is not built to be nonblocking.

So if callbacks aren't useful to us as a means of avoiding blocking code, then why should we use them at all? One remaining use is to observe state changes, and to notify listeners of these events. You can imagine how this might be useful. Take a look at the demonstration in Listing 19-15.

Listing 19-15. Listening for New States

```
addEvent("the.state.changed", function($message) {
    echo "state changed to: " . $message;
});

fireEvent("the.state.changed", array("new state"));
fireEvent("the.state.changed", array("another new state"));
```

We are dealing with a big framework, and possibly even a big application. There might be times when it is essential that we know when states change, and this is a perfect opportunity for us to use the Observer pattern.

Code

Understanding the usefulness of events is only half the battle. We need to build a class to manage the event listeners, and emit events. Take a look at this class in Listing 19-16.

Listing 19-16. The Events Class

```
namespace Framework
{
    class Events
    {
        private static $_callbacks = array();

        private function __construct()
        {
            // do nothing
        }

        private function __clone()
        {
            // do nothing
        }

        public static function add($type, $callback)
        {
            if (empty(self::$_callbacks[$type]))
            {
                self::$_callbacks[$type] = array();
            }
```

```
            self::$_callbacks[$type][] = $callback;
        }

        public static function fire($type, $parameters = null)
        {
            if (!empty(self::$_callbacks[$type]))
            {
                foreach (self::$_callbacks[$type] as $callback)
                {
                    call_user_func_array($callback, $parameters);
                }
            }
        }

        public static function remove($type, $callback)
        {
            if (!empty(self::$_callbacks[$type]))
            {
                foreach (self::$_callbacks[$type] as $i => $found)
                {
                    if ($callback == $found)
                    {
                        unset(self::$_callbacks[$type][$i]);
                    }
                }
            }
        }
    }
}
```

This class looks quite similar to the Registry class, but it's better that we keep them separated. The add() method adds the provided $callback to the $_callbacks array, so that it can be executed when any $type events happen.

The fire() method emits/triggers an event. If you provide an optional $parameters array, this array will be available to all the callbacks executed. The remove() method simply removes the stored $callback from the $_callbacks array. It requires a reference to the original callback that it should remove. Let's see how we can use this new class to listen for events and trigger them, as shown in Listing 19-17.

Listing 19-17. Using the Events Class

```
use Framework\Events as Events;

Events::add("the.state.changed", function($message) {
    echo "state changed to: " . $message;
});

Events::fire("the.state.changed", array("new state"));
Events::fire("the.state.changed", array("another new state"));
```

This matches our previous example, almost exactly. The order of array elements translates directly into the order of the callback's arguments. If you provide four array elements, you can expect four arguments in the callback.

Events

We should take this opportunity to add some events to our framework, so that other developers can create listeners for our framework classes. We will create the first two together. These events will be called `framework.controller.destruct.before` and `framework.controller.destruct.after`. This method should be fired as late as possible in the `__destruct()` method, and will look like that shown in Listing 19-18.

Listing 19-18. Modified Controller Class

```
namespace Framework
{
    use Framework\Events as Events;

    class Controller extends Base
    {
        /**
        * @read
        */
        protected $_name;

        protected function getName()
        {
            if (empty($this->_name))
            {
                $this->_name=get_class($this);
            }

            return $this->_name;
        }

        public function __destruct()
        {
            Events::fire("framework.controller.destruct.before", array($this->name));

            $this->render();

            Events::fire("framework.controller.destruct.after", array($this->name));
        }
    }
}
```

The new events will be fired before and after the templates are rendered, and the callbacks will be provided the name of the current controller. If there are no listeners waiting for this event, nothing will happen (no error messages either).

We should also see a useful way in which one of these new events can help us. If you consider the `Shared\Controller` class we created (in Chapter 15), you might remember that we connected to a database but never disconnected from it. We are essentially opening a connection to the database on each request, and then never closing any. This could be made more efficient by closing the connection after the templates are rendered, as shown in Listing 19-19.

Listing 19-19. Modified Shared\Controller Class

```
namespace Shared
{
    use Framework\Events as Events;
    use Framework\Registry as Registry;

    class Controller extends \Framework\Controller
    {
        /**
        * @readwrite
        */
        protected $_user;

        public function __construct($options = array())
        {
            parent::__construct($options);

            // connect to database
            $database = Registry::get("database");
            $database->connect();

            // schedule disconnect from database
            Events::add("framework.controller.destruct.after", function($name) {
                $database = Registry::get("database");
                $database->disconnect();
             });
        }
    }
}
```

Our modified `__construct()` method actually schedules a call to the `$database->disconnect()` method, using our new events. This is only safe to do if we are sure we won't need the database connection after it has been closed. What's cool about it is that we don't need to find a place to shove the disconnect code. We simply listen for the event, within the `__construct()` method, and it will be done.

We should add similar methods in as many classes as reasonably possible, such as the events listed in Table 19-1.

Table 19-1. *List of Events Added to the Framework*

Event	Signature
`framework.cache.initialize.before`	`function($type, $options)`
	`$type`—The type of driver required
	`$options`—Initialization options for the cache resource
`framework.cache.initialize.after`	`function($type, $options)`
	`$type`—The type of driver required
	`$options`—Initialization options for the cache resource

(*continued*)

Table 19-1. (*continued*)

Event	Signature
framework.configuration.initialize.before	function($type, $options) $type—The type of driver required $options—Initialization options for the configuration resource
framework.configuration.initialize.after	function($type, $options) $type—The type of driver required $options—Initialization options for the configuration resource
framework.controller.construct.before	function($name) $name—The name of the controller class
framework.controller.construct.after	function($name) $name—The name of the controller class
framework.controller.render.before	function($name) $name—The name of the controller class
framework.controller.render.after	function($name) $name—The name of the controller class
framework.controller.destruct.before	function($name) $name—The name of the controller class
framework.controller.destruct.after	function($name) $name—The name of the controller class
framework.database.initialize.before	function($type, $options) $type—The type of driver required $options—Initialization options for the database resource
framework.database.initialize.after	function($type, $options) $type—The type of driver required $options—Initialization options for the database resource
framework.request.request.before	function($method, $url, $parameters) $method—The request method (GET, POST, PUT, etc.) $url—The URL to send the request to $parameters—Parameters for the request

(*continued*)

Table 19-1. (*continued*)

Event	Signature
framework.request.request.after	function($method, $url, $parameters, $response)
	$method—The request method (GET, POST, PUT, etc.)
	$url—The URL to send the request to
	$parameters—Parameters for the request
	$response—The response received after making the request
framework.router.dispatch.before	function($url)
	$url—The URL to dispatch
framework.router.dispatch.after	function($url, $controller, $action, $parameters)
	$url—The URL to dispatch
	$controller—The intended controller
	$action—The intended action
	$parameters—The parameters supplied for the request
framework.session.initialize.before	function($type, $options)
	$type—The type of driver required
	$options—Initialization options for the session resource
framework.session.initialize.after	function($type, $options)
	$type—The type of driver required
	$options—Initialization options for the session resource
framework.view.construct.before	function($file)
	$file—The template file that should be rendered
framework.view.construct.after	function($file, $template)
	$file—The template file that should be rendered
	$template—The template that was instantiated
framework.view.render.before	function($file)
	$file—The template file that should be rendered

Plugins

Events may be useful for our framework/application needs, but they are essential for most plugin architectures. The very definition of a *plugin* is something that can attach itself to a functional system without requiring fundamental changes to the system.

To test this concept further, we will build an activity log plugin. The activity log will contain itemized information about each event fired, along with a timestamp for when the event occurred. It will also include some benchmarking information. Let's begin by creating the plugin loader shown in Listing 19-20.

Listing 19-20. /public/index.php (Extract)

```
$path = APP_PATH . "/application/plugins";
$iterator = new DirectoryIterator($path);

foreach ($iterator as $item)
{
    if (!$item->isDot() && $item->isDir())
    {
        include($path . "/" . $item->getFilename() . "/initialize.php");
    }
}
```

This code should be placed in the public/index.php file, just after the Core initialization code. This is so that plugins can immediately start listening for framework events, and act accordingly. The Directory Iterator class is simply an interface for reading directory information (in the file system). We use it to iterate through all the directories contained in the application/plugins directory. For each directory it finds there, we then include an initialization.php file. If plugins wish to be automatically loaded, they need to have their initialization logic in this file.

Using include allows execution of the application to continue, even if no initialize file was found in a plugin's directory. We should now add this initialization file, as shown in Listing 19-21.

Listing 19-21. Initializing the Logger Plugin

```
// initialize logger
include("logger.php");

$logger = new Logger(array(
    "file" => APP_PATH . "/logs/" . date("Y-m-d") . ".txt"
));

// log cache events

Framework\Events::add("framework.cache.initialize.before", function($type, $options) use
($logger)
{
    $logger->log("framework.cache.initialize.before: " . $type);
});

Framework\Events::add("framework.cache.initialize.after", function($type, $options) use
($logger)
{
    $logger->log("framework.cache.initialize.after: " . $type);
});

// log configuration events

Framework\Events::add("framework.configuration.initialize.before", function($type, $options)
use ($logger)
{
    $logger->log("framework.configuration.initialize.before: " . $type);
});
```

```
Framework\Events::add("framework.configuration.initialize.after", function($type, $options)
use ($logger)
{
    $logger->log("framework.configuration.initialize.after: " . $type);
});
```

The initialize.php file is quite simple. We include the logger.php and instantiate the Logger class. We can't depend on any of the framework classes, or even the class autoloader. We have to pretend they're not there! After initializing the Logger class, we need to add listeners for all the events we want to log. This leads to a lot of code (most of which is not here, yet remains trivial). So we know how to use the Logger class, but how does it actually log the messages? Let's take a closer look at the class in Listing 19-22.

Listing 19-22. The Logger Class

```
class Logger
{
    protected $_file;
    protected $_entries;
    protected $_start;
    protected $_end;

    protected function _sum($values)
    {
        $count = 0;

        foreach ($values as $value)
        {
            $count += $value;
        }

        return $count;
    }

    protected function _average($values)
    {
        return $this->_sum($values) / sizeof($values);
    }

    public function __construct($options)
    {
        if (!isset($options["file"]))
        {
            throw new Exception("Log file invalid.");
        }

        $this->_file = $options["file"];
        $this->_entries = array();
        $this->_start = microtime();
    }
```

```
    public function log($message)
    {
        $this->_entries[]=array(
            "message" => "[" . date("Y-m-d H:i:s") . "]" . $message,
            "time" => microtime()
        );
    }

    public function __destruct()
    {
        $messages="";
        $last=$this->_start;
        $times=array();

        foreach ($this->_entries as $entry)
        {
            $messages .=$entry["message"] . "\n";
            $times[]=$entry["time"] - $last;
            $last=$entry["time"];
        }

        $messages .="Average: " . $this->_average($times);
        $messages .=", Longest: " . max($times);
        $messages .=", Shortest: " . min($times);
        $messages .=", Total: " . (microtime() - $this->_start);
        $messages .="\n";

        file_put_contents($this->_file, $messages, FILE_APPEND);
    }
}
```

The Logger class has one public method (aside from the magic methods) that adds a log message (and timestamp) to the $_entries array. When the Logger is instantiated, it checks the supplied options for a "file" parameter, which is a reference to the file to which the log messages should be appended. If this option is not provided, an exception is raised. The __destruct() method renders the log messages to the target file, as well as some benchmarking information.

Note The benchmarking values are only estimates, based on when the logger was initialized and the timestamps stored with each message. The values remain useful for debugging, though.

We now have a reasonably useful plugin architecture, thanks to the events system we have going here. We also have a useful Logger class, which will help with future debugging!

Questions

1. Both the `files()` and `thumbnails()` actions rely on file I/O. How can we make these methods more efficient?
2. We did not actually change the structure of the Imagine classes. Wouldn't it be better (for our application) if we were to rewrite the Imagine classes so that they comply with our organizational system?
3. Should we be creating our `thumbnails()` action (and similar) to accept different `$width/$height` parameters?
4. PHP might not be built to be nonblocking, but is it possible to write all of our classes/functions as nonblocking to avoid the problem of synchronous execution?
5. We built a class that handles callbacks, but do any common PHP functions support callbacks as a means of delayed execution of code?
6. Given that the `Events` class looks quite similar to the `Registry` class, is there any reason why we didn't simply use the `Registry` class to store the callbacks?

Answers

1. The obvious answer is to use caching wherever possible. This could mean caching the response to font requests that have a consistent font face/user agent combination. It could mean caching the contents of an existing thumbnail after the first time it is read.
2. Given unlimited time and energy, it would often be preferable to rewrite libraries to match a consistent theme or structure. In this case, we simply had to make do with the existing structure. It came with some odd trade-offs (like the position of the autoloader function) but we were able to use Imagine without very much fuss.
3. Yes, we should. It was not important to this lesson, though.
4. While it might be possible to build all the classes/functions with callbacks, it does not avoid synchronous execution of code. There will still be aspects of PHP that are block (e.g., file I/O, databases, loops, etc.). This is not because we are unable to use callbacks, but rather that each request is handled on a single thread. We can allow more threads to be used, or even run multiple PHP servers on a load balancer, but none of these really solve the problem.
5. PHP has had the concept of callbacks for a while now. They weren't always as elegant (often times strings referring to function names), but the idea of passing a reference to another body of executable code is not uncommon in PHP.
6. We did not use the `Registry` class, purely to keep the events isolated from everything else. The moment we start sharing the same storage space, we need to start worrying about naming schemes, which would complicate our events system needlessly.

Exercises

1. We spoke a little about using caching to avoid expensive file I/O operations. Try implementing these ideas in your `Files` controller. It might also be useful to benchmark the difference between cached and uncached actions.
2. The addition of the Imagine's autoloader function presents an alternative means of specifying autoloader functions to `spl_autoload_register`. Try modifying the `Core` class to use a similar approach to defining its autoloader functionality.
3. Try modifying the `thumbnails()` action to allow for custom `$width`/`$height`, and the `fonts()` action to allow for multiple font faces in a single request.
4. We learned about the usefulness of the Observer pattern, yet built a single plugin. Try to leverage the power of the events system by creating another plugin that uses it.

CHAPTER 20

Administration

The word *administration* strikes fear in the hearts of many developers. The problem is that most large (or user content-driven) applications require some form of content review. Fortunately, this is a topic that has been explored at great length. There are entire applications developed to help with the review of content, from all of the prebuild CMS (Content Management System) systems, such as WordPress and PHP-Nuke, to frameworks that automatically generate these CMS areas, such as Django.

Goals

- We need to understand the fundamental components in any administration interface.
- We need to build the different models, views, and controllers to manage the submission of content by users.

What Is a CMS?

A CMS is a secondary, secure web site through which the contents of the primary web site can be reviewed and/or changed. It is not intended for a user base of equivalent size to that of the primary web site, and usually requires training of some description in order for administrative users to use efficiently.

A CMS usually provides an interface through which to add other administrative users, and sometimes it can even provide some statistics about how the primary web site is used. The CMS we will build in this chapter will only concern itself with the basics of content review and user creation, leaving the addition of statistics as an exercise.

Administrators

Only administrators should have access to a CMS. Administrators are defined as users with above-average permissions, allowing them access and control over the secondary, secured web site. Structurally, they do not have to be quite distinct from normal users, and (in our case) will be separated by a simple flag field in the User model. Let's look at how this will be defined in Listing 20-1.

Listing 20-1. User Model Admin Flag

```
class User extends Shared\Model
{
    /**
    * @column
    * @readwrite
    * @type boolean
    */
    protected $_admin = false;
}
```

The `$_admin` field is a simple, Boolean field that we will use to determine whether the user has access to the administration interface. We have provided a default value for it that will be used as the row is added to the database, should no admin value be provided.

Login

If you are wondering whether we need to create a completely separate login interface for these administrative users, the answer is simply that all users will log in through the same interface. We will not create a separate administrative web site, but rather a set of actions/views that only administrative users will have access to.

I do, however, have changes for us to make to the login system. To recap, the login code looks like that shown in Listing 20-2.

Listing 20-2. Current login() Action

```
use Framework\Registry as Registry;
use Framework\RequestMethods as RequestMethods;
use Shared\Controller as Controller;

class Users extends Controller
{
    public function login()
    {
        if (RequestMethods::post("login"))
        {
            $email = RequestMethods::post("email");
            $password = RequestMethods::post("password");

            $user = User::first(array(
                "email = ?" => $email,
                "password = ?" => $password,
                "live = ?" => true,
                "deleted = ?" => false
            ));

            if (empty($email) || empty($password) || empty($user))
            {
                $this->actionView->set("password_error", "Email address and/or password ➥
are incorrect");
            }
```

```
            else
            {
                $session = Registry::get("session");
                $this->user = $user;
                self::redirect("/profile.html");
            }
        }
    }
}
```

The login() action looks for posted form data and validates against it. If the data fails validation, an error message is presented to the user. If the data passes validation and a valid user row is found, the user row is saved to the session and assigned to the controller. Finally, the login() action redirects to the profile page. This is similar to the current settings() action, as shown in Listing 20-3.

Listing 20-3. Current settings() Action

```
use Framework\Registry as Registry;
use Framework\RequestMethods as RequestMethods;
use Shared\Controller as Controller;

class Users extends Controller
{
    /**
    * @before _secure
    */
    public function settings()
    {
        if (RequestMethods::post("update"))
        {
            $user = new User(array(
                "id" => $this->user->id,
                "first" => RequestMethods::post("first"),
                "last" => RequestMethods::post("last"),
                "email" => RequestMethods::post("email"),
                "password" => RequestMethods::post("password"),
                "live" => (boolean) RequestMethods::post("live"),
                "deleted" => (boolean) RequestMethods::post("deleted")
            ));

            if ($user->validate())
            {
                $user->save();
                $this->user = $user;
                $this->_upload("photo", $user->id);
                $this->actionView->set("success", true);
            }

            $this->actionView->set("errors", $user->errors);
        }
    }
}
```

Similarly, the `settings()` action validates posted form data, updates the user row, and stores the user data in the session as well as the controller. These actions are sufficient for the most part, but what I want to improve on is where an unmodified user object is saved to both the session and the controller. I want to make the following changes:

- Entire user objects shouldn't be stored directly in the session. What I mean to say is that we shouldn't keep details such as passwords and statuses in the session, in case that session data is ever compromised. Instead, what we should do is store a reference to the user row, and return that user row from the database or cache, as we need it.
- We don't need to duplicate code by saving the user account to the session as well as the controller. Sure, we need to store a reference to the user (in the session) at some point, but it doesn't need to be in multiple user actions. We will create some code to automatically store this reference toward the end of a request cycle.

In order to achieve both of these objectives, we need to make use of the events we created in the Chapter 19, and we need to address a bug in PHP to make it happen. First, let's add those events to the `Shared\Controller`, as shown in Listing 20-4.

Listing 20-4. Events in the Shared\Controller Class

```
namespace Shared
{
    use Framework\Events as Events;
    use Framework\Router as Router;
    use Framework\Registry as Registry;

    class Controller extends \Framework\Controller
    {
        public function setUser($user)
        {
            $session = Registry::get("session");

            if ($user)
            {
                $session->set("user", $user->id);
            }
            else
            {
                $session->erase("user");
            }

            $this->_user = $user;
            return $this;
        }

        public function __construct($options = array())
        {
            parent::__construct($options);

            // connect to database
            $database = Registry::get("database");
            $database->connect();
```

```
            // schedule: load user from session
            Events::add("framework.router.beforehooks.before", function($name, $parameters) {
                $session = Registry::get("session");
                $controller = Registry::get("controller");
                $user = $session->get("user");

                if ($user)
                {
                    $controller->user = \User::first(array(
                        "id = ?" => $user
                    ));
                }
            });

            // schedule: save user to session
            Events::add("framework.router.afterhooks.after", function($name, $parameters) {
                $session = Registry::get("session");
                $controller = Registry::get("controller");

                if ($controller->user)
                {
                    $session->set("user", $controller->user->id);
                }
            });

            // schedule: disconnect from database
            Events::add("framework.controller.destruct.after", function($name) {
                $database = Registry::get("database");
                $database->disconnect();
            });
        }
}
```

What we've done is add two new event listeners to the `__construct()` method of the `Shared\Controller` class. These hook the user session–related details into the request cycle. The first event, which retrieves a user row based on session data, happens when the event `"framework.router.beforehooks.before"` fires. This means that it will occur before any action hooks or actions are executed. The second event, which stores a user reference to the session, happens when the event `"framework.router.afterhooks.after"` fires. This means that it will occur after all the action hooks and actions are executed.

We've also overridden the `$_user` setter method. This is so that the `login()` and `logout()` actions can make immediate changes to the session. The save event is similar to the code we were repeating in the `login()` and `settings()` actions, in as much as it takes the user row and saves it to the session. We get this data from the controller's user property, which in this case is the user's `id`. This is much better than our previous approach because it allows us to deal just with the controller's user property, and we no longer need to even think about saving user rows to session!

We are also no longer saving all the user's information to the session, but rather just the user's id property. This means we also need to request the user row when we pull the reference from the session, but this is preferable to storing everything in the session. We could also store the user row in cache, to save the overhead of an additional database query, but that's not important right now.

Now we need to address that PHP bug. In Chapter 19, we added an event so that the database instance would disconnect when it was no longer in use (around the time the `"framework.controller.destruct.after"` event is fired). We are not going to change this approach, but it might surprise you to know that this isn't actually happening.

You see, because of how PHP is executed (and specifically how the garbage collection works), objects are unset in variable order as the request cycle ends. In addition to this, the PHP interpreter will also shut down all the PHP modules in use, before it garbage collects objects. This means that all of the PHP modules are already shut down by the time our `__destruct()` methods are called, and the `"framework.controller.destruct.after"` event is only called in the `__destruct()` method of the Controller class. The $database instance is never disconnected as the MySQL module (in this case) is already shut down. Oh dear!

There is a work-around to this, but it involves some extra code. The `__destruct()` magic method is run whenever an object is garbage collected, but also if the object is manually destroyed, via an `unset()` statement. If we want `__destruct()` events to be of any practical use to us, we need to `unset()` the objects manually, so that they are fired before all of the modules are shut down. In the case of the `Controller` `__destruct()` method, we need to modify the Router class. Take a look at how we accomplish this in Listing 20-5.

Listing 20-5. Unsetting the Controller

```
namespace Framework
{
    use Framework\Base as Base;
    use Framework\Events as Events;
    use Framework\Registry as Registry;
    use Framework\Inspector as Inspector;
    use Framework\Router\Exception as Exception;

    class Router extends Base
    {
        protected function _pass($controller, $action, $parameters = array())
        {
            $name = ucfirst($controller);

            $this->_controller = $controller;
            $this->_action = $action;

            Events::fire("framework.router.controller.before", array($controller, $parameters));

            try
            {
                $instance = new $name(array(
                    "parameters" => $parameters
                ));
                Registry::set("controller", $instance);
            }
            catch (\Exception $e)
            {
                throw new Exception\Controller("Controller {$name} not found");
            }
            Events::fire("framework.router.controller.after", array($controller, $parameters));
```

```
if (!method_exists($instance, $action))
{
    $instance->willRenderLayoutView = false;
    $instance->willRenderActionView = false;

    throw new Exception\Action("Action {$action} not found");
}

$inspector = new Inspector($instance);
$methodMeta = $inspector->getMethodMeta($action);

if (!empty($methodMeta["@protected"]) || !empty($methodMeta["@private"]))
{
    throw new Exception\Action("Action {$action} not found");
}

$hooks = function($meta, $type) use ($inspector, $instance)
{
    if (isset($meta[$type]))
    {
        $run = array();

        foreach ($meta[$type] as $method)
        {
            $hookMeta = $inspector->getMethodMeta($method);

            if (in_array($method, $run) && !empty($hookMeta["@once"]))
            {
                continue;
            }

            $instance->$method();
            $run[] = $method;
        }
    }
};

Events::fire("framework.router.beforehooks.before", array($action, $parameters));

$hooks($methodMeta, "@before");

Events::fire("framework.router.beforehooks.after", array($action, $parameters));
Events::fire("framework.router.action.before", array($action, $parameters));

call_user_func_array(array(
    $instance,
    $action
), is_array($parameters) ? $parameters : array());

Events::fire("framework.router.action.after", array($action, $parameters));
Events::fire("framework.router.afterhooks.before", array($action, $parameters));
```

```
            $hooks($methodMeta, "@after");

            Events::fire("framework.router.afterhooks.after", array($action, $parameters));

            // unset controller
            Registry::erase("controller");
        }
    }
}
```

We unset the controller by calling the `erase()` method on the `Registry` class. It will, in turn, unset the stored `Controller` instance, which means the `__destruct()` method will run immediately. The final thing we need to do, before we can start creating the secured actions/views, is to create a method we can use to ensure the user is a valid administrator. We will add this method to the `Shared\Controller` class, as demonstrated in Listing 20-6.

Listing 20-6. The _admin() Hook

```
namespace Shared
{
    use Framework\Events as Events;
    use Framework\Router as Router;
    use Framework\Registry as Registry;

    class Controller extends \Framework\Controller
    {
        /**
        * @protected
        */
        public function _admin()
        {
            if (!$this->user->admin)
            {
                throw new Router\Exception\Controller("Not a valid admin user account");
            }
        }
    }
}
```

We will use this method as a hook, and its meaning is simple: if the user's admin property is not truthy, the user will be redirected to a 404 error page, via a raised exception.

Users

There are some consistent elements to each CMS. These include interfaces through which to add, edit, view, and delete rows of a database table (sometimes referred to as *CRUD*, which stands for **C**reate, **R**ead, **U**pdate, **D**elete). Because we are not interested in adding either users or photos (as these are already available in a public interface), we will concentrate on viewing, editing, and deleting rows from the application. To begin with, we need to add some actions to the `Users` and `Files` controllers. Let's start with the `Users` controller, as shown in Listing 20-7.

Listing 20-7. The edit()/view() Actions

```
use Framework\Registry as Registry;
use Framework\RequestMethods as RequestMethods;

use Shared\Controller as Controller;

class Users extends Controller
{
    /**
    * @before _secure, _admin
    */
    public function edit($id)
    {
        $errors = array();

        $user = User::first(array(
            "id = ?" => $id
        ));

        if (RequestMethods::post("save"))
        {
            $user->first = RequestMethods::post("first");
            $user->last = RequestMethods::post("last");
            $user->email = RequestMethods::post("email");
            $user->password = RequestMethods::post("password");
            $user->live = (boolean) RequestMethods::post("live");
            $user->admin = (boolean) RequestMethods::post("admin");

            if ($user->validate())
            {
                $user->save();
                $this->actionView->set("success", true);
            }

            $errors = $user->errors;
        }

        $this->actionView
            ->set("user", $user)
            ->set("errors", $errors);
    }
    /**
    * @before _secure, _admin
    */
    public function view()
    {
        $this->actionView->set("users", User::all());
    }
}
```

The two new actions we've added are responsible for updating and listing user rows. The `edit()` action is very similar to the `settings()` action, except that it allows for two new form fields (live and admin). The `view()`

action is even simpler, returning all user rows to the view. For these actions to route successfully, we need to add a few extra routes to the `public/routes.php` file, as shown in Listing 20-8.

Listing 20-8. public/routes.php (Extract)

```
// define routes
$routes = array(
    array(
        "pattern" => "users/edit/:id",
        "controller" => "users",
        "action" => "edit"
    ),
    array(
        "pattern" => "users/delete/:id",
        "controller" => "users",
        "action" => "delete"
    ),
    array(
        "pattern" => "users/undelete/:id",
        "controller" => "users",
        "action" => "undelete"
    ),
    array(
        "pattern" => "files/delete/:id",
        "controller" => "files",
        "action" => "delete"
    ),
    array(
        "pattern" => "files/undelete/:id",
        "controller" => "files",
        "action" => "undelete"
    )
);
```

You will notice we also added routes for `delete()/undelete()` actions that will look like that shown in Listing 20-9.

Listing 20-9. The delete()/undelete() Actions

```
use Framework\Registry as Registry;
use Framework\RequestMethods as RequestMethods;
use Shared\Controller as Controller;

class Users extends Controller
{
    /**
    * @before _secure, _admin
    */
    public function delete($id)
    {
        $user = User::first(array(
            "id = ?" => $id
        ));
```

```
        if ($user)
        {
            $user->live=false;
            $user->save();
        }

        self::redirect("/users/view.html");
    }

    /**
    * @before _secure, _admin
    */
    public function undelete($id)
    {
        $user=User::first(array(
            "id=?" => $id
        ));

        if ($user)
        {
            $user->live=true;
            $user->save();
        }

        self::redirect("/users/view.html");
    }
}
```

The delete()/undelete() actions modify a user row's live property, so they won't actually delete a row but rather just hide it from the main application views. Both methods redirect back to the user list. Now, let's look at the view templates, beginning with the application/views/users/view.html template, as shown in Listing 20-10.

Listing 20-10. application/views/users/view.html

```
<h1>View Users</h1>
<table>
    <tr>
        <th>Name</th>
        <th>Change</th>
    </tr>
    {foreach $_user in $users}
        <tr>
            <td>{echo $_user->first} {echo $_user->last}</td>
            <td>
                <a href="/users/edit/{echo $user->id}.html">edit</a>
                {if $user->deleted}
                    <a href="/users/undelete/{echo $user->id}.html">delete</a>
                {/if}
                {else}
                    <a href="/users/delete/{echo $user->id}.html">delete</a>
                {/else}
            </td>
        </tr>
    {/foreach}
</table>
```

The user list is similar to the `application/views/users/search.html` template, except that it does not have an area for search filters. The `edit()` action template should look like that shown in Listing 20-11.

Listing 20-11. application/views/users/edit.html

```
<h1>Edit User</h1>
{if isset($success)}
    The user has been updated!
{/if}
{else}
    <form method="post">
        <ol>
            <li>
                <label>
                    First name:
                    <input type="text" name="first" value="{echo $user->first}" />
                    {echo Shared\Markup::errors($errors, "first")}
                </label>
            </li>
            <li>
                <label>
                    Last name:
                    <input type="text" name="last" value="{echo $user->last}" />
                    {echo Shared\Markup::errors($errors, "last")}
                </label>
            </li>
            <li>
                <label>
                    Email:
                    <input type="text" name="email" value="{echo $user->email}" />
                    {echo Shared\Markup::errors($errors, "email")}
                </label>
            </li>
            <li>
                <label>
                    Password:
                    <input type="password" name="password" value="{echo $user->password}" />
                    {echo Shared\Markup::errors($errors, "password")}
                </label>
            </li>
            <li>
                <label>
                    Live:
                    <input type="checkbox" name="live" {if $user->live} checked="checked"{/if} />
                </label>
            </li>
            <li>
                <label>
                    Admin:
                    <input type="checkbox" name="admin" {if $user->admin} ➥
checked="checked"{/if} />
                </label>
            </li>
```

```
            <li>
                <input type="submit" name="save" value="save" />
            </li>
        </ol>
    </form>
{/else}
```

The user edit view is similar to the register/settings templates, but also includes the `live/admin` fields. It's okay to include those here, as only administrators will be able to get here. We also populate the field values automatically. We should also add the admin links to the navigation template, as shown in Listing 20-12.

Listing 20-12. application/views/navigation.html

```
<a href="/">home</a>
<a href="/search.html">search</a>
{if isset($user)}
    <a href="/profile.html">profile</a>
    <a href="/settings.html">settings</a>
    <a href="/logout.html">logout</a>
    {if $user->admin}
        <a href="/users/view.html">view users</a>
        <a href="/files/view.html">view files</a>
    {/if}
{/if}
{else}
    <a href="/register.html">register</a>
    <a href="/login.html">login</a>
{/else}
```

If you have done everything correctly so far, and you navigate to the users/view action, you should see a list of the registered users, along with some links (in the Change column). Clicking on the edit link will take you to the edit action/view. It might surprise you to see that your account details are populated in the form fields, no matter which user row you selected to change. This is because of how we are automatically populating the view with the current user section.

There are a few alternatives to this behavior, but the approach we will take is checking whether the view already has a user property (before assigning the session user to the views) and renaming this variable accordingly. Take a look at Listing 20-13 to see how we accomplish this.

Listing 20-13. Setting the Session in the Shared\Controller Class

```
namespace Shared
{
    use Framework\Events as Events;
    use Framework\Router as Router;
    use Framework\Registry as Registry;

    class Controller extends \Framework\Controller
    {
        public function render()
        {
            /* if the user and view(s) are defined,
               assign the user session to the view(s) */
```

```
            if ($this->user)
            {
                if ($this->actionView)
                {
                    $key = "user";
                    if ($this->actionView->get($key, false))
                    {
                        $key = "__user";
                    }

                    $this->actionView->set($key, $this->user);
                }

                if ($this->layoutView)
                {
                    $key = "user";
                    if ($this->layoutView->get($key, false))
                    {
                        $key = "__user";
                    }

                    $this->layoutView->set($key, $this->user);
                }
            }

            parent::render();
        }
    }
}
```

To achieve this dynamic naming, we modify the `Shared\Controller` class to first check whether the `user` key exists and, if it does, to save the user session with the `__user` key. The same issue would reoccur if there were already a `__user` key stored in the view's data, but the chances are slim, and we are not looking to avoid any collisions, as we are to get the users/edit action working properly. Now, the edit, view, delete, and undelete actions/views should all be functioning as expected.

Photos

Photos will work slightly differently: we will do all our editing from a single view, with only three attached actions. Let's look at the actions in Listing 20-14.

Listing 20-14. The File view(), delete(), and undelete() Actions

```
use Shared\Controller as Controller;
use Fonts\Proxy as Proxy;
use Fonts\Types as Types;

class Files extends Controller
{
    /**
    * @before _secure, _admin
    */
```

```
    public function view()
    {
        $this->actionView->set("files", File::all());
    }

    /**
    * @before _secure, _admin
    */
    public function delete($id)
    {
        $file=File::first(array(
            "id=?" => $id
        ));

        if ($file)
        {
            $file->deleted=true;
            $file->save();
        }

        self::redirect("/files/view.html");
    }

    /**
    * @before _secure, _admin
    */
    public function undelete($id)
    {
        $file=File::first(array(
            "id=?" => $id
        ));

        if ($file)
        {
            $file->deleted=false;
            $file->save();
        }

        self::redirect("/files/view.html");
    }
}
```

These actions are almost exactly the same as their counterparts in the `Users` controller. The view we will need is the `view()` action's view, as shown in Listing 20-15.

Listing 20-15. application/views/files/view.html

```
<h1>View Files</h1>
<table>
    <tr>
        <th>Thumbnail</th>
        <th>Change</th>
    </tr>
```

```
    {foreach $file in $files}
        <tr>
            <td><img src="/thumbnails/{echo $file->id}" /></td>
            <td>
                {if $file->deleted}
                    <a href="/files/undelete/{echo $file->id}.html">undelete</a>
                {/if}
                {else}
                    <a href="/files/delete/{echo $file->id}.html">delete</a>
                {/else}
            </td>
        </tr>
    {/foreach}
</table>
```

This template allows administrators to see the thumbnails of files that users have uploaded, and delete/undelete those they feel need changing. This means we can now view/edit both users and photos they upload, concluding the work we need to do in order to administer our social network.

Questions

1. In previous chapters, we stored all of a user's information in session variables, but in this chapter we slimed it down to just storing a user's id property. Can you think of any advantages to this approach?
2. In this chapter, we also developed a means of automatically storing the user in the session by overriding/modifying some Shared\Controller methods. Can you think of any advantages of this approach?
3. Can you think of any other user-submitted data that we could build administration interfaces for?

Answers

1. Apart from the stated security benefit of not keeping items such as e-mail address and password in the session variables, it also speeds up storage/retrieval at the cost of extra database queries. We could also use cache to cut down on these extra queries.
2. We saw that this automatic storage/retrieval helped us to work with the user session, without the hassle of getting/setting the session details each time we worked with it. This benefitted our login, logout, settings, and profile actions/view. This will also help whenever we need to get or set any user session information.
3. We built administration interfaces for users and files, but we could also build them for messages and statistics. The sky's the limit!

Exercises

1. With the changes to how we stored user sessions came an increase in database queries for user account information. Try storing this information in the cache and retrieving it from cache on each page load, instead of additional database queries. Just be use to keep the session information secure!
2. In Chapter 16, we used a primitive form of pagination and neglected adding pagination to our administration interface. Try implementing the same primitive pagination or even something more creative.
3. We are displaying thumbnails for the files/view action, but it would be even better to have the thumbnails click through to a larger version of the uploaded file. Perhaps even using some form of JavaScript lightbox effect. Try implementing this.

CHAPTER 21

Testing

With our sample application progressing nicely along, we once again need to turn our attention back to the topic of testing. What you are likely to find is that testing abstract code is much easier than testing application logic. What's more, the tests we need to perform require a level of interaction that's difficult to simulate through code.

Goals

- We need to test the format of various input forms.
- We need to test the results of various user interactions with these forms.

One of the many ways in which we can test the validity of forms is by checking for certain elements within the returned body of HTML. To do this, we need to utilize our Request class (for making various HTTP requests to pages within our application) and we need to evaluate the HTML returned by the Request class to determine whether certain fields are provided for input.

These two goals can be achieved using the functions shown in Listing 21-1.

Listing 21-1. Testing with Request

```
$get = function($url)
{
    $request = new Framework\Request();
    return $request->get("http://".$_SERVER["HTTP_HOST"]."/{$url}");
};

$has = function($html, $fields)
{
    foreach ($fields as $field)
    {
        if (!stristr($html, "name=\"{$field}\""))
        {
            return false;
        }
    }

    return true;
};
```

The first function simply creates a new Request instance and makes a GET request to a path within our localhost. If you set up your sample application to run under a different host name, be sure to adjust this function accordingly.

The second function iterates over an array of field names, checking whether they are contained within the provided `$html` string. It converts them into a format of `"name=\"{$field}\""`, which targets form fields. With these functions in place, we can write the tests for our sample application's various forms, as demonstrated in Listing 21-2.

Listing 21-2. Testing Form Fields

```
Framework\Test::add(
    function() use ($get, $has)
    {
        $html = $get("register.html");
        $status = $has($html, array(
            "first",
            "last",
            "email",
            "password",
            "photo",
            "register"
        ));

        return $status;
    },
    "Register form has required fields",
    "Forms/Users"
);

Framework\Test::add(
    function() use ($get, $has)
    {
        $html = $get("login.html");
        $status = $has($html, array(
            "email",
            "password",
            "login"
        ));

        return $status;
    },
    "Login form has required fields",
    "Forms/Users"
);

Framework\Test::add(
    function() use ($get, $has)
    {
        $html = $get("search.html");
        $status = $has($html, array(
            "query",
            "order",
            "direction",
            "page",
```

```
            "limit",
            "search"
        ));

        return $status;
    },
    "Search form has required fields",
    "Forms/Users"
);
```

The first test gets the HTML in the `register.html` form and checks against a list of fields to make sure they are provided. The second and third tests do similar checks but on the `login.html` and `search.html` forms respectively.

The second thing we need to test for is the results of various user interactions within our sample application. To achieve this we need to add another function to the mix, as shown in Listing 21-3.

Listing 21-3. Testing POST Requests

```
$post = function($url, $data)
{
    $reques = new Framework\Request();
    return $request->post("http://".$_SERVER["HTTP_HOST"]."/{$url}", $data);
};
```

This function is quite similar to the `$get` function, but instead performs `POST` requests with provided data. We use this function in the tests shown in Listing 21-4.

Listing 21-4. Testing Form Posting

```
Framework\Test::add(
    function() use ($post)
    {
        $html = $post(
            "register.html",
            array(
                "first" => "Hello",
                "last" => "World",
                "email" => "info@example.com",
                "password" => "password",
                "register" => "register"
            )
        );

        return (stristr($html, "Your account has been created!"));
    },
    "Register form creates user",
    "Functions/Users"
);

Framework\Test::add(
    function() use ($post)
    {
```

```
        $html = $post(
            "login.html",
            array(
                "email" => "info@example.com",
                "password" => "password",
                "login" => "login"
            )
        );

        return (stristr($html, "Location: /profile.html"));
    },
    "Login form creates user session + redirect to profile",
    "Functions/Users"
);
```

The first test posts some user data to the `register.html` form and checks to see whether this leads to a response indicating a user account was created. The second test is similar except that it posts instead to the `login.html` form with user details matching those of the user account that was created by the first test. The validity of the second test is indicated by whether the `Request` instance is told to go to a new location.

Testing can initially seem daunting – it was for me before the first time I tried it. The truth is that it's really quite easy. We've not only managed to develop our own unit-testing framework code but also a handful of tests which will pave the way for you to be able to create even more tests for your projects in the future.

Questions

1. How does testing for the presence of certain fields help us to further ensure the stability of our application?

2. Is there a reason why we should avoid testing forms that require the user to be logged in?

3. What are some other ways in which we can test our application?

Answers

1. The fields contained in a form are indicative of the action a user should want to perform. While fields can change over time, this is a good way to know if something has broken the basic structure of each form.

2. On the contrary, we should be testing everything we can get our hands on. The problem is one of session management meeting our `Request` class. Session management is tricky even without the added proxy, and this presents problems with tests that require valid, secure sessions.

3. There are a number of things we didn't test for. One thing that would be relatively easy to test is the validity of posted form data. We could knowingly provide invalid form data and check the response for validation error messages concerning the invalid data. Another thing we could test for is the presence of interface elements (such as a consistent navigation menu across multiple pages).

Exercises

1. In this chapter, we tested for just two kinds of errors that could occur. Try writing some tests for form field validation.

2. In Chapter 11, we set about creating tests for framework classes. If you already have a place where these tests are represented, try integrating these new tests there.

CHAPTER 22

CodeIgniter: Bootstrapping

CodeIgniter is the first of three frameworks we will review in this book. It is arguably the least popular of the three, the smallest, the fastest (in comparative tests), and the least complex. It was created and is maintained by EllisLab (`http://ellislab.com`).

Our aim for the remaining chapters of this book will be to duplicate the majority of the functionality we created in our social network, to try and gain an understanding of some of the differences between the frameworks and our own. It will also serve as an opportunity to assess the strengths of each framework so you can better decide which framework suits the PHP MVC projects you undertake.

Goals

- We need to understand the philosophy and benefits of CodeIgniter.
- We need to review the requirements for URL rewriting within CodeIgniter applications.
- We need to create a few CodeIgniter routes that will allow us to access the controllers, actions, and views we create in future chapters.

Why CodeIgniter?

As I mentioned, CodeIgniter has a relatively small and simple codebase. This is due to one of their goals, which is to keep the framework lean. This is achieved through minimal automation, as well as a limited set of libraries that come bundled with the framework.

With good code conventions and a small codebase, it follows that the average execution time of an action is fairly low. This might not always be the case, especially when performing intensive operations.

CodeIgniter's documentation is exceptional. It's not merely API documentation, but provides the developer with an understanding of the practical implementation of MVC within the framework, as well as numerous code examples for the most common problems a developer will encounter when diving into CodeIgniter.

Note You can find the CodeIgniter documentation at `http://codeigniter.com/user_guide`.

When deciding whether to use CodeIgniter for your next project, it helps to consider the types of applications for which CodeIgniter is a good choice. CodeIgniter is ideally suited for small- to medium-sized applications that require minimal functionality without the use of third-party libraries. This is not because it is difficult to add additional third-party libraries but because CodeIgniter comes bundled with a small selection of libraries for only the most common of requirements.

Why Not CodeIgniter?

CodeIgniter does not include any automated build tools. These are scripts that can be used to create all the usual components that accompany MVC frameworks, leaving only the tricky bits for developers to concern themselves with. If you are new to MVC, then this is not something you will miss.

CodeIgniter has always been open source, but the framework hasn't been open for public contribution for very long at all. This continues to improve as the project is becoming active due to contributions streaming in from GitHub users.

■ **Note** You can contribute to CodeIgniter development at `https://github.com/EllisLab/CodeIgniter`.

URL Rewriting

The mechanisms we need to utilize for URL rewriting, in CodeIgniter applications, are much the same as we used for our own framework. CodeIgniter provides a single access point for our application, which is an `index.php` file in the root application directory.

We also need to use `.htaccess` (mod_rewrite) to transfer requests to this `index.php` file. EllisLab suggests the `.htaccess` configuration shown in Listing 22-1.

Listing 22-1. CodeIgniter .htaccess

```
RewriteEngine on
RewriteCond $1 !^(index\.php|images|robots\.txt)
RewriteRule ^(.*)$ /index.php/$1 [L]
```

This `RewriteRule` basically tells Apache to send requests for everything that is not `robots.txt` or within the `images` directory to the `index.php` file. This `.htaccess` file should reside in the same directory as the `index.php` file provided by CodeIgniter. This will ensure that the requests are served as recommended by EllisLab.

■ **Note** You can find more details about this `.htaccess` file at `http://codeigniter.com/user_guide/general/urls.html`.

Routes

In CodeIgniter, routes are defined as key/value pairs in an associative array configuration file format. This configuration file is typically found in `application/config/routes.php`, and should resemble what is shown in Listing 22-2.

Listing 22-2. application/config/routes.php (Extract)

```
$route['default_controller'] = "welcome";
$route['404_override'] = '';

// custom routes

$route['register'] = 'users/register';
$route['login'] = 'users/login';
$route['logout'] = 'users/logout';
$route['search'] = 'users/search';
$route['profile'] = 'users/profile';
$route['settings'] = 'users/settings';
$route['friend/(:num)'] = 'users/friend/$1';
$route['unfriend/(:num)'] = 'users/unfriend/$1';
$route['users/edit/(:num)'] = 'users/edit/$1';
$route['users/delete/(:num)'] = 'users/delete/$1';
$route['users/undelete/(:num)'] = 'users/undelete/$1';
$route['fonts/(:any)'] = 'files/fonts/$1';
$route['thumbnails/(:num)'] = 'files/thumbnails/$1';
$route['files/delete/(:num)'] = 'files/delete/$1';
$route['files/undelete/(:num)'] = 'files/undelete/$1';
```

The first two routes are automatically defined for us. The first is used to present the default landing page for new CodeIgniter installations. The second is merely a means of specifying a custom error page for missing controllers, actions, or views.

In some of the routes we have used things like `(:num)`, `(:any)`, and `$1`. These are used in the translation of routes to regular expressions. CodeIgniter uses regular expression matching to determine the correct controller and action to execute, much the same as our framework does. The values matched by `(:num)` and `(:any)` are sent to the action as arguments.

If you try to access any of these new routes, you will see an error. This is because we have not yet created the corresponding controllers, actions, and so on. In Chapter 23, we will create the controllers, models, and views required for most of these routes to function correctly.

■ **Note** You can find more details about this configuration file at `http://codeigniter.com/user_guide/general/routing.html`.

Questions

1. In the Chapter 21, we learned how CodeIgniter secures the application and system class files by a line of code in every file. Our framework handles this differently by restricting all web requests to a public folder. Does this mean CodeIgniter got it wrong?
2. In Chapter 4, we discussed the differences between associative array configurations and INI configurations. How might we represent the same routes in an INI configuration format?

Answers

1. The core team responsible for CodeIgniter development has been quite thorough in its application of this security technique. The problem is not that their system is insecure, but that securing it requires a combination of Apache security and the addition of security code to each class file. That does not mean this security check would be a bad thing if we decided to add it to our framework, but that forgetting to add it to any CodeIgniter application class files could create a security vulnerability.

2. There are a number of ways to approach this question, but the simplest would be to use a format resembling what is shown in Listing 22-3.

Listing 22-3. INI route configuration

```
route[register] = users/register
route[login] = users/login
route[logout] = users/logout
...
route[thumbnails/:id] = files/thumbnails/:id
route[files/delete/:id] = files/delete/:id
route[files/undelete/:id] = files/undelete/:id
```

Exercises

1. In this chapter, we created all the routes our example application requires. Now try creating a route that uses a username to invoke the users/profile action.

2. Having all these routes without any controllers and actions isn't very helpful to us. Try creating a controller and action to handle a few of the routes we defined.

CHAPTER 23

CodeIgniter: MVC

We have our work cut out for us, with CodeIgniter. It does provide us with controllers, models, and views with which to build all the functionality our social network needs, but they are little more than empty containers. We have grown accustomed to have an ORM in our models, yet CodeIgniter provides none of this. We are also used to having autoloaded classes within our controllers, yet CodeIgniter makes us load our own classes. We are used to a rich templating language in our views, yet CodeIgniter provides a stunted template parser and even encourages PHP directly in view templates.

Goals

- We need to recognize the differences between our framework and CodeIgniter when it comes to creating the controllers, models, and views for our example application.
- We need to create the models for users, friends, files, and messages.
- We need to create the corresponding views and controllers.

Differences

I have already mentioned three differences between CodeIgniter and our framework, but there are a few more things we need to consider. First, CodeIgniter does have form validation, but it is not linked to the models in any way. It is actually recommended that the validation should occur in the controller.

Second, CodeIgniter provides a form builder class that we can use to speed up development of our views. Furthermore, we are able to access validation error messages without assigning them to the view.

Models

Creating the models for our example application will be a bit of work. We do not have access to the ORM we are used to using in our framework, so we have to construct the database queries for each model manually. CodeIgniter helps us out with this by providing an expressive query generator (similar to the one we built for our framework).

We begin by defining our `User` model, as shown in Listing 23-1.

Listing 23-1. application/models/user.php (Extract)

```
class User extends CI_Model
{
    public $id;
    public $live = true;
    public $deleted = false;
    public $created;
    public $modified;
    public $first;
    public $last;
    public $email;
    public $password;

    protected function _populate($options)
    {
        // set all existing properties
        foreach ($options as $key => $value)
        {
            if (property_exists($this, $key))
            {
                $this->$key = $value;
            }
        }
    }

    public function __construct($options = array())
    {
        // be a good subclass
        parent::__construct();

        // populate values
        if (sizeof($options))
        {
            $this->_populate($options);
        }

        // load row
        $this->load();
    }

    public function load()
    {
        if ($this->id)
        {
            $query = $this->db
                ->where("id", $this->id)
                ->get("user", 1, 0);

            if ($row = $query->row())
            {
                $this->id = (bool) $row->id;
```

```
                $this->live = (boolean) $row->live;
                $this->deleted = (boolean) $row->deleted;
                $this->created = $row->created;
                $this->modified = $row->modified;
                $this->first=$row->first;
                $this->last=$row->last;
                $this->email=$row->email;
                $this->password=$row->password;
            }
        }
    }
}
```

This User model is fairly similar to the one we created for our framework, containing all the fields relating to the database table in which user rows are stored. CodeIgniter does have libraries to manipulate the structure of database tables, but we won't go as far as to build that functionality into our models.

The structure of the table can be achieved by running the SQL query, shown in Listing 23-2, on your local MySQL database.

Listing 23-2. User Table SQL

```
CREATE TABLE `user` (
    `id` int(11) NOT NULL AUTO_INCREMENT,
    `live` tinyint(4) DEFAULT NULL,
    `deleted` tinyint(4) DEFAULT NULL,
    `created` datetime DEFAULT NULL,
    `modified` datetime DEFAULT NULL,
    `first` varchar(32) DEFAULT NULL,
    `last` varchar(32) DEFAULT NULL,
    `email` varchar(100) DEFAULT NULL,
    `password` varchar(32) DEFAULT NULL,
    `admin` tinyint(4) DEFAULT NULL,
    PRIMARY KEY (`id`)
) ENGINE=InnoDB DEFAULT CHARSET=utf8 AUTO_INCREMENT=1 ;
```

To get a user row out of the database, we simply need to run the same code as we did in our framework, as shown in Listing 23-3.

Listing 23-3. Getting a User Row

```
$this->user = new User(array(
    "id" => $id
));
```

There are a few other methods that we need to add to this User model, which you can see in Listing 23-4.

Listing 23-4. application/models/user.php (Extract)

```
class User extends CI_Model
{
    public function save()
```

```
    {
        // initialize data
        $data = array(
            "live" => (int) $this->live,
            "deleted" => (int) $this->deleted,
            "modified" => date("Y-m-d H:i:s"),
            "first" => $this->first,
            "last" => $this->last,
            "email" => $this->email,
            "password" => $this->password
        );

        // update
        if ($this->id)
        {
            $where = array("id" => $this->id);
            return $this->db->update("user", $data, $where);
        }

        // insert
        $data["created"] = date("Y-m-d H:i:s");
        $this->id = $this->db->insert("user", $data);

        // return insert id
        return $this->id;
    }

    public static function first($where)
    {
        $user = new User();

        // get the first user
        $user->db->where($where);
        $user->db->limit(1);

        $query = $user->db->get("user");

        // initialze the data
        $data = $query->row();
        $user->_populate($data);

        // return the user
        return $user;
    }

    public static function count($where)
    {
        $user = new User();
        $user->db->where($where);
        return $user->db->count_all_results("user");
    }
```

```
    public static function all($where = null, $fields = null, $order = null, $direction = "asc",
$limit = null, $page = null)
    {
        $user = new User();

        // select fields
        if ($fields)
        {
            $user->db->select(join(",", $fields));
        }

        // narrow search
        if ($where)
        {
            $user->db->where($where);
        }

        // order results
        if ($order)
        {
            $user->db->order_by($order, $direction);
        }

        // limit results
        if ($limit && $page)
        {
            $offset = ($page - 1) * $limit;
            $user->db->limit($limit, $offset);
        }

        // get the users
        $query = $user->db->get("user");
        $users = array();

        foreach ($query->result() as $row)
        {
            // create + populate user
            $user = new User();
            $user->_populate($row);

            // add user to pile
            array_push($users, $user);
        }

        return $users;
    }
}
```

These methods are very similar to the methods we defined on our `Model` class, and perform various database queries that we will require in our controllers. Things start to deviate from what we are used to when we consider that CodeIgniter doesn't share our ideas for connectors and queries, but rather implements its own system for querying the database. CodeIgniter does have method chaining, though, so it's not all bad!

Controllers

With our User model in place, we can begin to work on our Users controller, as shown in Listing 23-5.

Listing 23-5. application/controllers/users.php (Extract)

```
class Users extends CI_Controller
{
    public $user;

    public static function redirect($url)
    {
        header("Location: {$url}");
        exit();
    }

    protected function _isSecure()
    {
        // get user session
        $this->_getUser();

        if (!$this->user)
        {
            self::redirect("/login");
        }
    }
    protected function _getUser()
    {
        // load session library
        $this->load->library("session");

        // get user id
        $id = $this->session->userdata("user");

        if ($id)
        {
            // load user model
            $this->load->model("user");

            // get user
            $this->user = new User(array(
                "id" => $id
            ));
        }
    }
}
```

The Users controller begins simply enough, containing similar "hook" methods to those we have in our framework. The _getUser() method accesses the session to retrieve the user ID and loads the User model to retrieve a user row. We proceed to the register() action and view next, as demonstrated in Listings 23-6 and 23-7.

Listing 23-6. application/controllers/users.php (Extract)

```
class Users extends CI_Controller
{
    //...

    public function register()
    {
        $success = false;

        // load validation library
        $this->load->library("form_validation");

        // if form was posted
        if ($this->input->post("save"))
        {
            // initialize validation rules
            $this->form_validation->set_rules(array(
                array(
                    "field" => "first",
                    "label" => "First",
                    "rules" => "required|alpha|min_length[3]|max_length[32]"
                ),
                array(
                    "field" => "last",
                    "label" => "Last",
                    "rules" => "required|alpha|min_length[3]|max_length[32]"
                ),
                array(
                    "field" => "email",
                    "label" => "Email",
                    "rules" => "required|max_length[100]"
                ),
                array(
                    "field" => "password",
                    "label" => "Password",
                    "rules" => "required|min_length[8]|max_length[32]"
                )
            ));

            // if form data passes validation...
            if ($this->form_validation->run())
            {
                // load user model
                $this->load->model("user");
```

```
                // create new user + save
                $user = new User(array(
                    "first" => $this->input->post("first"),
                    "last" => $this->input->post("last"),
                    "email" => $this->input->post("email"),
                    "password" => $this->input->post("password")
                ));
                $user->save();

                // indicate success in view
                $success = true;
            }
        }

        // load view
        $this->load->view("users/register", array(
            "success" => $success
        ));
    }
}
```

Listing 23-7. application/views/users/register.php

```
<h1>Register</h1>
<?php if ($success): ?>
    Your account has been created!
<?php else: ?>
    <form method="post" enctype="multipart/form-data">
        <ol>
            <li>
                <label>
                    First name:
                    <input type="text" name="first" />
                    <?php echo form_error("first"); ?>
                </label>
            </li>
            <li>
                <label>
                    Last name:
                    <input type="text" name="last" />
                    <?php echo form_error("last"); ?>
                </label>
            </li>
            <li>
                <label>
                    Email:
                    <input type="text" name="email" />
                    <?php echo form_error("email"); ?>
                </label>
            </li>
```

```
            <li>
                <label>
                    Password:
                    <input type="password" name="password" />
                    <?php echo form_error("password"); ?>
                </label>
            </li>
            <li>
                <input type="submit" name="save" value="register" />
            </li>
        </ol>
    </form>
<?php endif; ?>
```

We begin the `register()` action by loading the `form_validation` library. Next, we check whether the save button was clicked and define the validation rules for the posted field data. If validation is successful, we create a new `User` object and populate it with the posted data. Finally, we save the `User` object and indicate success to the loaded view. The view template includes everything our previous register view template did, while using CodeIgniter equivalent methods for displaying validation errors.

The next action and view we need is for login, as shown in Listings 23-8 and 23-9.

Listing 23-8. application/controllers/users.php (Extract)

```
class Users extends CI_Controller
{
    public function login()
    {
        $errors = null;

        // load validation library
        $this->load->library("form_validation");

        // if form was posted
        if ($this->input->post("login"))
        {
            // initialize validation rules
            $this->form_validation->set_rules(array(
                array(
                    "field" => "email",
                    "label" => "Email",
                    "rules" => "required|max_length[100]"
                ),
                array(
                    "field" => "password",
                    "label" => "Password",
                    "rules" => "required|min_length[8]|max_length[32]"
                )
            ));

            // load user model
            $this->load->model("user");
```

```
            // create new user+save
            $user = User::first(array(
                "email" => $this->input->post("email"),
                "password" => $this->input->post("password"),
                "live" => 1,
                "deleted" => 0
            ));

            // if form data passes validation...
            if ($user && $this->form_validation->run())
            {
                // load session library
                $this->load->library("session");

                // save user id to session
                $this->session->set_userdata("user", $user->id);

                // redirect to profile page
                self::redirect("/profile");

            }
            else
            {
                // indicate errors
                $errors = "Email address and/or password are incorrect";
            }
        }

        // load view
        $this->load->view("users/login", array(
            "errors" => $errors
        ));
    }
}
```

Listing 23-9. application/views/users/login.php

```
<h1>Login</h1>
<form method="post">
    <ol>
        <li>
            <label>
                Email:
                <input type="text" name="email" />
            </label>
        </li>
        <li>
            <label>
                Password:
                <input type="password" name="password" />
                <?php if ($errors): ?><?php echo $errors; ?><?php endif; ?>
            </label>
        </li>
```

```
        <li>
            <input type="submit" name="login" value="login" />
        </li>
    </ol>
</form>
```

The login() action works similarly to the register() action, except instead of saving the user row to the database, we retrieve a user row from the database that corresponds to the posted form data and store the user ID in the session. Finally, we redirect to the profile page after a successful login has occurred.

We follow this up with the logout() and profile() actions and the profile view template, as shown in Listings 23-10 and 23-11.

Listing 23-10. application/controllers/users.php (Extract)

```
class Users extends CI_Controller
{
    public function logout()
    {
        // load session library
        $this->load->library("session");

        // remove user id
        $this->session->unset_userdata("user");

        // redirect to login
        self::redirect("/login");
    }

    public function profile()
    {
        // check for user session
        $this->_isSecure();

        // load view
        $this->load->view("users/profile", array(
            "user" =>$this->user
        ));
    }
}
```

Listing 23-11. application/views/users/profile.php

```
<h1><?php echo $user->first; ?><?php echo $user->last; ?></h1>
This is a profile page!
```

The logout() action simply removes the user ID from the session, and the profile action loads the user session, passing it to the loaded view. The profile view is quite similar to our previous profile view, using the PHP methods corresponding to our previous template tags.

The last two actions and views relate to user settings and user search. These are demonstrated in Listings 23-12 through 23-14.

Listing 23-12. application/controllers/users.php (Extract)

```
class Users extends CI_Controller
{
    public function settings()
    {
        $success = false;

        // check for user session
        $this->_isSecure();

        // load validation library
        $this->load->library("form_validation");

        // if form was posted
        if ($this->input->post("save"))
        {
            // initialize validation rules
            $this->form_validation->set_rules(array(
                array(
                    "field" => "first",
                    "label" => "First",
                    "rules" => "required|alpha|min_length[3]|max_length[32]"
                ),
                array(
                    "field" => "last",
                    "label" => "Last",
                    "rules" => "required|alpha|min_length[3]|max_length[32]"
                ),
                array(
                    "field" => "email",
                    "label" => "Email",
                    "rules" => "required|max_length[100]"
                ),
                array(
                    "field" => "password",
                    "label" => "Password",
                    "rules" => "required|min_length[8]|max_length[32]"
                )
            ));

            // if form data passes validation...
            if ($this->form_validation->run())
            {
                // update user
                $this->user->first = $this->input->post("first");
                $this->user->last = $this->input->post("last");
                $this->user->email = $this->input->post("email");
                $this->user->password = $this->input->post("password");
                $this->user->save();
```

```
                // indicate success in view
                $success = true;
            }
        }

        // load view
        $this->load->view("users/settings", array(
            "success" => $success,
            "user" => $this->user
        ));
    }

    public function search()
    {
        // get posted data
        $query = $this->input->post("query");
        $order = $this->input->post("order");
        $direction = $this->input->post("direction");
        $page = $this->input->post("page");
        $limit = $this->input->post("limit");

        // default null values
        $order = $order ? $order : "modified";
        $direction = $direction ? $direction : "desc";
        $limit = $limit ? $limit : 10;
        $page = $page ? $page : 1;
        $count = 0;
        $users = null;

        if ($this->input->post("search"))
        {
            $where = array(
                "first" => $query,
                "live" => 1,
                "deleted" => 0
            );

            $fields = array(
                "id", "first", "last"
            );

            // load user model
            $this->load->model("user");

            // get count + results
            $count = User::count($where);
            $users = User::all(
                $where,
                $fields,
                $order,
                $direction,
```

```
                $limit,
                $page
            );
        }

        // load view
        $this->load->view("users/search", array(
            "query" => $query,
            "order" => $order,
            "direction" => $direction,
            "page" => $page,
            "limit" => $limit,
            "count" => $count,
            "users" => $users
        ));
    }
}
```

Listing 23-13. application/views/users/settings.php

```
<h1>Settings</h1>
<?php if ($success): ?>
    Your account has been updated!
<?php else: ?>
    <form method="post" enctype="multipart/form-data">
        <ol>
            <li>
                <label>
                    First name:
                    <input type="text" name="first" value="<?php echo $user->first; ?>" />
                    <?php echo form_error("first"); ?>
                </label>
            </li>
            <li>
                <label>
                    Last name:
                    <input type="text" name="last" value="<?php echo $user->last; ?>" />
                    <?php echo form_error("last"); ?>
                </label>
            </li>
            <li>
                <label>
                    Email:
                    <input type="text" name="email" value="<?php echo $user->email; ?>" />
                    <?php echo form_error("email"); ?>
                </label>
            </li>
            <li>
                <label>
                    Password:
                    <input type="password" name="password" value="<?php echo
$user->password; ?>" />
```

```
                <?php echo form_error("password"); ?>
            </label>
        </li>
        <li>
            <input type="submit" name="save" value="save" />
        </li>
    </ol>
</form>
<?php endif; ?>
```

Listing 23-14. application/views/users/search.php

```
<h1>Search</h1>
<form method="post">
    <ol>
        <li>
            <label>
                Query:
                <input type="text" name="query" value="<?php echo $query; ?>" />
            </label>
        </li>
        <li>
            <label>
                Order:
                <select name="order">
                    <option<?php if ($order == "created"): ?>selected="selected"<?php
endif; ?>value="created">Created</option>
                    <option<?php if ($order == "modified"): ?>selected="selected"<?php
endif; ?>value="modified">Modified</option>
                    <option<?php if ($order == "first"): ?>selected="selected"<?php
endif; ?>value="first">First name</option>
                    <option<?php if ($order == "last"): ?>selected="selected"<?php
endif; ?>value="last">Last name</option>
                </select>
            </label>
        </li>
        <li>
            <label>
                Direction:
                <select name="direction">
                    <option<?php if ($direction == "asc"): ?>selected="selected"<?php
endif; ?>value="asc">Ascending</option>
                    <option<?php if ($direction == "desc"): ?>selected="selected"<?php
endif; ?>value="desc">Descending</option>
                </select>
            </label>
        </li>
        <li>
            <label>
                Page:
                <select name="page">
                    <?php if ($count == 0): ?>
```

```
                        <option value="1">1</option>
                    <?php else: ?>
                        <?php for ($i = 1; $i<ceil($count / $limit); $i++): ?>
                            <option<?php if ($page == $i): ?>selected="selected"<?php
endif; ?>value="<?php echo $i; ?>"><?php echo $i; ?></option>
                        <?php endfor; ?>
                    <?php endif; ?>
                </select>
            </label>
        </li>
        <li>
            <label>
                Limit:
                <select name="limit">
                    <option<?php if ($limit == 10): ?>selected="selected"<?php
endif; ?>value="10">10</option>
                    <option<?php if ($limit == 20): ?>selected="selected"<?php
endif; ?>value="20">20</option>
                    <option<?php if ($limit == 30): ?>selected="selected"<?php
endif; ?>value="30">30</option>
                </select>
            </label>
        </li>
        <li>
            <input type="submit" name="search" value="search" />
        </li>
    </ol>
</form>
<?php if ($users): ?>
    <table>
        <tr>
            <th>Name</th>
        </tr>
        <?php foreach ($users as $user): ?>
            <tr>
                <td><?php echo $user->first; ?> <?php echo $user->last; ?></td>
            </tr>
        <?php endforeach; ?>
    </table>
<?php endif; ?>
```

The `settings()` action is almost identical to the new `register()` action we just created, yet instead of creating a new `User` object, we simply update `$this->user`, which is retreived with a call to the `_getUser()` method. The settings view template is also fairly similar to the register view template, with the addition of us populating the form fields from the provided `$this->user` object.

The `search()` action is similar to the previous `search()` action we created for our own framework. In order for proper searching to actually take place, we would probably need to define additional model methods to perform the searching, but for now we will just define simple search parameters.

This concludes the model, controller, and views required to do just about everything we could in the application we created on top of our framework. It should be clear that, while the differences between our framework and CodeIgniter are noticeable, the underlying principles are much the same. We still think in the same way when defining our controllers, models, and views, despite the additional coding we need to do in order to get CodeIgniter to behave as we have come to expect.

Questions

1. The `User` model we created in this chapter is similar to the `Model` class in our framework. Is it possible for us to make `CI_Model` similar to our `Model` class?
2. Is there something similar to the `Events` class (from our framework) in CodeIgniter?
3. The views we created in this chapter all have loads of PHP. Does CodeIgniter have any sort of template engine for us to use instead?

Answers

1. CodeIgniter's `CI_Model` class is quite lean when compared to our framework's `Model` class. CodeIgniter does allow us to extend this in the same way that they allow third-party libraries to be added. (We will cover this in Chapter 24)
2. CodeIgniter has what it calls "hooks," which are similar to the `Events` class, but aren't defined at runtime. Hooks are defined by adding references to classes/methods in an associative array configuration file.
3. CodeIgniter does have a template parser, but you're better off avoiding it.

Exercises

1. CodeIgniter's database class has methods to modify database structure, but we used a simple SQL query to create the database table for this chapter. Try using these methods to create a table.
2. In the interests of time, we didn't create any CMS actions or views. Try creating those now.

CHAPTER 24

CodeIgniter: Extending

CodeIgniter includes a wide assortment of libraries that cater to details such as file uploads, image manipulation, and e-mail sending. Let us see how to use these, as well as extend CodeIgniter to use third-party libraries.

Goals

- We need to learn how to use built-in CodeIgniter libraries.
- We need to learn how to include our own (third-party) libraries in our CodeIgniter applications.
- We need to learn how to extend core CodeIgniter classes.

File Uploads

We will begin by looking at how to use one of the built-in CodeIgniter libraries for file uploads. Our original sample application allows the user to upload a photo on registration, so that would be the perfect place to include this functionality. Our original application includes a `File` model, which we need to re-create with CodeIgniter.

It needs to include all the methods the `Files` controller will require in order to correctly process/query `photo` database table rows. After this, we need to modify the actions and views that are involved with file uploads to correctly intercept and process uploaded files. The `File` model should look like the code in Listing 24-1.

Listing 24-1. The File Model

```
class File extends CI_Model
{
    public $id;
    public $live = true;
    public $deleted = false;
    public $created;
    public $modified;
    public $name;
    public $mime;
    public $size;
    public $width;
    public $height;
    public $user;
```

```
    protected function _populate($options)
    {
        // set all existing properties
        foreach ($options as $key => $value)
        {
            if (property_exists($this, $key))
            {
                $this->$key = $value;
            }
        }
    }

    public function __construct($options = array())
    {
        // be a good subclass
        parent::__construct();

        // populate values
        if (sizeof($options))
        {
            $this->_populate($options);
        }

        // load row
        $this->load();
    }

    public function load()
    {
        if ($this->id)
        {
            // get corresponding row
            $query = $this->db
                ->where("id", $this->id)
                ->get("file", 1, 0);

            // populate properties with row data
            if ($row = $query->row())
            {
                $this->id = (bool) $row->id;
                $this->live = (boolean) $row->live;
                $this->deleted = (boolean) $row->deleted;
                $this->created = $row->created;
                $this->modified = $row->modified;
                $this->name = $row->name;
                $this->mime = $row->mime;
                $this->size = $row->size;
                $this->width = $row->width;
                $this->height = $row->height;
```

```
                $this->user = $row->user;
            }
        }
    }

    public function save()
    {
        // initialize data
        $data = array(
            "live" => (int) $this->live,
            "deleted" => (int) $this->deleted,
            "modified" => date("Y-m-d H:i:s"),
            "name" => $this->name,
            "mime" => $this->mime,
            "size" => $this->size,
            "width" => $this->width,
            "height" => $this->height,
            "user" => $this->user
        );

        // update
        if ($this->id)
        {
            $where = array("id" => $this->id);
            return $this->db->update("file", $data, $where);
        }

        // insert
        $data["created"] = date("Y-m-d H:i:s");
        $this->id = $this->db->insert("file", $data);

        // return insert id
        return $this->id;
    }

    public static function first($where)
    {
        $user = new File();

        // get the first user
        $user->db->where($where);
        $user->db->limit(1);
        $query = $user->db->get("file");

        // initialze the data
        $data = $query->row();
        $user->_populate($data);

        // return the user
        return $user;
    }
}
```

The File model is quite similar to the User model we created in the Chapter 23, except with a few methods excluded for the sake of simplicity. It allows us to save and load a single file row from the database. It expects the database table shown in Listing 24-2 to be in place, in order to function.

Listing 24-2. The file Table

```
CREATE TABLE `file` (
    `name` varchar(255) DEFAULT NULL,
    `mime` varchar(32) DEFAULT NULL,
    `size` int(11) DEFAULT NULL,
    `width` int(11) DEFAULT NULL,
    `height` int(11) DEFAULT NULL,
    `user` int(11) DEFAULT NULL,
    `id` int(11) NOT NULL AUTO_INCREMENT,
    `live` tinyint(4) DEFAULT NULL,
    `deleted` tinyint(4) DEFAULT NULL,
    `created` datetime DEFAULT NULL,
    `modified` datetime DEFAULT NULL,
    PRIMARY KEY (`id`),
    KEY `live` (`live`),
    KEY `deleted` (`deleted`)
) ENGINE=InnoDB  DEFAULT CHARSET=utf8 ;
```

With this model in place, we can now modify our register.html view and register() action (in the Users controller) in order to allow users to upload photos when they register. You can see we accomplish this in Listing 24-3.

Listing 24-3. The register.html View

```
<h1>Register</h1>
<?php if ($success): ?>
    Your account has been created!
<?php else: ?>
    <form method="post" enctype="multipart/form-data">
        <ol>
            <li>
                <label>
                    First name:
                    <input type="text" name="first" />
                    <?php echo form_error("first"); ?>
                </label>
            </li>
            <li>
                <label>
                    Last name:
                    <input type="text" name="last" />
                    <?php echo form_error("last"); ?>
                </label>
            </li>
            <li>
                <label>
                    Email:
```

```
                <input type="text" name="email" />
                <?php echo form_error("email"); ?>
            </label>
        </li>
        <li>
            <label>
                Password:
                <input type="password" name="password" />
                <?php echo form_error("password"); ?>
            </label>
        </li>
        <li>
            <label>
                Photo:
                <input type="file" name="photo" />
            </label>
        </li>
        <li>
            <input type="submit" name="save" value="register" />
        </li>
    </ol>
</form>
<?php endif; ?>
```

This view includes a new file input that is used in the Users controller, as shown in Listing 24-4.

Listing 24-4. The Users Controller

```
class Users extends CI_Controller
{
    protected function _upload($name, $user)
    {
        // load file upload helper
        $this->load->library("upload");

        // get extension
        $time = time();
        $path = dirname(BASEPATH)."/uploads/";
        $filename = "{$user}-{$time}";

        // do upload
        $this->upload->initialize(array(
            "upload_path" => $path,
            "file_name" => $filename,
            "allowed_types" => "gif|jpg|png"
        ));

        if ($this->upload->do_upload($name))
        {
            // get uploaded file data
            $data = $this->upload->data();
```

```
            // load file model
            $this->load->model("file");

            $file = new File(array(
                "name" => $data["file_name"],
                "mime" => $data["file_type"],
                "size" => $data["file_size"],
                "width" => $data["image_width"],
                "height" => $data["image_height"],
                "user" => $user
            ));

            $file->save();
        }
    }

    public function register()
    {
        $success = false;

        // load validation library
        $this->load->library("form_validation");

        // if form was posted
        if ($this->input->post("save"))
        {
            // initialize validation rules
            $this->form_validation->set_rules(array(
                array(
                    "field" => "first",
                    "label" => "First",
                    "rules" => "required|alpha|min_length[3]|max_length[32]"
                ),
                array(
                    "field" => "last",
                    "label" => "Last",
                    "rules" => "required|alpha|min_length[3]|max_length[32]"
                ),
                array(
                    "field" => "email",
                    "label" => "Email",
                    "rules" => "required|max_length[100]"
                ),
                array(
                    "field" => "password",
                    "label" => "Password",
                    "rules" => "required|min_length[8]|max_length[32]"
                )
            ));
```

```
            // if form data passes validation…
            if ($this->form_validation->run())
            {
                // load user model
                $this->load->model("user");

                // create new user + save
                $user = new User(array(
                    "first" => $this->input->post("first"),
                    "last" => $this->input->post("last"),
                    "email" => $this->input->post("email"),
                    "password" => $this->input->post("password")
                ));
                $user->save();

                // upload file
                $this->_upload("photo", $user->id);

                // indicate success in view
                $success = true;
            }
        }

        // load view
        $this->load->view("users/register", array(
            "success" => $success
        ));
    }
}
```

Similar to how we handled file uploads in our original application, the `register()` action does not actually perform the file upload logic, yet it calls a protected `_upload()` method. The `_upload()` method is slightly changed from our original implementation in that it has less flexibility before the file is uploaded and more information after the file is uploaded.

The built-in CodeIgniter file upload library is actually quite powerful in terms of validating uploaded files and handling all the PHP required to move the files around in the file system. We simply need to give the field name for the file we want to upload, and it will figure out the rest (with a little help from initialization parameters).

■ **Note** You can learn more about the CodeIgniter File Upload class at `http://codeigniter.com/user_guide/libraries/file_uploading.html`.

After the file is uploaded, we create a row in the file table, linking it to the user ID. Before we can use this photo on the profile page, we need to look at another aspect of extending CodeIgniter through third-party libraries.

Third-Party Libraries

Similar to our framework, CodeIgniter allows third-party libraries to be placed in a special directory so that they can be loaded within the actions where they are needed. The problem is that CodeIgniter makes no effort to autoload classes, so it would be far easier for us to create a façade class, as shown in Listing 24-5, to wrap Imagine thumbnail generation.

Listing 24-5. The Thumbnail Façade Class

```
require("imagine/image/imagineinterface.php");
require("imagine/image/manipulatorinterface.php");
require("imagine/image/imageinterface.php");
require("imagine/image/boxinterface.php");
require("imagine/image/box.php");
require("imagine/gd/imagine.php");
require("imagine/gd/image.php");
require("imagine/image/pointinterface.php");
require("imagine/image/point.php");

class Thumbnail
{
    protected $_filename;

    public function __construct($options = array())
    {
        if (isset($options["file"]))
        {
            $file = $options["file"];
            $path = dirname(BASEPATH)."/uploads";

            $width = 64;
            $height = 64;

            $name = $file->name;
            $filename = pathinfo($name, PATHINFO_FILENAME);
            $extension = pathinfo($name, PATHINFO_EXTENSION);

            if ($filename && $extension)
            {
                $thumbnail = "{$filename}-{$width}x{$height}.{$extension}";

                if (!file_exists("{$path}/{$thumbnail}"))
                {
                    $imagine = new Imagine\Gd\Imagine();
                    $size = new Imagine\Image\Box($width, $height);
                    $mode = Imagine\Image\ImageInterface::THUMBNAIL_OUTBOUND;

                    $imagine
                        ->open("{$path}/{$name}")
                        ->thumbnail($size, $mode)
                        ->save("{$path}/{$thumbnail}");
                }
```

```
                $this->_filename = $thumbnail;
            }
        }
    }

    public function getFilename()
    {
        return $this->_filename;
    }
}
```

The first thing you should notice about our façade class is that it requires multiple `Imagine` classes. We could create an autoloader, but manually including the `Imagine` dependencies is quicker and easier for this small thumbnail class.

The `Thumbnail` class is made to work with an instance of the `File` class, passed into `__construct()` as a value of the associative array. We will see how to call this in a moment, but it is important to note that CodeIgniter's library loader will automatically instantiate the `Thumbnail` class, so we need to make sure the file parameter is set before doing any image resizing.

After we have a file row to work with, we need to get the file name and extension. We then construct the thumbnail file name and check whether the thumbnail has been created yet. If the thumbnail hasn't already been created, we create the thumbnail with `Imagine` and, finally, we store the thumbnail's file name in a protected `$_filename` property.

Let's now see how to use this class in our `Users` controller, where we modify the `profile()` action. Take a look at Listing 24-6.

Listing 24-6. The Modified profile() Action

```
class Users extends CI_Controller
{
    public function profile()
    {
        // check for user session
        $this->_isSecure();

        // get profile photo
        $this->load->model("file");

        $file = File::first(array(
            "user" => $this->user->id
        ));

        // get thumbnail
        $this->load->library("thumbnail", array(
            "file" => $file
        ));

        $filename = $this->thumbnail->getFilename();
        // load view
        $this->load->view("users/profile", array(
            "user" => $this->user,
```

```
            "filename" => $filename
        ));
    }
}
```

There are two new aspects to our profile() action. The first is that we get the first File row from the database. The second is that we need to pass this to $this->load->library(). This will initialize the Thumbnail class with the file we want the thumbnail of.

Note You can learn more about the nuances of resource loading in CodeIgniter, at http://codeigniter.com/user_guide/libraries/loader.html.

Finally, we need to change the profile.html view and the main .htaccess files, as demonstrated in Listings 24-7 and 24-8.

Listing 24-7. The Modified .htaccess File

```
RewriteEngine on
RewriteCond $1 !^(index\.php|images|uploads|robots\.txt)
RewriteRule ^(.*)$ /index.php/$1 [L]
```

Listing 24-8. The Modified profile.html View

```
<?php if ($filename): ?>
    <img src="/uploads/<?php echo $filename; ?>" />
<?php endif; ?>
<h1><?php echo $user->first; ?> <?php echo $user->last; ?></h1>
This is a profile page!
```

The change we make to the .htaccess file (in the regular expression) allows calls to files in the uploads directory. We also add the profile photo to the profile.html view if it has been provided from the controller.

Note In terms of security, file upload directories shouldn't be web accessible, or should have strict .htaccess rules protecting against the execution of scripts within the uploads directory. Web sites often break when malicious users are able to upload scripts and execute them on the server, usually through interfaces designed specifically to allow file uploads!

Extending the Core

The last thing we need to cover is how to extend CodeIgniter core classes. The trick to this is to add classes in the application/core directory that match the name of the core classes, with a special prefix. If we wanted to create a controller from which our application can inherit, we simply need to create a MY_Controller.php file within this directory, as shown in Listing 24-9.

Listing 24-9. application/core/MY_Controller.php

```
class MY_Controller extends CI_Controller
{
    public $user;

    public static function redirect($url)
    {
        header("Location: {$url}");
        exit();
    }

    protected function _isSecure()
    {
        // get user session
        $this->_getUser();
        if (!$this->user)
        {
            self::redirect("/login");
        }
    }

    protected function _getUser()
    {
        // load session library
        $this->load->library("session");

        // get user id
        $id = $this->session->userdata("user");

        if ($id)
        {
            // load user model
            $this->load->model("user");

            // get user
            $this->user = new User(array(
                "id" => $id
            ));
        }
    }
}
```

The important things to note about extended core classes are that the file name must match the `my_*` pattern and that the custom core class must extend the built-in core class. We can move the `redirect()`, `_isSecure()`, and `_getUser()` methods into this new class, since any controller can reuse them.

■ **Note** There's a lot more to know about extending core classes, and you can learn more at `http://codeigniter.com/user_guide/general/core_classes.html`.

Questions

1. In our original application we also created a `File` model to store a reference to uploaded files in the database. Why do we not simply search the `uploads` directory for the file belonging to the user?
2. In our original application we also created a special `/thumbnails/*` route for thumbnail generation, and then integrated the thumbnail generation into the controller. Are there any drawbacks to this new approach?

Answers

1. We involve the database in file lookups simply because it is faster to query the database than it is to iterate over files in the file system. We could make things even faster by caching a list of files belonging to the user.
2. There are two drawbacks to this new approach. The first is that the controller now needs to be aware of how the thumbnails are generated. The second is that thumbnails are less dynamic—you can no longer simply request a new thumbnail size, because it has to be coded!

Exercises

1. We've learned about the drawbacks to this approach of thumbnail generation. Now re-create our previous approach with CodeIgniter MVC.
2. We also learned about how to extend core classes, and did so with the `CI_Controller` class. Try replicating this idea with the models we have created, by moving reusable code into an extended `CI_Model` subclass.

CHAPTER 25

CodeIgniter: Testing

We conclude the section on CodeIgniter by looking at how we can unit test our CodeIgniter applications with built-in CodeIgniter classes.

Goals

- We need to find out what CodeIgniter offers in the way of unit testing.
- We need to see what alternatives we have.

Tools

CodeIgniter provides a simple unit-testing class that you can use to write tests for your CodeIgniter applications. It has one method you can use to add more tests, and one method to return the formatted results. Let's look at an example of how to use it, as shown in Listing 25-1.

Listing 25-1. Using the CodeIgniter Unit-Testing Class

```
class Welcome extends CI_Controller
{
    public function index()
    {
        $this->load->view('welcome_message');
    }

    public function tests()
    {
        $this->load->library("unit_test");

        $test = $this->testing();
        $expected_result = "hello world";
        $test_name = "testing function returns hello world";
        $this->unit->run($test, $expected_result, $test_name);

        echo $this->unit->report();
    }
```

```
    public function testing()
    {
        return "hello world";
    }
}
```

As Listing 25-1 shows, you may use the unit-testing library supplied by CodeIgniter to compare only two values (one of them presumably the result of the call to an action or function). This is a little limiting in terms of testing how actions perform when supplied posted form data.

Another limitation that we need to be aware of is that the unit testing that CodeIgniter allows has to occur within the MVC architecture. This couples the tests closely with the framework they should be testing, which is never a good thing.

The Alternative

You are far better off using a third-party library to test the functionality of your CodeIgniter applications. A unit-testing library, such as PHPUnit, includes a multitude of different assertion functions to test not only the equality of two values but also the size of arrays, the type of exceptions thrown, whether files exist in a directory, and more.

■ **Note** If you would like to download or learn more about PHPUnit, you can do so at `https://github.com/sebastianbergmann/phpunit`.

You can utilize third-party unit-testing libraries by including them in the `application/libraries` folder (as we did in the Chapter 24), or even separating them out of the application altogether. The choice is yours.

If you compare the unit testing we implemented in our original sample application to something bundled in the `application/libraries` directory, you will see that the former operates completely outside of the application/framework architecture. This allows the tests to function, even if the application/framework isn't.

Questions

1. How are the CodeIgniter unit-testing class and our unit-testing class the same and how do they differ?

2. Why would it be a good idea to use a third-party unit-testing library when CodeIgniter already provides a unit-testing class?

Answers

1. Our unit-testing class performs two basic checks: whether an exception was raised, and whether the test returns true or false. It is also intended for use outside of the application architecture, and has minimal dependencies. CodeIgniter's unit-testing class is meant to work from inside CodeIgniter's MVC application code, and tests only the equality between two values.

2. Third-party unit-testing libraries offer many advantages over the simple unit-testing classes we have seen so far. They allow us to write more complicated tests that get to the heart of an application's functionality.

Exercises

1. CodeIgniter's unit-testing class is easy to set up and use. Try creating a few action tests using it.
2. PHPUnit is an exceptional alternative to CodeIgniter's built-in unit-testing class. Try integrating it into our application, and write some tests for it.

CHAPTER 26

Zend Framework: Bootstrapping

The makers and maintainers of PHP, as the name suggests, maintain Zend Framework. It is the only framework (of the three we are focusing on) where the application architecture isn't already created by the framework's download archive. This is due to a design goal of Zend Framework, which is to be a "use-at-will" architecture of loosely coupled components.

This does not mean we need to do anything special to get it to behave in the same manner as CodeIgniter or CakePHP, but it is simply a case of issuing the right commands in order to get the layout we want.

Note You can download Zend Framework from `http://framework.zend.com/download/overview`.

Goals

- We need to understand the philosophy and benefits of Zend Framework.
- We need to learn how to create the architectural requirements for our sample application.

Why Zend Framework?

Zend Framework is extremely well structured and includes many interfaces to popular third-party services. The philosophy behind the framework is that it should include 80 percent of the functionality everyone needs, while letting developers customize the other 20 percent to meet their specific business requirements.

The documentation for Zend Framework is extensive and also covers the intricacies of all the API classes provided alongside the core classes. It also includes numerous examples for the general-purpose use of the bundled classes.

Note You can find the Zend Framework documentation at `http://framework.zend.com/manual/en/introduction.overview.html`.

Why Not Zend Framework?

Zend Framework can be tricky to learn, simply due to the initial application layout (or lack thereof) and the sheer volume of bundled classes. Once you understand how to create MVC applications and how to navigate the documentation, these aren't really factors in the ongoing use of the framework.

Zend Framework (1.11) does not use namespaces, mainly due to how its classes are named.

Note At the time of writing, Zend Framework 2 is in beta testing, and fully supports namespaces. You can download version 2.0 from `http://packages.zendframework.com`. Be warned that it appears to differ significantly in terms of installation and use from the current version of Zend as used in this chapter.

Getting Set Up

Generating a functional application with Zend Framework is rather simple. The archives you can download all include a build script that will construct the recommended directory structure and even provide sample controllers, views, and configurations for your application. The steps we need to follow to begin building the sample application are as follows:

1. Download the Zend Framework Minimal Package (`http://framework.zend.com/download/current`) and extract it anywhere. Remember where you have extracted it to because you will need to go there in a minute.
2. Open terminal (if you are in Linux or OS X) or command prompt (if you are in Windows) and navigate to the `bin/` folder within the extracted directory.
3. Run the `zf.sh` (if you are in Linux or OS X) or the `zf.bat` (if you are in Windows) file with the following command:
   - α. Linux/OS X: `./zf.sh create project prophpmvc`
   - β. Windows: `zf.bat create project prophpmvc`

Note The second command might warn that PHPUnit was not found. This is okay, since we don't need to use it.

You will need to configure your web server to point to the `public/` directory in order for the generated bootstrapping code to execute.

Routes

Along with the directory structure generated by the `create project` command, a bootstrap file is created that allows us to specify any custom initialization logic for our application. It is the class in this file to which we must add the custom routes for our application (in `application/bootstrap.php`), as shown in Listing 26-1.

Listing 26-1. application/bootstrap.php

```
class Bootstrap extends Zend_Application_Bootstrap_Bootstrap
{
    protected function _initRouter()
    {
        $router = Zend_Controller_Front::getInstance()->getRouter();
```

```
        $routes = array(
            "register" => array("register", "users", "register"),
            "login" => array("login", "users", "login"),
            "logout" => array("logout", "users", "logout"),
            "search" => array("search", "users", "search"),
            "profile" => array("profile", "users", "profile"),
            "settings" => array("settings", "users", "settings"),
            "friend" => array("friend/:id", "users", "friend"),
            "unfriend" => array("unfriend/:id", "users", "unfriend"),
            "users/edit" => array("users/edit/:id", "users", "edit"),
            "users/delete" => array("users/delete/:id", "users", "delete"),
            "users/undelete" => array("users/undelete/:id", "users", "undelete'),
            "fonts" => array("fonts/:name", "files", "fonts"),
            "thumbnails" => array("thumbnails/:id", "files", "thumbnails"),
            "files/delete" => array("files/delete/:id", "files", "delete"),
            "files/undelete" => array("files/undelete/:id", "files", "undelete")
        );

        foreach ($routes as $name => $route)
        {
            list($pattern, $controller, $action) = $route;

            $router->addRoute($name, new Zend_Controller_Router_Route($pattern, ➥
array("controller" => $controller, "action" => $action)));
        }
    }
}
```

The process is simple: we get an instance of the `Zend_Controller_Router` class (via the `Zend_Controller_Front` class) and add a few `Zend_Controller_Router_Route` instances to it. The main application code will run after the `Zend_Application_Bootstrap_Bootstrap` class is executed, so these new routes will be available when the application is trying to figure out which controllers and actions should happen for requested URLs.

It is important to note that, out of the three frameworks we are focusing on, Zend Framework handles routes in a manner most similar to how our framework does. The important differences are that Zend Framework's router class is a singleton, where ours is managed by a registry, and that Zend Framework's routes are all named.

If you try to access any of these new routes you will see an error. This is because we have not yet created the corresponding controllers, actions, and so forth. In Chapter 27, we will create the controllers, models, and views required for most of these routes to function correctly.

■ **Note** You can find more details about Zend Framework routing at `http://framework.zend.com/manual/en/zend.controller.router.html`.

Questions

1. Why should we add routes in the `Zend_Application_Bootstrap_Bootstrap` class? Can't we simply define them in the `public/index.php` file?

2. Can you think of some ways in which automated build scripts (such as the one we used in this chapter) could speed up application development?

Answers

1. There is no hard and fast rule here. It's simply one of the ways in which Zend recommends the addition of custom routes. There is nothing stopping us from adding routes directly in the `public/index.php` file if we wanted to.

2. Apart from creating the initial structure of an application, automated build scripts could be used to create additional controllers, models, or even views. The Zend Framework command line tools can do all of these things.

Exercises

1. In this chapter, we created all the routes our example application requires. Now try creating a route that uses a username to invoke the users/profile action.

2. Having all these routes without any controllers and actions isn't very helpful to us. Try creating a controller and action to handle a few of the routes we defined.

CHAPTER 27

Zend Framework: MVC

Zend Framework is much closer to our framework than CodeIgniter, in terms of the tools it offers us with which to build a sample application. We've already seen the similarities between Zend Framework's routing system and that of our framework, but it also has an ORM system similar to our own. We will come to appreciate these things as we use them in this chapter.

Goals

We need to recognize the differences between our framework and Zend Framework when it comes to creating the controllers, models, and views for our example application.

- We need to create the models for users, friends, files, and messages.
- We need to create the corresponding views and controllers.

The Differences

Of the frameworks on which this book focuses, Zend Framework is actually the most similar to our framework. Where they differ, among other things, is how closely they follow the MVC pattern. It might be tempting to think that our framework does it better, but Zend has actually chosen a loosely coupled model for Zend Framework, and it is visible right out of the gate. You do not download an MVC framework, neatly organized in a familiar folder structure. Rather, you download a collection of classes that work really well when the MVC pattern is applied to them.

Because of this, it will seem like we are writing more code than we required getting our own framework to perform the equivalent actions concerning users, friends, files, and messages. This is simply because our framework couples things like the ORM and controllers more tightly than Zend Framework couples its ORM and controllers.

Models

We will begin our model work by looking at a few of the ways in which we can use Zend Framework's ORM to select and modify database records. Before we can alter the database records, we need to define the database tables our application will be using. For now, we need only the `user` table, which is shown in Listing 27-1.

Listing 27-1. The user Table

```
CREATE TABLE 'user' (
  'id' int(11) NOT NULL AUTO_INCREMENT,
  'live' tinyint(4) DEFAULT NULL,
  'deleted' tinyint(4) DEFAULT NULL,
  'created' datetime DEFAULT NULL,
  'modified' datetime DEFAULT NULL,
  'first' varchar(32) DEFAULT NULL,
  'last' varchar(32) DEFAULT NULL,
  'email' varchar(100) DEFAULT NULL,
  'password' varchar(32) DEFAULT NULL,
  PRIMARY KEY ('id')
) ENGINE=InnoDB  DEFAULT CHARSET=utf8 ;
```

With this table in place, we can perform database operations, such as the select operation shown in Listing 27-2.

Listing 27-2. Selecting Rows

```
$db = Zend_Db::factory(
    "pdo_mysql",
    array(
        "host" =>"localhost",
        "username" =>"prophpmvc",
        "password" =>"prophpmvc",
        "dbname" =>"prophpmvc-zendframework"
    )
);

$table = new Zend_Db_Table(array(
    "name" => "user",
    "db" => $db
));

$select = $table->select()
    ->where("first = ?", "Chris")
    ->order("id ASC");

$user = $table->fetchRow($select);
```

The first two statements aren't specific to selecting rows, but rather establish a connection to the database and request an interface for working with the `user` table. We will shortly move them to a better place, but it's important to understand how they work.

The `Zend_Db` factory class is used simply to return an instance of a database adapter, in a manner quite similar to our own database factory class. The `Zend_Db_Table` class likewise returns an interface with which to query/manipulate the user database table we created previously. It supports a similar query interface to our framework and CodeIgniter.

Listing 27-3 demonstrates how we can modify the user rows.

Listing 27-3. Modifying User Rows

```
$id = $table->insert(array(
    "first" => "Joe",
    "last" => "Blogs",
    "email" => "joe@example.com",
    "password" => "password",
    "live" => true,
    "deleted" => false,
    "created" => date("Y-m-d"),
    "modified" => date("Y-m-d")
));

$user = $table->find($id)->getRow(0);

$user->password .= "123";
$user->save();

echo $user->password; // output: password123

$user->delete();
```

When we built our sample application with CodeIgniter, we had to define our models by hand, creating each row function. We will do the same thing with our Zend Framework sample application, using the tricks we have just learned. Before we begin our user model, we will need to define a `DbTable` class.

`DbTable` classes are defined in Zend Framework as containers for database table metadata. We will save time using a `DbTable` class to generate the various database queries we will need, as opposed to using a database adapter directly (see Listing 27-4).

Listing 27-4. The Application_Model_DbTable_User extends Class

```
class Application_Model_DbTable_User extends Zend_Db_Table_Abstract
{
    protected $_name = 'user';
}
```

As you can see, this class needs little more than a table name in order to generate a full set of metadata for query generation. It's not really that interesting, so we will move on to the model itself, shown in Listing 27-5.

Listing 27-5. The Application_Model_User Class

```
class Application_Model_User
{
    protected $_table;

    public function setTable($table)
    {
        // if string is given, make new table class
        if (is_string($table))
        {
            $table = new $table();
        }
```

```
        // ...else if object is given that is not a valid table class...
        if (!$table instanceof Zend_Db_Table_Abstract)
        {
            throw new Exception("Invalid table specified");
        }

        $this->_table = $table;
        return $this;
    }

    public function getTable()
    {
        if (!$this->_table)
        {
            // define the DbTable the first time it is needed
            $this->setTable("Application_Model_DbTable_User");
        }

        return $this->_table;
    }
}
```

The Application_Model_User model class begins with a method for getting a table adapter, setting a table adapter as well as a protected property for storing a table adapter. The approach taken here is that the DbTable instance will be defined only the first time it is required, and will be cached for further reference. We continue by defining the initialization methods, as shown in Listing 27-6.

Listing 27-6. The Application_Model_User Class (Cont.)

```
class Application_Model_User
{
    public $id;
    public $first;
    public $last;
    public $email;
    public $password;
    public $live = true;
    public $deleted = false;
    public $created;
    public $modified;

    protected function _populate($options)
    {
        foreach ($options as $key => $value)
        {
            if (property_exists($this, $key))
            {
                $this->$key = $value;
            }
        }
    }
```

```
    public function __construct($options = array())
    {
        if (sizeof($options))
        {
            $this->_populate($options);
        }

        $this->load();
    }

    public function load()
    {
        if ($this->id)
        {
            // get the first row from id...
            $row = $this->first(array("id = ?" => $this->id));

            // if no row is found: abort!
            if (!$row)
            {
                return;
            }

            // populate the rest of the data
            $this->id = $row->id;
            $this->first = $row->first;
            $this->last = $row->last;
            $this->email = $row->email;
            $this->password = $row->password;
            $this->live = (boolean) $row->live;
            $this->deleted = (boolean) $row->deleted;
            $this->created = $row->created;
            $this->modified = $row->modified;
        }
    }
}
```

The initialization methods are quite similar to the model we created for CodeIgniter. The important differences are those relating to how we query the applicable row from the database table (within the `load()` method).

The structure of the table can be achieved by running the SQL query shown in Listing 27-7 on your local MySQL database.

Listing 27-7. user Table SQL

```
CREATE TABLE 'user' (
  'id' int(11) NOT NULL AUTO_INCREMENT,
  'live' tinyint(4) DEFAULT NULL,
  'deleted' tinyint(4) DEFAULT NULL,
  'created' datetime DEFAULT NULL,
  'modified' datetime DEFAULT NULL,
  'first' varchar(32) DEFAULT NULL,
```

```
  'last' varchar(32) DEFAULT NULL,
  'email' varchar(100) DEFAULT NULL,
  'password' varchar(32) DEFAULT NULL,
  'admin' tinyint(4) DEFAULT NULL,
  PRIMARY KEY ('id')
) ENGINE=InnoDB DEFAULT CHARSET=utf8 AUTO_INCREMENT=1 ;
```

Returning the first row in the user table will, therefore, be achievable with the code shown in Listing 27-8.

Listing 27-8. Retrieving the First User

```
$user=new Application_Model_User(array(
    "id" => $id
));
```

There are a few other methods, shown in Listing 27-9, that we need to add to this `Application_Model_User` model.

Listing 27-9. The Application_Model_User Class (Cont.)

```
class Application_Model_User
{
    public function save()
    {
        // initialize data
        $data = array(
            "first" => $this->first,
            "last" => $this->last,
            "email" => $this->email,
            "password" => $this->password,
            "live" => (int) $this->live,
            "deleted" => (int) $this->deleted,
            "modified" => date("Y-m-d H:i:s")
        );

        if ($this->id)
        {
            // update
            $where = array("id = ?" => $this->id);
            return $this->getTable()->update($data, $where);
        }
        else
        {
            // insert
            $data["created"] = date("Y-m-d H:i:s");
            return $this->getTable()->insert($data);
        }
    }

    public static function first($where = null)
    {
        $user = new self();
        $table = $user->getTable();
```

```
        $query = $table->select()->limit(1);

        // narrow search
        if (is_array($where))
        {
            foreach ($where as $key => $value)
            {
                $query->where($key, $value);
            }
        }

        // get the users
        if ($row = $table->fetchRow($query))
        {
            $user->_populate($row->toArray());
            return $user;
        }

        return null;
    }

    public static function count($where = null)
    {
        $user = new self();
        $table = $user->getTable();
        $query = $table->select()->from($table, array("num" => "COUNT(1)"))->limit(1);

        // narrow search
        if (is_array($where))
        {
            foreach ($where as $key => $value)
            {
                $query->where($key, $value);
            }
        }

        $row = $table->fetchRow($query);
        return $row->num;
    }

    public static function all($where = null, $fields = null, $order = null, ➥
                               $direction  = "asc", $limit = null, $page = null)
    {
        $user = new self();
        $table = $user->getTable();
        $adapter = $table->getAdapter();
        $query = $adapter->select();

        // select fields
        if ($fields)
        {
            $query->from("user", $fields);
        }
```

```
        // narrow search
        if (is_array($where))
        {
            foreach ($where as $key => $value)
            {
                $query->where($key, $value);
            }
        }

        // order results
        if ($order)
        {
            $query->order("{$order} {$direction}");
        }

        // limit results
        if ($limit && $page)
        {
            $offset = ($page - 1) * $limit;
            $query->limit($limit, $offset);
        }

        // get the users
        $users = array();
        $rows = $adapter->fetchAll($query);

        foreach ($rows as $row)
        {
            // create + populate user
            $user = new self();
            $user->_populate($row->toArray());

            // add user to pile
            array_push($users, $user);
        }

        return $users;
    }
}
```

The remaining methods are quite similar to the data access/modification methods we created for CodeIgniter. In fact, they differ only in the means used to return the rows from the `user` table or save new rows to the `user` table.

Controllers

With our `User` model in place, we can begin to work on our `UsersController` controller, as demonstrated in Listing 27-10.

Listing 27-10. application/controllers/UsersController.php (Extract)

```
class UsersController extends Zend_Controller_Action
{
    public $user;

    public static function redirect($url)
    {
        header("Location: {$url}");
        exit();
    }

    protected function _isSecure()
    {
        // get user session
        $this->_getUser();

        if (!$this->user)
        {
            self::redirect("/login");
        }
    }

    protected function _getUser()
    {
        // initialize session
        $session = new Zend_Session_Namespace("application");

        // get user id
        $id = $session->user;

        if ($id)
        {
            // get user
            $this->user = Application_Model_User::first(array("id = ?" => $id));
        }
    }
}
```

The `UsersController` class starts with methods for retrieving the user from the database and checking whether a valid session has been created. It is simpler than our CodeIgniter equivalent, mostly because of the lazy loading that Zend Framework is doing. We didn't need to explicitly load the model or session class. We continue with the `registerAction()` method, as shown in Listing 27-11.

Listing 27-11. application/controllers/UsersController.php (Extract)

```
class UsersController extends Zend_Controller_Action
{
    public function registerAction()
    {
        $valid = true;
        $errors = array();
        $success = false;
```

```
        $first = $this->_request->getPost("first");
        $last = $this->_request->getPost("last");
        $email = $this->_request->getPost("email");
        $password = $this->_request->getPost("password");

        // if form was posted...
        if ($this->_request->getPost("save"))
        {
            // ...enforce validation rules

            $alnum = new Zend_Validate_Alnum();
            $stringLength1 = new Zend_Validate_StringLength(array("min" => 3, "max" => 32));
            $stringLength2 = new Zend_Validate_StringLength(array("min" => 0, "max" => 255));

            if (empty($first) || !$alnum->isValid($first) || !$stringLength1->isValid($first))
            {
                $valid = false;
                $errors["first"] = "First field required";
            }

            if (empty($last) || !$alnum->isValid($last) || !$stringLength1->isValid($last))
            {
                $valid = false;
                $errors["last"] = "Last field required";
            }

            if (empty($email) || !$stringLength2->isValid($email))
            {
                $valid = false;
                $errors["email"] = "Email field required";
            }

            if (empty($password) || !$stringLength2->isValid($password))
            {
                $valid = false;
                $errors["password"] = "Password field required";
            }

            // if form data passes validation...
            if ($valid)
            {
                // ...create new user + save
                $user = new Application_Model_User(array(
                    "first" => $first,
                    "last" => $last,
                    "email" => $email,
                    "password" => $password
                ));
                $id = $user->save();
```

```
                // indicate success in view
                $success = true;
            }
        }
        // load view
        $this->view->errors = $success;
        $this->view->success = $success;
    }
}
```

These changes to the registerAction() method require additional changes to the register.phtml view template as well; demonstrated in Listing 27-12.

Listing 27-12. application/views/users/register.phtml

```
<h1>Register</h1>
<?php if ($this->success): ?>
    Your account has been created!
<?php else: ?>
    <form method="post" enctype="multipart/form-data">
        <ol>
            <li>
                <label>
                    First name:
                    <input type="text" name="first" />
                    <?php echo isset($this->errors["first"]) ? $this->errors["first"] : ""; ?>
                </label>
            </li>
            <li>
                <label>
                    Last name:
                    <input type="text" name="last" />
                    <?php echo isset($this->errors["last"]) ? $this->errors["last"] : ""; ?>
                </label>
            </li>
            <li>
                <label>
                    Email:
                    <input type="text" name="email" />
                    <?php echo isset($this->errors["email"]) ? $this->errors["email"] : ""; ?>
                </label>
            </li>
            <li>
                <label>
                    Password:
                    <input type="password" name="password" />
                    <?php echo isset($this->errors["password"]) ? $this->errors["password"] ➥
                        : ""; ?>
                </label>
            </li>
            <li>
                <input type="submit" name="save" value="register" />
```

```
            </li>
        </ol>
    </form>
<?php endif; ?>
```

The registerAction() method begins by retrieving some posted form values. Those values are then passed through some validation methods provided by Zend Framework, and error messages are created for each field that fails validation.

If the validation is successful and all the fields are in order, a new user record is created and saved in the database and confirmation is passed to the view. This is not the only way to validate posted form data with Zend Framework, but it is by far the simplest and closest to the other frameworks we have used.

Next, we need to create the action and view for login. You can see how we accomplish this in Listings 27-13 and 27-14.

Listing 27-13. application/controllers/UserController.php (Extract)

```
class UsersController extends Zend_Controller_Action
{
    public function loginAction()
    {
        $valid = true;
        $errors = array();

        $email = $this->_request->getPost("email");
        $password = $this->_request->getPost("password");

        // if form was posted...
        if ($this->_request->getPost("login"))
        {
            // ...enforce validation rules

            $alnum = new Zend_Validate_Alnum();
            $stringLength = new Zend_Validate_StringLength(array("min" => 0, "max" => 255));

            if (empty($email) || !$stringLength->isValid($email))
            {
                $valid = false;
                $errors["email"] = "Email field required";
            }

            if (empty($password) || !$stringLength->isValid($password))
            {
                $valid = false;
                $errors["password"] = "Password field required";
            }

            // if form data passes validation...
            if ($valid)
            {
                $user = Application_Model_User::first(array(
                    "email = ?" => $email,
                    "password = ?" => $password
```

```
                ));

                if ($user)
                {

                    // initialize session
                    $session = new Zend_Session_Namespace("application");
                    // save user id to session
                    $session->user = $user->id;

                    // redirect to profile page
                    self::redirect("/profile");

                }
                else
                {
                    // indicate errors
                    $errors["password"] = "Email address and/or password are incorrect";
                }
            }
        }

        // load view
        $this->view->errors = $errors;
    }
}
```

Listing 27-14. application/views/users/login.phtml

```
<h1>Login</h1>
<form method="post">
    <ol>
        <li>
            <label>
                Email:
                <input type="text" name="email" />
                <?php echo isset($this->errors["email"]) ? $this->errors["email"] : ""; ?>
            </label>
        </li>
        <li>
            <label>
                Password:
                <input type="password" name="password" />
                <?php echo isset($this->errors["password"]) ? $this->errors["password"] ➥
                    : ""; ?>
            </label>
        </li>
```

```
        <li>
            <input type="submit" name="login" value="login" />
        </li>
    </ol>
</form>
```

The loginAction() works in much the same way as the registerAction() method. First, the posted field values are retrieved, then they are validated, and if they are valid they are used to retrieve a user record from the database. If a user account is found, the user's ID is stored in the session, and finally the user is redirected to the profile page.

We follow this up with the logoutAction() and profileAction() methods and views, as shown in Listings 27-15 and 27-16.

Listing 27-15. application/controllers/UserController.php (Extract)

```
class UsersController extends Zend_Controller_Action
{
    public function logoutAction()
    {
        // unlock session
        $session = new Zend_Session_Namespace("application");
        $session->unlock();

        // kill session
        Zend_Session::namespaceUnset("application");

        // redirect to login
        self::redirect("/login");
    }

    public function profileAction()
    {
        // check for user session
        $this->_isSecure();

        // load view
        $this->view->user = $this->user;
    }
}
```

Listing 27-16. application/views/users/profile.phtml

```
<h1><?php echo $this->user->first; ?><?php echo $this->user->last; ?></h1>
This is a profile page!
```

The logoutAction() method differs from the CodeIgniter example in as much as it doesn't simply remove the user's ID from the session, but rather the entire session, after which it redirects back to the login page. The profileAction() method sets the user record that is represented in the simple profile.phtml template.

We finish off with the settingsAction() and searchAction() methods and views, as shown in Listing 27-17.

Listing 27-17. application/controllers/UserController.php (Extract)

```
class UsersController extends Zend_Controller_Action
{
    public function settingsAction()
    {
        // check for user session
        $this->_isSecure();

        $valid = true;
        $errors = array();
        $success = false;

        $first = $this->_request->getPost("first");
        $last = $this->_request->getPost("last");
        $email = $this->_request->getPost("email");
        $password = $this->_request->getPost("password");
        // if form was posted...
        if ($this->_request->getPost("save"))
        {
            // ...enforce validation rules

            $alnum = new Zend_Validate_Alnum();
            $shortString = new Zend_Validate_StringLength(array("min" => 3, "max" => 32));
            $longString = new Zend_Validate_StringLength(array("min" => 0, "max" => 255));

            if (empty($first) || !$alnum->isValid($first) || !$shortString->isValid($first))
            {
                $valid = false;
                $errors["first"] = "First field required";
            }

            if (empty($last) || !$alnum->isValid($last) || !$shortString->isValid($last))
            {
                $valid = false;
                $errors["last"] = "Last field required";
            }

            if (empty($email) || !$longString->isValid($email))
            {
                $valid = false;
                $errors["email"] = "Email field required";
            }

            if (empty($password) || !$longString->isValid($password))
            {
                $valid = false;
                $errors["password"] = "Password field required";
            }
```

```
            // if form data passes validation...
            if ($valid)
            {
                // save changes to user
                $this->user->first = $first;
                $this->user->last = $last;
                $this->user->email = $email;
                $this->user->password = $password;
                $this->user->save();
                // indicate success in view
                $success = true;
            }
        }

        // load view
        $this->view->errors = $errors;
        $this->view->success = $success;
        $this->view->user = $this->user;
    }
    public function searchAction()
    {
        // get posted data
        $query = $this->_request->getPost("query");
        $order = $this->_request->getPost("order");
        $direction = $this->_request->getPost("direction");
        $page = $this->_request->getPost("page");
        $limit = $this->_request->getPost("limit");

        // default null values
        $order = $order ? $order : "modified";
        $direction = $direction ? $direction : "desc";
        $limit = $limit ? $limit : 10;
        $page = $page ? $page : 1;
        $count = 0;
        $users = null;

        if ($this->_request->getPost("search"))
        {
            $where = array(
                "first = ?" => $query,
                "live = ?" => 1,
                "deleted = ?" => 0
            );

            $fields = array(
                "id", "first", "last"
            );
```

```
            // get count + results
            $count = Application_Model_User::count($where);
            $users = Application_Model_User::all(
                $where,
                $fields,
                $order,
                $direction,
                $limit,
                $page
            );
        }

        // load view
        $this->view->query = $query;
        $this->view->order = $order;
        $this->view->direction = $direction;
        $this->view->page = $page;
        $this->view->limit = $limit;
        $this->view->count = $count;
        $this->view->users = $users;
    }
}
```

The `settingsAction()` method resembles the `registerAction()` method in as much as it retrieves and validates posted form values. Where it differs is in what it saves. The `registerAction()` method saves a new user to the database, while the `settingsAction()` method updates the user row indicated by the session ID value (which is used in the `_getUser()` method).

The `searchAction()` method accepts a few query parameters and returns an array of matched user rows, which are presented in the `search.phtml` template.

These are all the methods and templates needed to build our sample application in Zend Framework. By comparison, the code we needed in this chapter was more succinct than the CodeIgniter equivalent, and this is indicative of the ease with which classes are autoloaded, as opposed to having to manually load models, libraries, and views.

Questions

1. Zend Framework's ORM model is different from CodeIgniter's and even our framework. Where we have a connector and query, CodeIgniter has a simple query interface and Zend Framework has both table adapters and model classes. What are the benefits and drawbacks of this approach?
2. Zend Framework loads views automatically (based on controller and action names) as does our own framework, where CodeIgniter requires explicit view loading. What are the benefits and drawbacks of this approach?

Answers

1. Having more classes/interfaces to deal with means more complication. Zend Framework has a steeper learning curve because of all the different classes you need to be aware of but this allows for greater granularity. We can, for instance, add methods to the table that do not belong in the model. Zend Framework even has a row-level interface (classes that extend `Zend_Db_Table_Row_Abstract`), which allows for row-level methods.
2. Loading views automatically is quite convenient but it does present a problem when we don't want a view to be loaded or when the view's name differs from the controller and action names. In such situations, it is good to know how to toggle automatic rendering or be able to override which view will be used.

Exercises

1. Our `User` model mirrors the behavior of our framework and CodeIgniter's models, but it would be better for this functionality to be in a class that is subclassed. Try doing this.
2. Take a look at the Zend Framework documentation and experiment with a few ways of disabling or preventing automatic view rendering.

▒ **Note** You can find out more about how action views and view templates interact, and how to disable automatic view rendering at `http://framework.zend.com/manual/en/zend.controller.action.html`.

CHAPTER 28

Zend Framework: Extending

In our attempt to understand the finer details of Zend Framework, we need to realize that it doesn't ship with a wide collection of libraries, but rather *is* a wide collection of libraries roughly arranged in a coherent MVC framework.

It should then come as no surprise that using internal libraries are no different from using third-party libraries. Let's see how we do this.

Goals

- We need to learn how to use built-in Zend Framework classes.
- We need to learn how to include our own (third-party) libraries in our Zend Framework applications.

File Uploads

One of the great classes provided in Zend Framework is the `File_Transfer` class. This class handles the usual file upload for most applications, allowing developers to focus on the business logic.

Similarly to how our CodeIgniter needed a `File` model to deal with file-related database data, our Zend Framework will also have this class (as well as a `Application_Model_DbTable` class), as shown in Listings 28-1 and 28-2.

Listing 28-1. The User Model

```
class Application_Model_File
{
    protected $_table;

    // define column fields
    // ...

    public function setTable($table)
    {
        // if string given, make new table class
        if (is_string($table))
        {
            $table = new $table();
        }
```

```
        // ...else if object given that is not a valid table class...
        if (!$table instanceof Zend_Db_Table_Abstract)
        {
            throw new Exception("Invalid table specified");
        }

        $this->_table = $table;
        return $this;
    }

    public function getTable()
    {
        if (!$this->_table)
        {
            // define the DbTable first time it is needed
            $this->setTable("Application_Model_DbTable_User");
        }

        return $this->_table;
    }

    protected function _populate($options)
    {
        // populate fields from $options
        // ...
    }

    public function __construct($options = array())
    {
        // populate and load model
        // ...
    }

    public function load()
    {
        if ($this->id)
        {
            // load fields from the database record with this id
            // ...
        }
    }

    public function save()
    {
        // initialize data
        $data = array(
            "name" => $this->name,
            "mime" => $this->mime,
            "size" => $this->size,
            "width" => $this->width,
            "height" => $this->height,
            "user" => $this->user,
```

```
            "live" => (int) $this->live,
            "deleted" => (int) $this->deleted,
            "modified" => date("Y-m-d H:i:s")
        );

        if ($this->id)
        {
            // update
            $where = array("id = ?" => $this->id);
            return $this->getTable()->update($data, $where);
        }
        else
        {
            // insert
            $data["created"] = date("Y-m-d H:i:s");
            return $this->getTable()->insert($data);
        }
    }

    public static function first($where = null)
    {
        $file = new self();
        $table = $user->getTable();
        $query = $table->select()->limit(1);

        if (is_array($where))
        {
            foreach ($where as $key => $value)
            {
                $query->where($key, $value);
            }
        }

        if ($row = $table->fetchRow($query))
        {
            $file->_populate($row->toArray());
            return $file;
        }

        return null;
    }
}
```

Listing 28-2. The File DbTable

```
class Application_Model_DbTable_File extends Zend_Db_Table_Abstract
{
    protected $_name = "file";
}
```

The File model is similar to the User model we created in Chapter 27, differing only with the table name used and the addition of a few Zend-specific utility methods for setting the table adapter. It allows us to save the details of a single file to the database, and link it to a user. The methods without any code in them are identical to the ones we created when working with CodeIgniter. This model expects the database table shown in Listing 28-3 to be in place, in order to function.

Listing 28-3. The file Table

```
CREATE TABLE 'file' (
    'name' varchar(255) DEFAULT NULL,
    'mime' varchar(32) DEFAULT NULL,
    'size' int(11) DEFAULT NULL,
    'width' int(11) DEFAULT NULL,
    'height' int(11) DEFAULT NULL,
    'user' int(11) DEFAULT NULL,
    'id' int(11) NOT NULL AUTO_INCREMENT,
    'live' tinyint(4) DEFAULT NULL,
    'deleted' tinyint(4) DEFAULT NULL,
    'created' datetime DEFAULT NULL,
    'modified' datetime DEFAULT NULL,
    PRIMARY KEY ('id'),
    KEY 'live' ('live'),
    KEY 'deleted' ('deleted')
) ENGINE=InnoDB  DEFAULT CHARSET=utf8 ;
```

With this model in place, we can now modify our register.phtml view and registerAction() method (in the Users controller) in order to allow users to upload photos when they register. You can see how we accomplish this in Listing 28-4.

Listing 28-4. The register.phtml View

```
<h1>Register</h1>
<?php if ($this->success): ?>
    Your account has been created!
<?php else: ?>
    <form method="post" enctype="multipart/form-data">
        <ol>
            <li>
                <label>
                    First name:
                    <input type="text" name="first" />
                    <?php echo isset($this->errors["first"]) ? $this->errors["first"] : ""; ?>
                </label>
            </li>
            <li>
                <label>
                    Last name:
                    <input type="text" name="last" />
                    <?php echo isset($this->errors["last"]) ? $this->errors["last"] : ""; ?>
                </label>
            </li>
            <li>
```

```
                <label>
                    Email:
                    <input type="text" name="email" />
                    <?php echo isset($this->errors["email"]) ? $this->errors["email"] : ""; ?>
                </label>
            </li>
            <li>
                <label>
                    Password:
                    <input type="password" name="password" />
                    <?php echo isset($this->errors["password"]) ? $this->errors["password"] : ""; ?>
                </label>
            </li>
            <li>
                <label>
                    Photo:
                    <input type="file" name="photo" />
                </label>
            </li>
            <li>
                <input type="submit" name="save" value="register" />
            </li>
        </ol>
    </form>
<?php endif; ?>
```

This view includes the new file input that is used in the Users controller, as shown in Listing 28-5.

Listing 28-5. The registerAction() Function

```
class UsersController extends Zend_Controller_Action
{
    protected function _upload($name, $user)
    {
        // get extension
        $time = time();
        $path = dirname(APPLICATION_PATH)."/public/uploads/";
        $filename = "{$user}-{$time}";

        // instantiate file transfer class
        $adapter = new Zend_File_Transfer_Adapter_Http(array(
            "useByteString" => false
        ));
        $adapter->setDestination($path);

        if ($adapter->receive())
        {
            // get file data
            $size = $adapter->getFileSize($name);
            $file = $adapter->getFileName($name);
```

```
            if (rename($file, "{$path}/{$filename}"))
            {
                // get image size/mime
                $dimensions = getimagesize("{$path}/{$filename}");

                // create new file + save
                $file = new Application_Model_File(array(
                    "name" => $filename,
                    "mime" => $dimensions["mime"],
                    "size" => $size,
                    "width" => $dimensions[0],
                    "height" => $dimensions[1],
                    "user" => $user
                ));

                $file->save();
            }
        }
    }

    public function registerAction()
    {
        $valid = true;
        $errors = array();
        $success = false;

        $first = $this->_request->getPost("first");
        $last = $this->_request->getPost("last");
        $email = $this->_request->getPost("email");
        $password = $this->_request->getPost("password");

        // if form was posted
        if ($this->_request->getPost("save"))
        {
            // enforce validation rules

            $alnum = new Zend_Validate_Alnum();
            $stringLength1 = new Zend_Validate_StringLength(array("min" => 3, "max" => 32));
            $stringLength2 = new Zend_Validate_StringLength(array("min" => 0, "max" => 255));

            if (empty($first) || !$alnum->isValid($first) || !$stringLength1->isValid($first))
            {
                $valid = false;
                $errors["first"] = "First field required";
            }

            if (empty($last) || !$alnum->isValid($last) || !$stringLength1->isValid($last))
            {
                $valid = false;
                $errors["last"] = "Last field required";
            }
```

```
            if (empty($email) || !$stringLength2->isValid($email))
            {
                $valid = false;
                $errors["email"] = "Email field required";
            }

            if (empty($password) || !$stringLength2->isValid($password))
            {
                $valid = false;
                $errors["password"] = "Password field required";
            }

            // if form data passes validation...
            if ($valid)
            {
                // create new user + save
                $user = new Application_Model_User(array(
                    "first" => $first,
                    "last" => $last,
                    "email" => $email,
                    "password" => $password
                ));
                $id = $user->save();

                $this->_upload("photo", $id);

                // indicate success in view
                $success = true;
            }
        }

        // load view
        $this->view->errors = $errors;
        $this->view->success = $success;
    }
}
```

Similar to how we have handled file uploads thus far, the register action does not perform the upload logic. That takes place in the protected `_upload()` method, which utilizes Zend Framework's `Zend_File_Transfer_Adapter_Http` class. This class deals mostly in file validation and uploading, but we need a very small cross-section of code for our purposes.

■ **Note** You can learn more about the Zend Framework File Transfer classes at `http://framework.zend.com/manual/en/zend.file.transfer.introduction.html`.

After the file is uploaded, we create a row in the database table, linking it to the user who uploaded the file. Before we modify the profile page to display the photo, we need to look at how we can use external libraries Zend Framework applications.

Third-Party Libraries

Using third-party libraries in a Zend Framework application is not at all unlike using the built-in libraries. We simply need to add another autoloader instance (aside from the one that Zend Framework configures by default) so that we can load classes without `include` statements. You can see this in the modified `application/Bootstrap.php` file, shown in Listing 28-6.

Listing 28-6. The Modified Bootstrap.php File

```
class Bootstrap extends Zend_Application_Bootstrap_Bootstrap
{
    protected function _initAutoloader()
    {
        $autoloader = Zend_Loader_Autoloader::getInstance();
        $autoloader->registerNamespace("Imagine");
    }
}
```

We need to add the namespace for Imagine to the autoloader so that it will recognize classes prefixed with `Imagine`, from within the `library/Imagine` directory, when instantiated by our application. We can now use Imagine classes to modify uploaded files, which we will do in a new protected method, and by modifying the `profileAction()` method in the `Users` controller, as shown in Listing 28-7.

Listing 28-7. Using Imagine in the profileAction() Method

```
class UsersController extends Zend_Controller_Action
{
    protected function _thumbnail($file)
    {
        $path = dirname(APPLICATION_PATH)."/public/uploads";

        $width = 64;
        $height = 64;

        $name = $file->name;
        $filename = pathinfo($name, PATHINFO_FILENAME);
        $extension = pathinfo($name, PATHINFO_EXTENSION);

        if ($filename && $extension)
        {
            $thumbnail = "{$filename}-{$width}x{$height}.{$extension}";

            if (!file_exists("{$path}/{$thumbnail}"))
            {
                $imagine = new Imagine\Gd\Imagine();

                $size = new Imagine\Image\Box($width, $height);
                $mode = Imagine\Image\ImageInterface::THUMBNAIL_OUTBOUND;
```

```
                $imagine
                    ->open("{$path}/{$name}")
                    ->thumbnail($size, $mode)
                    ->save("{$path}/{$thumbnail}");
            }

            return $thumbnail;
        }

    }

    public function profileAction()
    {
        // check for user session
        $this->_isSecure();

        // load thumbnail
        $file = Application_Model_File::first(array(
            "user = ?" => $this->user->id
        ));
        $filename = $this->_thumbnail($file);

        // load view
        $this->view->user = $this->user;
        $this->view->filename = $filename;
    }
}
```

■ **Note** Remember to secure your `uploads` directory!

The `_thumbnail()` method is similar to the façade class we created in our CodeIgniter application, and is also called internally by the profile action. This will produce a thumbnail should none already exist, and return it to our `profileAction()` method, which then assigns it to the view. We also need to modify our `profile.phtml` view, as shown in Listing 28-8.

Listing 28-8. The profile.phtml View

```
<?php if ($this->filename): ?>
    <img src="/uploads/<?php echo $this->filename; ?>" />
<?php endif; ?>
<h1><?php echo $this->user->first; ?> <?php echo $this->user->last; ?></h1>
This is a profile page!
```

We now know how to utilize built-in Zend Framework libraries, as well as third-party libraries with namespace support and class autoloading.

Questions

1. What are some of the differences between Zend Framework's namespace schema and the namespace schema PHP 5.3 provides?
2. We began our time with Zend Framework by using the Command Line Interface to create a project, yet most of the work we've done has been without the help of the CLI. Why might this be?

Answers

1. Zend Framework (1.11) uses underscores as namespace separators where PHP 5.3 namespaces are separated by backslash characters. Zend Framework's class libraries aren't technically namespaced in that they are all in the global namespace. Conflicts aren't likely to occur, though, as Zend Framework's class names tend to be verbose.
2. While the CLI provides a lot of helpful functionality, learning a framework has to be done by manual coding. We could have used the CLI, but then we would also have understood much less of Zend Framework.

Exercises

1. There is no way to generate thumbnails outside of the `profileAction()` method. Try creating a public action that allows for this functionality.
2. Take a look at some of the many class libraries bundled with Zend Framework. There are many helpful resources and the libraries can even be used alongside other frameworks.

CHAPTER 29

Zend Framework: Testing

We end our time with Zend Framework by looking at how to run unit tests in our application, using PHPUnit.

Goals

- We need to learn how to install PEAR and PHPUnit.
- We need to learn how to create and run tests on our controllers.

Installing PEAR

PEAR is the official distribution platform for reusable PHP libraries. You can think of it like Homebrew except instead of distributing packages that work with OS X, it distributes libraries tailored for use with PHP.

You can install PEAR in just a few steps, which we will detail next.

Windows

- After you have downloaded and installed PHP, you must manually execute the batch file located in, for example, `c:\php\go-pear.bat`. The setup will ask you some questions, after which the PEAR Package Manager will be installed in the path that you have specified during installation.
- Next, you must add the installation path to your PATH environment. Either do this manually (Start > Control Panel > System > Environment) or run (double-click) the newly generated `PEAR_ENV.reg` that's now found in the PHP source directory.
- After that, you can access the PEAR Package Manager by running the command `pear` in a Windows Command Prompt.
- To update your PEAR installation, request `http://pear.php.net/go-pear.phar` in your browser and save the output to a local file, `go-pear.phar`. You can then run the following line:

  ```
  php go-pear.phar
  ```

Unix/Linux/BSD

When using PHP, the PEAR Package Manager is already installed unless one has used the `./configure` option `--without-pear`.

If one uses a version of PHP that is supplied by Unix/Linux/BSD distributors, it may be necessary to manually install PEAR. Users should consult the documentation for the respective distribution in this case. If you want to reinstall PEAR, you can use the following method:

- `wget http://pear.php.net/go-pear.phar`
- `php go-pear.phar`

Mac OS X

On Mac OS 10.4 and earlier, the PEAR Package Manager is already installed in `/usr/bin/pear`.

If you are using Mac OS 10.5 (Leopard) and would like to install a new copy or reinstall the PEAR Package Manager, use the following command:

- `wget http://pear.php.net/go-pear.phar`
- `php -d detect_unicode=0 go-pear.phar`

Installing PHPUnit

Installing PHPUnit is even easier, at this point, since it requires only the following two commands:

- `pear config-set auto_discover 1`
- `pear install pear.phpunit.de/PHPUnit`

Running the Tests

When we initially set up our Zend Framework project, it notified us that PHPUnit was not found within the PHP `include` path. Now that we have installed PHPUnit (via PEAR) we should no longer have this problem.

Navigate to the tests directory that the Zend Framework CLI generated for us and run the following command:

- `phpunit`

Note Be sure to follow the instructions in `phpunit.xml` if your Zend Framework library files are within the `libraries` directory.

Adding Tests

Adding tests is a fairly straightforward process. We will add four tests to the `tests/controllers/IndexControllerTest.php` file, as shown in Listing 29-1.

Listing 29-1. Adding Unit Tests

```
class IndexControllerTest extends Zend_Test_PHPUnit_ControllerTestCase
{

    protected $_email = "testing_user";
    protected $_password = "testing_password";

    public function setUp()
    {
        $this->bootstrap = new Zend_Application(APPLICATION_ENV, APPLICATION_PATH .
"/configs/application.ini");
        parent::setUp();
    }

    public function testRegisterHasFields()
    {
        $this->dispatch("/users/register");
        $this->assertQuery("input[name='first']", "first name field not found");
        $this->assertQuery("input[name='last']", "last name field not found");
        $this->assertQuery("input[name='email']", "email field not found");
        $this->assertQuery("input[name='password']", "password field not found");
        $this->assertQuery("input[name='photo']", "photo field not found");
        $this->assertQuery("input[name='save']", "register button not found");
    }

    public function testRegisterWorks()
    {
        $this->request->setMethod("POST")
            ->setPost(array(
                "first" => "testing",
                "last" => "testing",
                "email" => $this->_email,
                "password" => $this->_password,
                "save" => "register"
            ));

        $this->dispatch("/users/register");
        $this->assertQueryContentContains("p", "account has been created");
    }

    public function testLoginHasFields()
    {
        $this->dispatch("/users/login");
        $this->assertQuery("input[name='email']", "email field not found");
        $this->assertQuery("input[name='password']", "password field not found");
        $this->assertQuery("input[name='login']", "login button not found");
    }

    public function testLoginWorks()
    {
        $this->request
            ->setMethod("POST")
```

```
            ->setPost(array(
                "email" => $this->_email,
                "password" => $this->_password,
                "login" => "login"
            ));

        $this->dispatch("/users/login");
        $this->assertRedirect($message = "not redirected");
    }
}
```

The setUp() method merely initiates the testing process for each unit test that will be run. This is automatically generated and doesn't need to be modified. The first and third tests assert that the register.phtml and login.phtml views have all the required fields to log in and register.

The second and fourth tests actually post data to the Zend Framework application and check that the response is in the expected format. You might need to modify your application to redirect in the way shown in Listing 29-2.

Listing 29-2. Redirecting the Zend Framework Way

```
// redirect to profile page
$this->_helper->redirector->gotoRoute(array(
   "controller" => "users",
   "action" => "profile"
));
```

■ **Note** If you would like to download or learn more about PHPUnit, you can do so at https://github.com/sebastianbergmann/phpunit.

Questions

1. In this chapter, we learned about a standard library distribution mechanism (PEAR) and used it to install a popular unit-testing framework (PHPUnit). What are some of the benefits and drawbacks of using a distribution system like PEAR?
2. What are the benefits of using PHPUnit to make remote requests to our application, as opposed to building the tests as part of the application itself?

Answers

1. Distribution systems are pretty useful—we have already used a few in this book! The problem is that each has its own learning curve and clutters the system up in its own special way. It would be ideal if we could depend on only a single distribution system to install everything for us, from Apache to PHP to PHPUnit.
2. Thinking back to our own unit-testing library. Comparing it to PHPUnit, we can see how easily advanced functionality (such as registration and login) can be tested without any messy database or configuration code. The base for our unit testing was set up for us by Zend Framework, and all the heavy lifting was done by PHPUnit.

CHAPTER 30

CakePHP: Bootstrapping

CakePHP was created and is maintained by a community of open source developers, and is geared toward rapid application development that favors convention over configuration.

It is feature rich and includes, among other things, an impressive ORM and a command-line interface for quickly creating models, views, and controllers.

Note You can download CakePHP from `http://cakephp.org/`.

Goals

- We need to understand the philosophy and benefits of CakePHP.
- We need to learn how to create the architectural requirements for our sample application.

Why CakePHP?

CakePHP is extremely popular, and as a result has developed a knowledgeable community and good documentation. The focus of CakePHP is on doing things by convention rather than forcing developers to configure everything. That is not to say that it cannot be configured, but rather that most of this will have been done before you even start to use CakePHP.

The documentation of CakePHP is quite comprehensive, ranging from simple API documentation to a cookbook of frequent programming tasks. There are also many popular screencast, book resources, and events designed to educate new and experienced CakePHP developers alike.

Note You can find the CakePHP documentation at `http://api20.cakephp.org/`.

Why Not CakePHP?

CakePHP is not for the faint-hearted. There is actually a huge amount of things going on behind the scenes and it's easy to get lost when needing to make simple configuration or behavioral changes to a CakePHP application.

The heavy focus on convention also means that CakePHP makes many assumptions about directory structure, file names, and actual code. This is not dissimilar to other frameworks (ours included), but where the assumptions we make number in the tens, CakePHP is literally built upon them. It assumes when you want to load a model. It assumes when you want to load helpers.

It almost seems like there is little to do when using CakePHP for an application's codebase, but that's because CakePHP is already making assumptions and doing it all.

Getting Set Up

Getting CakePHP up and running is trivial. The downloadable archives are organized in a ready-to-go project structure and you simply need to make the public folder contained therein web-accessible to begin seeing your application. To get CakePHP running, download the latest CakePHP Stable release (e.g., `https://github.com/cakephp/cakephp/zipball/2.1.3`) and extract it where you see fit.

You will need to configure your web server to point to the `webroot/` directory in order for the generated bootstrapping code to execute.

Routes

CakePHP routes can only be defined by function calls, which makes it different from all the other frameworks we have worked with so far. These function calls can theoretically be in any file before the request is dispatched, but are typically in the `app/Config/routes.php` file. When adding our routes, this configuration file should resemble what is shown in Listing 30-1.

Listing 30-1. Adding Custom Routes to CakePHP

```
/**
* Here, we are connecting '/' (base path) to controller called 'Pages',
* its action called 'display', and we pass a param to select the view file
* to use (in this case, /app/View/Pages/home.ctp)...
*/
Router::connect('/', array('controller' => 'pages', 'action' => 'display', 'home'));

/**
* ...and connect the rest of 'Pages' controller's urls.
*/
Router::connect('/pages/*', array('controller' => 'pages', 'action' => 'display'));

/**
* custom routes
*/
Router::connect('/register', array('controller' =>'users', 'action' =>'register'));
Router::connect('/login', array('controller' =>'users', 'action' =>'login'));
Router::connect('/logout', array('controller' =>'users', 'action' =>'logout'));
Router::connect('/search', array('controller' =>'users', 'action' =>'search'));
Router::connect('/profile', array('controller' =>'users', 'action' =>'profile'));
Router::connect('/settings', array('controller' =>'users', 'action' =>'settings'));
Router::connect('/friend/*', array('controller' =>'users', 'action' =>'friend'));
Router::connect('/unfriend/*', array('controller' =>'users', 'action' =>'unfriend'));
Router::connect('/users/edit/*', array('controller' =>'users', 'action' =>'edit'));
Router::connect('/users/delete/*', array('controller' =>'users', 'action' =>'delete'));
Router::connect('/users/undelete/*', array('controller' =>'users', 'action' =>'undelete'));
```

```
Router::connect('/fonts/*', array('controller' =>'files', 'action' =>'fonts'));
Router::connect('/thumbnails/*', array('controller' =>'files', 'action' =>'thumbnails'));
Router::connect('/files/delete/*', array('controller' =>'files', 'action' =>'delete'));
Router::connect('/files/undelete/*', array('controller' =>'files', 'action' =>'undelete'));

/**
* Load all plugin routes. See the CakePlugin documentation on
* how to customize the loading of plugin routes.
*/
CakePlugin::routes();

/**
* Load the CakePHP default routes. Remove this if you do not want to use
* the built-in default routes.
*/
require CAKE . 'Config' . DS . 'routes.php';
```

The first two routes are automatically defined for us. The first defaults requests to the URL / to the pages/home action. The second is used to display a named page, according to the pages/display action.

In some of the routes, we have used * to specify that a parameter will be passed to the action. This does not need to be echoed in the parameter array, yet is automatically passed as an argument to the action.

If you try to access any of these new routes, you will see an error. This is because we have not yet created the corresponding controllers, actions, and so on. In Chapter 31, we will create the controllers, models, and views required for most of these routes to function correctly.

■ **Note** You can find more details about CakePHP routing at `http://book.cakephp.org/2.0/en/development/routing.html`.

Questions

1. The CakePHP `Router` allows very detailed route specification. How can we add this sort of functionality to our framework's `Router` class?

2. What are the benefits of using function calls to add routes to an application, over using configuration files?

Answers

1. Our framework has two distinct types of routes: the `Simple` and the `Regex` `Route` subclasses. In order to enhance our router's functionality, we simply need to create more detailed `Route` subclasses that handle the extra functionality for us.

2. Function calls can allow much finer control over the specification of routes. We can do all sorts of cool things with function calls (such as passing callbacks or object instances), which configuration files won't allow.

Exercises

1. In this chapter, we created all the routes our example application requires. Now try to create a route that uses a username to invoke the users/profile action.
2. Having all these routes without any controllers and actions isn't very helpful to us. Try to create a controller and action to handle a few of the routes we defined.

CHAPTER 31

CakePHP: MVC

CakePHP is a powerful, semi-autonomous framework intended for rapid application development, favoring convention over configuration. What this means is there are many parts of CakePHP that make some assumptions and then move on. This includes areas such as ORM and view generation, where many of the decisions about how data should be handled and interfaces should be rendered are made for you before you open up your code editor.

Goals

- We need to understand how CakePHP's ORM system works so that we can create and use the models our sample application needs.
- We need to create the views and controllers, which talk to these models.

What's in a Model?

In the case of CakePHP, the model holds quite a bit more than we've seen or built before. It is seriously packed with functionality that can help us to develop complex relationships between data entities and extract data rapidly; however, this complexity can also possibly hinder development.

Consider the database table shown in Listing 31-1.

Listing 31-1. The users Table

```
CREATE TABLE 'users' (
  'id' int(11) NOT NULL AUTO_INCREMENT,
  'live' tinyint(4) DEFAULT NULL,
  'deleted' tinyint(4) DEFAULT NULL,
  'created' datetime DEFAULT NULL,
  'modified' datetime DEFAULT NULL,
  'first' varchar(32) DEFAULT NULL,
  'last' varchar(32) DEFAULT NULL,
  'email' varchar(100) DEFAULT NULL,
  'password' varchar(32) DEFAULT NULL,
  PRIMARY KEY ('id')
) ENGINE=InnoDB  DEFAULT CHARSET=utf8 ;
```

Up until now, all of our users tables have been singular in name. There is a set of conventions for how to name (among other things) database tables, when working with CakePHP. It allows CakePHP to infer names of things and generate code accordingly.

This database table can easily interface with ORM using the model class shown in Listing 31-2.

Listing 31-2. ~/app/Model/User.php

```
class User extends AppModel
{
    // nothing to see here
}
```

The model class is surprisingly sparse because of the naming convention we used for the users database table. If we were to create a sample action (shown in Listing 31-3), it is plain to see how the model can be used similarly to our previous sample applications.

Listing 31-3. ~/app/Controller/UsersController.php

```
App::uses("AppController", "Controller");

class UsersController extends AppController
{
    public $name = "Users";

    public $helpers = array("Html", "Form");
    public $uses = array("User");

    public function index()
    {
        $user = $this->User->find("first");

        print_r($user); // no users yet!

        $id = $this->User->save(array(
            "first" => "Chris",
            "last" => "Pitt",
            "email" => "cgpitt@gmail.com",
            "password" => "chris"
        )); // user saved

        $user = $this->User->find("first");

        print_r($user); // found Chris!

        exit();
    }
}
```

This shows us that we can not only use the models in CakePHP in a predictable manner, but also that they require even less setup than our other sample applications. On to the controllers and views!

Controllers

Now that we understand the basics of creating models in CakePHP, we can move on to the `UsersController` class our application will need to function, shown in Listing 31-4.

Listing 31-4. ~/app/Controller/UsersController.php (Extract)

```
class UsersController extends AppController
{
    public $name = "Users";

    public $helpers = array("Html", "Form");

    public $uses = array("User");

    public $user;

    protected function _isSecure()
    {
        $this->_getUser();
        if (!$this->user)
        {
            $this->redirect(array(
                "action" => "login"
            ));
        }
    }

    protected function _getUser()
    {
        $id = $this->Session->read("user");

        if ($id)
        {
            $this->user = $this->User->findById($id);
        }
    }
}
```

These methods, similar to the ones we created in our previous sample applications, are used simply to check whether a user session is valid and to extract user data from the database based on a session-stored user ID.

We continue with the `register()` action, as shown in Listing 31-5.

Listing 31-5. ~/app/Controller/UsersController.php (Extract)

```
class UsersController extends AppController
{
    public function register()
    {
        if ($this->request->is("post"))
        {
```

```
            if ($this->User->save($this->request->data))
            {
                $this->Session->setFlash("Your account has been created.");
            }
            else
            {
                $this->Session->setFlash("An error occurred while creating your account.");
            }
        }
    }
}
```

This register() action is vastly different than previous iterations, and while the code is significantly less, CakePHP is doing a lot of things behind the scenes. First, the register() action checks whether the form was posted, and then immediately tries to save the user data in the database. This requires that the form fields also follow a naming convention so that the model can infer database field values based simply on form field names. Next, a temporary (or "flash") message is stored in the session to inform the user as to the outcome of this action's processing.

In order to use this action, we need to create a view compatible with the ORM code, as shown in Listing 31-6.

Listing 31-6. ~/app/View/Users/register.ctp

```
<h1>Register</h1>
<?php
    echo $this->Form->create("User");

    echo $this->Form->input("first");
    echo $this->Form->input("last");
    echo $this->Form->input("email");
    echo $this->Form->input("password", array(
        "type" => "password"
    ));

    echo $this->Form->end("register");
?>
```

It is just as quick to automatically create forms and form fields as it has been for us to create models and controllers. The register view is no exception! Give it a try.

Finishing Up

We still need to create a few models and actions before our basic application is in place. Let us begin with the actions, as shown in Listing 31-7.

Listing 31-7. ~/app/Controller/UsersController.php (Extract)

```
class UsersController extends AppController
{
    public function register()
    {
        if ($this->request->is("post"))
```

```
    {
        if ($this->User->save($this->request->data))
        {
            $this->Session->setFlash("Your account has been created.");
        }
        else
        {
            $this->Session->setFlash("An error occurred while creating your account.");
        }
    }
}

public function login()
{
    if ($this->request->is("post"))
    {
        $email = $this->request->data["User"]["email"];
        $password = $this->request->data["User"]["password"];

        $user = $this->User->findByEmailAndPassword($email, $password);

        if ($user)
        {
            $this->Session->write("user", $user["User"]["id"]);

            $this->redirect(array(
                "action" => "profile"
            ));
        }
        else
        {
            $this->Session->setFlash("Logn details invalid.");
        }
    }
}

public function logout()
{
    $this->Session->delete("user");

    $this->redirect(array(
        "action" => "login"
    ));
}

public function profile()
{
    $this->_isSecure();
    $this->set("user", $this->user);
}
```

```
    public function settings()
    {
        $this->_isSecure();
        $this->set("user", $this->user);

        $this->User->id = $this->user["User"]["id"];

        if ($this->request->is("get"))
        {
            $this->request->data = $this->user;
        }
        else if ($this->request->is("post"))
        {
            if ($this->User->save($this->request->data))
            {
                $this->Session->setFlash("Your account has been updated.");
            }
            else
            {
                $this->Session->setFlash("An error occurred while updating your account.");
            }
        }
    }

    public function search()
    {
        $data = $this->request->data;

        if (isset($data["Search"]))
        {
            $query = !empty($data["Search"]["query"]) ? $data["Search"]["query"] : "";
            $order = !empty($data["Search"]["order"]) ? $data["Search"]["order"] : "modified";
            $direction = !empty($data["Search"]["direction"]) ?
$data["Search"]["direction"] : "desc";
            $page = !empty($data["Search"]["page"]) ? $data["Search"]["page"] : 1;
            $limit = !empty($data["Search"]["limit"]) ? $data["Search"]["limit"] : 10;
        }

        $users = null;

        if ($this->request->is("post"))
        {
            $conditions = array(
                "conditions" => array(
                    "first = ?" => $query
                ),
                "fields" => array(
                    "id", "first", "last"
                ),
                "order" => array(
                    $order . " " . $direction
                ),
```

```
                "page" => $limit,
                "offset" => ($page - 1) * $limit
            );

            $users = $this->User->find("all", $conditions);
            $count = $this->User->find("count", $conditions);
        }
        $this->set("query", $query);
        $this->set("order", $order);
        $this->set("direction", $direction);
        $this->set("page", $page);
        $this->set("limit", $limit);
        $this->set("count", $count);
        $this->set("users", $users);
    }
}
```

These actions mirror the functionality of the same actions in our previous frameworks, yet take much less code to achieve. They also request the view files in Listings 31-8 to Listing 31-12.

Listing 31-8. ~/app/View/Users/register.ctp

```
<h1>Register</h1>
<?php
    echo $this->Form->create("User");

    echo $this->Form->input("first");
    echo $this->Form->input("last");
    echo $this->Form->input("email");
    echo $this->Form->input("password", array(
        "type" => "password"
    ));

    echo $this->Form->end("register");
?>
```

Listing 31-9. ~/app/View/Users/login.ctp

```
<h1>Login</h1>
<?php
    echo $this->Form->create("User");

    echo $this->Form->input("email");
    echo $this->Form->input("password", array(
        "type" => "password"
    ));

    echo $this->Form->end("login");
?>
```

Listing 31-10. ~/app/View/Users/profile.ctp

```
<h1><?php echo $user["User"]["first"]; ?> <?php echo $user["User"]["last"]; ?></h1>
This is a profile page!
```

Listing 31-11. ~/app/View/Users/settings.ctp

```
<h1>Settings</h1>
<?php
    echo $this->Form->create("User");

    echo $this->Form->input("first");
    echo $this->Form->input("last");
    echo $this->Form->input("email");
    echo $this->Form->input("password", array(
        "type" => "password"
    ));

    echo $this->Form->end("save");
?>
```

Listing 31-12. ~/app/View/Users/search.ctp

```
<h1>Search</h1>
<?php
    echo $this->Form->create("Search");

    echo $this->Form->input("query");

    echo $this->Form->input("order", array(
        "options" => array(
            "id" => "id",
            "first" => "first",
            "last" => "last"
        )
    ));

    echo $this->Form->input("direction", array(
        "options" => array(
            "id" => "id",
            "first" => "first",
            "last" => "last"
        )
    ));

    echo $this->Form->input("limit", array(
        "options" => array(
            10 => 10,
            20 => 20,
            30 => 30,
            40 => 40
        )
    ));
```

```
    $range = range(1, ceil($count / $limit));
    $options = array_combine($range, $range);

    echo $this->Form->input("page", array(
        "options" => $options
    ));

    echo $this->Form->end("search");
?>

<table>
    <tr>
        <th>id</th>
        <th>name</th>
    </tr>
    <?php foreach ($users as $user): ?>
    <tr>
        <td><?php echo $user["User"]["id"]; ?></td>
        <td><?php echo $user["User"]["first"]; ?> <?php echo $user["User"]["last"]; ?></td>
    </tr>
    <?php endforeach; ?>
</table>
```

Questions

1. CakePHP makes a large number of assumptions about the naming conventions and default configuration of our application, allowing it to achieve very much with very little code. What are some of the benefits and drawbacks of this approach to application development?
2. CakePHP, like Zend Framework, uses a custom file extension for its template files. How could this introduce security errors for our applications?

Answers

1. CakePHP's approach to convention over configuration means that we can do very much with very little code. It's beneficial as developers can rapidly prototype applications without repeating the same tasks common to each application. It also requires that developers learn the conventions before being able to efficiently use the framework.
2. Files that contain PHP code, yet do not have the `.php` extension, could possibly be interpreted as plain text files or plain HTML files (by the web server responsible for serving the files). It is recommended that you use `.php` files for everything that contains PHP code, or at the very least ensure that every web-accessible folder that serves files containing PHP serves these files with the PHP mime type.

Exercises

1. CakePHP's ORM system is powerful and expressive, and we have used only a small portion of it here. Take a look at the documentation and try to extend the `search()` action.

2. CakePHP includes an authentication library quite dissimilar to the login system we have created here. Take a look at it and try to integrate it with our login system.

CHAPTER 32

CakePHP: Extending

Extensions to the core CakePHP functionality come in many forms. They can be in the form of Components, Helpers, Behaviors, or Tasks (which are all referred to as Collections).

Whether you require libraries bundled with CakePHP or intend to use your own (third-party) libraries, you will need to utilize the unified API that all of the Collections share, in order to load, unload, enable, disable, or invoke their functionality.

Goals

- We need to learn how to use built-in CakePHP functionality.
- We need to learn how to include our own (third-party) functionality in our CakePHP applications.

File Uploads

CakePHP has its own built-in library for dealing with files and folders. This library deals with all the hassle of creating and moving files, so we don't need to do any of that ourselves.

Before we can accept any file uploads, we need to create the database table in which references to files can be stored. This follows the predictable pattern set in the previous frameworks and applications, as shown in Listing 32-1.

Listing 32-1. The photos Table

```
CREATE TABLE 'photos' (
    'name' varchar(255) DEFAULT NULL,
    'mime' varchar(32) DEFAULT NULL,
    'size' int(11) DEFAULT NULL,
    'width' int(11) DEFAULT NULL,
    'height' int(11) DEFAULT NULL,
    'user_id' int(11) DEFAULT NULL,
    'id' int(11) NOT NULL AUTO_INCREMENT,
    'live' tinyint(4) DEFAULT NULL,
    'deleted' tinyint(4) DEFAULT NULL,
    'created' datetime DEFAULT NULL,
    'modified' datetime DEFAULT NULL,
```

```
    PRIMARY KEY ('id'),
    KEY 'live' ('live'),
    KEY 'deleted' ('deleted')
) ENGINE=InnoDB  DEFAULT CHARSET=utf8 ;
```

This table differs from the previous `file` tables we created; mainly, the name is now `photos` (due to the naming conventions in CakePHP) and the user field becomes `user_id` for the same reason. With the database table in place, we can look at the `Photo` model, shown in Listing 32-2.

Listing 32-2. ~/app/Model/Photo.php

```
class Photo extends AppModel
{
    public $belongsTo = "User";
}
```

The `Photo` model introduces a concept we haven't seen before: relationships. CakePHP's ORM model includes a wide array of relationship types between database objects, and `$belongsTo` denotes that each `Photo` object belongs to a single `User` object.

In order to solidify this connection between the two data types, we need to amend the `User` model as well, demonstrated in Listing 32-3.

Listing 32-3. ~/app/Model/User.php (Amended)

```
class User extends AppModel
{
    public $hasMany = "Photo";
}
```

The reciprocal relationship type (shown in the amended `User` model) is the `$hasMany` relationship type. This means that a single `User` object has many `Photo` objects. We could also have specified a `$hasOne` relationship in reciprocity to the `$belongsTo` relationship in the `Photo` model.

■ **Note** There are ways to deviate from the naming conventions of CakePHP and still utilize the relationships it provides. You can find out how here: `http://book.cakephp.org/2.0/en/models/associations-linking-models-together.html`

In order to allow file uploads from users, we need to modify the register and settings view templates, as shown in Listings 32-4 and 32-5.

Listing 32-4. ~/app/View/Users/register.ctp (Amended)

```
<h1>Register</h1>
<?php
    echo $this->Form->create("User" , array("type" => "file"));

    echo $this->Form->input("first");
    echo $this->Form->input("last");
    echo $this->Form->input("email");
```

```
    echo $this->Form->input("password", array(
        "type" => "password"
    ));
    echo $this->Form->input("photo", array(
        "type" => "file"
    ));

    echo $this->Form->end("register");
?>
```

Listing 32-5. ~/app/View/Users/settings.ctp (Amended)

```
<h1>Settings</h1>
<?php
    echo $this->Form->create("User" , array("type" => "file"));

    echo $this->Form->input("first");
    echo $this->Form->input("last");
    echo $this->Form->input("email");
    echo $this->Form->input("password", array(
        "type" => "password"
    ));
    echo $this->Form->input("photo", array(
        "type" => "file"
    ));

    echo $this->Form->end("save");
?>
```

There are two important changes to both of these views. The first is including the second parameter in the call to `$this->Form->create(...)`. The second is the input (of type `file`) added to each form. These allow us to create the function for processing file uploads (in the `UsersController`), as shown in Listing 32-6.

Listing 32-6. ~/app/Controller/UsersController.php (Extract)

```
class UsersController extends AppController
{
    protected function _upload($name, $user)
    {
        App::uses("File", "Utility");

        $meta = $this->request->data["User"][$name];
        $file = new File($meta["tmp_name"], false);

        if ($file)
        {
            $path = WWW_ROOT."uploads";

            if ($file->copy($path.DS.$meta["name"]))
            {
                $info = $file->info();
                $size = getimagesize($meta["tmp_name"]);
```

```
                $this->Photo->save(array(
                    "user_id" => $user,
                    "mime" => $info["mime"],
                    "size" => $info["filesize"],
                    "width" => $size[0],
                    "height" => $size[1]
                ));
            }
        }
    }
}
```

The _upload() method begins with us loading CakePHP's bundled File class. This is due to the fact that CakePHP does not support the class autoloading we have come to expect from our own framework or Zend Framework.

From there, we create a new File instance and use its copy() method to create a copy of the temporarily uploaded file within our ~/app/webroot/uploads directory. Finally, we save a reference to the uploaded file in the photos table. We call the _upload() method within our register() and settings() actions, as shown in Listing 32-7.

Listing 32-7. ~/app/Controller/UsersController.php (Extract)

```
class UsersController extends AppController
{
    public function register()
    {
        if ($this->request->is("post"))
        {
            if ($this->User->save($this->request->data))
            {
                $this->_upload("photo", $this->User->id);
                $this->Session->setFlash("Your account has been created.");
            }
            else
            {
                $this->Session->setFlash("An error occurred while creating your account.");
            }
        }
    }

    public function settings()
    {
        $this->_isSecure();
        $this->set("user", $this->user);

        $this->User->id = $this->user["User"]["id"];

        if ($this->request->is("get"))
        {
            $this->request->data = $this->user;
        }
```

```
        else if ($this->request->is("post"))
        {
            if ($this->User->save($this->request->data))
            {
                $this->_upload("photo", $this->User->id);
                $this->Session->setFlash("Your account has been updated.");
            }
            else
            {
                $this->Session->setFlash("An error occurred while updating your account.");
            }
        }
    }
}
```

Now, when new users register for an account in the sample application, and select a photo to upload, their user record will be created, their photo will be uploaded, and a reference to their photo will be created in the database (and assigned to the user account).

Third-Party Libraries

Using third-party libraries is a little different from using built-in libraries in CakePHP. There are two different ways of doing this, either with plugins or by placing them in a vendor directory.

Plugins

Creating a plugin is not unlike duplicating the structure of the app directory and filling it with the controllers, views, models, and collections that your plugin requires in order to function. The problem is that this approach generates a lot of work if all we want to do is use a preexisting PHP library.

■ **Note** You can find more about CakePHP plugins here: `http://book.cakephp.org/2.0/en/plugins.html`

Vendor Directory

The approach we will take is by placing the `Imagine` library within a `Vendor` directory. Begin by placing the `Imagine` library within the `~/app/Vendor` directory, followed by a new `_thumbnail()` method in our `UsersController`, as shown in Listing 32-8.

Listing 32-8. ~/app/Controller/UsersController.php (Extract)

```
class UsersController extends AppController
{
    protected function _thumbnail($photo)
    {
        App::uses("File", "Utility");

        App::import("Vendor", "Imagine/Image/ManipulatorInterface");
        App::import("Vendor", "Imagine/Image/ImageInterface");
```

```
        App::import("Vendor", "Imagine/Image/ImagineInterface");
        App::import("Vendor", "Imagine/Image/BoxInterface");
        App::import("Vendor", "Imagine/Image/PointInterface");
        App::import("Vendor", "Imagine/Image/Point");
        App::import("Vendor", "Imagine/Gd/Image");
        App::import("Vendor", "Imagine/Gd/Imagine");
        App::import("Vendor", "Imagine/Image/Box");

        $path = WWW_ROOT."uploads";

        $width = 64;
        $height = 64;

        $file = new File($path.DS.$photo["name"]);

        if ($file)
        {
            $name = $file->name();
            $extension = $file->ext();

            $thumbnail = "{$name}-{$width}x{$height}.{$extension}";

            if (!file_exists("{$path}/{$thumbnail}"))
            {
                $imagine = new Imagine\Gd\Imagine();

                $size = new Imagine\Image\Box($width, $height);
                $mode = Imagine\Image\ImageInterface::THUMBNAIL_OUTBOUND;

                $imagine
                    ->open("{$path}/{$name}.{$extension}")
                    ->thumbnail($size, $mode)
                    ->save("{$path}/{$thumbnail}");
            }

            return $thumbnail;
        }
    }
}
```

The `_thumbnail()` method is similar to the one we created in our Zend Framework application, with a few subtle differences. First, we accept the same types of arguments but they are named slightly differently in order to accommodate CakePHP conventions. Second, we utilize the `File` component in order to get the correct file name and extension. Third, we need to manually import all of the `Imagine` classes required to resize the uploaded photos, since there is no class autoloading to do this for us. Finally, there are a few small differences in the strings used to open and save our thumbnails.

This all comes together in the `profile()` action and the `profile.ctp` view template, as shown in Listings 32-9 and 32-10.

Listing 32-9 ~/app/Controller/UsersController.php (Extract)

```
class UsersController extends AppController
{
    public function profile()
    {
        $this->_isSecure();

        if (sizeof($this->user["Photo"]))
        {
            $this->set("photo", $this->_thumbnail($this->user["Photo"][0]));
        }

        $this->set("user", $this->user);
    }
}
```

Listing 32-10. ~/app/View/Users/profile.ctp

```
<?php if ($photo): ?>
    <img src="/uploads/<?php echo $photo; ?>" />
<?php endif; ?>
<h1><?php echo $user["User"]["first"]; ?> <?php echo $user["User"]["last"]; ?></h1>
This is a profile page!
```

We now know how to use built-in CakePHP collections, as well as how to include third-party (vendor) libraries.

Questions

1. CakePHP presents the first ORM library that handles relationships (out of all the frameworks we have built/used so far). What are some of the benefits and drawbacks of this concept?
2. We generated our forms quite differently in this chapter, compared to previous chapters. How is this good and bad?

Answers

1. Relationships are a complicated thing to get right in any ORM. The relationships we created in this chapter were easy to set up, but depended largely on naming conventions. The fact that we didn't have to do any work to retrieve related photos considerably lightened our workload. It also required a basic understanding of how the relationships work in CakePHP.
2. CakePHP is not the only framework we used to support automatic form generation. Zend Framework also facilitates this kind of thing; however, both frameworks require an in-depth knowledge of how to define these forms and how to use their various functionality. As with any automatically generated code, even small changes require lots of knowledge of what's being done automatically.

Exercises

1. In this chapter, we chose to use the `Vendor` directory as a home for the `Imagine` library. It is far better to use plugins for third-party code that you plan to reuse in other projects, but it also requires a lot of code. Try to convert our vendor-based `Imagine` code into a plugin.

2. CakePHP's ORM library also supports creating multiple database records by calling the `saveAll()` method on the main data object. Instead of separate `save()` calls for photos and users, try to combine them.

■ **Note** You can learn more about this method of creating related records here: `http://book.cakephp.org/2.0/en/models/saving-your-data.html#model-saveall-array-data-null-array-options-array`

CHAPTER 33

CakePHP: Testing

Similar to the testing we did in Zend Framework, CakePHP's unit tests depend on PHPUnit, making it an easy end to our time in CakePHP.

Goals

- We need to learn how to create and run tests on our controllers.

Testing

There are a few simple tests that we can create in order to validate the functionality of our CakePHP controllers. Because the majority of code we have written in CakePHP concerns the controller, we will only write tests for some of the actions in the `UsersController`.

CakePHP unit tests need to be placed n the `~/app/Test/` directory, and the first set of tests that we will create are shown in Listing 33-1.

Listing 33-1. ~/app/Test/Controller/UsersControllerTest.php (Extract)

```
class UsersControllerTest extends ControllerTestCase
{
    public function testRegisterGet()
    {
        $result = $this->testAction("/register", array(
            "method" => "get",
            "return" => "contents"
        ));

        $this->assertContains("data[User][first]", $result);
        $this->assertContains("data[User][last]", $result);
        $this->assertContains("data[User][email]", $result);
        $this->assertContains("data[User][password]", $result);
        $this->assertContains("data[User][photo]", $result);
    }
```

```
    public function testLoginGet()
    {
        $result = $this->testAction("/login", array(
            "method" => "get",
            "return" => "contents"
        ));

        $this->assertContains("data[User][email]", $result);
        $this->assertContains("data[User][password]", $result);
    }

    public function testLogoutGet()
    {
        $result = $this->testAction("/logout", array(
            "method" => "get",
            "return" => "contents"
        ));
    }

    public function testProfileGet()
    {
        $result = $this->testAction("/profile", array(
            "method" => "get",
            "return" => "contents"
        ));
    }
}
```

The tests shown here simply check that the actions can be called without raising errors, and that the register and login view templates contain various form fields. The `assert*()` methods are exactly the same as we saw when testing with Zend Framework and PHPUnit, since they are all provided by the PHPUnit library.

■ **Note** CakePHP also supports the testing of Collections, which is outlined here: `http://book.cakephp.org/2.0/en/development/testing.html#testing-components`

The second kind of test we need to set up checks the response of post requests, as shown in Listing 33-2.

Listing 33-2. ~/app/Test/Controller/UsersControllerTest.php (Extract) Class UsersControllerTest Extends ControllerTestCase

```
{
    public function testLoginPost()
    {
        $result = $this->testAction("/login", array(
            "method" => "post",
            "return" => "contents",
            "data" => array(
                "User" => array(
```

```
                "email" => "cgpitt@gmail.com",
                "password" => "chris"
            )
        )
    ));

    $this->assertEquals(true, isset($this->headers["Location"]));

    if (isset($this->headers["Location"]))
    {
        $this->assertContains("/profile", );
    }
  }
}
```

This test begins by posting some data to the `login()` action and checks to see that the form then redirects to the profile page. Your data will obviously need to reflect the details of a user account registered in your local database, but the logic remains the same.

At the end of the day, the more tests you write for your applications, the better they will be when the time comes to change or extend them. We wrote a paltry amount of tests in this chapter, but by now you should understand how they work and that it is up to the developer when deciding just how many tests to write and what functionality to cover.

■ **Note** You can learn more about PHPUnit tests in CakePHP here:
`http://book.cakephp.org/2.0/en/development/testing.html`

Questions

1. Both Zend Framework and CakePHP use the same unit-testing library PHPUnit. Why is this a good idea?
2. Is it technically possible to test things like login session management and settings page updates?

Answers

1. The benefit of many frameworks using PHPUnit is that developers can write unit tests in the same way, no matter the framework they are using. This has obvious benefits in time saved learning new testing frameworks, and also helps multiple competing frameworks know what their competition is testing for.
2. It is technically possible, while requiring a long chain of requests, to establish a successful login, followed by further session-based interaction. We have chosen not to go so in-depth in this chapter, as this kind of sustained request testing quickly shows subtle differences in the makeup of my codebase versus your codebase. Things as simple as route differences or as small as spelling differences can make or break unit tests.

Exercises

1. In this chapter, we created a mere five unit tests, but there is much room for improvement. Try to create at least ten unit tests in total, which cover the majority of your sample application's functionality.
2. We have spoken briefly about testing session-based interaction, but haven't written any tests for it. Try to create a test or two that depend on a successful login.

APPENDIX A

Setting Up a Web Server

In this chapter, we will learn how to install and configure a web server in Windows, Linux, and OS X.

Goals

- Install Apache 2.2+, MySQL 5+, and PHP 5.3+.
- Install Memcached.
- Run our unit tests to ensure everything is working as it should.

Windows

In this section, we will cover the installation process in Windows 7. The installation of these software packages is commonly known as WAMP (**W**indows **A**pache **M**ySQL **P**HP). Let's get started.

Step 1

Go to `http://www.wampserver.com/en/download.php` and download the version most applicable to your system. If you are running a 64-bit PC, then you will want the 64-bit installer. If you are unsure, stick with the 32-bit installer, which should work on both 64-bit and 32-bit PCs. After you have downloaded the installer, start it up, and start completing the steps, as shown in Figure A-1.

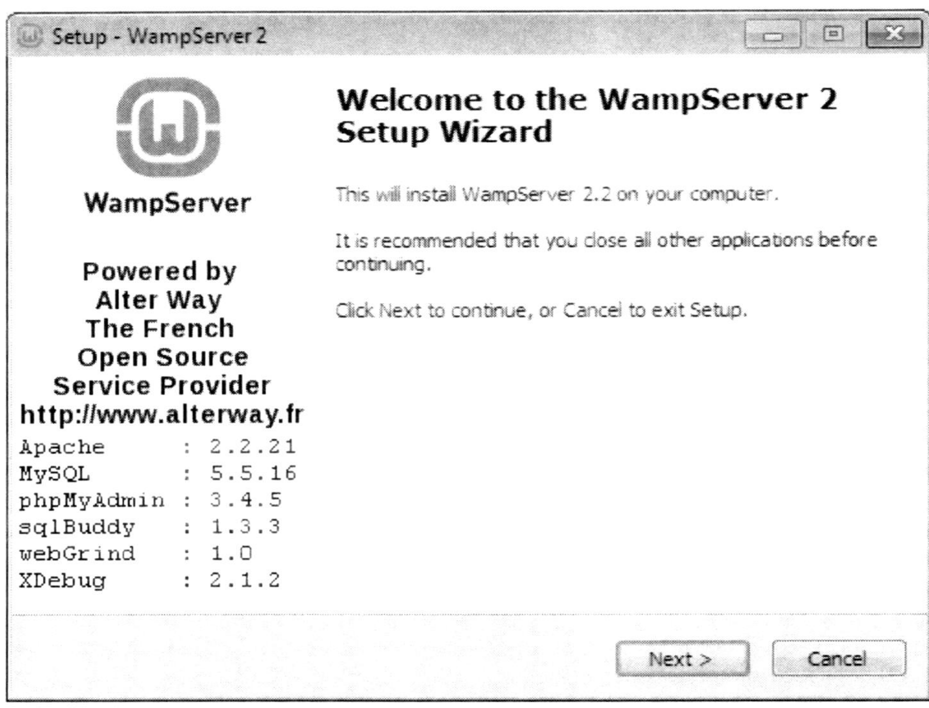

Figure A-1. *Setting up with the WAMP installer*

You can install WAMP to the default `c:\wamp` directory, which it suggests. You can also use the default SMTP and e-mail settings it suggests, which you can change later if you need to. At some point, it will ask you to choose your default browser. Since I have Google Chrome installed, I want to use that as my default. The quickest way to find that executable is to right-click the Google Chrome shortcut icon and select `Properties` ➤ `Shortcut`. Then copy the whole `Target` value and paste it into the `File name` box. This is demonstrated in Figures A-2 and A-3.

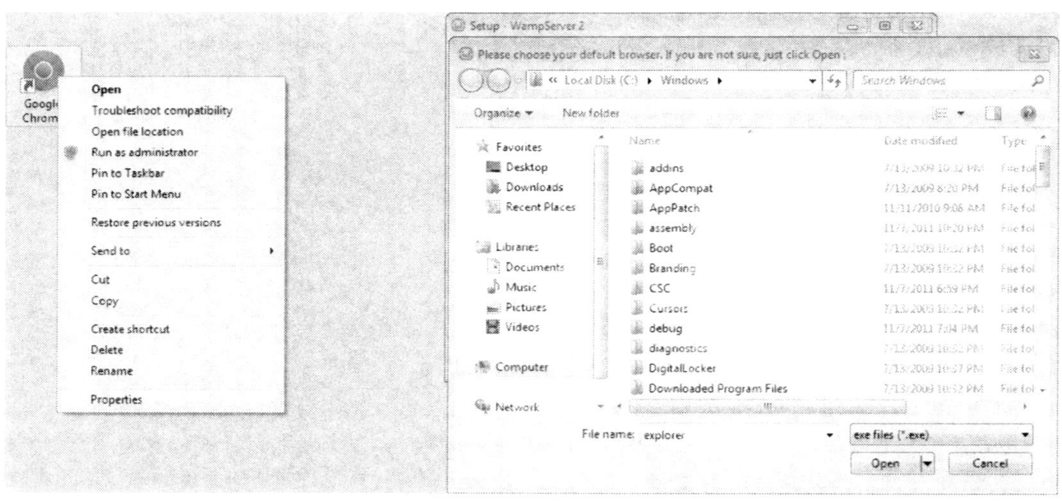

Figure A-2. *Choosing the default browser*

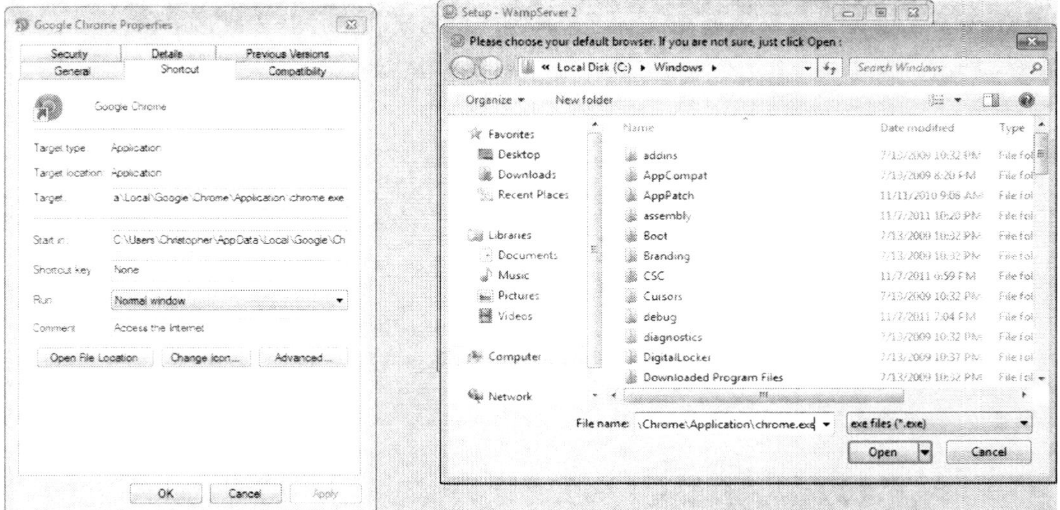

Figure A-3. *Getting the path to Google Chrome*

After you have completed the installation of WAMP, you will see a new icon in your system tray. If you left-click on this icon, you will see a pop-up menu. Click `localhost`.

■ **Note** You don't have to use Google Chrome. You can target any other browser in the same manner.

Naughty Skype!

A recurring problem I have encountered each time I installed WAMP on a Windows system, which also happened to be running Skype, was that Apache would not load. This is due to how browsers and Skype work.

It has long been standard for web servers to serve their content at port 80. Likewise, browsers request the web site from port 80, on a domain. You can easily change these, but they are the standards. Port 80 is, therefore, a popular port. Routers and security software frequently leave this port open for sending/receiving data, as they assume only HTTP traffic will happen here.

Seeing this, Skype opted to use port 80 as the default communications port, so it could bypass even the most difficult security software. The problem is that either Apache or Skype, but not both, may use port 80.

We can either run Apache at a different port, continuously changing the address bar of our browser to match, or we can change Skype settings. I recommend changing Skype! To make Skype use a different port, go to `Skype` ➤ `Options` ➤ `Advanced` ➤ `Connection` ➤ and uncheck `"Use port 80 and 443 as alternatives..."` (see Figure A-4). Now restart Skype and WAMP, and the problem should be rectified.

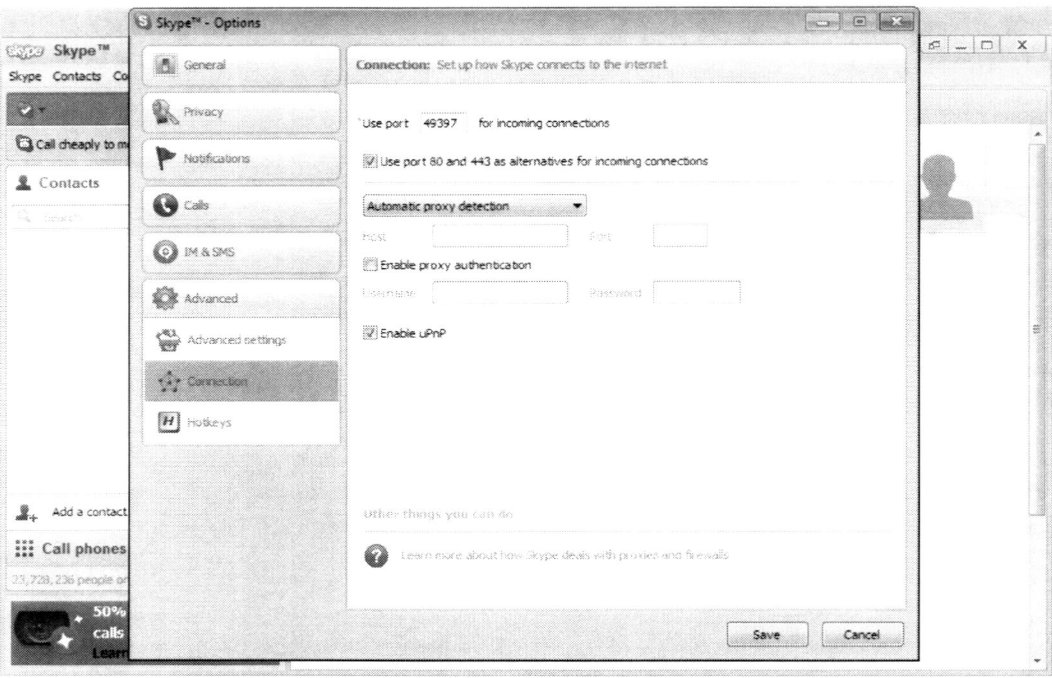

Figure A-4. *Kicking Skype off port 80*

Configuring Apache/PHP

We need to enable some modules and change some settings in both Apache and PHP. Let's first enable all the modules we need. Left-click on the WAMP icon again, and select Apache ➤ `Apache modules` ➤ `rewrite_module`. Repeat this process for `cache_module`, `headers_module`, and `expires_module`. Each time you enable a module, WAMP will restart the server. Then, left-click on the WAMP icon, and select PHP ➤ `PHP extensions` ➤ `php_memcache`.

We then need to update Apache's document root to point to the public folder within our application folder. Left-click on the WAMP icon and select Apache ➤ `httpd.conf`. Update both places you find the default path (`c:/wamp/www`) to the correct location, as shown in Figure A-5.

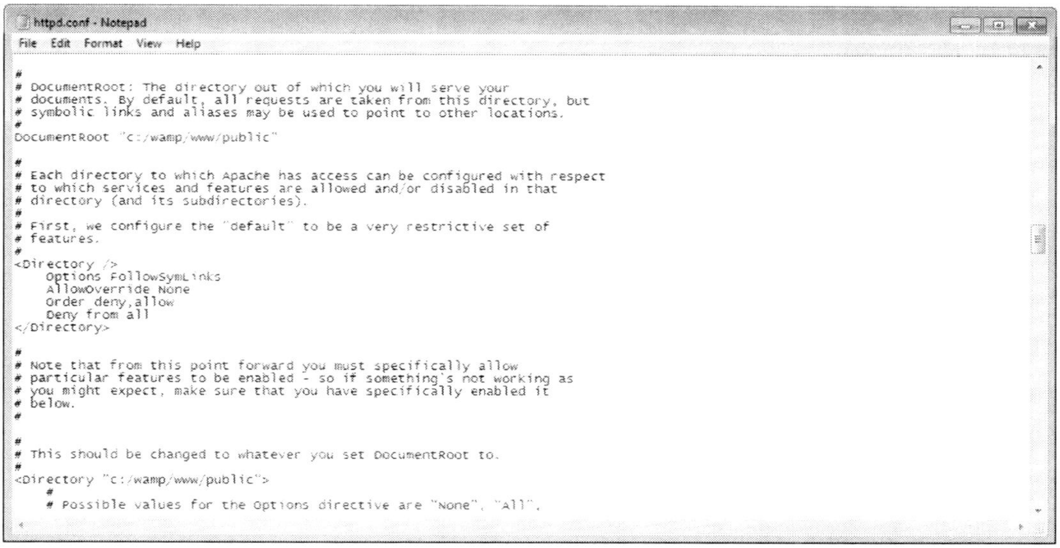

```
httpd.conf - Notepad
File Edit Format View Help

#
# DocumentRoot: The directory out of which you will serve your
# documents. By default, all requests are taken from this directory, but
# symbolic links and aliases may be used to point to other locations.
#
DocumentRoot "c:/wamp/www/public"

#
# Each directory to which Apache has access can be configured with respect
# to which services and features are allowed and/or disabled in that
# directory (and its subdirectories).
#
# First, we configure the "default" to be a very restrictive set of
# features.
#
<Directory />
    Options FollowSymLinks
    AllowOverride None
    Order deny,allow
    Deny from all
</Directory>

#
# Note that from this point forward you must specifically allow
# particular features to be enabled - so if something's not working as
# you might expect, make sure that you have specifically enabled it
# below.
#

#
# This should be changed to whatever you set DocumentRoot to.
#
<Directory "c:/wamp/www/public">
    #
    # Possible values for the Options directive are "None", "All",
```

Figure A-5. *Setting the correct DocumentRoot*

Step 2

Installing Memcached is slightly less user-friendly. Go to `http://code.jellycan.com/memcached/` and download the `win32 binary archive`. Once downloaded, extract it to `c:\memcached` (you might have to create this folder).

You will need to instruct Windows to run the Memcached executable as an administrator. To do so, right-click the executable and go to `Properties` ➤ `Compatibility` and check "`Run this program as an administrator`" (see Figure A-6).

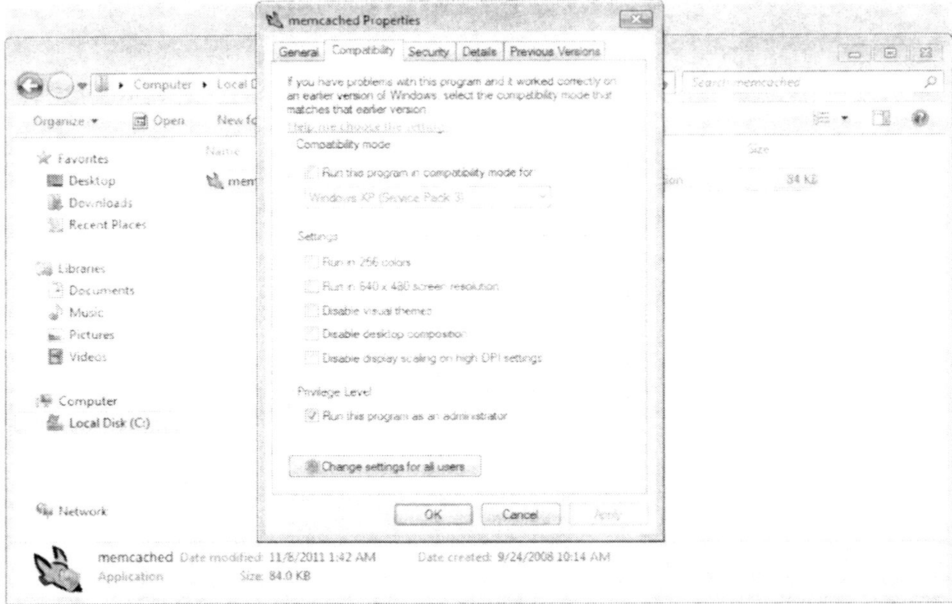

Figure A-6. *Running the executable as an administrator*

Next, open the command prompt and type the following commands, as shown in Figure A-7:

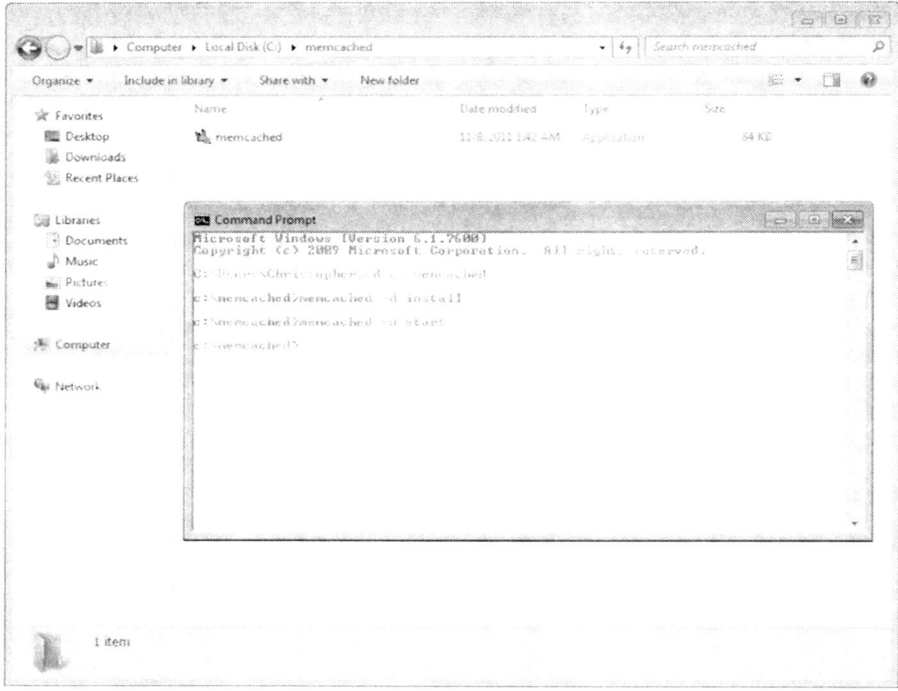

Figure A-7. *Installing and starting Memcached*

- `cd c:\memcached`
- `memcached -d install`
- `memcached -d start`

What Is MSVCP71.dll?

If you are seeing an error, referring to a similarly named missing file, do not be alarmed. It seems Microsoft left out some libraries that many third-party software packages (such a Memcached) make frequent use of. To install these missing libraries, go to `http://www.addictivetips.com/?attachment_id=38105` and download the archive containing two `.dll` files.

Once downloaded, extract these to either the `c:\Windows\System32` directory or the `c:\Windows\SysWOW64` directory (depending on whether you are running a 32-bit or 64-bit system). The Memcached executable should now work as expected.

Step 3

We need to create a database user and schema for our framework to use. Left-click on the WAMP icon and select `phpMyAdmin`. This interface lets you interact directly with the MySQL server that WAMP installed. Go to `databases` ➤ `Create new database`, and enter the database name (I have chosen `prophpmvc`), as shown in Figure A-8.

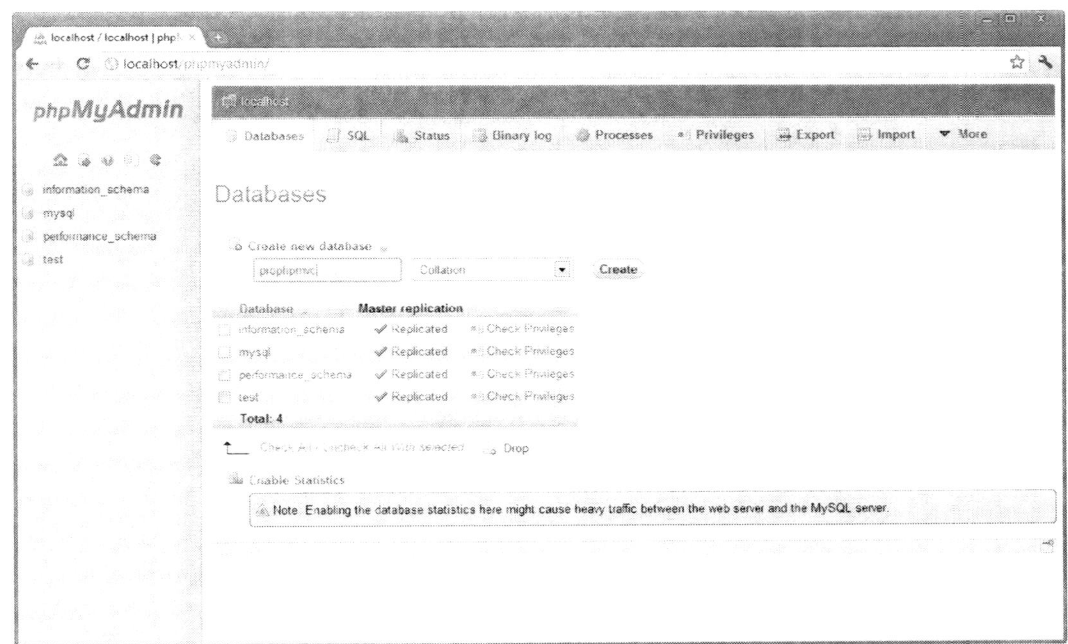

Figure A-8. *Creating a database and schema*

Next, go to `Privileges` ➤ `Add a new User` and fill in the username, password, and privileges, as demonstrated in Figures A-9 through A-11.

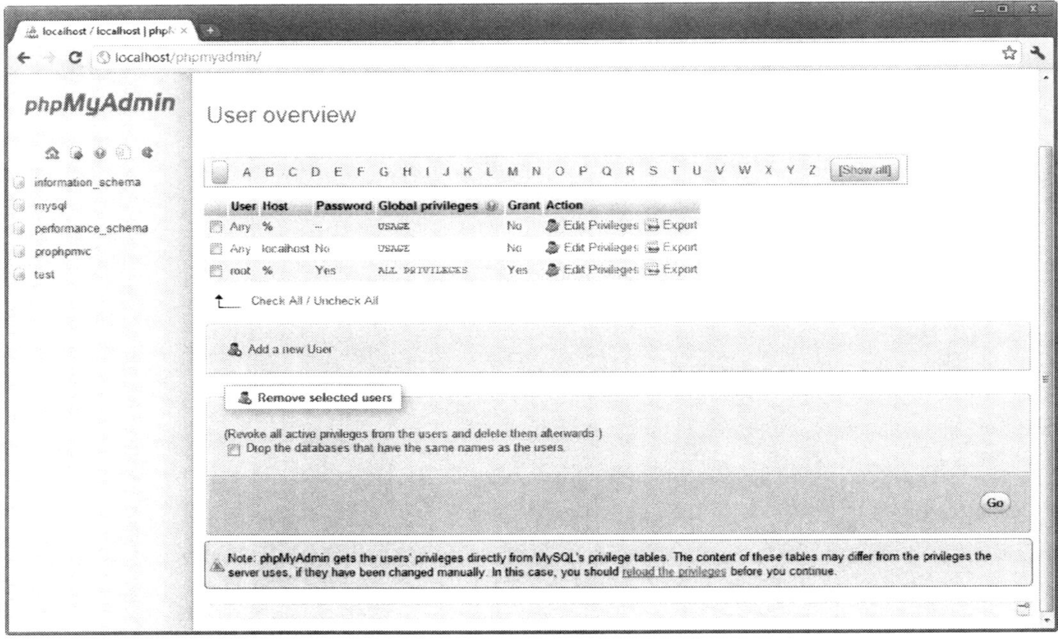

Figure A-9. User privileges hub

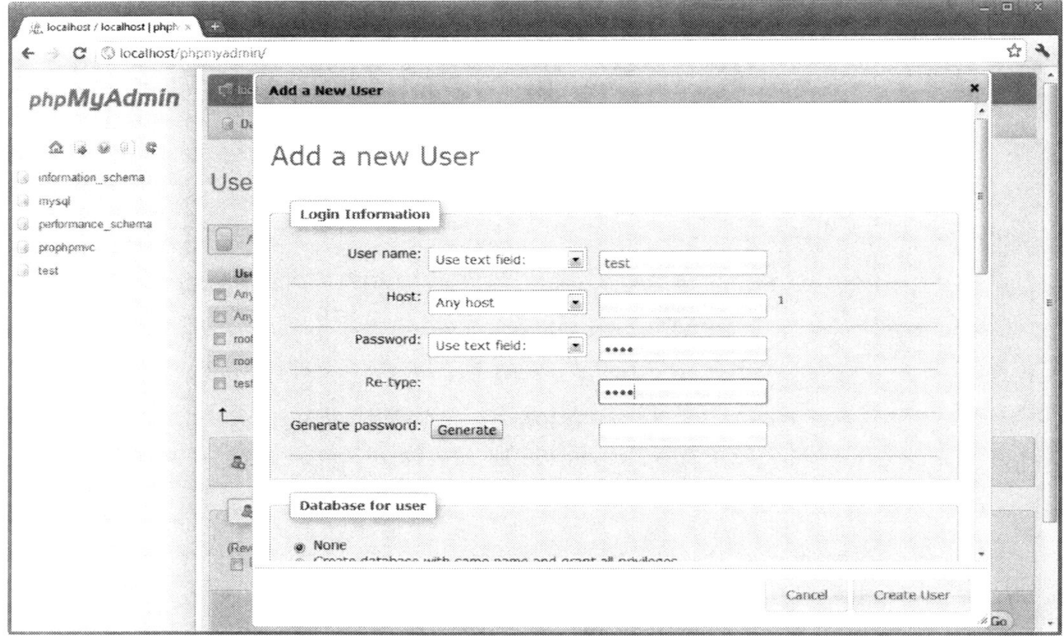

Figure A-10. Adding a username and password

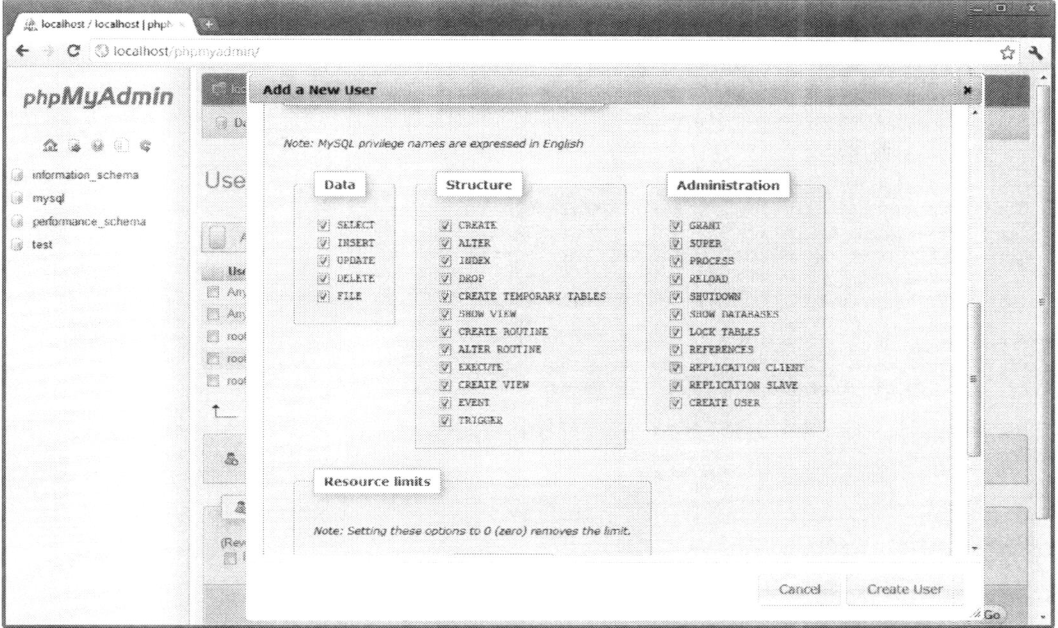

Figure A-11. *Privileges*

■ **Note** Be sure to update the unit tests with the correct database username, password, and schema.

Linux

In this section, we will be covering the installation process in Ubuntu 11.10. The installation of these software packages is commonly known as LAMP (**L**inux **A**pache **M**ySQL **P**HP). While there might be small differences, the methods described in this section should work on other Linux distributions.

Step 1

Switch to the root user account by typing `sudo -s`, and providing the root account password. The commands that follow require root access to install/configure correctly. After you have root access, type the following commands, answering `Y` when prompted:

- `apt-get update`
- `apt-get install tasksel` (see Figure A-12)
- `tasksel`

```
Hit http://za.archive.ubuntu.com oneiric-backports/restricted i386 Packages
Hit http://za.archive.ubuntu.com oneiric-backports/universe i386 Packages
Hit http://za.archive.ubuntu.com oneiric-backports/multiverse i386 Packages
Hit http://za.archive.ubuntu.com oneiric-backports/main TranslationIndex
Hit http://za.archive.ubuntu.com oneiric-backports/multiverse TranslationIndex
Hit http://za.archive.ubuntu.com oneiric-backports/restricted TranslationIndex
Hit http://za.archive.ubuntu.com oneiric-backports/universe TranslationIndex
Hit http://za.archive.ubuntu.com oneiric/main Translation-en
Hit http://za.archive.ubuntu.com oneiric/multiverse Translation-en
Hit http://za.archive.ubuntu.com oneiric/restricted Translation-en
Hit http://za.archive.ubuntu.com oneiric/universe Translation-en
Get:20 http://za.archive.ubuntu.com oneiric-updates/main Translation-en [67.3 kB
]
Hit http://za.archive.ubuntu.com oneiric-updates/multiverse Translation-en
Hit http://za.archive.ubuntu.com oneiric-updates/restricted Translation-en
Get:21 http://za.archive.ubuntu.com oneiric-updates/universe Translation-en [23.
0 kB]
Hit http://za.archive.ubuntu.com oneiric-backports/main Translation-en
Hit http://za.archive.ubuntu.com oneiric-backports/multiverse Translation-en
Hit http://za.archive.ubuntu.com oneiric-backports/restricted Translation-en
Hit http://za.archive.ubuntu.com oneiric-backports/universe Translation-en
Fetched 548 kB in 10s (53.0 kB/s)
Reading package lists... Done
root@Christopher:~# apt-get install tasksel
```

Figure A-12. *Installing tasksel*

Select LAMP server from the list of options shown in Figure A-13. At some point in the installation, you will be asked to provide a MySQL username and password. I chose to use `root/root`, as it's simple to remember and fine for a development environment.

```
Package configuration

            Software selection
 You can choose to install one or more of the following predefined
 collections of software.

 Choose software to install:

      [ ] Basic Ubuntu server
      [ ] OpenSSH server
      [ ] DNS server
      [ ] LAMP server
      [ ] Mail server
      [ ] PostgreSQL database
      [ ] Print server
      [ ] Samba file server
      [ ] Tomcat Java server

                         <Ok>
```

Figure A-13. *Selecting packages to install*

Step 2

Unlike WAMP, tasksel does not automatically install phpMyAdmin with the LAMP server software packages. To install phpMyAdmin, type the command `apt-get install phpMyAdmin`. Select `apache2` (see Figure A-14), configure with `dbconfig-common` (see Figure A-15), and provide the username/password you just set up for MySQL (see Figure A-16).

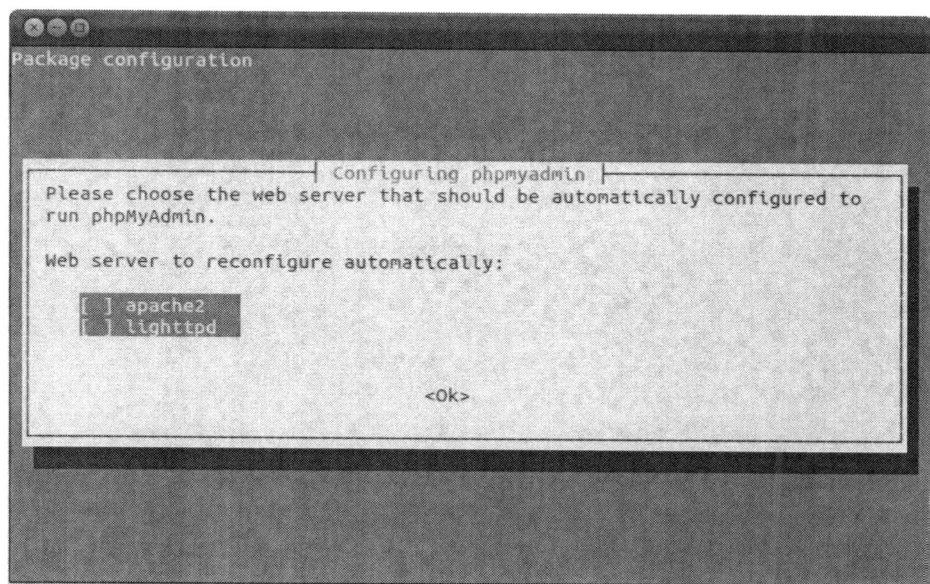

Figure A-14. *Integrating phpMyAdmin with Apache*

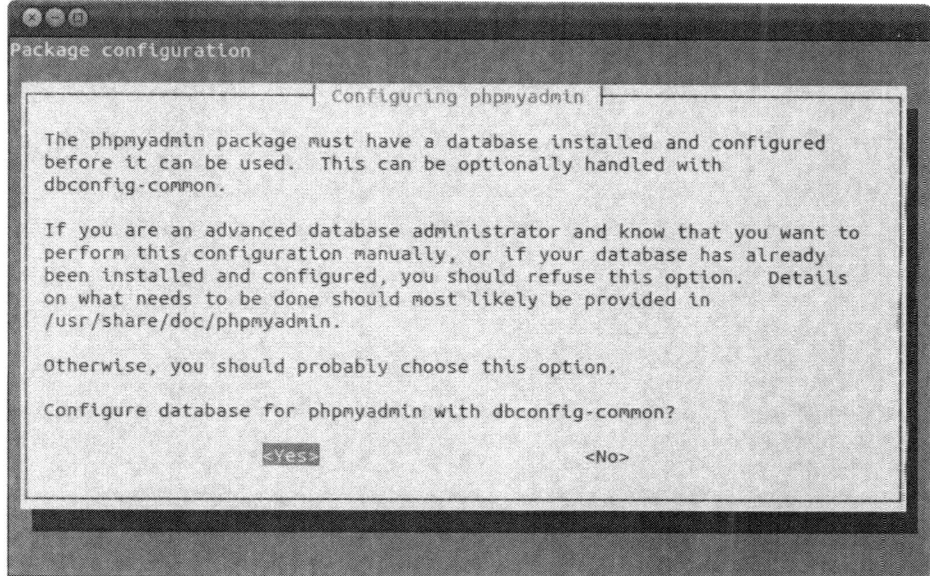

Figure A-15. *Using dbconfig-common*

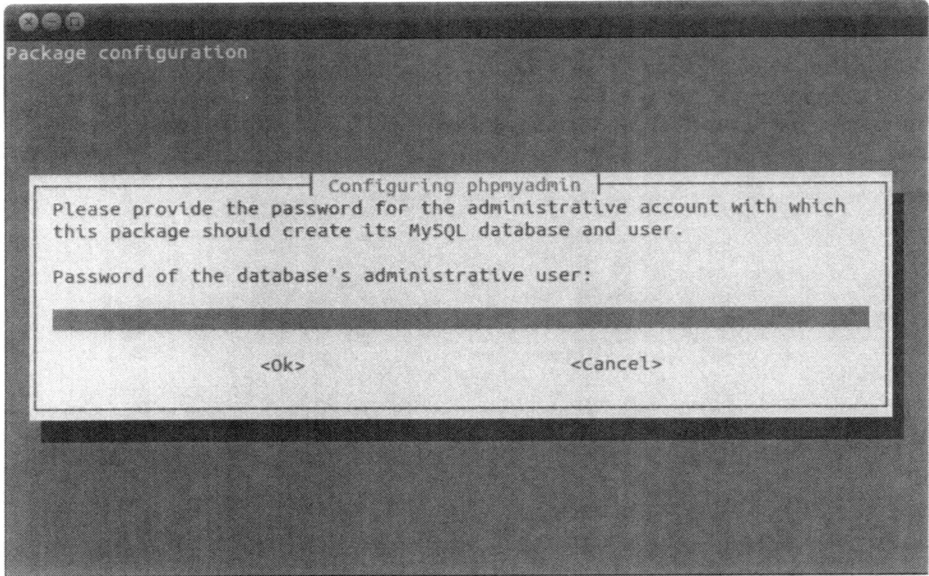

Figure A-16. *Providing the username/password for MySQL*

After setting up phpMyAdmin, feel free to create the prophpmvc database and username/password for your application/unit tests. You can do this in exactly the same way was we did for Windows 7, as phpMyAdmin should work similarly in both.

Step 3

Installing Memcached could not be easier. Simply type the command `apt-get install memcached php5-memcache`, and answer `Y` when prompted (see Figure A-17). Once installed, the Apache2 server (and the Memcached service) will restart and Memcached will be available for use.

```
  libcache-memcached-perl libmemcached
The following NEW packages will be installed:
  memcached php5-memcache
0 upgraded, 2 newly installed, 0 to remove and 195 not upgraded.
Need to get 119 kB of archives.
After this operation, 463 kB of additional disk space will be used.
Get:1 http://za.archive.ubuntu.com/ubuntu/ oneiric/main memcached amd64 1.4.7-0.
1ubuntu1 [69.9 kB]
Get:2 http://za.archive.ubuntu.com/ubuntu/ oneiric/universe php5-memcache amd64
3.0.5-1 [49.5 kB]
Fetched 119 kB in 0s (154 kB/s)
Selecting previously deselected package memcached.
(Reading database ... 126113 files and directories currently installed.)
Unpacking memcached (from .../memcached_1.4.7-0.1ubuntu1_amd64.deb) ...
Selecting previously deselected package php5-memcache.
Unpacking php5-memcache (from .../php5-memcache_3.0.5-1_amd64.deb) ...
Processing triggers for ureadahead ...
Processing triggers for man-db ...
Setting up memcached (1.4.7-0.1ubuntu1) ...
Starting memcached: memcached.
Setting up php5-memcache (3.0.5-1) ...

Creating config file /etc/php5/conf.d/memcache.ini with new version
root@Christopher:~#
```

Figure A-17. *Installing Memcached*

Step 4

The last thing we need to do in Ubuntu is set the ownership of the files to Apache2 and set the correct document root. Use the following command to change ownership of the files, from within the same folder:

```
chown -R www-data:www-data *
```

Next, type `vim /etc/apache2/sites-enabled/000-default` and change the line that shows `DocumentRoot` to the correct path of your application directory's public folder. Mine is at `/var/www/public`, so that line in the config file should read `DocumentRoot /var/www/public` (see Figure A-18).

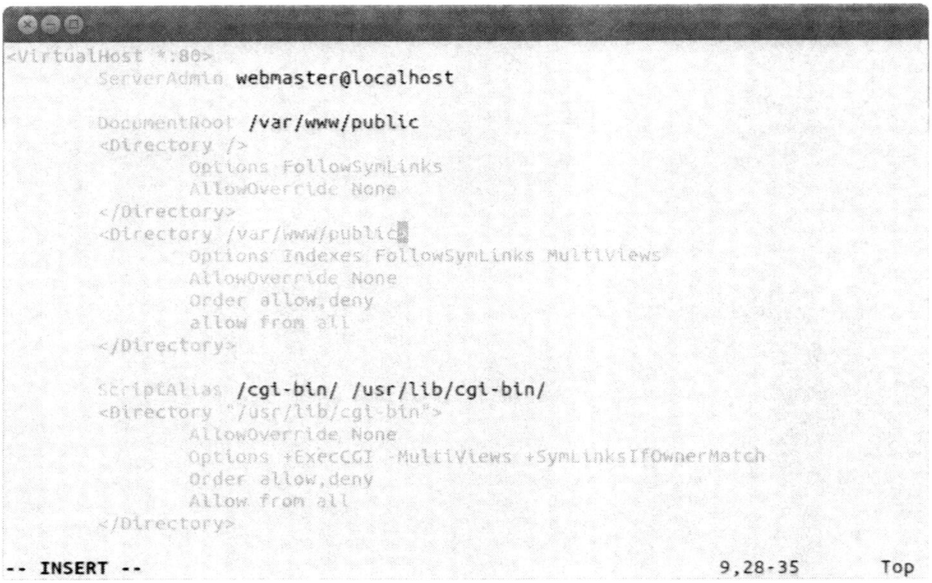

```
<VirtualHost *:80>
        ServerAdmin webmaster@localhost

        DocumentRoot /var/www/public
        <Directory />
                Options FollowSymLinks
                AllowOverride None
        </Directory>
        <Directory /var/www/public>
                Options Indexes FollowSymLinks MultiViews
                AllowOverride None
                Order allow,deny
                allow from all
        </Directory>

        ScriptAlias /cgi-bin/ /usr/lib/cgi-bin/
        <Directory "/usr/lib/cgi-bin">
                AllowOverride None
                Options +ExecCGI -MultiViews +SymLinksIfOwnerMatch
                Order allow,deny
                Allow from all
        </Directory>
-- INSERT --                                          9,28-35       Top
```

Figure A-18. *Setting the correct DocumentRoot*

■ **Note** Vim is a common text editor, installed on most Linux systems. If it is not installed, you can install it by typing `apt-get install vim`. Alternatively, you can use your favorite text editor, but the important thing here is that you update the `DocumentRoot` path to the correct location.

MAC OS X

In this section, we will cover the installation process in OS X. The installation of these software packages is commonly known as MAMP (**M**ac **A**pache **M**ySQL **P**HP).

Step 1

Installing our OS X web server is really simple. Begin by going to `http://www.mamp.info/en/downloads/index.html` and downloading the latest version of MAMP & MAMP PRO. Extract the contents of the downloaded archive and run the appropriate installer (32-bit or 64-bit).

The installer will place a MAMP folder within your `Applications` folder, and needs administrative privileges to do so. You will be prompted to provide an administrator password. When you open the MAMP application (which should now be in your `Applications` folder), you will easily be able to stop/start the servers, and view the landing page for your local web server (see Figure A-19). You can set the default ports to 80/3306 (see Figure A.20), as you would have them in Windows 7/Linux, and you can also select the appropriate version of PHP to run (you should select PHP 5.3+). Finally, you can also set the correct `DocumentRoot` folder from the Apache tab.

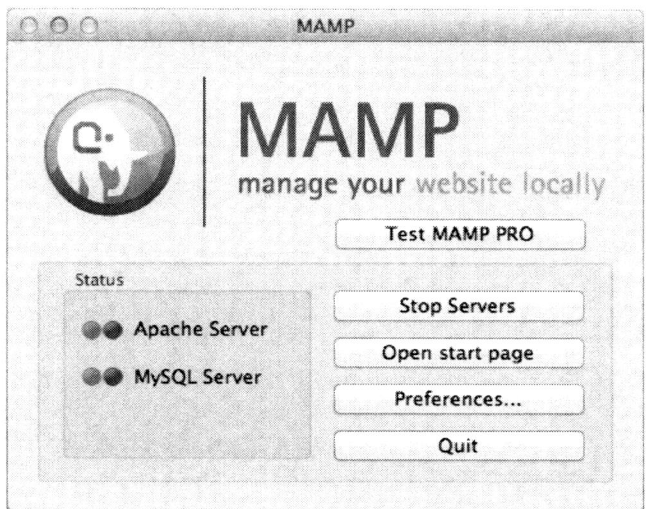

Figure A-19. *Memcached application*

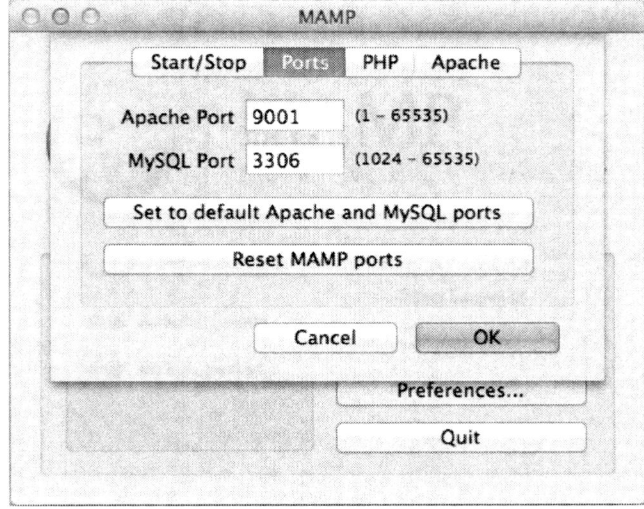

Figure A-20. *Setting server ports in OS X*

Repeat the same steps we performed for creating the database schema, username, and password for our application, through the phpMyAdmin that installs with MAMP.

Step 2

Installing the Memcached PHP extension in OS X is somewhat tricky. You will need to type in the following commands:

- `chmod u+x /Applications/MAMP/bin/php/php5.3.X/bin/p*` (where *5.3.X* is the version of PHP you selected in the MAMP application)

- `cd /tmp`
- `wget http://pecl.php.net/get/memcache-2.2.5.tgz`
- `tar -zxvf memcache-2.2.5.tgz`
- `cd memcache-2.2.5`
- `/Applications/MAMP/bin/php/phpX.X.X/bin/phpize`
- `MACOSX_DEPLOYMENT_TARGET=10.6 CFLAGS='-O3 -fno-common -arch i386 -arch➥ x86_64' LDFLAGS='-O3 -arch i386 -arch x86_64' CXXFLAGS='-O3 -fno-common➥ -arch i386 -arch x86_64' ./configure`
- `make`
- `cp modules/memcache.so /Applications/MAMP/bin/php/phpX.X.X/➥ lib/php/extensions/no-debug-non-zts-20060613/`
- `echo 'extension=memcache.so' > /Applications/MAMP/bin/php/phpX.X.X/➥ conf/php.ini`

After restarting the servers, through the MAMP application, the PECL Memcache class should be available to use in our code.

What If wget Is Missing?

It is possible that you will not have the `wget` command available to you, in which case you will be stuck at step 3. Not to worry; it's easy to install with the following commands:

- `/usr/bin/ruby -e "$(/usr/bin/curl -fsSL https://raw.github.com/mxcl/ homebrew/master/Library/Contributions/install_homebrew.rb)"` (see Figure A-21)

```
bash-3.2$ /usr/bin/ruby -e "$(curl -fsSL https://raw.github.com/gist/323731)"
-e:66: warning: Insecure world writable dir /usr/local/bin in PATH, mode 040777
-e:77: warning: Insecure world writable dir /usr/local/bin in PATH, mode 040777
==> This script will install:
/usr/local/bin/brew
/usr/local/Library/Formula/...
/usr/local/Library/Homebrew/...

Press enter to continue
-e:32: warning: Insecure world writable dir /usr/local/bin in PATH, mode 040777
```

Figure A-21. *Installing Homebrew*

- `brew install wget` (see Figure A-22)

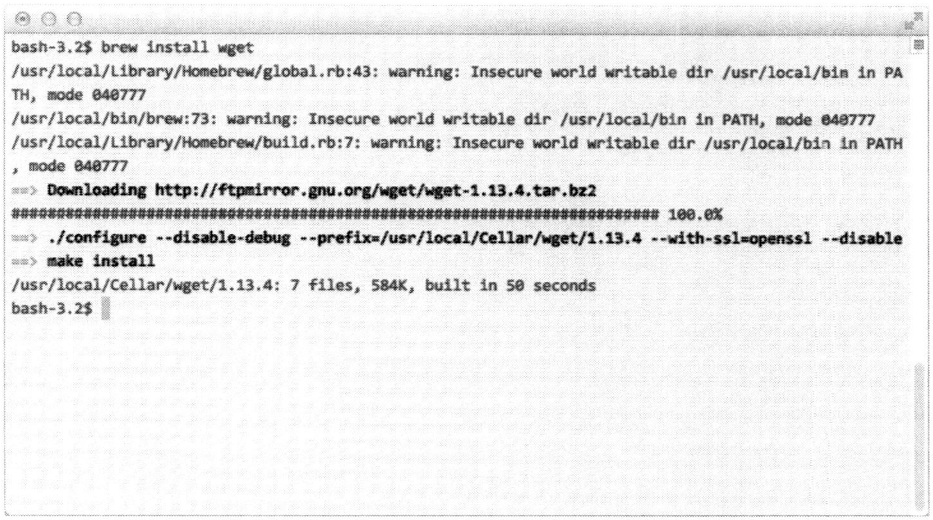

Figure A-22. *Installing wget*

What we're basically doing is installing an OS X package manager called Homebrew. Using Homebrew, we can install a drop-in replacement for Linux's `wget` command.

■ **Note** If would like more information on Homebrew, or are having trouble installing it, you can read more at `https://github.com/mxcl/homebrew/wiki`.

■ **Note** It is normal to see these warnings, and okay to ignore them.

The next 2 listings (A-23 and A-24) illustrate commands 3 through 6 in this step.

```
bash-3.2$ chmod u+x /Applications/MAMP/bin/php/php5.3.6/bin/p*
bash-3.2$ cd /tmp
bash-3.2$ wget http://pecl.php.net/get/memcache-2.2.5.tgz
--2011-11-09 19:51:54--  http://pecl.php.net/get/memcache-2.2.5.tgz
Resolving pecl.php.net... 76.75.200.106
Connecting to pecl.php.net|76.75.200.106|:80... connected.
HTTP request sent, awaiting response... 200 OK
Length: 35981 (35K) [application/octet-stream]
Saving to: `memcache-2.2.5.tgz'

100%[======================================================>] 35,981      22.9K/s   in 1.5s

2011-11-09 19:51:58 (22.9 KB/s) - `memcache-2.2.5.tgz' saved [35981/35981]

bash-3.2$
```

Figure A-23. *Downloading PECL Memcached extension*

```
bash-3.2$ cd memcache-2.2.5
bash-3.2$ /Applications/MAMP/bin/php/php5.3.6/bin/phpize
grep: /Applications/MAMP/bin/php/php5.3.6/include/php/main/php.h: No such file or directory
grep: /Applications/MAMP/bin/php/php5.3.6/include/php/Zend/zend_modules.h: No such file or director
y
grep: /Applications/MAMP/bin/php/php5.3.6/include/php/Zend/zend_extensions.h: No such file or direc
tory
Configuring for:
PHP Api Version:
Zend Module Api No:
Zend Extension Api No:
bash-3.2$ MACOSX_DEPLOYMENT_TARGET=10.6 CFLAGS='-O3 -fno-common -arch i386 -arch x86_64' LDFLAGS='-
O3 -arch i386 -arch x86_64' CXXFLAGS='-O3 -fno-common -arch i386 -arch x86_64' ./configure
```

Figure A-24. *Installing/configuring Memcached extention*

Step 3

Next, we need to install the Memcached server that will run in OS X. Do this by downloading `http://topfunky.net/svn/shovel/memcached/install-memcached.sh` to a local directory (such as `~/Desktop`) and executing it with the following commands:

- `chmod 744 install-memcached.sh`
- `sudo ./install-memcached.sh`

■ **Note** If the script did not execute correctly, you probably do not have xcode tools installed. Download them from `http://developer.apple.com/technologies/tools/`.

You can tell Memcached to run as a daemon by typing `memcached -d` in terminal.

You Passed, with Flying Colors!

To ensure that we have installed and configured everything correctly, we need to run the unit tests that we created in Chapter 21 (at `http://localhost/tests`). See Figure A-25 for Windows 7; see Figure A-26 for Linux; see Figure A-27 for Mac OS X.

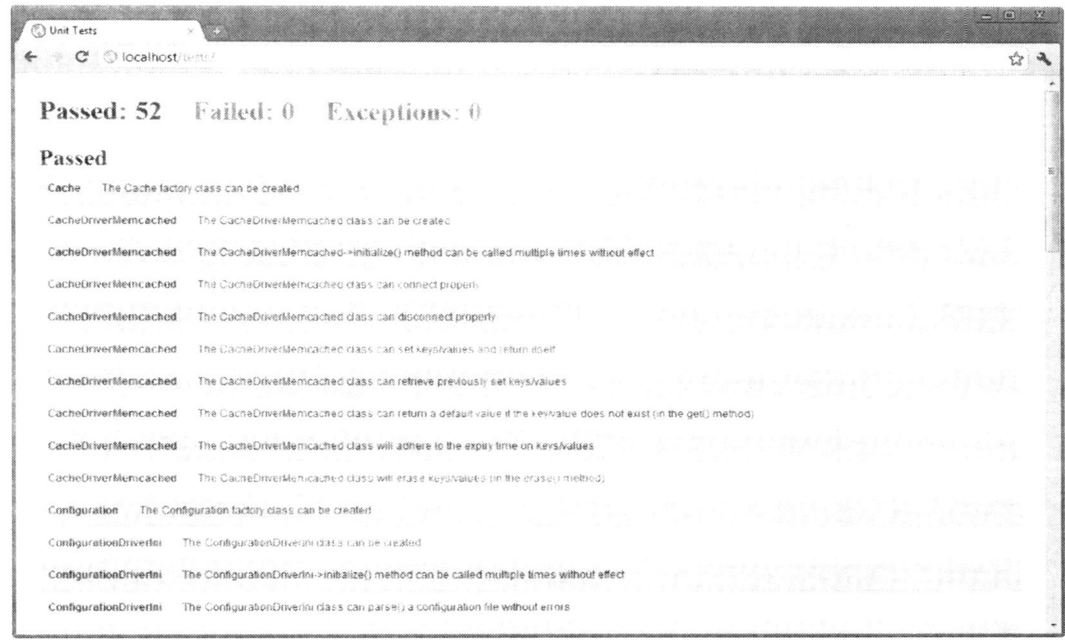

Figure A-25. *Tests passing in Windows 7*

Figure A-26. *Tests passing in Ubuntu 11.10*

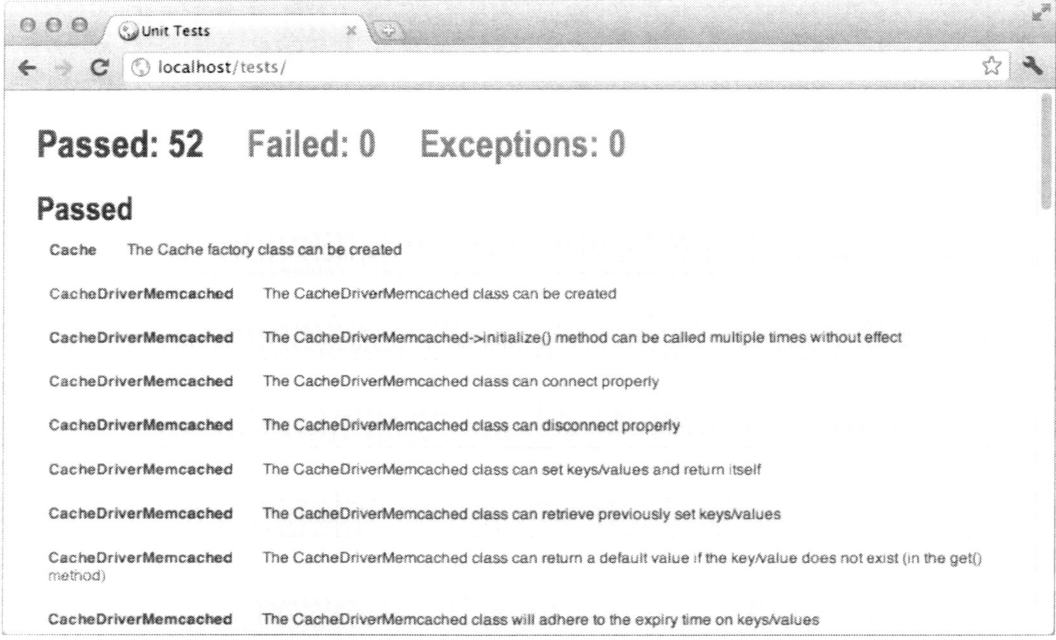

Figure A-27. *Tests passing in OS X*

Index

A

B

C

D

E

F

O

P

Q

R

S

T

U

V

W, X, Y

Z

CPSIA information can be obtained at www.ICGtesting.com
Printed in the USA
LVOW110010250413

330849LV00006B/53/P